Insurance Marketing

LOMA (Life Office Management Association, Inc.) is an international association founded in 1924. LOMA is committed to a business partnership with its worldwide members in the insurance and financial services industry to improve their management and operations through quality employee development, research, information sharing, and related products and services. Among LOMA's activities is the sponsorship of several self-study education programs leading to professional designations. These programs include the Fellow, Life Management Institute (FLMI) program and the Fellow, Financial Services Institute (FFSI) program. For more information on all of LOMA's education programs, please visit www.loma.org.

Statement of Purpose: LOMA Educational Programs Testing and Designations.

Examinations described in the LOMA Education and Training Catalog are designed solely to measure whether students have successfully completed the relevant assigned curriculum, and the attainment of the FLMI and other LOMA designations indicates only that all examinations in the given curriculum have been successfully completed. In no way shall a student's completion of a given LOMA course or attainment of the FLMI or other LOMA designation be construed to mean that LOMA in any way certifies that student's competence, training, or ability to perform any given task. LOMA's examinations are to be used solely for general educational purposes, and no other use of the examinations or programs is authorized or intended by LOMA. Furthermore, it is in no way the intention of the LOMA Curriculum and Examinations staff to describe the standard of appropriate conduct in any field of the insurance and financial services industry, and LOMA expressly repudiates any attempt to so use the curriculum and examinations. Any such assessment of student competence or industry standards of conduct should instead be based on independent professional inquiry and the advice of competent professional counsel.

Insurance Marketing

Sharon Allen-Peterson, FLMI, ACS, AIRC, PAHM
Kevin Head, Ph.D., FLMI, ACS, AFSI
Steven R. Silver, J.D., FLMI, AFSI, AIRC, AIAA, ACS

LOMA Education and Training
Atlanta, Georgia
www.loma.org

Information in this text may have been changed or updated since its publication date. For current updates visit www.loma.org.

PROJECT TEAM:

Authors:	Sharon Allen-Peterson, FLMI, ACS, AIRC, PAHM
	Kevin Head, Ph.D., FLMI, ACS, AFSI
	Steven R. Silver, J.D., FLMI, AFSI, AIRC, AIAA, ACS
Manuscript Editor:	Patsy Leeuwenburg, Ph.D., FLMI, FLHC, ACS, AIAA, ARA, AIRC, AAPA, PAHM
Examinations Editor:	JoAnn Appleton, FLMI, PCS, ALHC, HIA, CEBS
Project Managers:	Mark Adel, FLMI, FFSI, PCS, AAPA, AIRC, PAHM
	Julia K. Wooley, FLMI, ACS, ALHC, HIA, MHP
Copyeditor:	Eastman Communications
	Barbara Foxenberger Brown, FLMI, ACS, AIAA, AIRC
Indexer:	Robert D. Land, FLMI, ACS
AVP, Marketing:	Paul Wilson
Lead Graphic Designer:	Marlene McAuley
Typesetters:	Allison Ayers-Molette
	Amy Stailey
Product Sourcing Manager:	Carol Wiessner, ACS
Administrative Support:	Mamunah Carter
Cover Design:	Amy Stailey

ISBN: 978-1-57974-321-5

Contents

Chapter 9: Marketing Communications: Engaging the Customer 235

Chapter 10: Promotion Tools 255

Chapter 11: Regulation of Life and Health Insurance Marketing

Preface

Insurance Marketing delivers information about how insurance companies market their products, the environment in which insurance companies must accomplish that marketing, and the laws and regulations that surround almost every aspect of insurance marketing. We present this information in an understandable format that uses real-world insurance examples to convey important concepts. Although this text focuses primarily on marketing insurance in the United States, the underlying marketing principles and practices we describe generally apply worldwide. And, where appropriate, we included examples of practices in other countries.

Acknowledgments

LOMA's texts always are the result of a joint effort between industry experts and LOMA's own staff. Both groups made invaluable contributions to the success of LOMA's *Insurance Marketing* text.

Textbook Development Panel and Additional Contributors

Industry experts reviewed the entire text prior to publication. These individuals made many substantive comments on the outline and chapters, provided suggestions for content, submitted relevant research materials, and answered numerous questions from the authors during the course of the text's development. These industry experts served as our review panel and made the writing of this text possible. We are deeply grateful for the efforts of our reviewers, who cared enough about the educational needs of current and future industry employees to volunteer their time and expertise to this project. They improved the accuracy and clarity of the text, although the authors claim responsibility for any errors.

The following individuals devoted countless hours to reviewing *Insurance Marketing* for which we are most grateful:

Lydia Boyko, FLMI, APR
Professor, Faculty of Business
Seneca College of Applied Arts & Technology

M. Steven Brotherton, M.Tx., ChFC, CLU
Advanced Markets Consultant
New England Financial - Atlanta Agency

William T. (Bill) Burke, FLMI, ACS
Senior Systems Programmer
Southern Farm Bureau Life Insurance Company

Paul Clark, FLMI, CLU, AIE
Life Policy Analyst
Georgia Department of Insurance

Eric Cochran, FLMI, PMP, NASD 6 Registered Rep, NASD 26
Registered Principal
Senior Project Manager
Conseco Insurance Group

Julia Cornely, FLMI, AIRC
Assistant Vice President, Treaty Services
AXA Corporate Solutions Life Reinsurance Company

Philip J. Fernandez, FLMI, Associate, Institute of Bankers
Senior Business Consultant
The Manufacturer's Life Insurance Company Limited

Frankie Drinnen Graves, CLU, ChFC, FLMI, PCS, AIAA, AIRC, ARA,
AAPA

Fabian Ricardo Hilsenrat, Actuary, FLMI, PFSL, ACS
Assistant General Manager-Product Manager
Binaria Seguros de Retiro S.A.

Matthew Hughes, FLMI, ACS
Senior Writer & Analyst
Transamerica Occidental Life Insurance Company

Robert L. McPherson, CLU, ChFC, CPCU, PMP
Director, Process Management
Nationwide Insurance

Denise Olivares, CLU, ChFC
Vice President, Marketing
The Union Labor Life Insurance Company

Marcel Padilla, MBA, FLMI, FFSI, ACS, AAPA
Unit Head, Annuities and Cash, U.S. Policy Services
Industrial-Alliance Pacific Insurance and Financial Services, Inc.

Douglas A. Pennington, FLMI, CIC, CCP, AIRC, AAI, ARA, AIAA,
CISR, ACS, i-Net+
Chief Market Analyst
Washington State Office of the Insurance Commissioner

David J. Perhai, FLMI, CPCU, AIM, API, AIS
Senior Business Analyst, Marketing Projects
COUNTRY Insurance and Financial Services

Kimberly A. Reynolds, FLMI, ACS, HIA, CFCI
Senior Manager, Training Development
Aflac

Kyle H. Schultz, FLMI, FFSI, ACS, PCS, AAPA, AIAA, AIRC, ARA, MHP, HCSA
Manager
Great-West Healthcare

Mai-Han Shultz, FLMI
Marketing Director
Lincoln Financial Advisors

Lynn Toddie Splittstoesser, Ph.D., CPCU, CLU, ChFC, FLMI, AFSB
Director, Business Process Consulting
State Farm Insurance Companies

R. Maurice (Moe) Stebbins, FLMI, FLHC, ACS, HIA, ARA, AIRC,
Quality Assurance Auditor
CoreSource, Inc.

Thomas J. (TJ) Wood, FLMI, ACS
Business Solutions Manager
The Western and Southern Life Insurance Company

We also wish to thank the following individuals who reviewed portions of the text or provided guidance or other assistance with this project:

- Robert M. Baranoff, FLMI, LLIF; Senior Vice President, Member Benefits, LIMRA
- James W. (Jim) Colton
- William L. Evans, CLU, ChFC; Senior Compliance Analyst, RIS-Compliance
- Alan L. Fry, CLU, ChFC, CFP, FLMI/M, REBC, RHU, ACS, PCS, AAPA; Director, Advanced Sales Support, Variable Annuity Sales, Lincoln Financial Group
- M. Meaghan Kenagy, ACS
- Kathleen E. Krozel, FLMI, ARP; Associate Research Director, Distribution Research, LIMRA
- Patrick T. Leary, Associate Director, Distribution Research, LIMRA
- Tara M. Reynolds, CLU, ChFC, CASL, Vice President; Customer Marketing, Prudential Financial

- Harold D. Skipper, Jr., Professor Emeritus of Risk Management and Insurance, Georgia State University

- Cynthia E. Spires, CPCU, CLU, FLMI; Senior Analyst, State Farm Insurance

- Alison Stemp, FLMI, ACS, AIAA, ARA; Director, Traditional Markets, Unity Life of Canada

- Elaine F. Tumicki, CLU, ChFC, LLIF; Corporate Vice President, Product Research, LIMRA

LOMA Staff/Consultants

LOMA has talented staff members who contribute in many ways to ensure LOMA's products meet the highest possible standards for education and information about the financial services industry. Dennis W. Goodwin, FLMI, ACS, Assistant Vice President, Learning Support, deserves our special thanks for writing LOMA's very first text on insurance marketing entitled *Life and Health Insurance Marketing* on which the basic foundation of *Insurance Marketing* is based. Thanks also go to Jennifer W. Herrod, FLMI, PCS, AIAA, PAHM, ARA, AIRC; Sharon Allen-Peterson, FLMI, AIRC, ACS, PAHM, Senior Associate, Training Programs; Patsy Leeuwenburg, Ph.D., FLMI, FLHC, ACS, AIAA, ARA, AIRC, AAPA, PAHM, Senior Associate, Training Programs; and Mary Bickley Naismith, J.D., FLMI, FFSI, CLU, AIRC, ACS, AIAA, PAHM, AAPA, ARA, Senior Associate, Training Programs, for updating subsequent editions of that text.

Our heartfelt gratitude goes out to Patsy Leeuwenburg who served as our manuscript editor and brought the writing styles of multiple authors into a cohesive whole for this text. We also thank Kristen L. Falk, FLMI, FFSI, AAPA, ACS, AIAA, AIRC, ARA, Senior Associate, Training Programs, who was recruited near the end of the project to write a chapter for this text and delivered outstanding results.

We extend a very special thank you to the hard work of Mark Adel, FLMI, FFSI, PCS, AAPA, AIRC, PAHM, Assistant Vice President, Learning and Development Services, who served as Project Manager and provided excellent guidance throughout the project. We also thank Mamunah Carter, Administrative Assistant III, for her assistance with this project.

Special thanks also go to Julia K. Wooley, FLMI, ACS, ALHC, HIA, MHP, Assistant Vice President, Designation Programs, who served dual roles on the project—initially to oversee the project from an exams perspective and later as Project Manager for the final stages of the project. We appreciate her excellent leadership and flexibility.

Other individuals in LOMA's Designation Programs department who are responsible for examinations and related products who contributed to the text include Jo Ann S. Appleton, FLMI, PCS, ALHC, HIA, CEBS, Senior Associate. In her capacity as Exams Editor, Jo Ann made many valuable contributions to the chapters as they were developed and is a co-developer of the Test Preparation Guide (TPG) that accompanies this text. Other developers of the TPG are Sean Schaeffer Gilley, FLMI, ACS, HIA, CEBS, AIAA, MHP, AIRC, AAPA, ARA, FLHC, PAHM, Senior Associate, Designation Programs; and Martha Parker, FLMI, ACS, ALHC, AIAA, Senior Associate, Designation Programs. In addition, Lisa M. Kozlowski, FLMI, FFSI, CLU, ChFC, AIAA, AIRC, ARA, FLHC, AAPA, ACS, Senior Associate, Training Programs, contributed to the Exams review.

In LOMA's Production Department, thanks go to Carol A. Wiessner, Product Sourcing Manager, who coordinated printing of the text, Amy Stailey, Production Coordinator II/Scheduling Coordinator, who coordinated production of and typeset the text and Allison Ayers-Molette who also typeset portions of the text. In addition, we thank Eastman Communications and Barbara Foxenberger Brown, FLMI, ACS, AIAA, AIRC for their excellent copyediting of the manuscript; Steve Silver, an author of this text, also served as our permissions editor and secured the necessary permissions for material in the text from external sources. Finally, Robert D. Land, FLMI, ACS, a consultant, created the index for the text with his usual expertise.

We also thank the individuals in LOMA's Information Center who provided valuable research services: Jean Gora, ACS; Mallory Eldridge, Writer/Research Analyst; and Olivia Blakemore, ACS, Technical Administrator.

Special thanks go to Katherine C. Milligan, FLMI, ACS, ALHC, Vice President, Education and Training Division, who provided leadership, guidance, resources, support, and encouragement for this project.

Sharon Allen-Peterson, FLMI, ACS, AIRC, PAHM
Kevin Head, Ph.D., FLMI, ACS, AFSI
Steven R. Silver, J.D., FLMI, AFSI, AIRC, AIAA, ACS
Atlanta, Georgia
2010

Introduction

The purpose of *Insurance Marketing* is to provide an overview of the practices and procedures involved in marketing insurance. To enhance your learning experience, LOMA has developed a Course Portal for this course that is accessible upon enrollment in LOMANET. A LOMA Course Portal is an online resource from which learners access everything they need to study and prepare for the course examination. The 320 Course Portal contains an array of blended learning resources, including some multimedia features. The Course Portal provides access to:

■ An introductory course video

■ Protected PDFs of the assigned study materials that can be printed or read online

■ Access to the interactive Practice Questions and Sample Exams

■ Recommended study assignments to help you set goals and manage your learning experience

■ Review tools, including a "Top Ten Tough Topics" review

Students preparing to take the examination for LOMA 320—*Insurance Marketing*—which is part of the Fellow, Life Management Institute (FLMI) program, will find that the course materials include many features designed to help learners more easily understand the course material, organize their study, and help them prepare for the examination. These features include chapter outlines, learning objectives, key terms, figures containing real-world examples of course content, and a comprehensive glossary. As we describe each of these features, we give you suggestions for studying the material.

■ **Chapter Outline.** The first page of each chapter contains an outline of the chapter. Review this outline to gain an overview of the major topics that will be covered; then scan through the chapter to become familiar with how information is presented. By looking at the headings, you can gain a preview of how various subjects in each chapter relate to each other.

■ **Learning Objectives.** The first page of each chapter also contains a list of learning objectives to help you focus your studies. Before reading each chapter, review these learning objectives. Then, as you read the chapter, look for material that will help you meet the learning objectives.

- **Key Terms.** This text explains new marketing and insurance industry terms that apply to the text material and, where appropriate, reviews key terms previously presented in LOMA courses. Important terminology is highlighted with ***bold italic type*** when the term is defined, and a list of these key terms appears at the end of each chapter. All key terms also appear in a comprehensive glossary at the end of the text and are accessible from the Course Portal. As you read each chapter, pay special attention to the key terms.

- **Figures.** We include figures throughout the text to illustrate and bring a real-world perspective to the text's discussions of selected important topics. Information contained in figures may be tested on the examination for the course.

- **Glossary.** A comprehensive glossary that contains definitions of all key terms appears at the end of the book and is accessible from the Course Portal. Following each glossary entry is a number in brackets that indicates the chapter in which the key term is defined. The glossary also references important equivalent terms, acronyms, and contrasting terms.

LOMA may periodically revise the course materials and study aids for this course. To ensure that you are studying from the correct materials, check the current *LOMA Education and Training Catalog* available at www.loma.org/StudentServices.asp or the Course Portal for LOMA 320 for a description of the materials and study aids assigned for the examination for which you are preparing.

Using The LOMA Study Aid

LOMA has prepared a study aid designed to help students prepare for the LOMA 320 examination. LOMA recommends that you use this study aid. **Studies indicate that students who use LOMA study aids consistently perform significantly better on LOMA examinations than students who do not use these study aids.**

This study aid, LOMA's *Test Preparation Guide for LOMA 320*, is assigned reading for students preparing for the LOMA 320 examination. Used along with the text, the Test Preparation Guide (TPG) will help you master the course material. The TPG, which is accessible from the Course Portal, can be used online or printed as a PDF. It contains practice exam questions and a full-scale sample examination, along with answer explanations to every question in the TPG.

Chapter 1

An Introduction to Marketing

Objectives:

After studying this chapter, you should be able to

- ■ Define the four variables of the marketing mix
- ■ Explain the role of utility in the exchange process
- ■ Explain how factors in an insurance company's internal and external marketing environments can create marketing opportunities or constraints
- ■ Define corporate culture and distinguish between proactive and reactive companies
- ■ Describe how the business cycle and inflation influence an insurance company's marketing activities
- ■ Identify the four basic market structures found in the competitive environment and explain how product differentiation is used in monopolistic competition
- ■ Describe common barriers to entry that affect insurance companies
- ■ Identify several technological developments, social factors, and economic challenges that impact the marketing of insurance products

Outline

What Is Marketing?
- Marketing as a Process
- Creating Utility

The Marketing Environment
- Internal Environment
- External Environment

Marketing Challenges

Marketing slips into every day and every minute of our lives. Breakfast cereal boxes offer free gifts in exchange for proofs of purchase or provide entries for contests or sweepstakes. The morning newspaper advertises sales at local stores and promotes activities around town. Roadside billboards announce grand openings or encourage us to donate blood. Direct mail ads fill our mailboxes. The Internet offers online shopping and a way to share and obtain information about products and services worldwide. Radio, television, and the Internet include product ads and public service announcements. Companies sponsor sports and charity events to promote their company's image or products.

Most of us encounter marketing at work, too. For example, if you work in an insurance company, your boss may ask you to do marketing research for a new product or promotional idea. You may need to explain to a customer what a variable annuity is and why the customer needs it. Or, maybe you'll be asked to be in a video clip about the company that will be posted to your company's Web site. Marketing knowledge can benefit workers in a wide range of job functions.

What Is Marketing?

The American Marketing Association, which represents approximately 38,000 marketing professionals worldwide as of 2008, defines marketing as:

> *Marketing* is the activity, set of institutions, and processes for creating, communicating, delivering, and exchanging offerings that have value for customers, clients, partners, and society at large.[1]

Marketing as a Process

Marketing in successful companies starts with learning about and understanding the customer and the customer's needs. For most insurance customers, those needs relate to financial security and include

- Maintaining their current standard of living if a family member dies or becomes disabled

- Saving for retirement or education

- Growing and protecting assets to pass down to future generations

- Providing for business continuity in the event of the death or disability of a key person or owner

- Paying for health care and final expenses upon death

Next, the company develops the products or services it believes will best meet customer needs and offer value to the customer. Finally, the marketing staff puts into place ways to promote and distribute the products and services to prospective customers. Throughout this process, the company tracks how its products perform and how customers respond to those products.

Throughout the marketing process, companies manage four main variables—called the *marketing mix*, or *the Four Ps* of marketing:

- *Product* refers to the goods, services, and/or ideas that a seller offers to customers to satisfy their needs. *Customers* are the individuals and organizations that purchase a company's products.

- *Price* is the monetary value of whatever the customer exchanges for the product; usually price is an amount of money.

- *Place* refers to how and where customers purchase products. Insurance companies substitute *distribution*—the activities that make products available for customers to buy—for the term "place."

- *Promotion* refers to all the activities that companies use to make customers aware of their offerings and to influence customers to purchase, and distributors to sell, a product.

Each of "the Four Ps" affects and is affected by each of the other variables.

Creating Utility

As the marketing definition states, one goal of marketing is to exchange offerings that have value for the customer, client, company, and society. In an *exchange* one party gives something of value to another party to get something of value in return. Often, money is exchanged for either goods or services.

The product or service itself may not be the real value in an exchange. *Utility* is how well a product or service satisfies a customer's needs and is often the true value of an exchange. A product or service has utility (it satisfies customers' needs) if it has been produced, taken to a place where customers can buy it, stored until they are ready to buy it, and given to them so they can use it. In other words, utility is created when a customer can get the right product, at the right place, and at the right time. For example, a single mom who wants to financially provide for her two young children if she dies before they're grown may consider a term life insurance product that she can find using the Internet to have more utility than a similar product that would require her to meet in person with a sales agent.

The Marketing Environment

The marketing environment is always changing. Economic conditions change. Laws and regulations change. Technology creates newer, faster, and better ways of sharing and obtaining information and getting tasks done. As a direct result, customers expect speedier and more efficient service. To survive in this environment, insurance companies must adapt to changes. For example, today many customers expect a company to support its community by making charitable donations of money or services, or developing company-wide programs to conserve energy or resources.

A company's marketing environment includes all the factors that directly or indirectly affect the company's ability to carry out its marketing activities. The ***internal environment*** consists of all those elements that come from within the company and that it can control. Factors that exist outside a company and that it does not control make up the ***external environment***. Figure 1.1 depicts the influences in a company's internal and external environments.

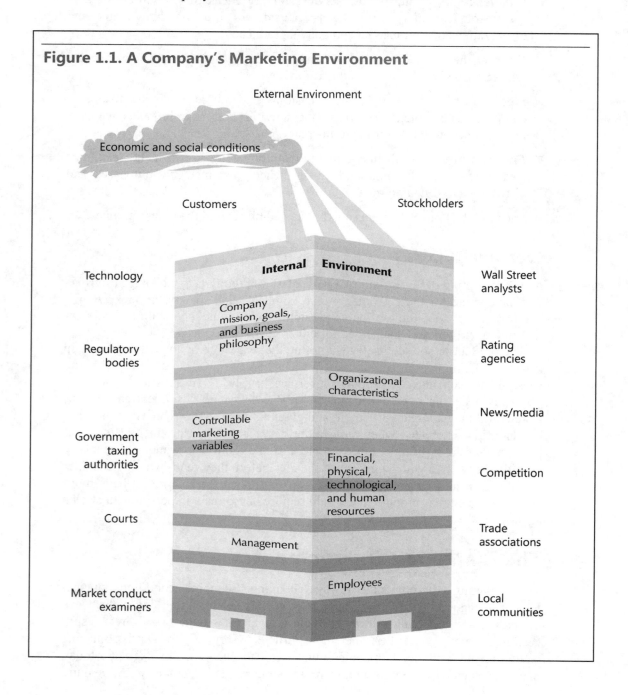

Figure 1.1. A Company's Marketing Environment

All these environmental factors offer marketing opportunities or constraints. A *marketing opportunity* arises when environmental conditions allow a company to use its strengths or capabilities to take advantage of current trends or expand its activities. A *constraint* is a factor that limits a company's activities.

Some constraints are outside a company's control. For example, companies have no control over whether a country is at war. However, companies can sometimes cause changes in the environment that reduce or remove constraints. For example, companies can use promotion to try to increase demand for products, or they can work toward regulatory changes by backing legislation or other efforts to reduce regulatory requirements. Sometimes companies can turn constraints into opportunities. A company may overcome a constraint by developing new products or targeting new markets. A company has more control over its internal environment than its external environment. So, it is easier for a company to remove internal constraints than external constraints.

Internal Environment

Within an insurance company's internal environment, marketing is supported by almost every functional department in the company. Figure 1.2 shows the marketing and marketing-related support activities that nonmarketing departments typically perform. As this figure illustrates, virtually every functional area in an insurance company is involved in some aspect of the marketing process. Similarly, the marketing process in some way affects virtually every functional area of an insurance company.

Because so many functional departments contribute to marketing efforts, the internal environment of a particular company can greatly affect whether an insurance company's marketing efforts succeed or fail. The parts of the internal environment that have the greatest impact on how a company can market itself and its products are

- Company traits
- Company resources
- Controllable marketing variables

Company Traits

Company traits such as a company's legal form, internal structure, and corporate culture all affect how the company markets itself and its products, as explained in the following chart.

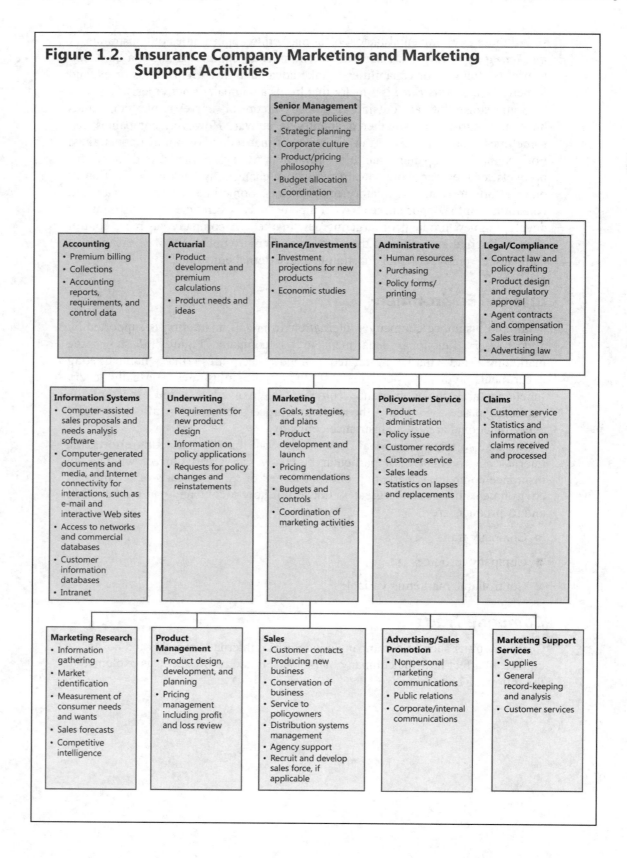

Figure 1.2. Insurance Company Marketing and Marketing Support Activities

Trait	Effect on Marketing Programs
Legal Form	- Affects how money can be raised for growth or stability
	Affects the number and type of marketing activities used
Internal Structure	- Affects how routine business is done including getting operating funds, governing the company, setting goals and objectives, and using profits
Corporate Culture	- Affects how well and quickly a company can put in place a new marketing program supported by all staff
	- Affects how a company reacts to or addresses changes in its environment

Legal form. *Legal form* refers to the way a company is legally set up to allow it to operate in a particular state or other jurisdiction. Laws in the United States and many other countries require insurance companies to be organized as corporations. Insurance companies can choose to be incorporated as stock companies or mutual companies. Stock companies sell stock (or shares of ownership) to raise money to operate and expand as needed. If a company needs more funds for operations or growth, it can issue and sell more shares of stock if company shareholders approve the sale. Mutual companies do not issue stock and cannot sell it to raise capital. So, mutual companies must sell additional products or use other funding sources, such as borrowing, to get additional funds. Many mutual companies have converted to stock companies in recent years, in part to be able to raise funds more easily by issuing additional stock.

Internal structure. The way a company chooses to structure its organization affects how it can perform routine business activities. The number of management layers a company has affects how quickly it can respond to its environment. A company that requires several management levels to approve new strategies may miss marketing opportunities. By the time a plan gets all the required approvals, a competitor may already have seized an opportunity or the opportunity may have disappeared.

Example: Suppose a huge natural disaster such as a hurricane, earthquake, or tornado strikes. A company with fewer layers of management may be able to act more quickly to provide immediate support and services to victims than companies with more layers of management from which approval for company activities must be obtained.

Corporate culture. A company's *corporate culture* describes the attitudes, values, perceptions, beliefs, and experiences shared by the company's employees and instilled in new employees when they join the company. Figure 1.3 provides some insight into how corporate culture affects the way business gets done in one company.

Corporate culture affects how a company reacts to or addresses changes in its environment. Some companies are more proactive; others are more reactive. A *proactive organization* anticipates changes in the environment, pioneers innovative activities, and encourages new approaches and ideas. A *reactive organization* is more passive, responds more cautiously, and is unlikely to anticipate changes before they occur. Few companies are consistently proactive or reactive. Instead, how a company responds to environmental changes depends on the situation.

Figure 1.3. How We've Always Done It

From their first day at Xylophone Insurance Company, employees learn that following established procedure to get things done is how work is accomplished. Marketing employees submit ideas for new products or product changes to their managers. Managers review the promising ideas with higher level managers to decide whether to pursue a new idea. A marketing panel with representatives from several different functional areas of the company makes the final decision whether to pursue a suggestion or not.

Dennis Hadley is a new employee at Xylophone with several years of marketing experience at other insurance companies. After his first few months at Xylophone, Dennis has an idea for marketing one of their products that he has analyzed thoroughly and believes will cut the company's marketing and distribution costs significantly. Although Dennis knows how things are done at Xylophone, he decides to skip a few levels of management and try to present his idea at the next marketing panel meeting instead of going through the chain of managers first.

Dennis has persuaded the administrative assistant for the company's marketing director to help him obtain a few minutes in front of the panel. He presents his idea and although everyone listens politely, he is quickly ushered back to his department. Later that same day his manager meets with him to explain again the company's procedure for new ideas and reinforces that no new ideas will be considered unless they go through the established procedure.

Dennis tried to go against the corporate culture at Xylophone and was not successful.

A company's culture can help it move ahead or can hold it back from opportunities. For example, when a reactive company faces a problem, it may look at how it handled similar problems in the past, or at how other companies have handled such situations. By using knowledge gained from past experiences, the company's corporate culture is a strength because the company is less likely to repeat past mistakes or waste resources solving problems that have already been solved. However, a reactive company may miss marketing opportunities, such as being an early entrant into a new market.

Company Resources

A company's resources include:

- Physical resources (facilities)
- Technological resources (information management and communications systems)
- Human resources (employees)
- Financial resources (assets and capital)

In general, companies with plenty of financial, technological, and human resources can enter more markets, with more products, and draw upon a larger customer base than companies with limited resources.

Resources, particularly financial resources, strongly influence the ratings that outside rating companies and regulators give to companies. Ratings give investors a way to evaluate the overall financial health of an insurance company before investing in that company. Ratings give customers a gauge to rate the stability of the company they are considering doing business with. For example, one rating company—A.M. Best—assigns a Financial Strength Rating (FSR) to insurance companies. The FSR represents how likely A.M. Best thinks it is that an insurer will be able to meet its obligations to policyowners. A.M. Best reviews a company's financial strengths and weaknesses to develop its opinion. A strong financial base indicates to potential customers that a company will be able to meet its financial obligations over the long term. Financial strength is especially important to potential buyers of insurance products, which are essentially promises of payments in the future, often the distant future. So, a company that receives a solid, high rating has a competitive advantage. A weak financial rating often negatively affects a company's ability to market its products.

Controllable Marketing Variables

A company's **controllable marketing variables** are parts of the marketing process that a company can define and manage for itself. For most insurance companies, their controllable marketing variables include

- **Market choice**. Most companies aim their marketing at specific segments of the population. To find a segment that is a good fit for a company's products, the company may divide the population into groups based on income level, type of employment, life cycle stage, or other factors. Some companies market only to educators or military personnel; others market to customers in all lines of work but may offer only a few products.

- **Products**. The products that a company offers depend on its resources and its marketing expertise. Some insurance companies offer only individual life insurance and group life insurance products. Others offer individual life, group life, individual health, group health insurance products, and annuities. Still other companies may add property/casualty products to their product lines.

- **Pricing.** A company's prices for its products affects both its sales and profitability. Prices also affect customer perception of products. Some companies use high prices to emphasize quality and prestige. Other companies use low prices as a way to attract customers and emphasize value.

- **Promotion**. A company's promotional efforts are influenced by all the other elements of the marketing mix. Some insurance companies promote the company and their products mostly to consumers to create demand and encourage product purchases. Other companies direct more product promotion to their distributors—sales intermediaries—and use sales incentives and other sales rewards to encourage product sales.

- **Distribution**. Insurance companies can deliver their products through a variety of distribution channels ranging from an Internet sale to a face-to-face meeting with an insurance producer. An *insurance producer*, also known as a *producer*, is any individual who is licensed to sell insurance products, solicit sales, or negotiate insurance contracts in a state. Companies that market complex products—such as variable universal life insurance—usually generate sales through face-to-face meetings between producers and prospective customers. Companies that offer simple, low-cost products may market their products through direct response channels such as the Internet, direct mail, or in-bound call centers. Many sales involve more than one channel—for example, a company may generate leads via the Internet for producers to contact to pursue a sale.

All of these elements interrelate. Changes in one variable may affect another variable, which could ultimately affect sales or company profitability. Some marketing variables are also influenced by elements in the environment over which the company has little or no control.

External Environment

News reports or other media coverage related to the economy, insurance in general, specific insurance companies, or insurance industry practices can all affect a company's decisions about how to market its products.

> **Example:** [*Excerpt from The Late Night News television news report:* "Analysts expect a continued downward trend in the nation's economy. Key economic indicators show that the economy is experiencing a slight contraction in growth. More on this after Sports...."]

The major areas of the external environment that impact how insurers market their products include

Economy   Competition   Regulation   Technology   Society

Because companies don't have control over these factors, they must find ways to anticipate, favorably influence, and respond to changes in the external environment.

Economic Factors

The *economic environment* includes all the parts of an economy that affect how products and services are produced, distributed, and used. To compete successfully, companies identify trends in the economy that are likely to affect their marketing activities. For example, an insurance company that sells products and services in more than one region should keep track of the current and projected economic conditions for those regions. Economic conditions that the insurer should review include regional and local growth, employment rates, spending levels, level and types of production, prices for goods and services, cost of living, income levels, interest rates, and other economic indicators.

> **Example:** The metropolitan area of Pitchawa, a college town with a population of over 200,000 and growing, is experiencing rapid economic growth. Demand for upscale housing is on the rise as more professionals move to the area, and it is becoming a regional hub for technology. Consumer spending in the area is up as more and more people commute to Pitchawa from neighboring areas to work. Income levels for various professions are exceeding the average for areas of similar size.
>
> **Analysis:** An insurance company that serves the Pitchawa area may want to increase its marketing and sales efforts there to inform new residents about the company's products and services. The company may consider adding to its sales force to handle the anticipated growth in business for the company. Also, the company may decide to repackage its product bundles to appeal to affluent families.

A company should also look at national and global economic factors that could affect its business. Companies with multinational operations have an even greater need to monitor the global economy and its national and regional components.

Two major economic factors that affect insurance companies are the business cycle and inflation.

Business Cycle. Companies attempt to predict economic trends by studying the business cycle. A *business cycle* is a recurring pattern of fluctuations in the economic activity of a nation over a specified period of time, generally a year or more. This pattern is shown in Figure 1.4.

The economic activity periods in a business cycle are called expansion, peak, contraction, and trough. Economists determine a nation's stage in the business cycle by measuring the nation's gross domestic product, unemployment and other variables that affect the total economy. The *gross domestic product (GDP)* is the total output of goods and services produced by labor and property located within a country, valued at adjusted market prices. Economists, looking at the same data, may differ in opinion as to which business cycle the economy reflects. Each insurance company must review the information and opinions that

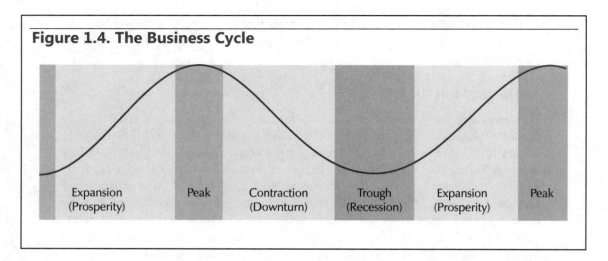

Figure 1.4. The Business Cycle

Expansion (Prosperity) — Peak — Contraction (Downturn) — Trough (Recession) — Expansion (Prosperity) — Peak

economists provide and determine where the business cycle is in relationship to the company and its marketing programs.

The business cycle is important to marketers because both consumer and organizational spending patterns differ depending on the economy's position in the cycle. Wealth, productivity, business growth, and overall spending typically increase during periods of expansion. Conversely, during a downturn or recession, overall spending, including spending on insurance and financial services products, decreases. Because of this pattern, most companies avoid a major marketing expansion during a down cycle, when unemployment rises and spending drops. However, downturns may offer opportunities for some companies. For example, discount retailers and used clothing stores may gain more customers during downturns because those new customers are not shopping at higher-cost retailers. Life insurance sales may also increase during a downturn, because people are less optimistic and want to protect, as much as possible, their existing assets. They also want products that will secure their financial future.

Business cycles are not completely regular or predictable in terms of:

- How long they last

- How many businesses they affect

- To what degree they affect those businesses

Yet, the business cycle still offers value. A company can form a clearer picture of the general trend of the economy if it knows (1) which period an economy is currently experiencing in the business cycle and (2) how long analysts expect that period to last.

Inflation. *Inflation*, a prolonged rise in the average level of prices in an economy, also affects marketing activities. The Consumer Price Index is the most widely quoted measure of inflation in the United States and Canada. The **Consumer Price Index (CPI)** is a number that results from comparing the average price of a "market basket" of goods and services at a stated point in time to the average price of the same market basket items at a different point in time.

$50 will buy basket
of goods in Year 1

$100 will buy same
basket of goods in Year 21

The market basket consists of hundreds of goods and services that an average family of four in a moderate-sized community would need. Many other countries throughout the world publish their own consumer price indexes, and some consumer price indexes are published for several countries combined. For example, the European Central Bank publishes the Harmonized Index of Consumer Prices (HICP), which shows money spent by households in the European Union member states.[2] A ***household*** is any single person who lives alone or any group of people, related or not, who share the same residence. During periods of inflation, a household's dollar, euro, yen, or peso cannot buy as much because the prices of goods and services rise faster than the household's income.

Inflation can negatively affect both the returns on, and the value of, the principal in fixed-rate financial products. As a result, owners may sell or give up guaranteed, fixed-rate products during high inflation periods in exchange for products whose value varies by market performance to try to earn better returns. When the rate of inflation drops, the process reverses, and some customers sell products tied to market performance and buy fixed-rate products that offer guaranteed returns. Occasionally, changes in inflation are big enough to cause large numbers of customers to remove money from an insurance product to earn higher returns on other investments. For insurers, this widespread movement of funds by customers can reduce premium income, prevent recovery of expenses, and possibly disrupt cash flows because of payments (surrender values) to customers who abandon the company or some of its products.

Competitive Factors

Just about every company faces competition from other companies that can provide alternative products or services to satisfy customer needs. In a competitive environment, companies can increase sales by (1) selling their products to new customers and/or (2) persuading current customers to buy more products.

Companies can sell to new customers by expanding into new markets, penetrating current markets more effectively, and/or adding new distribution channels. Companies increase sales to current customers by introducing new products the market wants, making product changes, lowering prices, and/or by getting customers to change what, how much, or how they buy. For example, a company may be able to convince its competitors' customers to buy its product by offering the product through a more convenient distribution channel. Some insurance companies expand their product line or increase their customer base by acquiring or merging with a competitor whose business complements their own.

The market for life insurance in North America is fairly mature and stable. To increase market share in this region, companies generally try to (1) differentiate their companies and products from competitors, (2) target faster-growing segments of the market, and (3) create innovative products or distribution channels that better meet market needs. Companies constantly monitor current and potential competitors' marketing activities, including new product offerings, special promotions, price changes, changes in distribution, and other actions, to ensure that their own marketing efforts exceed or at least meet competitors' offerings.

Market Structure. Market structure determines how many and what types of competitors a company will face. Economists generally divide market structures into four basic types: monopoly, oligopoly, monopolistic competition, and pure competition. Figure 1.5 shows these four basic structures and their characteristics. The structure of today's insurance and financial services market is best described as monopolistic competition. *Monopolistic competition* exists when a large number of competitors are present, who each sell similar but differentiated products and each have only a small percentage of the total market's sales.

Most marketing theorists believe the most effective practice for marketing in monopolistic competition is using product differentiation. *Product differentiation* is the practice of distinguishing a product from competing products using its form, style, quality, or some other characteristic, such as price, distribution, or promotion, so that the customer both understands and appreciates the difference. A company can also use price, distribution, and promotion to help differentiate itself from its competitors. This means that while the products offered in the market basically fulfill the same or similar needs, customers view the products and the company itself as different because of the way the company presents them.

How Much Competition is in the Market. The movement of competitors and competing products into and out of various markets is also an important part of the competitive environment. In theory, when competitors leave a market, competition is reduced, which makes it more likely that the remaining companies will achieve their sales objectives. As new competitors enter a market, competition increases, prices go down, and existing companies in the market find it harder to achieve their sales objectives.

The actual impact of changes in competition, however, depends on the number and kinds of competitors moving out of or into a market. For example, in markets that have many competitors, the entry or departure of one or two companies may have little effect. In markets with few competitors, the movement of a single company can make a dramatic difference. In the same way, a company that does not play a major role in a market may have little impact on the market if it leaves that market. However, if a company with a major role in the market leaves the marketplace, there may be a profound effect on the market itself. If a major competitor enters a new market, it may boost both the market's status and overall potential simply by being a part of that market.

Competing companies are less likely to enter a market with strong barriers to entry. A *barrier to entry* is a business practice or condition in a market that hinders new companies from entering the market. Common barriers to entry that affect insurance and financial services companies include

Figure 1.5. The Four Basic Market Structures

	Type of Market Structure			
Characteristics	**Monopoly**	**Oligopoly**	**Monopolistic Competition**	**Pure Competition**
Number of Competitors	One	Few	Many	Great many
Barriers to Entry	Many	Some	Few	None
Share of Market Sales	Total	Large percentage by each seller	Small percentage by each seller	Very small percentage by each seller
Product	No substitutes	Similar products	Similar products	Nearly identical products
Price	Not very important	Important, but sellers seek to avoid price competition	Very important	Important
Distribution	May have considerable control	Considerable control	Some control	Little control
Promotion	Not very important	Product differentiation important	Product differentiation extremely important	No product differentiation

- **Customer/brand loyalty.** In markets where strong product differentiation exists, customers are often extremely loyal to their favorite brands of particular products. For example, an owner of a BMW automobile might not even consider driving a Cadillac automobile instead. Large insurance companies can afford expensive national advertising that results in name recognition among potential buyers, which gives the company an advantage over smaller, less well-known companies. Customers may be more willing to purchase the products of companies with known names and may view the smaller, less-known companies as less desirable.

- **Access to distribution channels.** When the current major competitors in a market own or control the key distribution channels for a particular type of product, or the cost of developing a distribution channel is high, then the cost for companies to enter that market is likely to be high.

Example: In insurance, it is very expensive to build a personal selling distribution system because insurers must train and support sales agents even before they earn a profit for the company. Many new insurance companies cannot afford such an expense and enter the business by creating alternate distribution channels, such as third-party distributors or direct response distribution.

■ **Economies of scale**. When the costs per unit of producing, selling, distributing, and promoting a product decrease as the number of units of the product sold increases, *economies of scale* exist. In most industries, many units of sales are needed to reach this best level of operation. New companies that enter an industry often do not have enough resources and production or service capacity to create economies of scale. This lack of resources and capacity is often a disadvantage for a company when it competes against established sellers. New companies also find it more difficult to introduce and support related products than do established companies that have higher sales volume and the staff and technology needed to handle multiple products.

■ **Ownership advantages**. New competitors may not be able to enter an industry if companies already in the industry control sources of natural resources, raw materials, patents, or other special rights to any proprietary technology needed to compete in the industry. The barrier created by ownership advantages does not often apply to the insurance industry, because particular natural resources, raw materials, patents, and so on, are rarely required to offer insurance products. However, an insurer that controls the "talent" or expertise in a particular area may have an ownership advantage if the level of expertise in the market is limited. For example, a company with an experienced and productive sales force may have an ownership advantage if the number of experienced salespeople in the market is limited.

■ **Government regulations**. Laws that effectively discourage new companies from entering into certain markets exist. In the insurance industry, many regulatory barriers to entry have been changed to allow more types of players (banks, credit unions, and others) to market insurance products. However, barriers do still exist and only insurance companies can create and administer (or "issue") insurance products.

Examples:

Strict capital requirements that insurance companies must meet to operate in some jurisdictions are still potential barriers to entry.

Many countries have laws in place that discourage foreign companies from entering domestic markets.

Regulatory Factors

Regulation affects product development, pricing, distribution, and sales and marketing activities. For example, companies must be licensed in every jurisdiction in which they do business and sales intermediaries must be licensed and meet other requirements in many jurisdictions throughout the world. In addition, before a company can offer certain products for sale to the public, it must submit them for regulatory approval by the appropriate jurisdiction. Regulation touches almost all marketing materials that go out to the public, from printed brochures to Web sites, blogs, and other interactions with the public. The time and costs of meeting regulatory requirements are usually quite high.

Technological Factors

Technology is the application of knowledge, particularly scientific knowledge, to practical purposes. It is one of the most powerful forces affecting insurance marketing today. However, insurance companies are more limited in how they can use online interactions and marketing technology than other types of companies because regulatory authorities set stringent rules for insurers' operation and behavior.

In recent decades, technology has redefined the way customers seek and receive services as well as the ways companies develop, price, distribute, and promote new products. For example, using the Internet and other computer-based technologies, a potential consumer can learn about insurance, shop for insurance products online, and, in some situations, complete the entire insurance purchase electronically, including printing a policy. Insurance companies can use technology to

- Improve service to help retain customers

- React quickly to changing market demands

- Differentiate products more effectively (for example, by showing computerized visual sales illustrations)

- Provide timely information to management

- Explore new distribution channels

- Process new business electronically to increase productivity

- Tailor customer promotions to a narrowly targeted audience

- Educate producers and home office staff

- Generate leads and assist the sales process by using e-mail, database-generated mailings, and advanced telephone technologies

- Sell products

Companies use **electronic commerce**, also known as *e-commerce, e-business,* or *"B to B" (business to business),* which is the use of computer networks to perform business transactions and help deliver products and services to customers. Most insurance companies have created their own Web sites. These sites allow companies to display information about their businesses and to transmit data to and collect data from their internal and external customers. Most companies offer customer service via their Web sites, which may include real-time access to a customer service representative via a live Internet chat. Customers can also find information that offers reviews and comparisons of insurance products at various Web sites. In addition, computer networks allow customers to retrieve account information, including payments due and historical account data. Often, customers can combine information about their particular investments from multiple insurance and financial services companies on their own computers using financial software to monitor investment performance over time.

Computer software now allows people with similar interests to interact with each other online via social networks where they can share opinions and information, possibly about an insurance company and its products or competitor products. In addition, companies can provide information about themselves and their products and keep up with the changing desires of customers through podcasts, blogs, and mobile marketing. *Podcasts* are audio or video broadcasts about a particular subject or topic that are sent to a user's computer via an audio or video file in a format that can be transferred to and played on portable digital media devices such as the iPod™ and Zune™. Users can subscribe to a provider's podcast feed, also called an *RSS feed*. Companies or industry groups can also create their own podcasts that apply to their industry. For example, A.M. Best offers several podcasts related to insurance topics and the American Marketing Association sponsors podcasts on marketing themes.

A **blog**, also known as a *Web log*, is a Web site or a portion of a Web site that provides news or commentary on a particular subject with the entries displayed in reverse chronological order, beginning with the most recent entry. Often visitors to the site can post their own comments about the blog content. In addition to learning more about their customers and markets, interactive technology forums allow companies to have dynamic two-way information exchanges in which customers learn more about their options and companies learn more about their customers and markets. An insurance company that is considering adding a blog section to its Web site must carefully consider the advantages and disadvantages of such an addition. For example, because insurance is an intangible product, any blog posts that an insurance company's employees make could be regarded by customers as a warranty of performance and subject the company to unintended liability.

Some companies are starting to use mobile marketing to connect with their customers. **Mobile marketing** is the use of wireless technology to deliver advertising messages in a particular place, such as an airport, concert venue, or sports arena, usually with the intended receiver's consent. For example, a company might send a text message to the mobile devices of attendees at a music concert, advertising the company and directing attendees to a kiosk where they can receive a small free gift.

Social Factors

The **social environment** consists of the demographic traits, values, beliefs, and shared and learned norms of behavior of various groups of customers who make up a population. Peoples' beliefs about who bears the responsibility for the economic well-being of individuals and families—the individuals and families themselves, their employers, or government, and to what degree each is responsible—will shape the opportunities for the types of financial services products that can be marketed and who the purchaser will be.

Demographics. *Demographics* are measurable traits that describe or define a given population. Demographic traits used often in marketing include age, income and assets, life-cycle stage, household size and composition, gender, education, birth and death rates, race, nationality, occupation, and marital status.

In most countries, the government regularly collects demographic data through a census of the population and much of that data is readily available to marketers. Insurance companies consider a population's demographic traits when making marketing decisions. Two of the demographic traits that insurance companies focus their attention on when choosing markets to pursue are (1) age and (2) income and assets.

Age. The world's population is growing older. According to the United Nations (UN) Population Division the number of people age 60 or older is expected to triple and reach almost 1.9 billion by the year 2050.[3] Factors driving the overall aging of the world population include

- Decreasing birthrates. The **birthrate**, which is the number of babies born per 1,000 people in the population, is decreasing in almost all developed countries. Fertility is below replacement level in all countries considered to be developed countries by the UN. And, in at least 28 of the developing countries, including China, fertility is below replacement level.[4] *Replacement-level fertility* refers to the number of births required per woman to maintain the current population.

- Increasing life expectancies. Life expectancy is a description of how many years the average person is expected to live. For example, in the past, a person age 65 could expect to live an additional 5 to 10 years. Today, especially in most developed countries, people age 65 often live an additional 20 years or more. Aging populations are most common in more developed countries.

Age distribution, which refers to the proportion of people in certain age ranges in a given population, affects the type of products that insurance companies need to market to meet that population's needs and goals. For example, a population made up of retirees and workers nearing retirement generally needs products to help them manage and protect their resources rather than replacing future earned income. Markets with aging populations often need products for retirement and asset protection. Younger people, who are building their careers, raising families and planning for their future, need products that help them protect their assets and provide income for family members in the event of the death or disability of a primary financial provider or caretaker, such as a non-working spouse taking care of children. They also need products that help them save for major purchases, education, retirement, and transfer of wealth from one generation to the next. In particular, Generation Y—which refers to the generation in the United States born between about 1979 and 1995—includes a significant number of people who work as consultants or are self-employed and do not receive health benefits from an employer. Generation Y is a viable market with distinct needs for health and business insurance products.

Finally, health care is a priority for all age groups. In the United States, for example, health care costs keep rising at twice the rate of inflation. The aging population in the United States and other developed countries requires more and more health care services as they live longer. Affordable health insurance products that provide adequate coverage to meet the needs of specific populations are needed.

Income and assets. A population's assets and income level affect the ability of consumers in that population to buy insurance products and the types of products they need. For example, a population with low income levels and few assets may not be able to afford any, or only the least costly, insurance products. In contrast, a population with higher income and more assets can afford higher-priced products and may need and be able to afford multiple insurance products. In the United States, for example, there is a middle-income market for insurance products that is especially underserved and represents an opportunity for insurance companies. Some insurers are successfully targeting low-income markets in some countries, often with government subsidies or incentives for entering such a market. For example, India requires such a strategy from all market entrants to ensure that the benefits of life insurance extend beyond the cities into rural areas as well.

Shared and Learned Norms of Behavior. The social environment directly affects buying behavior and also sets standards for what a population expects from business and marketing in terms of the marketing mix. Social norms affect whether people in a particular society view the purchase of insurance as a responsible way to provide for one's family or whether such a purchase is discouraged, perhaps because the society considers it unseemly to discuss the inevitability of death, as many societies throughout the world do. Companies that use their marketing mix to influence potential customers' attitudes about openly discussing such issues are trying to affect social norms.

Shared norms of behavior also affect the way companies plan their marketing mix to appeal to potential customers. For example, Apple, Inc.—a United States-based company that designs, manufactures, and markets personal computers, portable digital music players, and mobile communication devices and sells a variety of related software, services, peripherals, and networking solutions—has positioned itself as an innovative company that creates cutting-edge technology products. Its customers expect something unique and different from an Apple marketing mix. When Apple introduced its first I-Phone it used only one retail vendor to distribute the product, creating an aspect of exclusivity to this product. Also, by leaking brief details about the product a few at a time in the months before the product launch, Apple created a lot of word-of-mouth promotion for the product in the form of publicity. Much of this chatter about the I-Phone occurred on Internet blogs and on social networking Web sites.

The growth in the popularity of blogs has resulted in rapid changes in social environment norms. Using blogs, customers can shape or create opinions—positively or negatively—about companies that may interfere with the messages that companies want consumers to receive. For example, customers who have positive experiences with a company, and write positive remarks about the company on a blog, are promoting the company and its products to millions of people worldwide in a way that many find more credible than other more traditional means of promotion. Of course, a bad experience that is described on a blog can have just the opposite effect on a company's reputation.

Marketing Challenges

One challenge insurers face is dealing with the trend in the financial services industry toward *convergence*—the creation of a single financial institution being able to serve all of a customer's banking, securities, and insurance needs. Convergence has dramatically affected competition, resulting in downsizing, mergers and acquisitions, and company re-engineering.

However, convergence has produced different outcomes than expected. For example, widespread convergence has not occurred largely because

- It is difficult for one company to do a superior job of fulfilling all the financial needs of the customer.

- Historically distinct industries have different cultural views of the products, and their varying priorities create barriers to convergence.

- Laws in the United States and some other countries restrict the sharing of customer information unless the customer specifically authorizes such sharing or takes an action that implicitly authorizes the company to obtain customer information, such as requesting a life insurance quote.

- Recent economic downturns in the United States have made consumers reluctant to put all their money or assets with one financial institution. In a period of economic uncertainty, a consumer might choose to spread assets among several different companies.

Another challenge for insurers is managing their profitability while complying with the many laws and regulations that apply to their operations, including marketing. For example, in the United States, federal laws prohibit telemarketers from calling consumers to sell products under certain circumstances, and laws and regulations also affect the storage, use, and dissemination of personal, financial, and health information. Insurers must develop processes for complying with such laws and regulations and join in the conversation about whether or not regulatory oversight is needed for various activities.

Insurers also have a duty and an opportunity to shape their own regulatory environment. On a worldwide level, the International Association of Insurance Supervisors (IAIS) is preparing recommendations for more global uniformity of solvency standards and insurance supervision, some of which seek to address market conduct. The ***International Association of Insurance Supervisors (IAIS)*** was created in 1994 to develop international principles and standards for insurance supervision and improve supervisory systems for the insurance industry.[5] Suitability standards typically require sales personnel to have a basic understanding of a customer's current financial situation, investment objectives, and future financial needs and obligations before making any product recommendation. Federal, state, and other regulations may impose suitability requirements.

Economic downturns present additional challenges. To successfully withstand economic downturns, such as that in Japan prior to 2005 and that experienced by the United States beginning in 2007, businesses must have adequate financial reserves in place as well as sound financial policies. In addition, solvency crises have caused the public to question the financial stability of specific companies. Publicized news stories of inappropriate market conduct are causing the public to question the ethics of the insurance industry as a whole. Companies must address the concerns of various individuals and groups, such as stockholders, policyowners, employees, regulators, and rating agencies, and find ways to keep valuable employees, operate profitably, and earn the loyalty of customers.

Key Terms

marketing
marketing mix
product
customer
price
place
distribution
promotion
exchange
utility
internal environment
external environment
marketing opportunity
constraint
legal form
corporate culture
proactive organization
reactive organization
controllable marketing variable
insurance producer
economic environment

business cycle
gross domestic product (GDP)
inflation
Consumer Price Index (CPI)
household
monopolistic competition
product differentiation
barrier to entry
economies of scale
technology
electronic commerce
podcast
blog
mobile marketing
social environment
demographics
birthrate
age distribution
convergence
International Association of
      Insurance Supervisors (IAIS)

Endnotes

1. American Marketing Association, "The American Marketing Association Releases New Definition for Marketing," *MarketingPower*, press release, 14 January 2008, http://www.marketingpower.com/AboutAMA/Documents/American%20Marketing%20 Association%20Releases%20New%20Definition%20for%20Marketing.pdf (8 June 2009).

2. European Central Bank, "Harmonised Index of Consumer Prices (HICP) and prices," http://www.ecb.int/stats/prices/hicp/html/index.en.html (13 June 2008).

3. United Nations Population Fund, "Population Ageing: A Larger—and Older Population," http://www.unfpa.org/pds/ageing.html (16 June 2008).

4. United Nations Population Fund, "Population Trends: Rapid Growth in Less Developed Regions," http://www.unfpa.org/pds/trends.htm (16 June 2008).

5. International Association of Insurance Supervisors, "New IAIS Framework for Insurance Supervision," press release, 7 October 2004, http://www.iaisweb.org/__temp/ IAIS_announces_new_framework_for_insurance_supervision.pdf (8 June 2009).

Chapter 2

How Companies Manage Marketing

Objectives:

After studying this chapter, you should be able to

- Identify the four basic stages in the marketing management process
- Describe situation analysis and business portfolio analysis and explain how each is used during the marketing planning process
- Describe the two major approaches to business portfolio analysis: the market share/market growth matrix and the market attractiveness/business strength matrix
- Identify and describe the parts of strategic marketing planning and tactical marketing planning and distinguish between the two
- Describe how companies use function, product, geographic area, customer type, and matrix structures to organize marketing operations and explain the advantages and disadvantages of each method
- Explain how management uses performance standards to evaluate marketing activities
- Describe how insurers use different types of control tools to measure marketing performance
- Identify the characteristics of effective marketing reporting systems

Outline

Marketing Planning

Planning Tools
- Situation Analysis
- Business Portfolio Analysis

Strategic Marketing Planning
- Set Marketing Goals
- Develop Marketing Strategies
- Select Target Markets
- Determine Resource Needs

Tactical Marketing Planning
- Creating Tactical/Action Programs
- Managing the Marketing Mix

The Marketing Plan

Organizing Marketing Operations
- Organizing by Function
- Organizing by Product Lines
- Organizing by Geographic Area
- Organizing by Customer Type
- Combination Structures

Putting Marketing Strategies in Action

Controlling Marketing Activities
- Evaluating Performance
- Reporting Systems

Suppose that your manager asks you to conduct an employee opinion survey in your department to find out how satisfied you and your coworkers are with the company and its environment. How would you do it? You could go from office to office and sit down for a chat with each employee. Or, you could create a written survey for coworkers to complete and return to you. Maybe you decide that your coworkers might share more of their concerns if you put an anonymous suggestion box for ideas to improve the department in the break room and compile the results in a report for your boss. Each of these ideas would provide answers, but before you start collecting information, you need to decide what information you need to get, the best way to get that information, and how it will be used. In other words, you need a plan. Just as you would need a plan to effectively conduct an opinion survey, companies need to plan how they will meet their corporate and marketing goals.

Planning is a system a company uses to evaluate opportunities, assess resources, set goals, and create strategies for action. When companies plan, they look at what tasks or activities they must perform to create their desired future. Planning is an essential and ongoing process for successful marketing because the environment within which marketing operates continually changes. *Marketing management* is the process companies use to plan, organize, implement, and control their marketing activities to create effective and efficient exchanges. An *effective marketing exchange* achieves a company's goals; an *efficient marketing exchange* uses the least amount of resources to achieve those goals. Figure 2.1 shows the four basic stages of the marketing management process and how they flow together. Planning builds the foundation from which the other stages flow, so let's look at planning first. Planning consists of three parts: corporate planning, marketing planning, and tactical planning. For this course we focus on marketing planning and tactical planning.

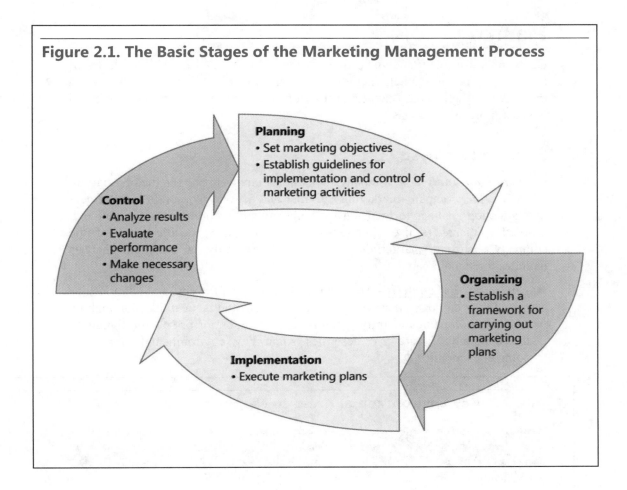

Figure 2.1. The Basic Stages of the Marketing Management Process

Planning
- Set marketing objectives
- Establish guidelines for implementation and control of marketing activities

Control
- Analyze results
- Evaluate performance
- Make necessary changes

Organizing
- Establish a framework for carrying out marketing plans

Implementation
- Execute marketing plans

Marketing Planning

In **marketing planning** a company sets goals and strategies for producing, distributing, promoting, and pricing its products and services, and determines the resources it needs to support these activities. By going through the marketing planning process, a company gets the information it needs to write a marketing plan for each product or product line. A **marketing plan** is a written document that states the marketing goals for a product or product line. The marketing plan also describes the strategies the company will use, the ways it will put the plan into action, and how it will set controls to make sure goals are achieved. Later in this chapter we discuss how companies create marketing plans.

Marketing planning and corporate planning overlap and support each other, so they must be consistent. Essentially, companies use marketing planning to identify the steps they must take to accomplish day-to-day marketing activities in line with strategies in the corporate plan and base their steps on the company's mission statement, corporate planning goals, and corporate strategies. A **company mission statement** answers the question "What is our fundamental purpose or why do we exist?" A mission statement should be broad enough to cover all the businesses the company engages in, but specific enough to focus company activities.

Planning Tools

Companies use many analytical tools in the corporate and marketing phases of the planning process to help them form a clearer picture of their environment and their own strengths and weaknesses. Two of these tools are situation analysis and business portfolio analysis.

Situation Analysis

In a ***situation analysis*** a company looks at its environment for factors that are likely to affect company marketing activities and actions. Corporate management uses situation analysis to focus on the company's overall business environment. Marketing managers use situation analysis to gauge specific parts of the company's current marketing environment. Generally, a situation analysis includes three main parts:

■ ***Environmental analysis*** - An ongoing examination of events and relationships outside the company that can influence strategic and tactical decision making and help companies identify potential opportunities for or specific threats to the company. Figure 2.2 describes some key environmental areas that companies monitor.

Figure 2.2. Key Environmental Areas to Monitor

ENVIRONMENTAL AREAS	KEY QUESTIONS RELATED TO ENVIRONMENTAL AREAS
Economy	■ What is the rate of inflation? ■ Are interest rates expected to rise or fall? ■ Is the stock market steady or erratic? ■ In the current state of our economy, are consumers able to purchase our products?
Competition	■ Who are our strongest competitors? ■ What are their strengths and weaknesses? ■ How are they advertising/promoting their products? ■ What is their special competitive advantage?
Society	■ What are the current trends in demographics? ■ Are the demographics of our target market changing? ■ Are there areas of growth we are currently neglecting?
Regulation	■ What is the current political/legal environment? ■ Do any recent government regulations affect our company? ■ Are we aware of pending government regulations that will affect us?
Technology	■ Are we keeping up with innovative technological advances that affect our business? ■ What types of new technology would enhance our performance?

■ ***Environmental forecast*** - A prediction about major environmental trends that will affect a company's future business activities, which helps a company reduce uncertainty and better manage risk by estimating the type, extent, and timing of expected environmental changes.

■ ***Internal assessment*** - A company's examination of its current activities, strengths and weaknesses, and ability to respond to potential threats and opportunities in the environment, called a SWOT Analysis.

SWOT analysis is a tool that allows a business to assess its internal strengths and weaknesses in the context of the environment in which it operates. A ***SWOT analysis*** gathers and organizes information so planners can easily identify matches between a company's strengths and specific environmental conditions. The acronym SWOT stands for strengths, weaknesses, opportunities, and threats. Corporate management uses SWOT analysis to help evaluate the overall strong and weak aspects of the company. To take advantage of current market trends, marketing managers may use SWOT analysis to find marketing opportunities in their environment. People often use the term ***strategic window*** to describe the time period during which an optimum "fit" exists between a company's distinct strengths and the key requirements of a marketing opportunity. A company can use a SWOT analysis to identify the best possible places to use resources to enter a strategic window before it closes. Figure 2.3 shows the areas a company must evaluate to determine its strengths, weaknesses, opportunities, and threats based on a SWOT analysis.

Figure 2.3. SWOT Analysis Model

Strengths	**Weaknesses**
■ Resources?	■ Cash flow?
■ Financial Assets?	■ Quality of product/service?
■ Location?	■ Emphasis on other products/activities?
■ Size?	■ Internal or external communication?
■ Market strength?	■ Innovation?
■ Product/service price?	■ Lack of financial or human resources?
■ Technology?	■ Size or location?
■ Reputation?	
Opportunities	**Threats**
■ Vulnerable competitors?	■ Downward turn in economy?
■ Expanding in international market?	■ Slower response than competitors?
■ Capitalizing on current market developments?	■ Unknown market demand?
■ Creating new partnerships?	■ Potential changes in government regulations?
■ Developing new target markets (demographically or geographically)?	■ Technological developments?
■ Actively responding to industry trends?	■ Changes in external marketing environment?

Companies often use a **PEST analysis**, also known as the *STEP analysis method*, to assess their current external business environment, evaluate their current position in relation to that environment, and predict future environmental trends for marketing. In other words, the company asks, how can we work with the external environment to benefit our company, and how might the external environment negatively affect our business? A PEST analysis examines and evaluates **P**olitical, **E**conomic, **S**ocial and **T**echnological factors, known as PEST factors.

Business Portfolio Analysis

Companies that use **business portfolio analysis** analyze the strengths and weaknesses of their separate business units to find out what contribution each unit can make to the company, based on current market trends. To conduct business portfolio analysis, a company must identify its strategic business units. A **strategic business unit (SBU)**, also known as a *profit center*, *division*, *product line*, or *line of business*, is an area of business that is distinct from other areas within a company. An SBU generally

- Is operated as a profit center separate from the rest of the company

- Has its own set of customers and competitors

- Has its own management and a distinct mission statement and goals

- Is capable of having its own marketing strategy

> **Examples**:
>
> **Corporate SBUs** for an insurance company might be individual or group divisions, life insurance or health insurance operations, pension division, property/casualty insurance operations, corporate markets division, new ventures division, consumer financial services operations, disability income division, payroll deduction division, company-owned life insurance, and asset management operations.
>
> **Marketing-level SBUs** for an insurance company consist of individual products and target markets.

Although SBUs are separate profit centers, they usually depend on their parent company for financial resources. Business portfolio analysis lets company planners assess each unit's potential for (1) generating financial resources and (2) consuming financial resources from the company. This type of analysis assumes that a company should shut down SBUs that are a financial drain on the company and should support profitable SBUs. Generally, companies invest more resources in business units and products that have growth potential and withdraw from business units and product lines with little or no growth potential.

Two commonly used methods of business portfolio analysis are

- Boston Consulting Group's **market share/market growth matrix**, which places each business unit or product line in one of four quadrants on a matrix based on (1) the growth rate of the market the business unit competes in, and (2) the business unit's relative share of that market compared to its largest competitor.

- General Electric and McKinsey & Company's *market attractiveness/business strength matrix* which places each business unit or product line into one or more of nine matrix cells based on two complex sets of criteria. One criteria set represents how attractive the market is that the business unit operates in; the other represents the SBU's business strengths.

Where an SBU is plotted on a matrix influences the company's marketing strategies for that and other SBUs.

Market Share/Market Growth Matrix

Figure 2.4 illustrates Boston Consulting Group's market share/market growth matrix. The horizontal axis on the matrix shows the business unit's market share (from high to low) related to its largest competitor's market share. The vertical axis shows the market's expected annual growth rate. Circles represent the business units or product lines, and the circles vary in size based on the dollar sales volume of each business unit they represent (larger sales volume = a bigger circle, smaller sales volume = a smaller circle).

The matrix categorizes each business unit or product line as a star, cash cow, question mark, or dog, depending on the quadrant in which it appears. A business unit or product line is a

- *Star* if it has a high market share in a high-growth market. Stars usually generate a lot of income and may be able to fund their own cash needs, but they may also need additional corporate resources to keep or increase their market share as the market grows. Stars usually become cash cows when market growth slows.

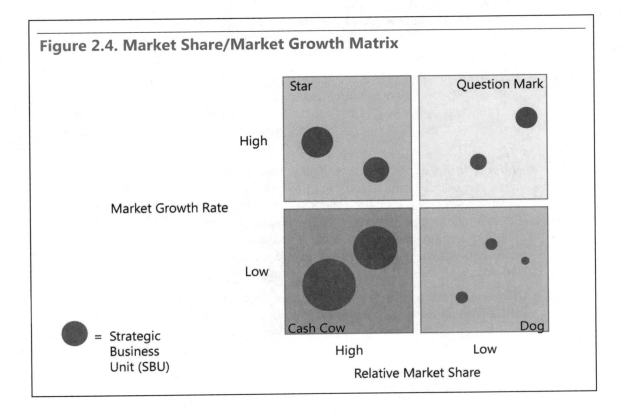

Figure 2.4. Market Share/Market Growth Matrix

- *Cash cow* if it has a high market share in a low-growth market. Cash cows generally produce a lot more profit than they need to keep their market share. Cash cows provide income to cover corporate overhead, pay dividends to stockholders (in a stock company), finance research and development, and fund needs of other business units that have high growth potential.

- *Question mark* (also called a *problem child*) if it has a low market share in a high-growth market. Most business units and products start off as question marks because companies usually try to enter growing markets. Question marks have high growth potential—because they are in high-growth markets—but they need more cash than they generate. Companies must decide which question marks they will try to convert into stars and which question marks to sell or phase out.

- *Dog* if it has a low market share in a low-growth market. Dogs may generate enough money to cover their own expenses, but their low market shares, coupled with their low growth rates, make them unlikely to become stars or cash cows, or for being very profitable.

Many SBUs begin as question marks, grow into stars, mature as cash cows, and spend the end of their life cycles as dogs before they are sold or discontinued. Companies can use the results from the market share/market growth matrix along with the expected potential for future growth to set strategies for their business units. Four basic strategies are the:

- *Build strategy* in which a company seeks to increase a business unit's market share. With this strategy a company usually gives up immediate earnings to fund growth it needs to improve a business unit's market position. Build strategies work best for SBUs with relatively low market shares in markets with relatively high growth potentials, such as a question mark. The goal is to increase the business unit's market share and turn the question mark into a star or cash cow.

- *Hold strategy* in which a company tries to hold a business unit's market position. The company usually invests only enough to keep promotional activities and customer services constant. A hold strategy works best for SBUs with high market shares in low market growth markets—for example, a cash cow.

- *Harvest strategy* in which a company tries to take advantage of a business unit's short-term earnings and cash flow. Using this strategy a company often cuts the resources it spends on the SBU and allows its market share to decline. For example, a company may stop allocating money to the SBU or product line for promotional activities. A harvest strategy works best for business units with weak growth potential (weak cash cows and sometimes question marks and dogs).

- *Withdrawal strategy* in which a company decides to sell or discontinue its SBUs with the weakest growth and investment potential because the company can better use the resources somewhere else.

Corporate managers use the market share/market growth matrix to help them estimate how much potential profit each business unit in the company might generate. Marketing managers use the matrix to find out which products generate a profit and which ones drain company finances.

Critics caution companies considering this approach, saying the market share/market growth matrix is too simplistic. For example, a business unit might hold a middle market share position instead of a high or low position. The matrix does not address this situation. Also, markets can just as easily have average growth rates instead of high or low growth rates, and market growth rates can change. In addition, factors other than market growth rate and market share also exert strong influences on the potential profit of a company's business units.

Market Attractiveness/Business Strength Matrix

General Electric and McKinsey & Company's market attractiveness/business strength matrix is illustrated in Figure 2.5. Notice that the matrix plots market attractiveness on the vertical axis in categories of high, medium, or low. The matrix shows business strength on the horizontal axis in categories of strong, average, or weak. The nine cells in the matrix are divided into three zones, each of which reflects different growth and investment opportunities. Business units or products located in the three cells labeled "A" represent good investment and growth opportunities; units located in "B" cells represent average opportunities; units in "C" cells have little growth or investment potential. This matrix is a more comprehensive business portfolio analysis technique than the market share/market growth matrix.

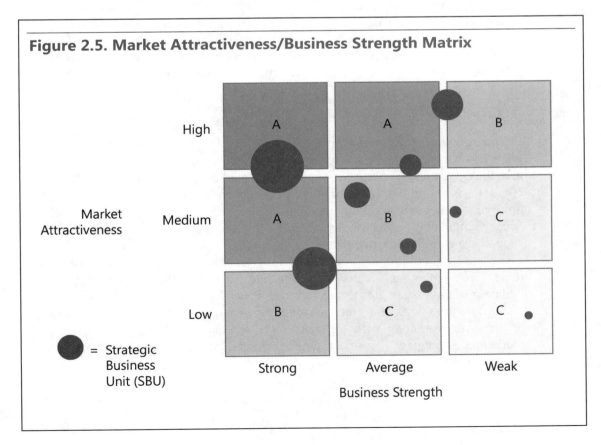

Figure 2.5. Market Attractiveness/Business Strength Matrix

A market's attractiveness is a composite index made up of a number of uncontrollable environmental factors and its strength is made up of controllable factors as shown in the following table

Market Attractiveness	Business Strength
Uncontrollable Environmental Factors ■ Market size ■ Market growth rate ■ Government regulation ■ Market stability ■ Competitive intensity ■ Technological requirements	Controllable Factors ■ Price competitiveness ■ Product quality ■ Customer loyalty ■ Marketing skills ■ Sales growth rate ■ Relative cost advantages ■ Technological resources ■ Financial resources

To develop each index, a company must determine which factors are relevant for a particular business unit, weigh each of the factors selected, rate the business unit according to the factors selected, and then combine the weights and ratings to determine the overall index rating for the business unit.

Planning tools help companies evaluate their strengths and weaknesses in relation to their environments, including competition. Once a company better understands its potential in relation to market opportunities, it may begin its specific marketing planning. Although marketing approaches differ from company to company, most companies do two types of marketing planning: strategic marketing planning and tactical marketing planning.

Strategic Marketing Planning

In *strategic marketing planning* a company sets its major long-term marketing goals and chooses the overall strategies it will follow to reach those goals. Some activities a company performs in strategic marketing planning overlap with corporate planning, because corporate planning covers *all* company operations; however, strategic marketing planning focuses only on marketing activities. Strategic marketing plans usually cover one to five years into the future, and they support the overall corporate plan.

Because the environment constantly changes, a company must regularly (1) review long-range goals and strategies to find out if they are still valid, and (2) update goals and strategies to meet current conditions. Many companies review and update their goals and strategies quarterly or semi-annually. The basic phases of strategic marketing planning are to (1) set marketing goals, (2) develop marketing strategies, (3) select target markets, and (4) determine financial resource needs.

Set Marketing Goals

Marketing goals are the specific written goals or objectives that a company wants to achieve using marketing efforts and activities. As a company translates its corporate goals into marketing goals, they become more detailed, cover a shorter time period, and are easier to plan and control. Like corporate goals, marketing goals should be clearly stated, specific and measurable, and realistic, as shown below.

Adonix Life Insurance Company

Corporate Goal: To increase overall sales by 25 percent during the next 3 years.

Related Marketing Goal: To increase the number of policies in force by 10 percent in the Viking Series I product line during the next 12 months beginning March 1.

Marketing goals cover the four basic marketing functions: product, pricing, distribution, and promotion. Marketing goals for insurance companies include such measurable factors as total premium income collected, persistency, market share, and number of new customers insured. Marketing goals also focus on best use of capital, customer retention, customer acquisition, expenses, customer satisfaction and service, and corporate image. A company uses marketing goals to create the outline of its marketing plans then uses marketing strategies to add the specific details it will use to reach those goals.

Develop Marketing Strategies

Marketing strategies are a company's plans for reaching its marketing goals. The following example shows one of the Adonix Life Insurance Company's goals and a related strategy for the next year.

Marketing Goal: Increase the number of policies in force in Viking Series I product line by 10 percent during the next 12 months beginning March 1.

Related Marketing Strategy: Use market penetration strategy and increase advertising for the Viking Series I product line during the next 12 months.

A *market penetration strategy* is a corporate growth strategy in which a company aims to increase sales of current products to current markets.

Marketing strategies are more specific than goals. In effect, strategies explain the actions needed to achieve a goal. For example, if a marketing goal is to increase sales of a product in a particular market, marketing strategies would describe how to deliver and promote the product to target customers in that market.

Select Target Markets

Because no company can serve all customers or markets equally well, senior management chooses the markets a company will pursue, such as the organizational market or the consumer market. Marketing managers then identify one or more segments of those large markets, called *target markets*, in which to market and sell its products.

To ensure that a company picks markets that best match its resources and expertise, it should consider and answer three important questions:

- Does this market have opportunity for an additional entrant or is it already saturated?

- Does this market fit in well with our overall corporate mission and goals?

- Do the individuals in this target market need our products or services?

  We discuss how to analyze potential target markets in more detail in Chapter 3.

Determine Resource Needs

A company must have enough financial and other resources to act on its plans. In planning, a company must determine what human and financial resources it needs to put into marketing activities during a particular planning period. Budgeting is one tool that management can use to weigh the costs against the potential profit for marketing activities. Companies usually use one of two general approaches to budgeting:

- *Bottom-up approach to budgeting.* Marketing managers communicate to senior management (1) the amount of resources they will need to execute a marketing plan and (2) when they will need those resources. Senior managers then allocate funds for the various elements in the marketing mix—for example, personal selling and advertising—and allocate funds for ongoing marketing department tasks.

- *Top-down approach to budgeting.* Marketing managers divide the funds they receive from senior management to cover all individual marketing activities.

  From a marketing perspective, the bottom-up approach is the preferred method because it takes into account the money the company actually needs to put specific strategies in place to reach marketing goals.

Tactical Marketing Planning

Tactical marketing planning translates strategic marketing decisions into a set of specific, detailed, action-oriented activities a company will follow to reach its target markets and satisfy customer needs. Tactical marketing planning is used for day-to-day marketing activities, and usually extends one to two years into the future. For example, an insurer's tactics for training and supporting insurance producers might include:

- Hosting a Web conference for sales intermediaries to announce a new product line and its features

- Creating and printing direct response mail materials for producers to use

- Hosting a product kickoff meeting to inform and motivate producers

Each task performed brings a company one step closer to reaching a marketing goal. Tactical marketing planning is made up of two important activities: (1) creating tactical/action programs and (2) managing the marketing mix.

Creating Tactical/Action Programs

A *tactical/action program* puts goals and strategies into action by describing

- How the company will perform planned activities

- How, when, and where each activity will be performed

- Who will be responsible for performing each activity

- How much an activity costs

- Results expected from each activity

- The unknowns or uncertainty of each activity

- How and with what frequency the company will monitor and evaluate results

A company's product or marketing managers usually develop the tactical/action programs for a particular product or in a specific market. Managers of a marketing team organized by function, such as sales, advertising, agency, or marketing research, may also develop tactical/action programs. Managers who coordinate, integrate, and continually review their tactical/action programs reap the greatest success with these programs.

Schedules are an important part of tactical/action programs. Schedules help marketing managers plan for the time and resources needed to execute the marketing goals and strategies in the real world. For example, a manager can schedule the roll-out of marketing activities based on the company's priorities.

Before a company puts tactical/action programs into action, it may want to benchmark what activities and processes other companies or competitors use. Using *benchmarking* a company

- Identifies the best outcomes that other companies have achieved for a specific activity and what practices they used to cause those outcomes

- Copies the best practices to equal or surpass the best outcomes

For example, suppose an insurance company wants to benchmark how claims resolution processes affect customer satisfaction. First, the insurer finds a company with extremely high customer satisfaction in claims resolution. Then, the insurer's marketing managers analyze the successful company's practices. If the insurer can put the best practices into action in its own organization, it can improve its marketing performance.

Managing the Marketing Mix

Tactical marketing planning describes how a company will manage its marketing mix. Marketing managers juggle and balance the marketing mix parts—product, price, promotion and place—to come up with the best combination of "the four Ps" to reach marketing goals and deliver customer value to target markets. Those marketing mix choices must also mesh with the company's corporate and marketing goals and strategies. Figure 2.6 lists some questions that marketing managers answer to manage the marketing mix.

Figure 2.6. Managing a Marketing Mix

Product	■ Do our products satisfy customer and producer needs? ■ What changes/improvements can we make to better meet customer demands and expectations?
Price	■ Are our current prices appropriate for our target market? ■ Are our prices competitive with those for similar products our competitors offer? ■ Are our prices and current sales volumes generating profits?
Promotion	■ Which types of advertising and sales promotions will be most effective for our products and markets? ■ Are there new technologies that will enhance our promotion efforts?
Distribution (Place)	■ What are the best ways to distribute our products? ■ Are our products available to our customers at the right time and in the right places? ■ Do we need more distributors or other distribution channels?

The four marketing mix variables are interdependent. So, decisions related to one variable also affect the decisions related to the other three variables.

The Marketing Plan

Marketing planning should result in a marketing plan that provides direction and clarity about future marketing goals and strategies to everyone within a company. The marketing plan focuses on strategies related to target markets and parts of the marketing mix. It outlines the programs and activities that the company needs to perform to reach those goals. Marketing plans range in length from short-range (six months to one year) to long-range (one to five years). Small companies may develop one marketing plan to cover all their marketing operations. Larger companies usually develop marketing plans for each SBU or division, each product line or product item, and each target market.

Most marketing plans seek to answer two main questions:

■ How will the company compete with similar companies?

■ How will the company handle the daily activities it needs to perform to meet its marketing goals?

The answers to these questions build the foundation for the marketing plan.

Most marketing plans include an *executive summary* that briefly states the plan's purpose and recommendations. It is designed to help senior management clearly understand what the plan proposes to do, how much the activities in the plan will cost, and what results the company expects to achieve. The remainder of the marketing plan includes more detailed reports on planning activities such as situation analysis, goals, strategies, tactical action programs, implementation schedules, evaluation and control mechanisms, and a budget.

The marketing plan coordinates all the areas in the company that will have roles in the marketing process. For example, in an insurance company, sales projections for a particular product can affect employees in sales because they have to create their own plan to reach those projections, employees in advertising because they have to plan for and design advertising to support the product for sale, as well as employees in other areas, such as distribution or underwriting. Ideally, a company communicates its marketing plans to all affected employees at the outset of a marketing campaign. By letting employees know what tasks they will be asked to perform and when they need to be completed, the company has a much better chance of succeeding in its plan.

Organizing Marketing Operations

Plans are only useful if they are translated into actions to reach goals. *Organizing* is the process of lining up corporate resources to put company plans into action effectively and efficiently. Most companies organize their marketing operations in a way that coordinates and assigns responsibility for marketing activities in the company, but this can be done in many different ways. In a very small company, marketing may be just one part of one manager's job. A larger company might create a separate department or division to do marketing. Whatever organizational structure a company chooses, that structure must allow a company to perform the essential marketing functions, including:

■ Information management	■ Marketing research
■ Sales and distribution	■ Customer relations
■ Market development (choosing where or to whom to sell)	■ Product development and pricing
■ Advertising, sales promotion, and publicity (sometimes called marketing communications or marketing support services)	■ Marketing personnel development ■ Marketing management and administration

How well a company organizes its marketing operations strongly affects its ability to develop and implement marketing strategies and respond to opportunities or threats in the environment. A company's structure determines who has the authority to make specific marketing decisions and who has the responsibility to complete specific marketing tasks. Companies often create organization charts to make sure everyone understands these lines of authority and responsibility. An *organization chart* visually represents an organization's structure. Insurance companies may organize their marketing operations by (1) function, (2) product, (3) geographic area, and (4) customer type, or some combination of these forms. Some companies also use matrix structures to organize marketing activities in some situations.

Organizing by Function

The most common way that companies set up their marketing operations is by function. Organizing by function means that a company groups personnel and other resources by the type of work they do. In a functional organizational structure, personnel who manage major functional areas, such as sales or advertising, report directly to the company's chief marketing officer (CMO). The CMO integrates and coordinates all marketing activities. Functional organization is a centralized approach to the marketing structure.

The advantages and disadvantages of organization by function are listed in the following boxes.

Advantages of Organizing by Function:
■ Simple to understand with clear lines of authority and responsibility
■ Works well in small companies with centralized marketing operations
■ Works well in large companies offering a few product lines to fairly identical groups of customers
■ Offers managers and staff the opportunity to develop expertise in each specialized area of marketing, such as sales, product development, or other areas
■ Little duplication of marketing activities

Disadvantages of Organizing by Function:
■ Less effective as the size and diversity of a company's product offerings, marketing approaches, and target markets increase
■ Marketing staff may have less opportunity for gaining expertise in other functional areas
■ Functional groups within a company may compete against each other for a larger share of limited corporate financial resources, which can hurt the company as a whole, for example, new or specialty products may be unintentionally neglected

Figure 2.7 shows an organization chart of an insurance company's marketing operations by function.

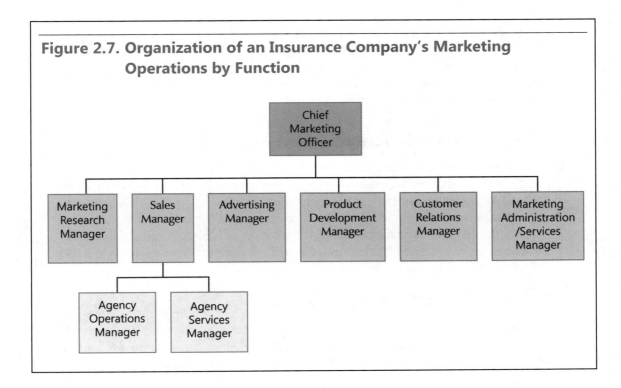

Figure 2.7. Organization of an Insurance Company's Marketing Operations by Function

Organizing by Product Lines

Companies with more than one product line may find it difficult to coordinate marketing for several different types of products using functional organization. To reduce conflict and increase efficiency, multi-product-line companies often organize their marketing activities by product.

Advantages of Organizing by Product:
■ Employees who work most closely with a particular product type make the marketing decisions related to that product
■ Product managers can react quickly to opportunities and challenges for their specific products
Disadvantages of Organizing by Product:
■ Communication may suffer because product managers may be less aware of the actions and concerns of other product areas
■ Can lead to unproductive duplication of effort

Insurance companies that offer both individual and group insurance often divide their operations into individual insurance operations and group insurance operations. Then, they further subdivide each operational group into separate product lines. Each division performs most of its own marketing functions, including planning, sales, advertising, sales promotion, product development, and pricing. With product line organization, a company may coordinate activities such as marketing research, advertising, customer relations, and administrative services through centrally managed departments, or each department may handle those types of activities for each product category. To organize marketing by product, each product line in a company must be large enough, distinct enough, and profitable (or promising) enough to support its own separate management and marketing activities.

Organizing by Geographic Area

A company that operates nationally or internationally, or serves regions with distinct legislative or language differences, may choose to organize some or all of its marketing operations by geographic area or region. Usually, this involves assigning a marketing manager to each regional area. These regional managers report directly to the company's chief marketing officer. A company that does business in the United States and Canada, for example, may have a U.S. marketing division and a Canadian marketing division.

Advantages of Organizing by Geographic Area:
■ Reduces span of control normally required to manage a company's sales force, which permits quicker reactions to local market changes. *Span of control* refers to the number of people a manager directly supervises.
■ Regional marketing managers better understand their region's regulatory and cultural environment, which allows them to find and implement the most effective marketing activities for the region.
Disadvantages of Organizing by Geographic Area:
■ Marketing activities are often duplicated.
■ There are multiple levels of functional management.
■ It is difficult to standardize activities or processes in different markets.
■ Corporate identity or image may be damaged or diluted if it varies significantly from region to region.

Organizing by Customer Type

Companies that market products to diverse customer groups with distinct needs most often choose to organize by customer type. This structure ties employee responsibilities to a common set of customer needs. For example, a company might create one marketing division for household markets, another division for medium-size and large corporations, and a third division for the small business market. Each division's marketing manager directs all marketing activities for one specific customer group. Often, division managers report directly to the company's chief marketing officer.

Advantages of Organizing by Customer Type:
■ It is customer-centric, which means it focuses on the specific needs of a particular customer group, and can quickly respond to customer wants and needs.

Disadvantages of Organizing by Customer Type:
■ Marketing efforts may be duplicated and result in inefficient use of resources.

Combination Structures

Insurance companies often use a combination of organizational structures for marketing. For example, a company might organize its marketing functions by product or region and then organize each product or region by function. A company that uses combination structures can create a flexible marketing organization that meets both customer and company needs.

To create a new product or finish a company-wide marketing project, a company may need input from many different functional areas in the company. In such situations, companies often use a ***matrix organizational structure***, an organizational form that has vertical and horizontal lines of authority flowing down and across the organization chart.[1] In a matrix organizational structure (shown in Figure 2.8), the company assigns individuals from various functional areas to form a cross-functional team. A ***cross-functional team*** is a group made up of employees from different functional areas who work together on a common assignment led by a project manager. The team members report to the project manager of the cross-functional team *and* to their functional department manager.

> **Example:** An underwriting employee who works on a cross-functional team to develop a new product reports to the project manager on project issues. The employee reports to the underwriting department manager for all other work assignments. When the project ends, the employee no longer reports to the project manager. Project managers generally report to a head projects manager, who coordinates and oversees several projects in the company.

Advantages of Matrix Organizational Structures:
■ Excellent project coordination because the project manager brings together many related but separate project parts and uses the wide-ranging skills of different employees
■ Team members can share information easily across functions
■ Uses corporate resources wisely because individual employees work on teams together on a project-by-project basis

---

Disadvantages of Matrix Organizational Structures :

■ Violates principle of **unity of command**, which states that employees should have only one manager to avoid confusion, and may cause an employee to have conflicting loyalties and create communication problems between the two managers

■ Can be inefficient because it requires double management

Figure 2.8. Organization of an Insurance Company's Marketing Operations by Matrix Structure

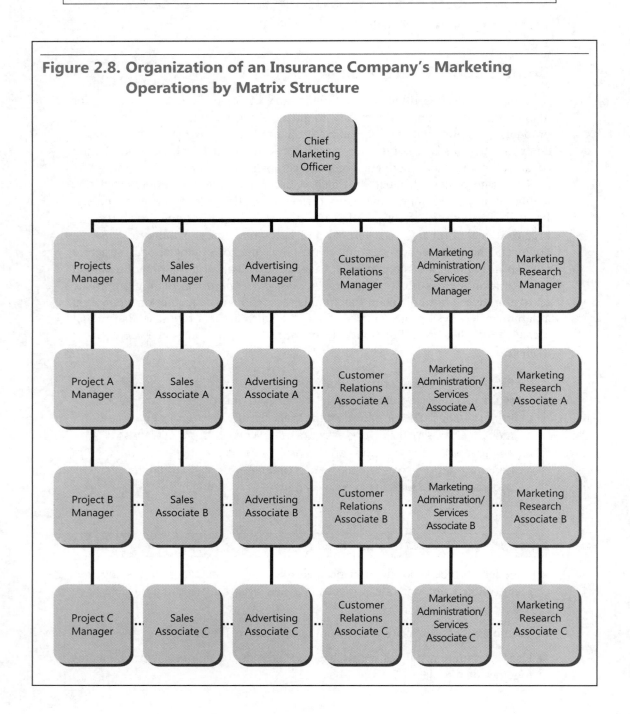

Putting Marketing Strategies in Action

In *marketing implementation*, a company puts its marketing plans and strategies into action. The following two factors affect how easy or difficult it may be to put strategies into action in a company:

- Corporate culture defines the company's personality, what the company holds important, and how the company believes things should be done. To make drastic changes in the way a company operates, it must first lay groundwork to convince employees that the proposed changes will ultimately be in the company's and their own best interests.

- Marketing managers hold a critical position between senior management and staff employees, and have the opportunity and responsibility to create an environment that encourages marketing staff to successfully implement strategies and tactical/action programs that support corporate goals.

A company implements plans through the day-to-day tactical/action programs and activities of marketing managers, distributors, customer service personnel, product development staff, advertising, and other marketing personnel. All of the company's employees must work together to implement and support successful marketing plans.

A company must carefully integrate the many different activities required to reach marketing plan goals so that confusion is minimized and marketing efforts are efficient and do not overlap or duplicate other actions.

Controlling Marketing Activities

Changes in the marketing environment or flaws in the marketing strategy itself can disrupt a well-planned implementation. Companies use *marketing control* to monitor the results of their marketing plans and take corrective action as needed to make sure their marketing goals are reached. Marketing control consists of two primary activities, evaluating performance and reporting results.

Evaluating Performance

Marketing managers compare the performance standards set out in the marketing plan against what actually happens. If what actually happens is what they planned, then their tactical/action programs meet their stated goals. A *performance standard* is an ideal level of performance against which actual performance is measured. Companies can use internal or external standards to measure and evaluate performance. An *internal standard* is a standard a company sets and is based on how the company performed in the past. An *external standard* is a standard based on outside information such as published industry-wide averages or best practices. Companies commonly use benchmarking to judge marketing performance.

Most companies combine performance standards into their marketing plan goals. Companies gauge whether they achieve their goals by comparing actual performance with the standard. A comparison like this lets managers determine if

- Sales are at, above, or below projections

- The effect of advertising or other promotion is increasing, holding steady, or falling

- The ratio of premium income received to expenses incurred is improving, stable, or declining

Marketing managers usually set a range of acceptable performance on either side of the standard. Performance within the range is not studied further. Managers investigate performance that falls outside the acceptable range. This technique of investigating only if there is very good or very poor performance is called *management by exception*. Management by exception saves time by directing managers' focus to potential opportunities or problems.

If performance does not match the standard, then a company must determine why. In some cases, unrealistic performance standards, inaccurate projections, stronger competition, or unexpected changes in the environment may explain the difference. In other cases, exceptional or unacceptable performance causes performance outside the set standards. For example, one company with great marketing strategies may not do a good job of putting the strategies in action. Another company may develop poor strategies but do a great job of implementing its strategies. Both companies fall outside the acceptable performance range, but the reasons why they are outside the standards are quite different.

To determine what causes performance to fall outside set standards, managers must distinguish problems from symptoms. For example, premium income that is below expected levels is usually a symptom of an underlying problem. The real problem may be an outdated product, poor sales training, noncompetitive pricing, poor compensation plans, or other factors. If a company identifies a problem, it can be corrected by taking one or more of the following actions:

- Changing the tactical/action programs designed to carry out a strategy

- Creating new ways to put tactical/action programs in action

- Developing new products, marketing strategies, or marketing goals

- Changing how it collects and analyzes performance data if the current way doesn't reflect true performance

- Reviewing the performance standards to make sure that they are valid and realistic. Standards should reflect challenging, but obtainable, goals.

If a company finds an opportunity, it can be explored further.

> **Example:** After reviewing producers' performance, a manager determines that their producers need more product training. She can then create a new tactical/action program to improve training or adjust the current program to add training.

Control Tools

Control tools help managers answer the questions: "How well is the company performing?" and "How well does a particular department perform?" Marketing managers use tools such as sales analysis, expense analysis, profitability analysis, Web site monitoring, and marketing audits to measure marketing performance.

Sales Analysis. In a *sales analysis* a company examines its sales numbers to evaluate current performance. To conduct a sales analysis, a company compares its current actual sales with one or more performance measures, including

- Forecasted sales

- Sales in previous years

- Expenses incurred to generate the sales

- Current competitors' sales

- Estimated market or sales potential for a particular geographic area or customer segment

- Current industry sales

Sales analysis helps a company answer the question: "How well are our marketing strategies working?" by showing how much product is being sold, where it is being sold, who is selling it, and who is buying it.

Insurance companies usually measure sales for their products by number of products sold, first-year commissions, total face amount sold, number of new cases generated, market share, average premium per case or product unit, and average policy size. Companies can also measure sales in terms of "close ratios," which are the percentage of bids or quotes that result in sales. Companies often further sort total sales numbers by region, district, producer, product, product line, customer segment, type of distribution system, or some other factor or combination of factors. Using this approach, management gets detailed information about where sales originate.

Expense Analysis. Most insurance companies maintain a *cost accounting system* that keeps track of the expenses they incur to develop, market, and sell a product, which helps the company effectively monitor and control costs. These expenses include specific product costs such as commissions, salaries, lead generation expenses, training expenses, employee benefit costs, product development costs, advertising expenses, direct response marketing expenses, sales promotion expenses, policy acquisition expenses, and marketing research expenses. A company can further sort its expenses by region, agency, producer, product, product line, distribution system, customer segment, or some other factor or combination of factors.

Expense analysis, which ties marketing costs to particular marketing activities, helps marketing managers decide if a cost is worth the value the activity provides. Expense analysis can also locate possible performance problems. Functional areas that incur large expenses to generate sales may not operate as effectively or efficiently as they should. In an expense analysis, marketing managers often use *expense ratios*, which are mathematical comparisons that divide the amount of expenses by a certain unit of measure, such as level of sales. Figure 2.9 shows examples of expense analysis for insurance marketing activities.

Profitability Analysis. *Profitability analysis* compares the sales an activity generates with the expenses it incurs to make those sales. This analysis helps the company figure out which activities lose money or make money for the

---

Figure 2.9. Examples of Expense Analysis Using Expense Ratios.

These types of ratios can be broken down by insurance producer, agency, field expenses, home office expenses, and so forth. Total sales and marketing expenses can also be broken down into more detailed categories, such as agency manager compensation, supervisor compensation, field operating expenses, and data processing.

- Ratio of marketing expenses per $1,000 face amount sold

- Ratio of marketing expenses per $100 of new premium income

- Ratio of marketing expenses per $100 of renewal premium income

- Ratio of marketing expenses per application received

- Ratio of marketing expenses per policy issued or paid for

- Average marketing expense per call

---

company. A company can use profitability analysis to measure how profitable a region, agency, insurance producer, product, product line, distribution system, or customer segment is. Management uses profitability analysis results to help decide when to change, maintain, expand, reduce, or discontinue marketing activities or operations.

Because profitability analysis uses sales volume and control of expenses to analyze profit, it can help predict how successful a company will be. However, profitability analysis is not an appropriate tool to evaluate short-term results because it can provide misleading information. For example, first-year expenses for many distribution systems are higher than first-year revenues, because the costs of acquiring new business are high for insurers. A company that compares its first-year sales of a new product with its first-year expenses would get a misleading view of the product's profitability. Companies should also use caution when they compare first-year sales to agency expenses. An agency that appears to have much higher expenses than other agencies might be spending money to ensure persistency and policy renewals. The persistency and policy renewals could lead to long-term profitability. Also, remember that other factors such as the company's environment, product mix, market segment, distribution systems, persistency, and service standards[2] affect a company's success.

Web Site Monitoring. Today, most insurance companies have Web sites and increasingly use these Web sites to market products to customers. *Web site monitoring* tests and tracks how customers use a company's Web site. Web site monitoring helps a company evaluate how well its Web site generates new business for the company.

Web site monitoring gives marketing managers valuable information about visitors to the company's Web site, including the number of

■ Visitors

■ First-time visitors

■ Pages viewed by each visitor

■ Visitors who requested more information on products

■ Purchases made through the Web site

Marketing Audit. When a company conducts a ***marketing audit***, it creates a system to examine and appraise its marketing environment, goals, strategies, tactical/action programs, organizational structure, and personnel on a very broad basis. Marketing audits can be company-wide, full-scale reviews of strengths and weaknesses, or smaller-scale audits that look at operating problems or review marketing operations. The factors that determine whether a full-scale or small-scale audit needs to be done are (1) a company's need for feedback on the environment and (2) how well its activities are reaching goals. An independent authority, such as an outside business consultant, or a corporate unit can perform marketing audits.

Auditors may interview managers, distributors, customers, and other individuals about a company's marketing operations and performance. The auditors also may conduct mail, Internet, or telephone surveys with customers and other individuals. Figure 2.10 lists some types of information that auditors gather for a full-scale marketing audit. Auditors keep senior management up-to-date on their progress and their preliminary findings, and send management a final report that outlines findings and recommendations.

Reporting Systems

Control tools are only useful if they provide information that can help management plan and make decisions. So, any control tools a company uses must include a way to report results back to management. A reporting system can be informal and consist mostly of meetings with marketing staff, members of the sales force, and other company employees and customers. Or, the reporting system can be a formal part of the company's overall control system.

Reporting systems must include the amount and types of information that management and staff need to make reliable decisions. Generally, lower-level managers need detailed information and higher-level managers need summary information. For example, an insurance company branch office manager usually needs weekly, detailed reports on each producer's sales-related activities. A district or regional sales manager might need only monthly summary reports. A national sales manager would need monthly reports with less detail but more summary information.

In some companies, a corporate controller decides the type of control information needed, how often it is needed, and which marketing managers or staff members need information. This controller creates and manages the corporate control system. In other companies, marketing management works with management information systems personnel to design and develop a formal

Figure 2.10. Key Areas of a Marketing Audit

Marketing Environment

- What threats and opportunities exist for the company with existing demographic, economic, political, technological, and cultural trends?
- What are the strengths and weaknesses of the company's major competitors?
- What are the major factors that affect the company's suppliers?
- What is happening to the size and growth of the company's major market segments?
- What is the economic condition of customers in the company's target market?

Marketing Structure

- How is the marketing department organized?
- Is the marketing department efficient and effective in its activities?
- Are lines of authority and responsibility consistent and clear?
- Are marketing communications effective?
- Does the company have the right people working in the right areas?
- Do marketing personnel work well with people in other non-marketing areas?
- Are marketing employees well-trained and properly supervised?

Marketing Systems

- What is the company's long-term, strategic marketing plan?
- Is the plan supported by the company's executives?
- Is the marketing planning information accurate and timely?
- What progress is being made in meeting the company's strategic marketing plans?
- Does the management of the company analyze marketing progress?

Marketing Expenses

- Does the marketing budget supply the needed resources to meet marketing goals?
- Are the company's product/services profitable?
- Does the company need to expand or reduce any product lines?
- Are any marketing expenses too high and can they be reduced?

Marketing Mix

- What are the objectives for each product line?
- Is the price for each product competitive with the prices of similar products?
- Does the company have distribution goals and strategies?
- What efforts does the company use for advertising and publicity?
- Is the sales force accomplishing the sales goals?

reporting system for control. This type of system produces computer-generated reports from a central database of information. In either scenario, the company, its systems, or personnel must be able to quickly design reports and studies to respond to emerging opportunities and threats in the marketing environment.

Key Terms and Concepts

planning

marketing management

effective marketing exchange

efficient marketing exchange

marketing planning

marketing plan

company mission statement

situation analysis

environmental analysis

environmental forecast

internal assessment

SWOT analysis

strategic window

PEST analysis

business portfolio analysis

strategic business unit (SBU)

market share/market growth matrix

market attractiveness/business
    strength matrix

star

cash cow

question mark

dog

build strategy

hold strategy

harvest strategy

withdrawal strategy

strategic marketing planning

marketing goal

marketing strategy

market penetration strategy

target market

bottom-up approach to budgeting

top-down approach to budgeting

tactical marketing planning

tactical/action program

benchmarking

executive summary

organizing

organization chart

span of control

matrix organizational structure

cross-functional team

unity of command

marketing implementation

marketing control

performance standard

internal standard

external standard

management by exception

sales analysis

cost accounting system

expense analysis

expense ratio

profitability analysis

Web site monitoring

marketing audit

Endnotes

1.   Robert Kreitner, *Management Principles & Practices*, 3rd LOMA ed. (Boston: Houghton Mifflin Custom Publishing, 2007), 298.

2.   Gregory P. Storey, "Expense Management: Industry Trends, Part II," *Resource*, February 1997, 46.

Chapter 3

Market Segmentation and Target Marketing

Objectives:

After studying this chapter, you should be able to

- Define market segmentation and explain the benefits and drawbacks of using single-variable and multivariable segmentation
- Identify the conditions required for effective market segmentation and describe the five bases used to segment consumer markets
- Identify the bases used to segment organizational markets and describe the similarities and differences between organizational market segmentation and consumer market segmentation
- Define target marketing and identify factors insurers use to evaluate potential target markets
- Describe three primary types of target marketing strategies and the factors that influence an insurance company's choice of a particular target marketing strategy
- Describe organizational market segments targeted by insurance companies

Outline

Market Segmentation
- Segmenting Markets Effectively
- Segmenting Consumer Markets
- Segmenting Organizational Markets

Target Marketing
- Evaluating Potential Target Markets
- Target Marketing Strategies
- Target Markets for Insurance Products

Years ago, companies employed salespeople to go door-to-door to meet with potential customers in person to explain and demonstrate their products or services. The market for the product was everyone who lived on the block, in the neighborhood, or in the town. Companies put little thought into determining whether customers had a desire for their product or could afford it.

Times have changed and so have the people who make up today's markets for insurance products and services. Insurance customers now want a choice of what they buy, and how, when and where they buy it. In today's competitive environment, successful insurance companies (1) identify unmet needs in existing markets and (2) identify growth markets that aren't being reached.

> **Example:** Growing affluence among certain ethnic groups increases their interest in and need of risk protection products, such as insurance
>
> **Market Found:** Life insurance companies identified increasing life insurance needs among Hispanic and Asian populations in the United States and began marketing to these groups
>
> **Benefit to the Company:** By expanding sales of existing products into growth markets, companies increased their customer base and reduced new product development costs

Market Segmentation

The potential market for many insurance products is large. For example, in 2007, term life policies accounted for 5 million of the new individual life insurance policies purchased.[1] People with different personal characteristics—ages, incomes, education levels—purchased these policies. And, they had many different reasons for buying insurance. Because this market is so large and so diverse, it is very difficult for insurance companies to try to sell to everyone in this market in the same way effectively. For this reason, marketers use *market segmentation* to create a more reachable, profitable market. ***Market segmentation*** is the process of dividing large, diverse markets into smaller submarkets that are more alike and need similar products or marketing mixes. A ***market segment*** is a submarket or group of customers with similar needs and preferences. Companies use market segmentation mainly to find out what kinds of customer groups exist within the total market for a product. Then they use this information to determine which market segments to pursue and how to adjust their marketing mix to appeal to those segments.

Companies often use one or several customer characteristics, such as income level, years of education, age, or gender, to segment a market. *Single-variable segmentation* uses only one characteristic, such as income level, to segment a market. *Multivariable segmentation* uses a combination of characteristics, such as income level and gender, to segment a market.

Example: **Goal**: Identify a market for online insurance quotes.

Single-Variable Segmentation: Company divides the total market of Internet users into segments, based on whether individuals are 40 years old or younger, or over the age of 40. This produces two segments: people 40 or under, and people over 40.

Multivariable Segmentation: Company divides the total market of Internet users into segments, based on age and income. This produces several segments in each age group, such as individuals over 40 who make less than $50,000, between $50,000 and $150,000, or more than $150,000.

Analysis: Using only the single variable of age would make it more difficult for the company to develop an effective marketing mix to best meet the specific needs of individuals at certain income levels and potential sales may be lost.

Figure 3.1 shows the benefits and drawbacks of single-variable and multivariable segmentation.

The more common characteristics and shared needs that a company can identify for a market segment, the easier it is to create a marketing mix that will appeal to that segment.

Segmenting Markets Effectively

In theory, segmenting a market sounds simple: Choose a large market and use one or more customer characteristics to divide the large market into smaller submarkets likely to buy your company's products. However, it is not as easy as it sounds. Effective segmentation requires that

- Customers in the segment have similar product needs and preferences or purchase products in similar ways

- The company is able to distinguish the needs and behaviors of customers in the segment from those of customers in other segments

- The potential sales, costs, and profits for the segment are large enough to measure and compare with those for other potential market segments

- The profit potential for the segment is high enough to offset the expense a company incurs to develop and maintain a tailored marketing mix for a segment

- Customers in the segment can be reached using available distribution channels or promotion efforts and are likely to respond favorably to the marketing mix planned for the segment

Figure 3.1. Single-variable and Multivariable Segmentation: Benefits and Drawbacks

Single-Variable Segmentation	
Benefits	**Drawbacks**
■ Simple ■ Easy to perform	■ Fewer separate segments ■ More people in each segment ■ Less precise marketing mix due to larger segment ■ May not adequately identify market segments with the most potential for profit because only one variable is used to segment
Multivariable Segmentation	
■ Provides more detailed information about customers in each segment ■ Fewer customers in each segment so marketing mix can be tailored to market needs ■ Customers are more likely to buy products because the products more precisely match the segment's needs ■ Marketing results (that is, sales) will be higher because more effective and efficient targeting of markets identifies markets with the most opportunity for growth	■ Costs more to perform ■ Run the risk of over-segmenting markets which can lead to targeting markets that are not profitable enough to justify segmenting

■ The size and composition of the market is expected to remain relatively stable over time at least for as many years as the company's planning period spans

Marketers use segmentation in both consumer markets and organizational markets. A **consumer market** is a market that consists of individuals who buy products or services for personal or family use. **Organizational markets** are markets that consist of individuals or formal organizations that purchase products and services for business purposes.

Segmenting Consumer Markets

Today, marketers can obtain information about a person's interests and personal data in many ways, including collecting data by

■ Tracking usage on Web sites using software that collects consumer information

- Conducting market research using traditional methods such as focus groups and surveys

- Extracting information from customer interactions, such as call center interactions, correspondence, and responses to satisfaction surveys

- Reviewing purchase history records, such as those available from a credit reporting agency or other type of information vendor (such information may be used for marketing, product development, and even underwriting)

One challenge for companies is sifting through all of this information to determine the best way to segment a market to meet customer needs and earn a profit. Effective segmentation identifies a market using characteristics that are (1) relevant to customer needs and behaviors and (2) measurable or observable. For example, one characteristic used to segment markets is by family status—whether a person is single, married, married with grown children, and so on. Before an insurance company decides to segment a market by family status, it would need to know if different types of families differ in how they prepare for, make decisions on, or evaluate purchases of the particular insurance product to be offered. If their behaviors are the same, this type of segmentation would not work very well. If their behaviors are different, segmenting by family status would be appropriate. Studies have shown that different types of families have different priorities related to insurance and financial services products, so segmenting by family status would be appropriate for marketing some insurance products. Two risks associated with any segmentation are: (1) the risk of drawing generalities (or stereotypes) based on information that may not be true or accurate because it is based on limited knowledge, and (2) the risk of over-segmenting a market or not segmenting a market enough to reach potential customers.

The five primary categories of consumer market segmentation are geographic, demographic, geodemographic, psychographic, and behavioristic segmentation. Figure 3.2 shows the characteristics (variables) included in each of these categories.

Geographic Segmentation

Geographic segmentation divides the total market for a product based on the needs and desires of populations in different jurisdictions or physical locations. Geographic differences can affect the marketing mix a company uses. For example, the sales, advertising, and distribution channels that a company would use to successfully market a product or service in a sparsely populated area such as a small town in Nebraska may differ significantly from the marketing mix it would use in a densely populated area such as New York City. Differences in population and growth rates give certain areas higher or lower market potential. In Canada, for example, 62 percent of the population of the entire country lives in Ontario and Quebec. So, the bulk of Canada's market potential lies within only 2 of its 10 provinces.

Figure 3.2. Primary Categories for Segmenting Consumer Markets

Geographic Segmentation	Demographic Segmentation	Geodemographic Segmentation	Psychographic Segmentation	Behavioristic Segmentation
Country	Age	Economic means	Behaviors	Benefits sought
Region	Gender	Cultural background	Activities	Usage rate
Province or state	Marital status	Perspective	Interests	Buyer readiness
County	Household composition	Neighborhood	Attitudes	Preferred method of purchase
City	Income			Risk tolerance
ZIP or postal code	Education			Buyer loyalty
Legal boundaries	Occupation			
Rural/ suburban/ urban	Family life cycle			
	Nationality			
	Cultural origin			
	Social class			

The laws and regulations that apply in various locations also influence how companies develop and market their products. Insurance companies must comply with applicable laws and regulations in the markets they serve. Such compliance requirements can affect everything from the wording in insurance policy forms to statements made in advertisements.

Many companies adjust their promotion efforts to match the regional flavor and geographic differences of the segments they serve. For example, in rural areas, an insurer might use an advertisement showing people in a diner discussing a retirement plan. In urban areas, an insurer might run an advertisement showing commuters on a train engaged in a similar conversation.

Advantages of Geographic Segmentation	Disadvantages of Geographic Segmentation
■ Relatively inexpensive ■ Easy to perform ■ Easy for local sales force to relate to customers in their same geographic area	■ Geographic differences do not greatly influence customer needs and desires ■ May not adequately subdivide the market to allow marketer to target viable potential customers

Demographic Segmentation

Demographic segmentation is segmentation based on the personal characteristics of people in the market. Demographic variables are closely associated with consumers' product needs and purchase behavior, and they identify a lot of potential segments. Consumer demographics include characteristics such as age, income, life cycle stage, gender, marital status, household composition, education, occupation, nationality, cultural origin, and social class. Some demographic characteristics are more useful in segmenting insurance markets than are others. Age and life cycle stage, for example, are two demographic variables frequently used to segment life insurance markets.

Advantages of Demographic Segmentation	Disadvantages of Demographic Segmentation
■ Relatively easy to identify and measure	■ May not adequately segment the market
■ Information about many demographics are easy to obtain from government and private sources	■ May not capture the differing needs of market members

In Figure 3.3, we describe some of the demographic segments in the United States that result from segmenting by age, income, life cycle stage, household composition, and cultural origin. Each of these segments offers marketing opportunities for insurance companies. As the size or the characteristics of a population change, new market segments may present opportunities for growth and some existing market segments may be less desirable.

Geodemographic Segmentation

Geodemographic segmentation divides consumer markets into segments by classifying people with similar demographic characteristics into geographically defined clusters. Geodemographic segmentation is based on the idea that people who share similar values, cultural origins, household income levels, and attitudes tend to live in the same areas. They also tend to adopt the social values, tastes, and behaviors toward products, services, media, and promotions of those who live near them.

Marketing research and other companies have developed a variety of classification systems to help companies cluster neighborhoods and households for marketing purposes. These systems provide information not only about the demographics of people in a particular geographic location, but also about the likes, dislikes, behaviors, and attitudes that affect the purchases those people make. Many of the classification systems note the differences as well as the similarities in consumer behavior within the neighborhood or cluster. Generally, the consumer behaviors, values, and lifestyle within a neighborhood remain very similar. Besides using this information to segment and identify target markets, insurance companies can also use this information to determine where to open office locations or build a sales force. They can also overlay information such as income ranges and crime statistics for a specific area on maps to help identify suitable office sites.

Figure 3.3. Some Consumer Market Segments for Insurance Products Based on Demographics

Segmenting by Age

Generation Y. The Generation Y population consists of people born between 1979 and 1995 and represents about 75 million people. Some Generation Y members are getting married and starting families and need life and health insurance. Individuals just entering the work force need retirement planning products. Generation Yers have grown up with information technology playing an integral role in their lives. They are tech savvy and value learning and education. So, products for this group must incorporate these elements (for example, Web-based product offerings) into the marketing mix. Products for this group include health insurance, term life products, and annuities.

Generation X. The Generation X population consists of people born between about 1964 and 1979. Represented by about 50 million people, this generation is very comfortable with technology, values individualism and self-expression, and is retiring at younger and younger ages. Quite a few have their own businesses; some are starting second careers. This group needs term life products, individual and group retirement products, and annuities to protect the family in the event of a loss of income, save funds for children's college education, have resources to care for aging parents, and amass retirement income. Self-employed Generation Xers need health care, retirement planning, and disability products.

Baby Boomers and Seniors. The Baby Boomer segment consists of people born between 1946 and 1964 and represents approximately 80 million people. Generally affluent and educated, this group's needs include estate planning, retirement products, and health and long-term care insurance. They may also still need life insurance to protect a spouse and/or other dependens. Older Boomers are entering retirement.

Seniors, people 65 years and older, have needs for supplemental life and health insurance, lifetime income distribution products, and long-term care insurance. Estate planning products are beneficial to this segment, and some members of this population purchase life insurance for their children or grandchildren.

Segmenting by Income

High-income households (annual incomes of $100,000 or more). In recent years, researchers have identified a growing affluent market consisting of the mass affluent and high-net-worth households.

The mass affluent market (liquid assets worth $100,000 to $1 million) consists of only 10 percent of American households, but they control 70 percent of total assets in the United States. In this market segment, 20 percent of the members own businesses and 75 percent have children.[2] According to a 2005 AIG American General study, consumers in this market are underinsured.

High-net-worth households (more than $1 million in liquid household assets) include 9.3 million households in the United States. Over the last eight years, the median age of members of this segment has moved down from the upper 50s to age 54. The Generation X group within this segment is growing although they represent the smallest portion of the segment.[3]

High-income households offer a significant market for companies that are able to (1) offer a full array of traditional and nontraditional products, (2) expand their distribution systems to include alternative channels, and (3) establish strong networks of financial advisors. On the downside, this market is highly competitive with sophisticated buyers who may not see a need for any insurance. Key products for this market are those that help minimize taxes and grow, preserve, and protect net worth.

continued on next page

Figure 3.3. (*continued*) Some Consumer Market Segments for Insurance Products Based on Demographics

Middle-income households (annual incomes between $36,000 and $100,000). This segment needs life insurance products to protect against the premature death of a sole income provider, disability products, health and supplemental health insurance products, and retirement products such as annuities.

Low-income households (annual incomes below $36,000). Low-income households have the strongest need for insurance because they have the least amount of resources to rely on in the event of a loss. They have a great need for life and health insurance but often are the least able to afford such protection. Some insurance companies throughout the world are beginning to offer micro-insurance to these populations. ***Micro-insurance*** refers to protection against insurable risks of assets and lives of target populations such as micro entrepreneurs, small farmers, the landless, women, and low-income earners through formal, semi-formal or informal institutions. This type of insurance typically offers poor populations a low premium and modest coverage for loss. Typically, micro-insurance must have a high sales volume to make it profitable for a company, but some jurisdictions are requiring insurers to offer coverage to the poor. For example, in India insurers are required by law to address the needs of the poorer segments of the population.

Segmenting by Life Cycle and Household Composition

Many insurance and financial services companies market to consumers based on events in a person's life cycle or household composition. Life cycle events include high school or college graduation, marriage, birth of a child, divorce, and retirement. Major events like these can cause a person to reevaluate his insurance and financial needs as circumstances change. Insurers who can tap into these life-event changes in a timely manner with a compelling marketing message may find a market for various life, health, and disability insurance; retirement planning products; and other financial products specific to each person's situation.

Household composition also creates a need for insurance and financial products. People with dependents, whether those dependents are aging parents or young children, need to protect their dependents in the event of the death of a financial provider. People who live in the same household may have needs that create an insurable interest or needs that call for protection of assets, such as their home, or products that help them save for education, retirement, or other major savings goals. For example, in the United States, single-parent families totaled about 12 million as of 2003.[4] These households typically need a large amount of insurance protection on the single wage earner, as well as education and retirement funding strategies tailored to their needs.

Segmenting by Cultural Origin

In the United States, both the Asian and Hispanic populations are growing rapidly. Hispanic-Americans total 41 million in the current population. According to U.S. Census Bureau data as of 2002, one in eight people in the United States is Hispanic.[5] The Asian-American population totals over 13 million.[6]

The growing Hispanic population represents an attractive market for companies offering life, health, and disability insurance as well as retirement planning products. Psychographic studies of the Hispanic-American population have shown that this group has a strong desire to financially protect their families. Additionally, in choosing a financial services advisor, this group looks largely to family recommendations.[7] Opportunities exist within this market for a range of insurance and financial services products. Challenges in marketing to this group include language barriers, breaking into the close-knit community to reach potential customers, and creating or identifying distribution channels acceptable and accessible to this population.

Studies have shown that major concerns of the Asian-American population include supporting family members and relatives and being able to pay for their children's education.[8] This market may need life, health, and disability insurance, as well as savings products for education.

Advantages of Geodemographic Segmentation	Disadvantages of Geodemographic Segmentation
■ Segments can be very well defined	■ Cost is high ■ Takes more time to develop segments than other segmentation types so a company must commit to following this approach over time as people's lives change and they fit into different segments

Psychographic Segmentation

Psychographic segmentation divides consumer markets based on several characteristics that describe consumers' attitudes, beliefs, opinions, values, lifestyles, activities, and interests. Psychographic segmentation views lifestyle as the outward display of individual psychological characteristics. As a result, consumers' lifestyles reflect their needs, values, attitudes, motives, and perceptions as affected by social factors in their environment.

The theory behind psychographic segmentation is that consumer markets consist of certain types of consumers and that different consumer types exhibit different purchasing behavior based on their attitudes, values, beliefs, activities or lifestyle choices. Companies can construct a profile of the consumers in a particular lifestyle segment by asking them the degree to which they agree or disagree with statements concerning their attitudes, values, beliefs, activities, or lifestyle choices or by using other psychographic measurement tools. For example, to create a profile of insurance customers for segmenting purposes, insurance companies might use a psychographic survey that measures the variety and degree to which consumers are interested in providing for their families' future financial security. Figure 3.4 shows a sample of a psychographic survey that a company might use to obtain information about a person's interests, values, beliefs and other psychological characteristics.

Much of the psychographic research available has come from the VALS™ Program of SRI Consulting Business Intelligence. The VALS™ system segments consumers based on personality traits that affect a person's behavior in the marketplace and is described in more detail in Figure 3.5. The segment into which a person is categorized is based on the person's (1) primary motivation, which includes ideals, achievement, or self-expression and (2) level of resources, which includes personality traits—such as energy, self-confidence, intellectualism, novelty-seeking, innovativeness, impulsiveness, leadership and vanity—and key demographic information. Different levels of resources enhance or hinder a person's expression of his primary motivation.[9]

Using psychographic profiles, a company can match a product's image with the type of consumer who buys or uses the product. For example, people who consider themselves environmentally responsible may choose to buy household cleaning products with minimal packaging and that contain no chemicals known as harmful to the environment. In this way, companies give brands of products "personalities" to match the profiles or personalities of the consumer segments for which they are designed.

Figure 3.4. Sample Portion of a Psychographic Survey

Following each of the statements below is the associated lifestyle component (shown in brackets) that can be used to determine an individual's orientation to a specific trait being measured. Such surveys typically use a five-to-seven point scale for responses that allows marketers to determine to what degree the statement describes the respondent.

	NEVER	RARELY	OCCASIONALLY	FREQUENTLY	ALWAYS
I enjoy going to the opera. [*Cultural orientation*]	____	____	____	____	____
I buy many things with a credit card. [*Credit orientation*]	____	____	____	____	____
I do volunteer work on a fairly regular basis. [*Community orientation*]	____	____	____	____	____
I enjoy talking about sports with others. [*Sports orientation*]	____	____	____	____	____
I attend a religious service [*Religious/Spiritual orientation*]	____	____	____	____	____

Some companies are starting to use personas to better understand the consumers in a particular segment and design a more appropriate marketing mix to appeal to them. ***Personas*** are models that represent the habits, needs, and motivations of a particular demographic portion of a market segment and that a company's marketing staff creates to better understand the habits, needs, and motivations of consumers in that segment. A persona is given a name and history by the marketer based on the marketer's assumptions and observations of how a person with these particular geographic, demographic, and psychographic characteristics would act in the marketplace. Some organizations call this process taking a "deeper dive" into a typical consumer's personality, habits, and needs.

By creating a persona that matches the target market's needs, attitudes, and other characteristics, the company can determine

- The products that will satisfy the target market's needs

- The message it should communicate to, and the product benefits it should highlight for the target market

- The promotion tools (personal selling, advertising, sales promotion, and publicity) it should use to reach the target market

- The distribution channels it should use to offer the product to the target market

Advantages of Psychographic Segmentation	Disadvantages of Psychographic Segmentation
- Gives a much deeper understanding of consumers than demographic or geographic segmentation information	- More difficult to measure psychographic factors than geographic or demographic factors

Figure 3.5. VALS™ Typology for U.S. Adult Consumers

The VALS™ typology uses "primary motivation" and "resources" to divide U.S. adult consumers into eight segments, each of which exhibits distinctive attitudes, behaviors, and decision-making patterns. The three primary motivations are ideals, achievement, and self-expression, and resources range from high to low. The typology segments are described below:

- **Innovators.** Motivated by ideals, achievement, and self-expression. High resources. Innovators are successful, sophisticated, take-charge people with high self-esteem. Because they have such abundant resources, they exhibit all three primary motivations in varying degrees. They are change leaders and are the most receptive to new ideas and technologies. Their purchases reflect cultivated tastes for upscale, niche products and services.

- **Thinkers.** Motivated by ideals. High resources. Thinkers are mature, satisfied, comfortable, and reflective. They tend to be well-educated and actively seek out information in the decision-making process. They favor durability, functionality, and value in products.

- **Believers.** Motivated by ideals. Low resources. Believers are strongly traditional and respect rules and authority. Because they are fundamentally conservative, they are slow to change and technology averse. They choose familiar products and established brands.

- **Achievers.** Motivated by achievement. High resources. Achievers have goal-oriented lifestyles that center on family and career. They avoid situations that encourage a high degree of stimulation or change. They prefer premium products that demonstrate success to their peers.

- **Strivers.** Motivated by achievement. Low resources. Strivers are trendy and fun loving. They have little discretionary income and tend to have narrow interests. They favor stylish products that emulate the purchases of people with greater material wealth.

- **Experiencers.** Motivated by self-expression, High resources. Experiencers appreciate the unconventional. They are active and impulsive, seeking stimulation from the new, offbeat, and risky. They spend a comparatively high proportion of their income on fashion, socializing, and entertainment.

- **Makers.** Motivated by self-expression. Low resources. Makers value practicality and self-sufficiency. They choose hands-on constructive activities and spend leisure time with family and close friends. Because they prefer value to luxury, they buy basic products.

- **Survivors.** Show no strong primary motivation. Low resources Survivors' lives are constrained by limited economic, social, and emotional resources and often by poor health. Survivors experience the world as pressing and difficult. Because they are so constrained, they show no evidence of a strong self-orientation, but rather focus on the needs of the present moment. Survivors are cautious consumers, representing a very modest market for most products and services.

Source: Adapted from SRI Consulting Business Intelligence, "The VALS™ Segments," © 2001-09 SRI Consulting Business Intelligence, http://www.sric-bi.com/VALS /types.shtml (17 June 2009). Used with permission.

Behavioristic Segmentation

Behavioristic segmentation divides markets according to consumers' behavior toward a product or company. The most commonly used factors in behavioristic segmentation include:

■ Benefits—the needs a consumer seeks to fill

■ Usage rate—how often or how much of a product a consumer buys

■ Buyer readiness—the stage of the purchase decision-making process a consumer is in

■ Preferred method of purchase—where or by what means a consumer wishes to buy products

■ Risk tolerance—how much or how little risk a consumer is willing to accept to achieve a desired outcome

■ Customer loyalty—how likely a customer is to buy from a company because of the trust they have in the company or their past experience with the company

Benefit Segmentation. ***Benefit segmentation*** is a way to segment markets by the benefits prospective customers seek from a product or service. Although most forms of segmentation try to show a relationship between one or more variables and consumers' needs, benefit segmentation is unique because the variables used to segment consumers into groups *are* their product needs. Insurance companies often segment markets according to the benefits sought by consumers. For example, the consumer market for whole life insurance can be divided into segments that consist of people who seek insurance for the following benefits

■ Tax or estate planning

■ Survivorship planning

■ Retirement purposes

■ Business continuity

■ Funds for college education

The benefits sought from the product vary from one segment to another, even though the product itself remains the same.

Usage Rate. Markets segmented by usage rate divide all the consumers in a market into smaller groups categorized as heavy users, light users, and nonusers. Each of these groups has different characteristics and different product needs that can help companies design product mixes that will appeal to the user group. In insurance markets, heavy users are known as *multiple purchasers* or *repeat users*—people who buy multiple products from the same company. Repeat users are important for insurance companies because it costs a company much less to sell additional products to current customers than to sell to new customers.

Buyer Readiness. Subgroups of consumers within a particular segment may be at different stages of readiness to buy a product. Some consumers may be unaware of a product; some will know a little about the product; some will know about the product but will not have tried it; and others will know a lot about the product and will have already purchased it. Each stage of buyer readiness needs a different marketing mix strategy. The marketing mix strategy for insurance products, in particular, must focus on promotion that educates consumers about insurance and the need for insurance products.

Preferred Purchase Method. Companies often segment markets based on how their customers prefer to purchase specific types of products. Insurance companies, for example, segment consumer markets according to whether consumers prefer to purchase insurance products (1) from insurance producers, (2) through direct response methods, such as direct mail, bill inserts, advertising postcards, and Internet quote systems or Web sites, (3) in retail settings, (4) from "one-stop" financial outlets, which are companies that offer multiple types of financial services (banking, insurance, financial planning, brokerage accounts, or other services) from one source, (5) at their place of employment, (6) via the Internet or by phone with contact initiated by the consumer, or (7) through a bank.

Risk Tolerance. Many financial products and services, including certain types of insurance, contain some level of financial risk. The risk is that the product will not attain the expected value or earnings sought, or that it will lose value. The amount of risk that consumers are willing to accept varies from one person to the next. Some consumers can tolerate high levels of risk, while others' tolerance for risk is low. Companies can use risk tolerance to match specific products and marketing strategies with specific consumer market segments. For example, insurers often market fixed-rate or guaranteed products to consumers with low risk tolerance, and emphasize the strength and stability of their products and companies in their marketing messages. For consumers comfortable with higher levels of risk, insurance companies market products such as variable life or variable universal life, mutual funds, and variable annuities, and promote the potential earnings of these products and the investment skills of their companies.

Risk tolerance may also be viewed from the perspective of risk of loss, instead of just risk associated with the performance of various insurance and financial or investment products. For example, not taking into account product type or types of risk by product, the death of a primary breadwinner may be financially devastating to new parents or people planning for future tuition needs. In such a situation, the family or household may be more averse to having such a risk occur and possibly more open to buying insurance and financial products to protect their standard of living if such an event were to occur. On the other hand, households with no children or grown children and with a house that has been paid for and assets in a variety of investment vehicles may be more risk tolerant of the loss of income of a primary breadwinner and, as a result, less willing to buy certain insurance and financial products designed to protect their income.

Customer Loyalty. Some insurance companies segment groups of customers based on how likely they are to remain a customer of a particular company. The groups of customers may range from price shoppers who will switch their insurance to whichever company offers the lowest price to customers who have a great relationship with a particular company or agent and will remain a customer of that company for a very long time. For insurance companies in particular, keeping a current customer is much less expensive than acquiring a new customer. Also, a customer who purchases life insurance from an insurance company is much more likely to buy from that same company in the future than another potential customer with similar demographic and psychographic characteristics. Most companies want to determine which customer segments are most likely to leave, often by using predictive models. Then, they can try to give those customers reasons to remain a customer of the company. Larger companies may have more resources than smaller companies to devote to this issue.

Advantages of Behavioristic Segmentation	Disadvantages of Behavioristic Segmentation
■ For existing customers, company already has some information about preferred purchase method, usage rate, and risk tolerance ■ Past behavior is often a good predictor of future behavior ■ General information about behavior patterns of customer groups is available from a variety of commercial sources; however, privacy laws prevent the sharing of specific information about customers	■ May cost more to obtain information about customer behavior than geographic or demographic segmentation because secondary research information about specific customer behavior is not available for purchase, so an insurer usually must conduct primary research to obtain such information ■ It is difficult for insurers to accurately gauge consumer behavior and use it to effectively segment markets because the information systems that most companies use do not support such data gathering and because there is not frequent enough contact with customers ■ It is difficult to collect behavioristic information for insurance products, unlike in retail situations where there may be cameras in stores or other means of tracking which products a customer purchases together. Also, most information comes self-reported from customers who may not accurately report their actual behavior.

Segmenting Organizational Markets

Organizational buyers have two main purposes for buying financial products and services: (1) to provide benefits for group members (such as a company's employees) and (2) to attract and retain talent, ensuring the continuation of business operations. These two purposes create two markets: the group market and the business market.

Insurance companies segment the group and business markets into smaller divisions based on the geographic, demographic, and behavioral characteristics of potential buyers. Figure 3.6 shows the specific factors included in each of these segmentation categories. As you can see from this figure, the characteristics used to segment organizational markets are similar to those used to segment consumer markets.

Figure 3.6. Categories Used to Segment Group and Business Markets

Geographic Characteristics	Demographic Characteristics	Behavioristic Characteristics
Country	Type of business activity	Benefits sought
Region	Type of group:	Patterns of usage
	Single-employer group	
Province or state	Multiple-employer group	Product preferences
	Debtor-creditor group	
County	Affinity group	
	OR	
City	Type of Organization:	
	-Corporation	
ZIP or postal code	-Partnership	
	-Sole Proprietorship	
Legal boundaries	-For-profit corporation	
	-Not-for-profit corporation	
	Size of group:	
	-Number of group members	
	OR	
	-Organization (number of employees)	

The divisions created by segmenting organizational markets are not mutually exclusive. As a result, insurance companies can market multiple group and business products to a single prospect.

Geographic Segmentation for Organizational Markets

The same geographic characteristics—such as location, population density and growth, and regulatory requirements—used in consumer marketing affects the way insurers market their products and services to both group and business markets. A company that identifies and accommodates geographic differences can focus its marketing activities on the segments that represent the greatest potential markets for its products.

Demographic Segmentation for Organizational Markets

Demographic variables most often used to segment organizational markets include

- The type of business activity—such as technology, manufacturing, agriculture, banking, insurance, government, or entertainment—in which companies are involved

- The type and size of groups and companies in the market

Segmentation by Business Activity. The *North American Industry Classification System (NAICS)* is the official system used in North America to categorize businesses according to the type of economic or business activity in which they are involved. Adopted by the United States in 1997, the NAICS groups together companies that use the same or similar processes to produce goods and services for thousands of types of business activities in Canada, Mexico, and the United States.[10]

Segmenting by business activity lets a company develop expertise in the needs of a particular industry, for example law firms or dental practices. Such businesses may have needs for insurance products that are similar to other businesses of the same type.

Segmentation by Type of Group. The group market for financial products and services consists of the following four types of groups:

- *Single-employer groups* are made up of the employees of one company and are the largest segment of the group insurance market.

- *Multiple-employer groups* consist of the employees of: (1) two or more employers in the same industry, (2) two or more labor unions, or (3) one or more employers and one or more labor unions. They represent only a small percentage of total insurance contracts in force but represent a high percentage of total group insurance premiums because they cover large numbers of employees.

- *Debtor-creditor groups* consist of lending institutions—banks, credit unions, savings and loan associations, finance companies, retail merchants, and credit card companies—and their debtors.

- *Affinity groups* are formed when individuals with common needs, interests, and characteristics communicate regularly with each other. Civic groups, professional associations, and social organizations, such as religious, ethnic, or educational groups, are examples of affinity groups. Typically, members of affinity groups are covered by large-group plans established on a state-wide, regional, or national basis. Such plans are marketed to the groups through highly specialized broker-consultants. Insurance companies market to the individual group members in an affinity group usually by using direct mail offers or by having agents contact eligible members to enroll them in the plan.

Segmentation by Group Size. Segmentation of the group market by size produces the following three primary segments:

- **Small groups** are usually defined as groups with 100 or fewer members and represent a large segment of the overall business market. A 2001 LIMRA research report revealed that there are an estimated 5.4 to 6.4 million small businesses with fewer than 100 employees in the United States.[11] Fifty-two percent of small businesses offer at least one group insurance benefit.[12] Small-group contracts generally provide standardized benefits, but group members can select from a menu of coverages and features. The insurer's home office or a third-party administrator hired by the insurer typically administers the plan.

- **Medium-sized groups** include groups with 101 to 499 members. Contracts for medium-sized groups offer greater flexibility—both in plan design and plan administration—than do small-group contracts. Traditionally, medium-sized to large companies have been an important market segment for insurance products. Today, this segment is becoming increasingly saturated and insurers are turning their attention to the growing small business segment.

- **Large groups** are defined as groups with 500 or more members. This segment includes only a small percentage of all group insurance contracts in force, but represents a large percentage of total group insurance premium volume. Insurers generally tailor benefits to the buyer's specifications and modify administrative procedures to meet the group policyholder's needs. Most large-group insurance programs are partially or fully self-funded.

An insurance company's goal is to most effectively meet the needs of its group customers. It is not uncommon for an insurance company to issue a large-group contract to the employees of a large organization, and also issue a small-group-type product only to the executives of that same organization.

Segmentation by Company Type. Insurers frequently segment a business market according to the legal and structural characteristics of organizations in the market. For example, organizations can be divided into three main legal forms—corporations, partnerships, and sole proprietorships. Organizations also can be classified as for-profit or not-for-profit organizations. These legal forms affect taxation, property ownership, and succession-planning strategies. As a result, each segment has distinct business needs for financial services products. Corporations, for example, offer a potential market for a variety of business insurance products and employee retirement plans. Sole proprietorships are more likely to need business continuation products and may also need retirement planning products.

Segmentation by Company Size. Business markets can be segmented by company size into two main segments:

- Small companies, with fewer than 100 employees

- Large companies, with 100 or more employees

Traditionally, large companies have been an important market segment for insurance products because they were a quick way to make a large sale. However, the reverse is also true—losing such a client may dramatically decrease the insurer's group business revenue. Also, a large-company client may require more service support than a small-company client, so the insurer must have the resources to provide such service. As mentioned previously, the large-company segment is becoming more saturated and the number of small businesses is growing. The small-company segment represents a market not only for life and health insurance products but also for property and casualty insurance, and bank and mutual fund products.

The insurance products and marketing methods a company uses for small business markets are basically the same as those it develops for consumer markets. We discuss the small business segment as an organizational target market later in this chapter.

Behavioristic Segmentation for Organizational Markets

Like consumer markets, group and business markets can be segmented based on their purchase behavior, which includes benefits sought, usage rate, risk tolerance, and buyer readiness. Buyers' use of specialized products, such as accidental death and dismemberment insurance, travel medical insurance, dental and vision insurance, is especially important. Within the group market, employer groups and affinity groups are interested mainly in group life and health insurance products and group pension plans. Organizations that provide charge accounts or make installment or mortgage loans to consumers use group credit life, group credit health, and group credit disability income insurance products. Within the business market, the demand for specialized products is even greater, with different types of companies purchasing different types of products. A group that buys one specialized product is a likely candidate to purchase additional specialized products.

Target Marketing

Market segmentation helps insurers identify smaller segments of the total market for a product or service. *Target marketing* is the process companies use to evaluate each identified market segment and then select one or more segments, called target markets, on which to focus their marketing efforts.

Each target market that a company selects to pursue generally needs its own marketing mix. As a result, the markets that an insurer chooses affect the

- Products it develops

- Prices it charges

- Distribution channels it uses

- Advertising and promotion it creates to market and sell its products

Evaluating Potential Target Markets

To select which market segment or segments to target, a company evaluates the segments to determine which of them offer the greatest (1) size and growth potential, (2) attractiveness, (3) compatibility with company goals and resources, and (4) market penetration. Before investing resources in a particular market segment, insurers need to ensure that buyers in the segment

- Have a specific need for the proposed product or service

- Are able and willing to buy the product or service

- Have the authority and/or means to buy the product or service

- Understand the product or service (or can be educated easily to understand the product or service) and how it may meet a need

Market Size and Growth Potential

A company should select target markets that offer the combination of size, growth, and profitability that best match the company's goals and resources. For example, if a company has expertise in a particular product type or particular type of market, it should probably concentrate its efforts on the markets that match its expertise to grow its business. Also, a company should consider if a potential market (1) has enough customers to generate the amount of sales needed to support the cost of marketing to that segment and (2) will help grow the company's business.

Market Attractiveness

How attractive a market segment is depends on a variety of factors, including the level of competition in the market and the buying power of customers. Aggressive competition can limit a company's ability to price and promote its products effectively. If buyers in the market have bargaining power over sellers, they can demand lower prices and greater quality and services. Meeting such demands can erode a company's profitability. In general, companies should enter only those segments in which they can gain a competitive advantage or offer superior value to customers.

Company Goals and Resources

A company may choose to *not* enter a particular market even it appears to be profitable because the potential market and the company's long-term goals do not mesh. For example, a company may not market to an otherwise attractive segment if it considers the segment to be politically, socially, or environmentally unsuitable. Companies typically also avoid segments that cannot be reached within the limits of company resources. For example, a home service insurance company that markets and sells low-face-amount, cash-value life insurance likely would not enter the high-net-worth markets with complex variable universal life insurance product offerings because it has neither the product design experience nor the appropriate distribution channel to support those types of products. A company should only pursue a target market if it has, or can easily obtain, the financial, technological, and human resources necessary to compete successfully.

Market Penetration

Market penetration strategies focus on increasing sales of current products to current markets. An insurance company may choose to target a market that is large and growing to increase its penetration of that market; however, if a company already has a significant percentage of that market, further targeting of that market may not be necessary.

Target Marketing Strategies

How many target markets a company chooses to pursue depends on the strategy it adopts to define its market. Target marketing strategies can be divided into three primary types: undifferentiated marketing, concentrated marketing, and differentiated marketing.

Undifferentiated marketing, also known as *mass marketing*, involves defining the total market for a product as the target market and designing a single marketing mix directed toward the entire market. Although undifferentiated marketing was widely used in the past, fewer insurance companies practice it today. In mature markets, such as the United States, even "low-cost" insurance providers try to differentiate themselves from competitors by advertising quality service and extra product features. However, undifferentiated marketing is still used in developing countries. As the insurance market in such countries opens to private-sector companies, demand for differentiated products and marketing mixes is being generated.

Concentrated marketing involves focusing all of a company's marketing resources on satisfying the needs of one segment of the total market for a particular type of product. *Niche marketing* is a form of concentrated marketing in which companies target small, narrowly defined subgroups within a segment that attract only one or a few competitors. An example of a niche marketer is the United Services Automobile Association (USAA), which offers insurance and other financial products only to members of the United States military and their families.

Most companies today follow a differentiated marketing strategy. *Differentiated marketing* aims to satisfy the needs of a large part of the total market for a particular type of product by offering a number of products and marketing mixes designed to appeal to different segments of the total market. Going one step further with differentiated marketing, some companies may choose to narrowly target consumers in a particular segment of the market. *One-to-one marketing*, also known as *micromarketing*, customizes the marketing mix for each individual consumer or consumers in a specific location. One-to-one marketing can be extremely effective if enough relevant information about the consumer is known; however, it is very expensive to market to each individual customer. Few companies use one-to-one marketing; however, companies do use *one-to-few marketing*, also known as *one-to-some marketing*, in which companies tailor their marketing mixes to a particular group of customers with similar characteristics, needs, or past purchase behavior, and personalize the message to some extent. For example, a company that offers life insurance may customize direct mail pieces for existing pre-selected customers who already have term life insurance with the company to offer them the opportunity to convert their term life policies to whole life or universal life policies for an additional premium charge without providing evidence of insurability. The following chart shows the advantages and disadvantages of each target marketing strategy.

Type of Target Marketing Strategy	Advantages	Disadvantages
Undifferentiated Marketing	■ Cost savings that result from developing a single marketing mix ■ Cost savings can be passed along to customers in the form of lower prices	■ Ignores any differences that exist among various segments of the total market ■ Must compete with companies who offer specialized products and marketing mixes
Concentrated Marketing	■ Company may be better able to serve the market because of its expertise in and understanding of the segment	■ Profitability is tied to only one segment ■ A change in the size, buying power or patterns of buyers, or other market conditions of the segment can negatively affect companies with this narrow focus
Differentiated Marketing	■ Customers can be better served with a variety of products, pricing, and distribution options that closely match their needs resulting in increased customer satisfaction and increased sales	■ Costs more to implement than other strategies ■ Requires large amounts of data to mine appropriate information ■ Requires constant monitoring and updating of strategy and message to customer

The particular target marketing strategy a company adopts depends on the following factors:

■ **Company resources.** For new, small companies that lack the financial and other resources needed to develop multiple products and marketing mixes, concentrated marketing is typically the best target marketing strategy to follow. Concentrated marketing also works well for older, more established companies that offer only one product.

■ **Product form or design variability.** Undifferentiated marketing is more appropriate for products, such as soybeans, cucumbers, steel, and commodities, that typically are offered in only one form. Differentiated and concentrated marketing are more appropriate for products that vary in design, such as insurance products and services.

■ **Market variability.** If most buyers of a particular product purchase, use, and respond to marketing for the product in a similar way, undifferentiated marketing may be appropriate. If buying behavior varies across market segments, concentrated or differentiated marketing strategies are likely to be more successful.

- **Stage in the product's life cycle.** New products often call for concentrated or undifferentiated marketing strategies, while mature products often require a differentiated marketing strategy.[13]

Target Markets for Insurance Products

Insurance companies may target consumer markets, organizational markets, or both, depending on their company mission and goals. In Figure 3.3, we described some consumer market segments that are produced using demographic segmentation. Many insurers choose to target such consumer markets for their products. Companies that serve consumer markets may identify subsets of these demographic markets by combining multiple segmentation methods allowing them to target more precisely defined consumer markets.

We illustrate this in Figures 3.7 and 3.8, which bring the concepts of market segmentation and target marketing in the consumer market, together, to show how using more than one type of segmentation method to identify target markets can deliver a richer market in terms of opportunity and profitability. Figure 3.7 explains the information a company might obtain using only demographic segmentation, and why that information may not be sufficient to effectively target a market segment. Figure 3.8 illustrates how overlaying geographic, demographic, psychographic, and behavioristic segmentation information can highlight market segments that are more narrowly defined and easier to target.

Figure 3.7. Using Only One Segmentation Method May Not Adequately Define a Target Market

The Spindle Company has developed a long-term care product that it believes will be most attractive to and needed by customers aged 50 to 85. Within the 50-to-85 age group, Spindle further refines its segmentation by eliminating prospective customers whose household income is less than $35,000 or whose investable assets are less than $75,000—suggesting these individuals could not afford the product. The company also eliminates individuals whose household income exceeds $250,000 or who have investable assets of more than $2 million—reasoning that these people can afford to pay for long-term care out of their current income. Spindle defines investable assets as all assets excluding a person's principal place of residence and funds in an employer-sponsored or other retirement savings plan. All of these decisions have been made based on demographic variables. This segment looks promising to Spindle.

However, because Spindle is using only one form of segmentation (that is, demographic), it may be missing important information. For example, using only demographic segmentation, Spindle still does not know

- The distribution channel from which these individuals wish to buy this type of product
- The values that are important to them
- The types of media they view, read, or are exposed to
- The geographic location of these customers

Spindle can address these issues by analyzing the interaction of several types of segmentation methods and by using powerful statistical and analytical tools, such as geodemographic classification systems to more accurately identify the needs, behaviors, and characteristics of potential customers for the long-term care product.

Figure 3.8 describes how the Spindle Company might now target two consumer markets that were identified using cluster analysis, which uses several segmentation forms combined to obtain information about customers in particular geographic locations.

Figure 3.8. Targeting Two Different Segments for the Same Product

Using a type of cluster analysis that combines demographic, geographic, behavioristic, and psychographic information to derive segments, the Spindle Company has now identified two promising segments for its long-term-care insurance product. Spindle is ready to finalize its marketing mix for each segment.

Segment A consists of college-educated individuals and couples of various cultural origins, aged 50–85 who reside in major metropolitan areas. This segment has annual household incomes of between $75,000 and $250,000 and investable assets from $350,000 to $2 million. The members of this segment actively read a major newspaper in their region, and watch some, but not a significant amount of, television on a daily basis. They also attend theater and symphony performances, travel internationally on a regular basis, and prefer to buy insurance and financial products through face-to-face meetings.

To successfully market to Segment A, Spindle must use a personal-selling sales force that is well represented in major metropolitan areas. It can promote the long-term care product in major newspapers, theater playbills and upscale travel magazines. Television advertising would be wasted on this segment because they do not watch it frequently. Because this market has medium-to-high income and a substantial amount of investable assets, these customers may welcome sophisticated products that include features such as compound interest on earnings and inflation riders.

Segment B consists of individuals who live in rural or small towns and who generally have a high school education or less. These individuals watch television on a daily basis for entertainment and information. They take pride in their military service and never want to be a burden on others. Their household incomes range from about $35,000 to $50,000 annually, and they have investable assets of at least $75,000 up to $100,000.

To successfully market to Segment B, Spindle will probably use direct response television advertisements, selecting markets and television stations based on where the potential customers reside and which programs they prefer to watch. The long-term care product will need to be modestly priced and easy to understand without face-to-face selling. An endorser who is a celebrity and who also is associated with the military would be a powerful draw for this segment.

The organizational market segments most often targeted by today's insurance companies are employer groups and small businesses.

Employer Groups

Employers can provide insurance coverage for their employees independently or by joining with other employers from the same or similar industries to form multiple-employer groups. Multiple-employer groups take one of the following three forms:

- A *negotiated trusteeship (Taft-Hartley Group)* results from a collective-bargaining agreement between one or more unions and employers of union members. The employees served by a negotiated trusteeship are usually in the same or related industries.

- A *voluntary trade association* is an association of individual employers that work in similar industries and have common business interests. Membership in such associations allows small companies to offer their employees better and less expensive group insurance benefits than the companies could purchase on their own.

- A *multiple-employer welfare arrangement (MEWA)* is formed when small employers band together to offer group insurance and other benefits to their employees.

Small Businesses

The small business market is a large and rapidly growing segment of the overall business market. According to U.S. Census Bureau data, three-fourths of all businesses in the United States have no payroll and most of these businesses are unincorporated and run by self-employed people.[14] These small businesses represent an opportunity for sales of life, health, disability, and retirement products.

Of all the businesses with employees in the United States, there are approximately 5 million firms with between 1 and 99 employees. As a group, small businesses offer a significant market for insurance products designed to

- Protect the business against the potential loss of earnings if an owner or key person dies prematurely or becomes disabled

- Prevent the liquidation of a business if an owner or partner dies, and preserve the value of the deceased's share of the business

- Preserve a disabled owner's or partner's financial interests in the business by facilitating funding for the buyout of the deceased owner's share of the business

- Allow surviving shareholders of closely held corporations to retain management control while providing a fair price for the shares purchased from a deceased shareholder's estate

- Prevent the estate tax burden on an inherited business from forcing the sale of the business

- Improve the credit rating and general financial stability of a business by helping to assure banks, suppliers, and other creditors that the business has the ability and resources to continue operations

- Provide a source of emergency funds

■ Provide various types of executive benefit plans to attract and keep key employees

■ Provide a variety of employee health, life, and disability insurance products and qualified retirement plans

Small businesses provide potential for multiple types of product sales. For example, a small corporation might be a prospect for (1) key-person life and disability insurance, (2) personal disability income insurance, (3) a buy-sell agreement funded with life and disability insurance, (4) group life and health insurance, and (5) group pension or retirement products. Insurers can also meet the diverse needs of small businesses by providing valuable advisory services. Small businesses often need help creating formal business continuation, retirement, asset protection, and employee retention plans.

Key Terms

market segmentation
market segment
single-variable segmentation
multivariable segmentation
consumer market
organizational market
geographic segmentation
demographic segmentation
geodemographic segmentation
micro-insurance
psychographic segmentation
persona
behavioristic segmentation
benefit segmentation
North American Industry
  Classification System (NAICS)

single-employer group
multiple-employer group
debtor-creditor group
affinity group
target marketing
undifferentiated marketing
concentrated marketing
niche marketing
differentiated marketing
one-to-one marketing
one-to-few marketing
negotiated trusteeship
  (Taft-Hartley Group)
voluntary trade association
multiple-employer welfare
  arrangement (MEWA)

Endnotes

1. *ACLI Life Insurers Fact Book 2008* (Washington, DC: American Council of Life Insurers, 2008), 66, http://www.acli.com/NR/rdonlyres/66E129A1-58EA-4AF2-BC38-F568FD185762/16461/FactBook2009.pdf (8 June 2009).

2. Walter H. Zultowski, "2007 Phoenix Wealth Survey Executive Summary: Optimism Returns for High Net Worth, but Where are the Baby Bulls?" *Phoenix High-Net-Worth Market Insights*, June 2007, https://www.phoenixwm.phl.com/servlet/DocDelivery?DocId=docu_publ_advi_survey_insight_0607.pdf&DocType=0 (10 June 2009).

3. Ibid.

4. Jason Fields, *America's Families and Living Arrangements: 2003*, Current Population Reports P20-553, U.S. Bureau of the Census, (Washington, DC: GPO, 2003), http://www.census.gov/prod/2004pubs/p20-553.pdf (10 June 2009).

5. Roberto R. Ramirez and G. Patricia de la Cruz, *The Hispanic Population in the United States: March 2002*, Current Population Reports P20-545, U.S. Bureau of the Census, (Washington, DC: GPO, 2002), http://www.census.gov/prod/2003pubs/p20-545.pdf (10 June 2009).

6.   Rick Niu, "A Perfect Match: Independent Distribution and Multicultural Marketing," *Perspectives*, March/April 2007, 27, http://www.nailba.org/content/perspectives/downloads/2007march/nibs0207.pdf (10 June 2009).

7.   Ibid.

8.   Allianz Life Insurance Company of North America, "New Survey Offers Significant Insight into the Financial Values and Concerns of Multicultural America," January 2005, http://www.allianzlife.com/ToolsInsights/Roperstory.aspx (18 June 2008).

9.   SRI Consulting Business Intelligence (SRIC-BI), "The VALS™ Segments," http://www.sri-bi.com/vals/types.shtml (10 June 2009).

10. U.S. Bureau of the Census, "North American Industry Classification System (NAICS)," http://www.census.gov/eos/www/naics/ (10 June 2009).

11. Nilufer R. Ahmed, *U.S. Small Businesses in 2000: A Dynamic Market*, Detailed Report (Windsor, CT: LIMRA International, 2001), 3, http://www.limra.com/members/abstracts/reports/3405a.pdf (10 June 2009). Used with permission.

12. Shawn P. Flynn, *Serving Up Small Businesses: Marketing Insurance and Employee Benefits to the Small-Business Market* (Windsor, CT: LIMRA International, 2006), 5, http://www.limra.com/members/abstracts/reports/5282.pdf (11 June 2009). Used with permission.

13. Philip Kotler and Gary Armstrong, *Principles of Marketing*, 9th ed. (Upper Saddle River, NJ: Prentice-Hall, 2001), 268.

14. U.S. Bureau of the Census, "Statistics about Business Size (including Small Business) from the U.S. Census Bureau," http://www.census.gov/epcd/www/smallbus.html (12 June 2009).

Marketing Information and Research

Objectives:

After studying this chapter, you should be able to

- Describe a marketing information system and explain how companies use internal databases, external databases, and marketing intelligence to obtain marketing information

- Describe the major information technologies that allow companies to access and evaluate information to help make marketing decisions

- Distinguish primary research from secondary research and identify several sources for secondary research

- List the six stages in the marketing research process and describe activities that commonly occur in each stage

- Distinguish among exploratory research, descriptive research, and causal research and explain how to determine which type of research to conduct

- Describe the major qualitative and quantitative methods researchers use to collect primary marketing research data

- Describe some types of marketing research services provided by external vendors

- Identify limitations associated with the use of marketing research

Outline

Suppose the company that you work for is considering developing hybrid life and annuity products that have Long Term Care (LTC) options or features. You have been selected to lead a team of company employees assigned to gather information about the potential markets for such products. Your primary goal is to identify the types of features and product solutions that will be the most appealing to those markets. The challenge for your team is to find the information that your company needs to

- Assess the proposed product enhancements

- Develop a profile of potential end-user customers

- Determine what producers and competitors are doing with similar product offerings

Where do you start?

Your company accumulates a lot of data in its day-to-day operations from both internal and external sources. Unfortunately, that information is in many different forms and not necessarily in the form that you need. To find the information that your team needs to accomplish its mission, you can turn to the company's marketing information system.

Marketing Information Systems

A *marketing information system* is an interactive system of people, software and equipment, and procedures that provides managers with a continuous flow of information to help them manage marketing activities. Marketing information systems help companies

- Assess what information they need

- Receive and store marketing data from sources inside and outside the company

- Classify, index, restructure, and retrieve data to produce timely, relevant information to support marketing decision making

- Distribute marketing information to the right people at the right time and in the right format

Three parts of a company's marketing information system have the greatest impact on marketing operations:

(1) The types and sources of marketing data the system collects and stores,

(2) How the system uses technology to help marketing decision-makers capture, store, analyze, and integrate usable information

(3) How marketing information is communicated to decision-makers.

Although companies can obtain much of the information they need to develop and implement marketing programs via the company's marketing information system, companies sometimes use the marketing research process to get information about specific problems or opportunities, which we discuss later in this chapter.

Sources of Marketing Information

Most of the information in marketing information systems comes from (1) internal databases, (2) external databases, and (3) marketing intelligence.

Internal Databases

Companies computerize and store internal records and reports in extensive internal databases. An *internal database* houses information in a central source that is meant to be shared by many users within the company. These records and reports provide detailed information about a wide variety of company activities as shown in Figure 4.1. Information that a company stores in its internal databases can be sorted and analyzed according to specific marketing factors—such as product or product line, geographic area, type of customer, target market, distribution channel, producer, or compensation plan—and then used by marketing managers to plan and monitor marketing programs.

Figure 4.1. Sources and Uses of Internal Information

Source	Use
Accounting Records & Financial Statements	■ Determine Sales by Product ■ Determine Expenses by Product ■ Calculate Profit by Product
Call Center Logs*	■ Assess Customer Satisfaction ■ Identify Products and Services Generating Complaints
Customer Applications*	■ Obtain General Demographic Data about Customers
Research Reports	■ Learn about Customer Preferences ■ Assess Past Market Conditions ■ Determine Effectiveness of Promotion Efforts
Sales Force Reports	■ Assess Customer Needs for Product Enhancements/Modifications

* Note that information from call center logs and customer applications is often not stored in an electronic format (much of it may be on paper) so it may be more difficult to retrieve such data easily.

Because marketing managers can access and work with internal database information easily and quickly, these databases usually provide information at a lower cost than other information sources. However, companies collect much of the internal information—such as customer service phone-log data, underwriting information, and credit information—for purposes other than marketing. Often, managers must change or adapt such information to use it to evaluate marketing activities or make marketing decisions. For example, sales and cost data that a company uses to produce its financial statements are often incomplete or in the wrong form to use for evaluating the company's sales force or distribution channels. In addition, a manager must often combine data from multiple sources, gathering internal and external data.

Insurance companies must always comply with current privacy regulations and procedures when accessing or using customers' personal information stored in internal databases. Most companies have implemented a personal information protection, or privacy, policy based on the Organization for Economic Co-Operation and Development (OECD) guidelines governing the protection of privacy and transborder flows of personal data. The OECD is an organization made up of government representatives of 30 member countries around the world. The organization promotes sustainable economic growth globally, supports world trade, seeks to boost employment and living standards, and is involved in other matters that affect international commerce. Insurance companies must obtain customer consent to collect, store, and use any information provided to them by their customers.

Using Technology to Find Information in Databases

Information technology offers marketing managers many ways to access and use information for marketing. In particular, marketing personnel use business intelligence, data warehouses, and data mining to find information they need in internal databases.

Business Intelligence

Business intelligence (BI), formerly known as *decision support systems (DSS)*, is an organized collection of procedures, software, databases, and devices that support problem-specific decision making. Forecasting is one of the most important applications of BI as described in the following example.

Example: Goal: Use BI to forecast the effect on sales of adding new producers to a particular sales territory.

The Process: A manager enters known information about the market, product, available resources, and competition into the BI system. Then, the manager adds information about the industry and competitors from internal databases, external databases, and marketing intelligence. The BI system processes the data, using marketing models or expert systems, and arrives at a recommendation.

> **The Results:** The manager can use the information obtained and alter the variables to see how different conditions may affect the proposed decision.

Although basic BI systems may only retrieve information, analyze files, and prepare reports from multiple files, more sophisticated BI systems include marketing models and expert systems. A ***marketing model*** is a statistical or management science tool that describes the mathematical relationships between certain variables (such as price, cost, or demand) that affect marketing decisions. An ***expert system*** is a knowledge-based computer system designed to provide expert consultation to information users for solving specialized and complex problems.[1] This means that the computer can actually suggest alternative actions or help solve problems based on the information or knowledge stored in its database. Insurance and financial services companies often use expert systems to perform credit evaluations, develop marketing plans for new products or new investment strategies, and evaluate insurance applications and claims.

By using BI, companies can simulate recommended actions on a computer before spending time and money implementing an action.

Data Warehouses

Most insurance companies have legacy technology systems that have evolved over time. A ***legacy system*** is a combination of computer hardware and software that a company has used for a long time to perform specific tasks. Often, different functional areas within a company maintain different legacy systems because the best system for one function is not the best for another function. Most legacy systems are no longer the best or most modern systems for processing information, but they have not been replaced because they continue to perform necessary functions and would be extremely costly to replace. In fact, replacing a legacy system in some companies would require that their entire information technology systems be overhauled. However, some components of legacy systems are replaced or updated as time and money allow and competitive pressures dictate.

Using multiple legacy systems often leads to the creation of distinct, unlinked databases. To find company-wide information, managers must search some or all of these separate databases. In some cases, managers may not have ready access to all of a company's different databases, and even when they do, the data they receive may not be in consistent, usable formats. Managers must manually sort through and analyze such information. As a result, multiple database searches often increase the time and cost of getting information for marketing purposes.

To address the problems of retrieving or obtaining information associated with multiple, often unlinked databases, many companies use data warehouses. A ***data warehouse*** is an integrated, subject-oriented database (or set of databases). Although some data warehouses are built just to store information, most are designed to support the functions performed by BI. Data warehouses broadly summarize by subject matter (for example, by client or policyowner) separate pieces of information from otherwise incompatible internal and external sources. Users can then apply common business models or business rules to process the information into a nonrepetitive, standardized form. A marketing professional with a specific marketing objective that does not violate the privacy protection applying to an individual's personal information could use query applications to extract information from the data warehouse for marketing purposes.

> **Example**: A marketing professional extracts a list of all the company's female policyholders over age 40 living in the state of Kentucky who own term life insurance products to find out if marketing a conversion option to those policyholders to change their term policies to permanent life policies would be profitable or feasible.

Although companies use legacy systems to create data warehouses, a company also can create a data warehouse using information from other sources such as newly acquired information not yet in the system, external information, and information from third parties associated with the insurer's business, all subject to privacy preferences and protection afforded by law. The following table describes some of the advantages and disadvantages of data warehouses:

Advantages of Data Warehouses	Disadvantages of Data Warehouses
■ More effective fraud detection and prevention ■ Greater flexibility to enter new business areas, such as Internet marketing or investments because information about customers and market potential is more readily accessible ■ Faster response time because users can access information from multiple sources from one central location with only one database query ■ More efficient operations because deleting repetitive information across departments reduces the size of department databases ■ Better business decisions because employees and managers have access to adequate, timely information ■ More accurate performance evaluation because of the standard format of the information ■ Managers can compare current and historical information across different products, markets, and distribution channels	■ Cost of creating them (including financial and other resources) ■ Amount of time and technological expertise needed to create and maintain such complex systems. Building a data warehouse can take two or more years and often requires the use of an external vendor. Once created, the data warehouse must be continually updated to include new information, and must be supported by multiple staff members of the information technology department.

Data Mining

Data mining is the process of analyzing the variables in a database or data warehouse to discover patterns and relationships. Data mining is a great tool for identifying unsuspected buying behavior patterns. Companies can then direct their efforts toward prospects that fit the patterns.

For example, using data mining tools, and open-ended questions, a marketer can query the data warehouse to identify prospects that are most likely to be interested in (1) purchasing a particular product and (2) purchasing multiple products. A marketer who intends to sell multiple products to an existing customer should notify the producer and ask for his or her input on the potential sale. In this way, the company honors any privacy preferences the customer has already stated. For example, a company with sophisticated technology can store input the producer conveys about a customer's privacy preferences in its customer database. When the company runs a query to the database, such preference information appears so the company does not have to contact the producer each time for this information.

External Databases

A wealth of marketing information is available from external organizational sources, including government agencies and industry trade associations.

In the United States, the federal government provides free access to the external databases of some of its agencies such as:

- The Bureau of Labor Statistics, whose Web site provides statistics on unemployment rates, the consumer price index, consumer expenditures, and much more

- The Census Bureau, whose Web site provides current industry reports and economic census data

- The Department of Commerce, whose Web site provides business and economic data for the United States and other countries

Industry trade associations are primary sources of industry-specific research. Research from LOMA and LIMRA, insurance industry trade associations, provides broad-based marketing intelligence for the financial services industry. For example, LIMRA offers MarketScans, which are fast-turnaround research projects that member companies can request to get specific information on a research topic. One recent MarketScan provided information from 15 companies on the underwriting, application, and placement of life insurance policies for applicants ages 61–75. Accessing industry trade association databases may require membership fees or transaction fees.

Marketing Intelligence

Marketing intelligence, also known as *competitive intelligence*, is the systematic collection and analysis of publicly available information about competitors and ongoing developments in the marketing environment.[2] Marketing intelligence helps companies discover how other companies in their industry operate. Usually, companies collect information on competitors' prices, product specifications, product performance, service quality, market characteristics, market share and trends, distribution channels, and marketing strategy. Companies also gather information about competitors' plans for new products and approaches to competition.

Today, most marketing intelligence information comes from public sources, such as

- Industry and private-sector publications
- Company Web sites
- Informal observations and questioning of customers
- Industry and professional association meetings
- Trade associations such as LOMA and LIMRA
- Competitors' advertisements and sales promotion materials
- Suppliers of goods and services, such as consultants, advertising agencies, public relations firms, and management service companies
- Competitors' annual reports to shareholders and filings required by the Securities and Exchange Commission for publicly owned entities (for example, Forms 10-K, 10-Q, and 8-K)
- Statutory reports to state regulatory agencies

An insurance company's sales force and even large brokerage agencies can obtain marketing intelligence information in their daily interactions with others in the industry, especially information about competitors' customer service programs, sales promotion, compensation systems, sales force training, and product portfolio. Also, a manager's personal and professional contacts with current and former managers and producers who work at other companies often provide information about the current competitive environment.

To remain competitive, companies must carefully monitor competitors' actions. However, laws and regulations or industry codes of conduct prohibit certain methods of monitoring competitors' actions. For example, insurers commonly can't hire employees away from competitors to get competitor information, interview a competitor's employees without intending to hire them, pay existing or former employees of competitors to disclose company secrets, or pretend to be interested in purchasing a competitor company to get details about the competitor's financial position.

Reporting Marketing Information

Much of the information that marketing information systems create comes in the form of regular reports. The system automatically produces such reports based on information stored in internal databases or accessed from external sources. These marketing information system reports concern topics that managers monitor on a regular basis. Occasionally, however, managers need the customized information that a business intelligence (BI) system can provide to make decisions.

A company feeds information from managers and other users back into the marketing information system to evaluate and improve its performance. Feedback from managers and other users can be used to update databases and reduce redundant information, modify and improve BI, or make necessary changes in the amount or types of information collected as input from internal databases, marketing intelligence, and marketing research.

At some companies top management is beginning to use information dashboards to access and monitor internal information about critical elements pertaining to company performance and financial health on a daily, or sometimes real-time, basis. An ***information dashboard*** is a visual representation, usually in the form of graphs or charts, of key information managers need to make decisions. In fact, some information dashboards actually resemble automobile dashboards. An ***enterprise dashboard*** allows at-a-glance visualization of company health and monitoring of key performance indicators.[3] These dashboards visually display key performance indicators for the entire company—such as sales and lapses by line of business, numbers reflecting agent recruiting and attrition of the agent workforce, and other information—that management wishes to constantly monitor. The enterprise dashboard may be set up to report all indicators that management has pre-identified as indicators to monitor, or it may just display indicators that show actual performance values that reflect a huge positive or negative deviation from their expected values.

Marketing Research Projects

Sometimes marketers need information that is not readily available through the marketing information system. In such cases, marketers may conduct or hire a third-party to conduct marketing research. Regardless of whether the research is done internally or externally, understanding how and why it is performed and the right way to conduct such research can greatly increase its effectiveness.

Marketing research is the discipline that focuses on collecting, analyzing, interpreting, and reporting information related to specific marketing problems or opportunities. For example, marketing research can provide information about customer needs, perceptions, attitudes, motivations, purchase behavior, and satisfaction with products and services. Marketing research helps a company

- Develop an appropriate marketing mix to appeal to its customers
- Identify marketing opportunities, analyze target markets, evaluate existing market strategies, and measure marketing performance to support strategic decision making
- Maintain or increase profitability by delivering products and services that best meet the targeted customers' needs and eliminating products and services that the target market no longer desires or that the company can no longer profitably deliver

Companies input information they obtain through marketing research projects into the company's formal database of information. However, marketing research projects themselves are not part of the standard operations of a marketing information system.

Secondary Research

For most companies marketing research projects begin with reviewing available secondary research. ***Secondary research*** is market research already performed for another purpose, and often by another entity, that may apply to the present question or opportunity. Secondary research data can come from a company's internal sources, such as internal databases or marketing intelligence reports, or from external sources. The primary external sources for secondary research data include (1) government sources, (2) syndicated sources, (3) industry and trade associations, (4) private publications, including published surveys of customers and sales people, and (5) online services.

Secondary research data provides valuable background information on environmental conditions and market trends at a much lower cost than conducting customized research. For some companies, using secondary research data available from government or industry sources may be the only realistic way to conduct marketing research. However, secondary research data generally relates to past conditions and marketing issues. As a result, secondary research typically is not the best way to evaluate current marketing concerns. Secondary research data may not be effective for a research project if:

- The units in which the data is measured are not specific enough for the current inquiry.

- How the data is categorized or its variables are defined do not match current research needs.

- The marketing environment has changed enough to make existing secondary data out of date.

- The accuracy of the secondary data is questionable, especially if the data collector, purpose for data collection, and method of data collection are unknown.

- The population sampled does not closely match the population currently under consideration. A *population* is the total group of individuals or organizations who are relevant to the research question and about whom a researcher wants to draw a conclusion. A *sample* is a subset of a population that a researcher studies to develop conclusions about the total population.

Companies use secondary research to help determine what, if any, primary research will be needed. Secondary research is also used to develop hypotheses to test. A *hypothesis* is an informed guess or assumption about a problem or set of circumstances that can be accepted or rejected based on empirical data. *Empirical data* is information, gathered through observation or experiment, that confirms or disproves a hypothesis.

Primary Research

When secondary data is not available or does not resolve an issue, companies turn to primary research to fill the information gaps. *Primary research* is original research that a company engages in or the company requests from an external vendor to answer the current research question. Primary research data can provide information specifically tailored to the research question, but it is very expensive to perform.

Before committing resources to primary marketing research, companies should be able to answer "yes" to the following questions:

- Is the value of the research worth its cost?

- Is the information and secondary research currently available from internal and external sources insufficient to guide development of new products and services, especially in highly specialized markets?

- Is the current budget for the research enough to do a technically adequate job?

- Is there enough time available to complete the project when needed?

- Is the company willing and able to act on the research findings, if action is indicated by the research results?
- Can the marketing problem or opportunity and project objectives be clearly and accurately defined?
- Are the research conditions likely to represent reality?
- Will the market and/or distribution channel respond to the product, feature, or service enhancement or change indicated by the research findings?
- Have findings from previous research changed enough to justify a new research study?

In the following sections, we discuss some of the highlights of the marketing research process.

Marketing Research Process

The marketing research process consists of a series of interrelated and overlapping steps or stages. For our discussion, we divide the marketing research process into six stages.

Stages 1 and 2: Determine Objectives and Identify/ Define the Research Question

Before conducting research, marketing managers must decide the goals, purposes, and objectives of the research. For example, are they trying to find an answer to a question about a specific product, or is their purpose to get information about changes in their customer base, or do they have some other objective? Clearly and concisely stating the research purpose and objectives helps a company determine and allocate the most appropriate resources—human, financial, and others—to the research project, saving time and money as a result. Also, after managers determine the objectives and purpose of the research, they must create a specific research question that defines the situation, opportunity, or problem to be studied.

Stage 3: Determine Research Purpose

Generally, primary marketing research projects serve three major purposes: (1) to explore a situation, opportunity, or problem, (2) to describe a situation or better understand a situation or trend, or (3) to determine the cause or causes of a particular situation, occurrence, or behavior. To help researchers achieve these three purposes they use one or more of three types of research: exploratory research, descriptive research, and causal research.

Exploratory Research. *Exploratory research* is intended to provide insight into the general nature of a problem and identify the variables that need to be considered in addressing the problem. Researchers use exploratory research when they recognize symptoms, or indicators, of a problem or opportunity (such as declining sales, increasing expenses, or a possible new distribution option), but they do not know the extent of the situation, its root causes, or exactly what additional information they need to help them solve the problem or take advantage of an opportunity.

> **Example:** Sales of a competitor's term-life insurance product similar to the company's own term-life product have increased dramatically in the last six months. Exploratory research can help the company identify possible reasons for the increase in the competitor's sales.

Exploratory research can provide direction for additional research, but is not intended to be used to develop conclusions. Companies often use exploratory research as a first step toward other, more specific research activities.

Descriptive Research. *Descriptive research* provides a picture of or describes the nature of a market or marketing problem or opportunity. It can be used to show that two or more marketing variables, such as purchase patterns and demographic characteristics, are related, but it does not attempt to establish a cause-effect relationship between the variables.

> **Example:** An insurance company conducts a study to determine the demographic characteristics of customers for different types of financial services products.

Causal Research. *Causal research* is used to identify factors or variables that affect the values of other variables. In a marketing situation, causal research seeks to determine cause-effect relationships between marketing variables.

> **Example:** A company conducts research to determine if a change in the timing or amount of advertising for a particular product affects product sales.

The variables used in causal research are classified as either independent or dependent. An *independent variable* is a marketing variable that influences the behavior of another variable and is not itself affected by changes in other variables. Independent variables used in insurance research include price, sales approach, distribution method, producer experience, commission rates, promotions, regulations, customer income, competitive activity, and product features. A *dependent variable* is a marketing variable that reacts to or is influenced by another variable (for example, changes in independent variables). Common dependent variables in insurance research include sales volume, policy persistency, producer retention, producer income, and repeat business.

The goal of causal research is to isolate the independent variables and determine the degree to which changes in the independent variables cause changes in the dependent variable or variables. A causal relationship is established if the researcher can prove that (1) a change in the independent variable preceded a change in a dependent variable and (2) no other factors or variables could have accounted for that change in the dependent variable.

When discovered, causal relationships provide insights into the behavior of individual and organizational buyers. However, it is difficult to prove causal relationships because unrelated and unobserved factors, rather than the independent variable identified in the study, may be the real cause of changes in the dependent variable. For example, research might indicate that an increase in the number of insurance producers in a particular market created an increase in the sales volume of a particular insurance product when, in fact, removal of a competitor's product from the market actually caused the increased sales. Causal research design must identify all possible independent variables that could impact the dependent variable and either control or eliminate them.

Stage 4: Research Design and Data Collection

In the research design stage, marketing researchers determine the sample population and the data collection methods they will use to collect and analyze information.

In most cases, observing or questioning every person in the total population is not practical. So, researchers typically collect data from a representative sample of the total population. Researchers use statistical inference to link the research sample to the total population. *Statistical inference* is a statistical process that allows researchers to draw conclusions and to make estimates and predictions about a population based on a sample taken from the population.

To draw accurate conclusions about a population, the research sample must adequately represent the population being studied in terms of demographics and other characteristics. For example, if the population being studied is college-educated female executives, then including women without a college education or who are not executives would not accurately represent the targeted population. In drawing the sample, researchers must ensure that

- The sample members accurately represent the population on all dimensions being studied in the research
- Each member of the sample had an equal and random chance of being included in the sample

If the sample does not represent the population, bias or errors can be introduced into the research design and the information derived from the sample will not accurately reflect whatever factors are being measured.

To collect primary data, marketing researchers can use qualitative research methods, quantitative methods, or both.

Qualitative Research

Qualitative research, most often used for exploratory research, examines what people think and how they feel about the subject being studied and the words they use to express their thoughts and feelings. Because qualitative research deals with data that is often difficult to quantify or summarize in numerical form, this research is sometimes called *soft research*. Researchers often perform qualitative research before doing quantitative research to ensure that questions reflect the language and thought processes of the target population.

For insurance and financial services marketing research, the data collection methods for qualitative research include focus groups, in-depth interviews, observational research, and ethnographic research.

Focus Groups. Focus groups are a frequently used qualitative research method. A *focus group* is an informal session during which a small group of people, usually no more than 8 to 10 individuals, are led through a guided discussion in which they are asked to discuss their opinions or feelings about a given topic, product, or service. An objective, professional moderator leads the group by asking questions and encouraging responses. Two-way mirrors and videoconferencing technology allow marketers to observe the sessions in progress, without disrupting the flow of the discussion.

For research related to insurance and financial services, either producers or end-user customers may be participants. Focus groups seeking end-user customers as participants have traditionally selected participants based on demographic data and history of product use. Today, researchers are adding psychographic information into the mix when they screen for focus group participants.

In-Depth Interviews. Researchers conduct in-depth interviews with individuals who are difficult to bring together in a single location at a single time, such as top insurance producers, business owners, or senior executives of large corporations. An *in-depth interview*, also known as a *one-on-one interview*, is qualitative research in which the researcher interviews individual study participants to collect information about their attitudes, experiences, or expertise. For in-depth interviews, the interview questions are loosely structured and may consist only of a checklist of topics relevant to the research topic. During the interview, the interviewer encourages the participant to speak freely and provide as much information as possible on the research topic. Although the in-depth interview provides valuable information, it is a very expensive data collection method.

Observational Research. Another type of qualitative research is *observational research,* a method that involves the study of the activities and behaviors of research participants with or without their knowledge, in natural or artificial settings, and through the use of human observers or mechanical devices.

A common observational tool that insurers use to perform observational research is mystery shoppers. A *mystery shopper* is a researcher disguised as a customer who (1) investigates what happens during an actual interaction between a customer and a salesperson or customer service representative and (2) records his or her observations on a standardized response form. The form focuses on the specific responses the company wants to investigate. For example, does the customer service representative greet the customer in a friendly manner or ask if the customer is interested in other products? Is the customer service representative courteous, knowledgeable, and effective?

Ethnographic Research. An emerging but not yet widely used qualitative method is ethnographic research. *Ethnography* is a process by which a researcher observes how people act in their natural environments. *Ethnographic research* combines ethnography with observational research to deliver insights into a person's or group's attitudes, beliefs, motivations, and values that may affect their decisions or actions. Observation of customers in purchasing or decision-making situations has revealed that they do not always act in the way they say they would act in that particular situation. Using ethnographic research a researcher can observe how a person naturally reacts to some change in the environment, especially decision-making situations involving a product or service.

Some companies that perform focus group research are borrowing from ethnographic research to try to make the focus group environment more comfortable or like the environment in which the focus group topic would be discussed in real life.

> **Example:** An insurance company may request that a focus group interview room be set up like a living room or a children's play room to facilitate a more open, natural discussion of the topic being researched. A few companies go one step further and actually study people and their habits and interactions in their own environments or in a simulated natural environment to gain insights into their needs and desires for products or services, such as a soap manufacturer observing how someone washes her hands with the soap. For insurance and financial services, a company may observe the behavior of customers who research insurance products online by tracking their online research or buying activities.

Quantitative Research

Quantitative research, sometimes called *hard research*, is designed to generate concrete information about population characteristics and behaviors that can be analyzed, summarized in the form of numbers, and projected to a population with a known level of error. Typically, both descriptive and causal research rely on quantitative research methods. Surveys are the quantitative data-collection method most commonly used in primary research for insurance and financial services products. Figure 4.2 summarizes the distinctions between qualitative and quantitative research and provides examples of potential applications for insurance companies.

Surveys

A *survey* is a primary research data-collection method that gathers data about a person's attitudes, knowledge, buying behavior, and preferences toward a particular topic, product, or service directly from the population being studied. A company or external vendor may conduct surveys by mail, telephone, or on the Web. The instrument used to collect survey information is the *questionnaire*, which is a set of specific questions that are asked of individual study participants. The questions included in a questionnaire can be either structured or unstructured. A *structured question* is a question that offers fixed alternatives. The following is an example of a structured question

> 1. Which of the following medical care benefits do you value most highly? (Please check only your top five choices and then rank those five benefits using the numbers "1" through "5", with "1" being the benefit you value most and "5" being the benefit you value least.)
>
> __ Hospital benefits   __ Major medical benefits
>
> __ Surgical benefits   __ Dental benefits
>
> __ Maternity benefits   __ Home health care benefits
>
> __ Vision care benefits   __ Hospice care benefits
>
> __ Prescription drug benefits   __ Survivor health benefits

An ***unstructured question*** is usually open-ended and provides no answer choices. The following is an example of an unstructured question:

1. Which medical expense benefits do you value most highly?
_____

Figure 4.2. Primary Differences Between Qualitative and Quantitative Research

Area of Distinction	Qualitative Research	Quantitative Research
Type of research project	Exploratory	Descriptive or causal
Main purpose served	Develops an initial understanding of a research question in order to provide guidance for any further research; adds insight	Suggests a course of action
Frequently used data-collection methods	Focus groups, in-depth interviews, observational and ethnographic research	Surveys
Findings	Provide insights; may not be generalizable	Generalizable to population as a whole (if sample is properly defined and sufficiently large)
Applications	**Qualitative Research**	**Quantitative Research**
Product planning and promotion	Develops insights into the kinds of benefits and features that customers look for in a new interest-sensitive life insurance product	Determines which of the most preferred benefits are sought by the largest percentage of target market respondents
Advertising	Gathers ideas on how best to present in a television commercial the idea that an insurance company had broadened its product offerings to include a wide range of financial services	Determines which of two magazine advertisements was more effective in generating leads for prospecting
Personal selling	Identifies how customers view the role of a producer in selling a product or providing a service	Helps identify which sales practices are likely to have the greatest effect in producing sales
Consumer attitudes	Explores the problems or apprehensions that customers face and the vocabulary they use when discussing their needs for life and health insurance	Determines which aspects of death and sickness are most difficult for customers to face and how best to approach them regarding these topics during an advertising or personal selling situation

Figure 4.3 shows an excerpt of one type of written survey about attitudes toward life insurance.

Figure 4.3. Example of a Questionnaire Survey of Attitudes Toward Life Insurance

Please place an "X" in the box beside each statement that most closely describes your feelings about that statement.

	Strongly Agree	Agree	Neither Agree Nor Disagree	Disagree	Strongly Disagree
1. I understand my life insurance needs.	❏	❏	❏	❏	❏
2. My family is adequately protected in the event of my death.	❏	❏	❏	❏	❏
3. Affordable life insurance is easy to find.	❏	❏	❏	❏	❏
4. I pay all my bills on time.	❏	❏	❏	❏	❏
5. I would purchase life insurance if I could afford it.	❏	❏	❏	❏	❏

About You:
Place an "X" to the left of the item that best describes you.

Age: ___ 18–25 ___26–34 ___35–43 ___ 44–52 ___53–61 ___ 62 and over

Gender: ___ Male ___ Female

Annual Income: ___ Under $20,000 ___$20,000–$49,999

___$50,000–$75,000 ___Over $75,000 ___Over $100,000

___Over $151,000

Number of members in household: ___1 ___2 ___3 ___4 or more

Marital status: ___Never Married ___ Married ___ Widowed ___Divorced

---

Stage 5: Process, Analyze, and Evaluate Data

After research data has been collected, it must be processed, analyzed, and evaluated to produce usable information. For example, the researcher must code unstructured questions into common response categories before quantitative analysis can be performed. Because coding is a time-consuming process, research designers carefully weigh the benefits versus the potential additional time and cost of including unstructured questions in their research. Also, researchers must check quantitative data for incomplete, missing, or multiple answers before they can analyze and evaluate the information.

In this stage of the marketing research process, researchers who are conducting exploratory research typically share preliminary findings with the research sponsor. Based on the preliminary results, the sponsor or researcher may decide to go back to the research design stage to ensure that the methodology used to obtain the findings did not negatively affect the research purpose or objectives.

Stage 6: Report Research Results

Marketing managers report information gained from a completed marketing research study in both oral and written form. The written reports usually include an executive summary. The executive summary provides an overview of the research project, including any study limitations, as well as the purpose and objectives, design, and conclusions of the research.

Using External Vendors for Research

Although companies with large, sophisticated marketing research departments may be able to conduct some marketing research projects internally, almost all companies depend to some degree on research services provided by outside suppliers. Small companies will most likely rely on a full-service research vendor to perform all aspects of a research project, including defining the research questions and the research design, choosing the best research approaches (qualitative or quantitative), designing the data collection devices, conducting the data collection and analysis, evaluating the research results, and reporting those results to the sponsoring company. Whether a company has the resources to perform the research in-house or it contracts with a full-service vendor for the project, typically the cost of research projects are quite high—ranging from about $10,000 for qualitative research to many times that amount for a large quantitative research project, depending on the scope of the project and the type of data collection method used.

Large insurance and financial services companies contract with external vendors for such tasks as conducting telephone interviews, recruiting focus group participants, and providing focus group facilities, as well as mailing, collecting, and analyzing data. The vendor also presents the data obtained from the research study in a form that allows the company to compare the research results by various dimensions. This presentation by each dimension measured in the study allows a company to investigate different variables that may be affecting a marketing research question.

In situations where research goals, or budgets, are more limited, a company may access professional research assistance through omnibus surveys and syndicated research. ***Omnibus surveys*** are surveys conducted regularly by a research company with a given target population. They may be targeted to a particular market segment, or focused on the research interests of a particular industry. The surveys are repeated periodically so that *longitudinal changes*, which refer to changes over a period of time, are evident. The company performing the research compiles the results and sells them.

Unlike the omnibus survey, the results of a syndicated study are revealed only to the participants. *Syndicated research* is research performed to obtain information about major topics that, because of their breadth, would be beyond the ability for a single company to fund, yet involve an area of study in which many companies are interested. For example, an industry association or external research vendor might initiate a proposal to target companies and offer to conduct the research if, for example, 10 or more companies agree to participate at a cost of $40,000 each. Participating companies have considerable input into the creation of the survey device used and may even be given the opportunity to have additional questions added, for a fee. The results related to those specific questions will be reported only to the companies that paid the extra fee.

Firms that provide a full range of marketing research services to client companies on a customized, special-project basis are known as *custom research firms*. These firms generally handle all aspects of the project design, data collection, and data analysis and may also develop final reports of research findings.

Firms that offer limited-services marketing research often specialize in one area of research—for example, providing centers for telephone surveys, conducting focus group research or Internet surveys, providing focus group facilities, or processing the information obtained from surveys and analyzing results from research—and are called *limited-services research firms*. For example, in the insurance industry, it is common for external vendors to perform focus group research related to producer and client groups to assess their responses to product, service, or feature changes.

Limitations of Marketing Research

Marketing research helps companies determine the most effective and efficient combination of marketing mix variables. However, before undertaking a research project, insurance and financial services companies must consider the pitfalls associated with marketing research. For example, attitudinal and survey research are more reliable in identifying customer perceptions, attitudes, and motivations than they are in predicting behavior. *Attitudinal research* is research designed to collect information about a person's or a group's attitudes. An *attitude* is a learned predisposition to respond to an idea, object, or class or group of objects in a consistent manner. Because people may not accurately recall their behavior in given situations, observational research may be a better source for accurately studying behavior. Although new research techniques, such as ethnographic research and tracking Web users' actions, are providing more insights into customer behavior, many customers are not knowledgeable about insurance and financial services, and customers sometimes do not do what they say they will do. Companies are more likely to find accurate information about buyer behavior through data mining because such information describes how people have behaved, rather than how they believe they will behave.

In addition, marketing research is generally more difficult to conduct for service products than for tangible products. Study participants can easily compare a company's tangible product to a competitor's offering, but they cannot compare services unless they have experienced them. Customers also generally find it difficult to consider a service product without considering the provider of that product. Companies must consider these difficulties to ensure that marketing research yields the most reliable, relevant, and timely information possible.

Ultimately, marketing research is only useful if the data collected through research studies allows managers to make decisions and take action. Collecting meaningful data through appropriate methods can improve the chances that those decisions and actions will be effective.

Key Terms

marketing information system
internal database
business intelligence (BI)
marketing model
expert system
legacy system
data warehouse
data mining
marketing intelligence
information dashboard
enterprise dashboard
marketing research
secondary research
population
sample
hypothesis
empirical data
primary research
exploratory research
descriptive research
causal research

independent variable
dependent variable
statistical inference
qualitative research
focus group
in-depth interview
observational research
mystery shopper
ethnography
ethnographic research
quantitative research
survey
questionnaire
structured question
unstructured question
omnibus survey
syndicated research
custom research firm
limited-services research firm
attitudinal research
attitude

Endnotes

1.   Joseph K. H. Tan, *Health Management Information Systems: Theories, Methods, and Applications* (Vancouver, BC: Aspen Publishers, 1995), 50.

2.   Philip Kotler and Gary Armstrong, *Principles of Marketing*, 9th ed. (Upper Saddle River, NJ: Prentice-Hall, 2001), 133.

3.   The Dashboard Spy, "Dashboards By Example: Volume 1," http://www.enterprise-dashboard.com (11 June 2009).

Customer Behavior and Customer Relationship Marketing

Objectives:

After studying this chapter, you should be able to

- ■ Identify different types of customers and describe the roles customers play in the exchange process

- ■ Describe four types of purchase decisions and three types of problem-solving strategies customers use to make a purchase decision and identify the circumstances in which a customer is likely to use each strategy

- ■ Identify the internal and external factors that influence purchase decisions and explain how each factor may influence a purchase decision

- ■ Describe Maslow's hierarchy of needs concept and explain how physiological and psychological needs motivate purchase decisions

- ■ Identify and describe the three stages of the perception process

- ■ Describe the five stages of the purchase decision process: problem recognition, information search, evaluation of alternatives, purchase decision, and postpurchase evaluation

- ■ Describe customer relationship marketing

- ■ Distinguish between low-value customers and high-value customers and explain how companies calculate lifetime customer value to target valuable customers

- ■ Describe five elements common to most customer relationship marketing strategies

- ■ Identify the benefits to a company of customer retention and describe ways in which companies measure and improve persistency

- ■ Describe the benefits companies receive from customer loyalty

Outline

Today, most companies use a customer-centric approach to marketing. A company that adopts a *customer-centric marketing approach* bases all its plans and actions on customer wants and needs and how to fill those wants and needs.[1] Companies that choose to focus on the customer must:

- Consider how their operations and business processes affect a customer's purchasing experience

- Understand how a customer behaves in purchase situations

All the mental, emotional, and physical activities that people go through to choose, purchase, and use products and services make up *customer behavior*, or *buyer behavior*. Before a company can understand how its customers behave, it must understand who its customers are. Broadly speaking, a customer is a person or organization that purchases a company's products.[2] Customers can be either individual consumers or organizational buyers. A *consumer* is an individual who purchases products and services for personal or household use. Individuals who purchase products and services for business purposes are *organizational buyers*.

Using a customer-centric approach, companies (1) develop goals and strategies based on perceived customer needs, (2) use technology to support their customer-focused approaches, and (3) identify key measures that will help them gauge their success in identifying and meeting customer needs from the point of view of both the company and the customer. Ideally, companies would like to be able to predict customer behavior so they can better develop their marketing mixes to appeal to the customers they have targeted. Also, a company that can, to some extent, predict customer behavior can provide better service to its customers and improve customer loyalty.

Unfortunately, no one can predict with 100 percent accuracy what products a customer will purchase. But, most companies still spend a lot of time and effort to determine who their customers are, the types of purchase decisions they face, and how and why they buy products and services. Such customer behavior information can help companies focus their marketing efforts on markets that offer the most promise for growth and profit.

Types of Purchase Decisions

Consumer and organizational customers make different types of purchase decisions for different situations. Some decisions are routine and made from habit, such as which brand of toothpaste or coffee to buy. Other decisions are more complex, such as—which car, computer system, or financial product to buy.

In general, consumers and organizational buyers make one of four types of purchase decisions, as described in the following table: [3]

Type of Purchase Decision:	Description:	Example:
Major New Purchase	A very important purchase decision on which the customer spends more time than any other type of buying decision and has little or no past experience making such a purchase	A customer purchases cash value life insurance
Major Rebuy	An important purchase decision but customer has some past experience with the product or service and feels more certain about the decision	A customer renews a term life insurance policy
Minor New Purchase	The product or service is new to the customer but not as important as a major new purchase or major rebuy; requires little time or thought to make decision	A customer decides to try a new brand of soft drink
Minor Rebuy	Requires the least amount of time and thought to make the decision because the product or service has been purchased repeatedly	A customer repeatedly purchases the same meal at a favorite restaurant

Problem-Solving Strategies

Customers use problem-solving strategies to make purchase decisions. In customer behavior, a ***problem-solving strategy*** is a means of getting information to use in making a purchase decision.[4] Generally, customers use one of three problem-solving strategies when they make a purchase decision: (1) a routine response strategy, (2) a limited problem-solving strategy, or (3) an extensive problem-solving strategy.

Routine Response Strategy

Description & Characteristics	Applications/Uses	Examples
A *routine response strategy* involves decisions that are automatic or require little or no thought. **Characteristics:** ■ Consumer generally does not consider any new information ■ Consumer relies on past experience or buying habits ■ It is the least complex problem-solving strategy	Most often used for *Minor Rebuy* purchases Also used to purchase *low-involvement products*, which are low-price, frequently purchased products that require little information for a customer to decide to purchase	Used by consumers for low-involvement purchases such as soft drinks, detergent, bubble gum, beer, and gasoline Used by organizational buyers for recurring low-involvement purchases, such as office supplies, when brand or product used in the past performed well Used by organizational buyers for more expensive products or services, such as legal advice or business or group insurance coverage for small organizations. In such situations, a company often develops a list of acceptable suppliers and only buys from those suppliers.

To keep their customers happy and coming back, insurers that sell to buyers who use a routine responses strategy should meet the buyer's expectations, keep up a good relationship with the buyer, and be alert and respond to changes in the buyer's needs. Competitors face a difficult task—they must convince the buyer to consider their products as acceptable alternatives, at a time when the least complex action—rebuying—is so easy to do.

Limited Problem-Solving Strategy

Description & Characteristics	Application/Uses	Examples
Customers use a *limited problem-solving strategy* when they acquire and use information to evaluate product alternatives before making a purchase decision. **Characteristics:** ■ Requires more time and thought (often at purchase time) than routine response ■ Used to evaluate alternatives before purchasing a product, especially if not satisfied with current product or supplier	Used when customer has a lot of experience with the product or service category, but needs to evaluate specific products within that category Most often used for *Minor New Purchases* or can be used for *Major Rebuy* purchases if customer has a lot of previous experience with the product or service May be used for a *Minor New Purchase* of a low-involvement product or a *Major Rebuy* of a high-involvement product. *High-involvement products* are items bought infrequently, that are in an unfamiliar product category, and require a large cash outlay.	Used by consumers for the purchase of most clothing and small appliances Used by organizational buyers in the purchase of group life and health insurance because: ■ Each renewal is a distinct rebuy situation because policies are written on a one-year or monthly renewable term ■ Coverage is frequently transferred from one insurer to another because of intense competition ■ Producers frequently sell group insurance plans and present proposals from several insurers to clients for comparison

Insurers that supply products or services to buyers who use a limited problem-solving strategy should immediately address customer product or service concerns because a dissatisfied customer is more likely to shop for alternatives. A competitor who can identify the sources of customer dissatisfaction and develop a plan to eliminate them may be able to win the customer's business.

Extensive Problem-Solving Strategy

Description & Characteristics	Application/Uses	Examples
Using an *extensive problem-solving strategy*, customers gather a lot of information before making a purchase	Used to purchase high-involvement products Most often used for *Major New Purchases* and *Major Rebuys*	Used by consumers for the purchase of cars, houses, computers, furniture, major appliances, and

and may use several criteria to evaluate alternative brand choices. **Characteristics:** -It is the most complex problem-solving strategy - Used when purchaser needs products that can perform a new job, solve a problem, or meet a new need		financial products, including many life and health insurance products Used by organizational buyers to purchase group and business insurance products—producers often can tailor proposals and marketing strategies to fit buyer's needs (and even influence plan design and specifications if involved early enough in the process)

The problem-solving strategy that a customer adopts depends on the type of product to be purchased and the customer's experience with the product. Usually, first-time customers with no product knowledge or experience use limited problem-solving or extensive problem-solving methods to make initial decisions. For later purchases of a specific type of product, customers may repeat their initial purchase strategy or switch to another problem-solving strategy.

> **Example:** Hélène Parent plans to purchase a term life insurance policy. She is using extensive problem-solving to gather information and compare products and rates because the product is unfamiliar to her. If she buys the policy and is satisfied with her purchase, she may use a routine response strategy when it is time to renew the policy. Or, she could use limited problem solving to evaluate current product alternatives before deciding to renew the policy. However, if later she becomes dissatisfied with the term policy's provisions or the insurer's customer service and decides to explore other options, she may use an extensive problem-solving strategy again.

Customers may also use extensive problem-solving strategies when they want to buy a combination of fairly simple and familiar products to meet a complex need. For example, suppose a customer who is familiar with mutual funds and life insurance products is nearing retirement age. This customer needs a combination of investment and insurance products to meet estate planning needs. Although the products the customer eventually chooses to buy may be familiar to the customer, the right type and combination will depend on the customer's estate planning goals. Figure 5.1 illustrates how the problem-solving strategies most commonly relate to the four types of purchase decisions.

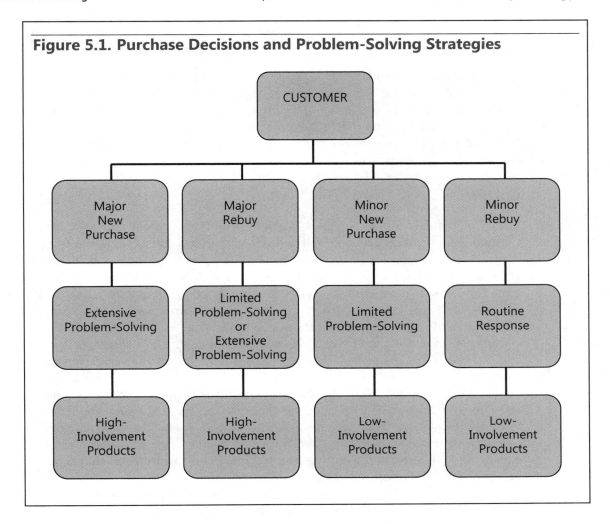

Figure 5.1. Purchase Decisions and Problem-Solving Strategies

Factors that Influence Customer Behavior

Both external and internal factors may influence a customer's decision to purchase a product or service. Figure 5.2 summarizes these key factors that influence purchase decisions.

Figure 5.2. Major Factors That Influence Purchase Decisions

EXTERNAL FACTORS	INTERNAL FACTORS
■ Culture	■ Motivation
■ Reference Groups	■ Perception
■ Customer Relationships	■ Learning
■ Demographics	■ Attitudes

External Factors

External factors are factors that exist apart from an individual or organization that influence purchase decisions and can be measured and observed. These external influences help companies develop a clear picture of who buys what, where, when, and how. As shown in Figure 5.2, some external factors that greatly influence purchase decisions include culture, reference groups, customer relationships, and demographics.

Culture

Culture determines which forms of behavior are acceptable and unacceptable. Cultural values and concepts are forms of learned behavior that are passed from one generation to another. For consumers, culture influences where people live, what they eat, what they wear, how they spend and save money, and what features they value in products and services. For organizations, corporate culture defines the attitudes, values, perceptions, beliefs, and experiences of company employees and shapes how organizations respond to change.

Subcultures and social classes are two subsets of culture. A *subculture* is an ethnic, regional, religious, racial, age, or social group that exhibits characteristic patterns of behavior strong enough to set its members apart from others within the overall culture or society. Although all consumers belong to more than one subculture, individuals often relate more closely to one particular subculture than to others. Generally, subculture has a greater impact on purchases of tangible products, such as food, clothing, and household goods; however, certain racial, ethnic, and age subcultures are increasingly important to insurance companies because of their increased size and purchasing power.

A *social class* is a social division in which individuals or groups fit into a distinct societal hierarchy based on characteristics—such as wealth, education, and occupation. No one is quite sure of the degree to which social class influences consumer behavior. However, studies show that the markets for certain types of products—for example, real estate, clothing, food, air travel, home furnishings, automobiles, leisure, and financial investments—do vary from one social class to another.

For organizations, companies can be divided into subgroups based on the industry in which they operate or the types of products they produce. For example, a group of manufacturing companies will need different types of products or services than a group of technology companies. Companies that recognize and meet the differing needs of subgroups gain a valuable marketing advantage.

Reference Groups

A *reference group* is any group that an individual identifies with so closely that the person adopts many of the beliefs, values, and norms held by the group as a whole. Reference groups can be either primary or secondary:

■ A *primary group* is a reference group that is small enough to let group members interact with each other face to face. Primary groups are usually informal, but they exert a major impact on customer behavior.

- **Examples of Consumer Primary Reference Groups**: Family, close friends, coworkers, neighbors

- **Examples of Organizational Primary Reference Groups**: Buying centers, executive committees, standards groups, product evaluation committees

- A *secondary group* is a reference group made up of members who share common interests or skills. Secondary groups tend to be more formal than primary groups and generally allow less continuous and direct interaction among members. They also have less influence on customer behavior.

  - **Examples of Consumer Secondary Reference Groups**: The company for which a person works; professional and trade associations; political, social, and religious groups

  - **Examples of Organizational Secondary Reference Groups**: Companies in the same industry, professional and trade associations that serve the company's industry

Within each reference group, an individual fills a certain role and has a certain status. A *role* is a socially expected behavior pattern that an individual in a particular position is supposed to follow. *Status* is the socially defined position an individual holds in relation to other members of the reference group. Status is reflected in the types of products consumers and organizations buy. For example, certain makes of cars, brands of clothing, types of food or beverages, and other products that are conspicuously consumed are considered to be symbols of a consumer's status.

Generally, consumers and organizational buyers make purchases that are in line with what they perceive to be the values and norms of their reference groups. For example, if members of a customer's reference groups (or groups to which a customer aspires) do not use certain products or brands of products, do not shop at certain stores, or do not purchase products through certain distribution channels, the customer will likely avoid those products, stores, and distributors as well. Advertisers who suggest that certain groups of people buy a particular product or brand and are quite satisfied with it are using reference group influence to try to affect a purchase decision.

The Impact of Family as a Primary Reference Group. Generally, consumers purchase life insurance and financial services products in family situations, and, often, family members make those decisions jointly. A family can consist of two or more related people or be single people or groups of unrelated people living together.

Family influences develop early in life. Through *consumer socialization*—the process by which young people develop the skills, knowledge, and attitudes they need to function as consumers in the marketplace—children learn important consumer concepts and behavior norms such as

- The behaviors the family considers to be "in good taste"—for example, purchasing life insurance to protect one's family

- The companies that the family considers acceptable to purchase products from—for example, purchasing insurance products from the same company or agent that the family has always used or buying from companies that market "American made" products or companies that support the local community

- The brands or products that are acceptable—for example, one family may view annuities as the best way to fund retirement and another family may view investments in stocks or bonds via an individual retirement account (IRA) as the best choice

Consumer behavior patterns that a family passes on to its children can profoundly affect the children's product and brand preferences.

The Impact of Buying Centers as Primary Reference Groups. Relationships among members of an organization's buying center exert the strongest influence on organizational buyers. A *buying center* is an informal, cross-departmental decision unit whose main goal is to acquire, spread, and process information for purchase decisions. Generally, a buying center consists of several people who have specific responsibilities in the purchase decision. However, as an organization moves from one stage in its purchase decision process to another, the role and importance of each member in a buying center tends to change. Also, each member may perform more than one role. Companies that market insurance products to organizational buyers must understand the characteristics of both the organization and the members of the buying center.

The larger an organization grows, the more complex its purchase process becomes and the more influence the buying center has on purchase decisions. For example, small organizations make insurance purchases using a process similar to the one that consumers use—one sales representative sells a product to one buyer who initiates the purchase process, generates specifications for the product, selects suppliers, and makes the final decision. The buyer may informally consult with family members, friends, or coworkers, but these people have little or no formal authority or responsibility for the purchase decision.

Buying center members at medium or large organizations may be responsible and accountable for various aspects of the purchase. Individuals within and outside the organization, including insurance company group sales representatives, insurance producers, consultants, and third-party administrators, provide additional input.

Customer Relationships

Customer relationships influence both the consumer and organizational insurance purchase decisions. A *customer relationship* is a mutual bond that forms as a result of all interactions between a customer and a business organization.[5] Typically, an insurer must work to positively maintain three essential relationships: (1) producer/customer relationships, (2) insurer/producer relationships, and (3) insurer/customer relationships.

Producer/Customer Relationships. Insurance companies rely to a large degree on producers to generate leads, make initial contact with prospective customers, gather information about customers' needs, and present the company's proposal for satisfying those needs. Producers also manage negotiations between the customer and the issuing company, close the sale, complete necessary paperwork, oversee employee enrollment in group plans, and provide follow-up service. In each of these activities, the producer serves as a vital communication link between the customer and the company.

Customers often view producers as trusted sources of advice and guidance. For example, a customer faced with two equally attractive purchase choices may ask the producer for advice. If the customer considers the producer to be competent, professional, experienced, knowledgeable, concerned, and honest, the producer recommendation may determine which option the customer chooses. The opposite is also true. If a producer is seen as unprofessional or incompetent, the company's products may not even receive consideration.

In organizational purchases, as in consumer purchases, individuals make buying decisions. If an organizational customer is faced with two equally attractive options, the relationship between the organizational customer and producer can be critical. Here again, recommendations made by professional, knowledgeable producers may carry more weight than recommendations from a less effective producer.

Insurer/Producer Relationships. Because producers exert so much influence in the buying process, insurers spend a significant amount of time and money to attract, retain, and build long-term relationships with their producers. Insurers also use marketing campaigns to convince producers to recommend the insurers' own products. These marketing campaigns involve providing information about the company, its products, and its service capabilities and offering a competitive compensation package to producers. Insurers also provide producer support that includes

■ Efficient and timely communication	■ Effective marketing materials
■ Continuing education	■ Sales convention opportunities
	■ Prizes, subject to regulatory conditions and restraints

Insurers that offer competitive marketing mixes, have high ratings, and maintain a reputation for ethical conduct and financial soundness have an advantage in the producer recruiting process. In addition, companies known for their ability to support and maintain mutually beneficial relationships with producers are more likely to retain producers.

Insurer/Customer Relationships. Although historically the producer/customer relationship has been the most important relationship, insurance companies have recognized the value of developing a direct relationship with the customer. Insurer/customer relationships can be built on interactions with the customer including e-mail messages or phone calls from the customer to the company, complaints made by the customer to the company, customer visits to a branch office or the company's Web site, or many other forms of contact. Each interaction between the company and the customer helps to mold the insurer/customer relationship.

Insurers generally build customer relationships on clear and effective communication and on the services they provide. To satisfy customer needs, companies must listen to their customers, acknowledge their concerns, and provide solutions for their needs. Companies can accomplish these tasks by clearly communicating the information customers need so that customers can buy the most appropriate and effective products that meet their particular insurance needs.

Customers expect to receive service from the company or the company's producer, or both, after their purchase of a product. In fact, many companies use their service capabilities to differentiate themselves from the competition. Insurance companies that meet or surpass customer expectations can establish a relationship of trust and effective communication between themselves and their customers, whether individuals or organizations. Insurers must also provide ongoing administrative support and continuous quality customer service to individual policyowners and organizational policyholders. An insurer that provides poor service to a policyowner or buying organization may cause serious financial problems for that organization and its employees. For this reason, group policyholders evaluate not only the cost of insurance, but also the level and quality of services an insurer and its representatives provide. Insurers who claim to offer quality service must actually deliver that service and be careful not to supplant the producer/customer relationship. Because group contracts must be resold to organizational buyers each year, an insurer that does not meet a group insurance customer's service expectations may lose the contract to another provider. Most companies provide specialized training for employees who interact with customers on a regular basis.

Ultimately, the length of time a customer's business stays in force and the profits that business generates reflect the quality and value of the information and service a company provides to its customers. If a company meets customer expectations, the customer is likely to remain with the company. If a company doesn't meet customer expectations, the customer may select a competitor's product, costing the company an entire stream of future purchases. Over a lifetime of potential purchases, such a loss can be significant. In the fast food industry, a single lost customer can represent hundreds of lost dollars. In the insurance industry, a lost customer can represent thousands of dollars.

Demographics

The demographic characteristics that describe various customer groups also affect customer behavior. These effects are direct, observable, and measurable. Organizational demographics include number of employees, number and types of products, organizational structure, size and concentration of markets, and market share.

Demographic characteristics such as age, marital status, and family structure significantly affect insurance purchase decisions. According to a recent study by LIMRA, statistics indicate that the majority of people who purchase insurance policies are married, young adults in the prime working years of life[6] who have children. These families are more likely to buy insurance policies than are singles or older people with grown children. As people age, their concerns shift from providing financial support for their families to providing financial resources for retirement.

Internal Factors

Internal factors, also known as *psychological factors,* are influences on purchase decisions that operate within the minds of consumers or organizational buyers and affect their behavior. The effects of internal influences on customer behavior cannot be measured or observed; they can only be inferred. The primary internal factors that affect customer behavior are motivation, perception, learning, and attitudes.

Motivation

In the study of customer behavior, researchers examine what factors motivate a particular customer to buy a specific product or service. In terms of customer behavior, **motivation** is the internal force that drives people to exhibit certain behavior or take certain actions to reach a purchase decision. A central component of motivation is need. A **need** is an unsatisfactory condition within a customer that leads to a specific action to improve the customer's condition.[7] Generally, a person's unfulfilled needs create tension that motivates the person to purchase particular products or services. Personal needs, including the need to purchase "the right quality in the right quantity at the right price for delivery at the right time from the right service,"[8] motivate both consumers and organizational buyers. However, if what constitutes "right" is not clear to an organizational buyer, that individual's personal motives come into play in the purchase decision process.

Needs that motivate purchase decisions can be physiological or psychological. A **physiological need** is physically or biologically determined. The need for food, shelter, sex, and clothing are examples of consumers' physiological needs. Adequate financial, human, and operational resources are examples of an organization's physiological needs. A **psychological need** arises from a customer's social environment. Psychological needs include the need for belonging, fulfillment, affiliation, and achievement. For insurance purposes, need is a critical factor for customers who are considering the purchase of an insurance policy. A report by LIMRA stated that 66 percent of customers who recently purchased life insurance made the purchase for income replacement for a dependent or dependents.[9] In other words, the need to provide financial security for one's survivors led to a decision to purchase life insurance.

One of the most widely accepted descriptions of needs is the **hierarchy of needs** concept developed by noted psychologist Abraham Maslow. Maslow classified needs into five hierarchical categories, as shown in Figure 5.3. These categories, starting at the bottom of the hierarchy, include

1. Physiological needs, such as hunger, thirst, sex, and shelter
2. Security or safety needs, such as protection, order, stability, and freedom from harm
3. Social needs, such as love, affection, belonging, and friendship
4. Esteem needs, such as success, self-respect, recognition, prestige, and achievement

5. Self-actualization needs, such as the desire to obtain self-fulfillment, maintain personal value systems, or maximize whatever potential an individual possesses[10]

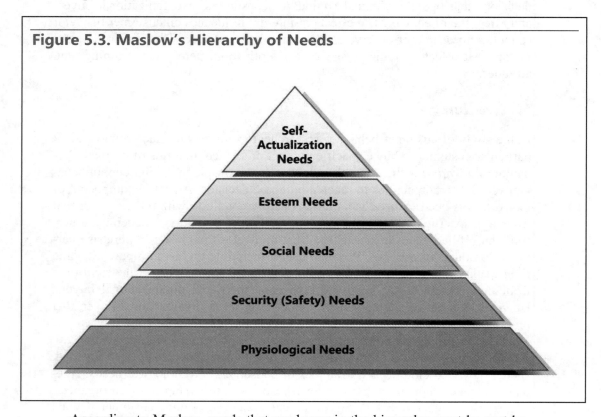

Figure 5.3. Maslow's Hierarchy of Needs

According to Maslow, needs that are lower in the hierarchy must be met before higher-order needs will emerge. Most customers seem to follow this general hierarchy in purchasing goods and services. Today, many consumers have little problem meeting their physiological needs. As a result, higher-order needs have become the major forces affecting consumer behavior. For this reason, companies market products that are designed to meet our most basic needs as a way of improving the quality of life rather than as a means of satisfying hunger or providing shelter. For example, foods are not described as being "life-sustaining" or "stomach-filling," but as "quick and easy to prepare," "fat-free," or "new and improved." In using such approaches, companies have changed consumer perceptions of basic products so that these products appeal to needs that are higher in the hierarchy. Figure 5.4 illustrates the ways that consumers meet the needs identified by Maslow's hierarchy.

Wants also motivate customers. A *want* is a desire to have more than is absolutely necessary to improve a condition that is unsatisfying.[11] Wants vary from person to person and, because they are learned, can be changed depending on what products are available. Marketers try to determine the underlying needs that customers are trying to satisfy so they can create wants for the company's products. For example, insurers try to translate the need for financial security into a desire for their insurance products.

Figure 5.4. Methods of Satisfying Customer Needs

1. Physiological Needs
Buying and using food, clothing, and shelter

2. Security or Safety Needs
Purchasing life, health, and disability insurance
Investing for retirement
Working for a company that offers 401(k), pension, or profit-sharing plans

3. Social Needs
Buying products that are well–regarded by friends and coworkers
Buying a home in a particular neighborhood
Joining a social, political, or religious group

4. Esteem Needs
Graduating from a prestigious university
Purchasing a mutual fund portfolio to show financial responsibility and foresight

5. Self-Actualization Needs
Maximizing intellectual and physical performance
Engaging in self-improvement or continuing-education activities
Establishing an estate plan that includes philanthropic goals such as a charitable remainder trust
Writing a book

Perception

Perception is the process by which people select, organize, and interpret information to give it meaning. No two people will see a product, advertisement, salesperson, company, or anything else in exactly the same way because perceptions vary from person to person. Companies must seek to understand what creates perceptions and how they can be influenced. The perception process can be divided into three stages: information selection, information organization, and information interpretation.

Information Selection. The perception process begins when an object or event in the environment stimulates one or more of the five senses: sight, hearing, smell, taste, or touch. Although people are exposed to many different stimuli at the same time, they will respond to only a few.

A typical customer is exposed to thousands of marketing communications each week, including radio, television, magazine, and Internet advertisements, newspaper articles, supermarket coupons, store displays, and special product promotions. A customer will actively seek out some of these information sources and avoid others, depending on the person's current needs. For example, a customer interested in purchasing term life insurance may suddenly notice direct mail inserts that offer a free quote or typical rates by age and gender and not even notice marketing materials about home repair services or travel insurance. A person's decision to acknowledge certain pieces of information and ignore the rest is known as *selective perception*.

Selective perception is a challenge for companies that must find ways to gain a customer's attention so the customer will read an advertisement or a sales promotion offer or agree to meet with a salesperson. To gain attention, companies try to make their marketing communications stand out from the messages of other companies by running advertisements repeatedly, offering special sales promotion incentives to customers, or using eye-catching pictures or bold statements that attract curiosity or interest.

Information Organization. Customers tend to organize bits of information into groups or categories with similar meaning. This grouping of information helps a person remember the information. For example, most people can remember their telephone number because they divide the number into several groups of digits instead of trying to remember one long series of numbers.

Effective marketers want customers to group their product with similar products that the customer perceives as positive, worthwhile, affordable, or some other desirable attribute. For example, The Travelers Companies Inc., created a television advertisement that shows a man holding a gigantic, red umbrella over himself and, as he walks along, he meets people who he helps by using the umbrella to solve problems or protect them. In this instance, one of the company's intentions may be that potential customers will see this advertisement and group The Travelers Companies Inc., with other companies and products they associate with protection, assistance, and safety.

Information Interpretation. The way people organize information directly affects how they interpret information. Over time, most people develop *preconceptions*, or preconceived ideas about what is reality based on their own needs, values, attitudes, beliefs, learning, and previous experiences. They tend to interpret new information in ways that fit in with, rather than differ from, their preconceptions. As a result, a person typically blocks out or modifies information that conflicts with his or her preconceptions until it supports those perceptions. This process is called *selective distortion*. All customers exhibit selective distortion. *Selective retention* is the process by which customers remember and internalize information that supports their preconceptions. The processes of selective perception, selective distortion, and selective retention serve as perceptual filters that reduce the amount of information customers absorb as they proceed through the perception process.

Companies care about these perceptual filters because they affect the way customers absorb and use information about companies, products, and services and, consequently, determine which products they buy.

> **Example:** An insurance producer discusses with a customer the need for money to pay for the college education of the customer's child. During this discussion the producer recommends several options, including a variable annuity. Because the customer has heard coworkers and family members talk favorably about annuities, the customer has formed an opinion that annuities are highly profitable (a preconception). Based on this opinion, the customer may focus on the proposed annuity product and dismiss other options for saving money for college such as mutual funds (selective perception). As the producer describes the advantages and risks of the proposed annuity, the customer may block out information about the losses that could occur under certain market conditions (selective distortion) and remember only the details related to the potential earnings the annuity could provide (selective retention). The producer must be aware of how the customer processes information and continue to talk with him until he fully understands the product.

Learning

The information customers receive from friends, relatives, books, and other sources and the things they learn through their own experiences largely determine the wants and needs that will motivate them to purchase products and the perceptions they form about those products. Companies influence what customers learn through product information and advertising and also by satisfying the customer. If customers are satisfied with a particular product and the service associated with the product, their purchase behavior is reinforced, and they tend to buy the same product again. Depending on the type of product involved, satisfied customers usually continue to buy a product until it no longer satisfies their needs. Customers who consistently and habitually purchase the same product over an extended period are said to exhibit brand loyalty. *Brand loyalty* is a customer's favorable attitude toward a specific brand usually leading to a consistent and habitual purchase of the same product over an extended period.

Almost all consumers are brand loyal to at least a few different types of products. Typically, organizational buyers are more brand loyal to distributors than to various manufacturers or service vendors. Brand loyalty depends primarily on the level of interaction a customer has with a particular company. For example, consumers tend to interact regularly with insurers that provide automobile and homeowner's insurance and often are brand loyal to those companies, especially if the companies offer quality service. Brand loyalty is often lower for life insurance companies because the relationship with a life insurer does not offer the insurer as many opportunities to interact with its customers or for companies to reinforce their brand. In fact, the only interaction after the initial purchase of the policy may be at the time a claim is submitted after the insured's death. The degree of brand loyalty for health insurance companies varies depending on whether the product is group health insurance or individual health insurance. Little brand loyalty exists in group health because benefits and costs are controlled by employers rather than employees. Alternatively, brand loyalty may be higher for health insurance companies that deal with individual health insurance policies.

Attitudes

Many experts believe that attitudes are the most significant factor in determining customer behavior. Attitudes are more strongly held than perceptions, and they generally remain stable over time. For example, customers who have good experiences with a product tend to develop positive attitudes toward the product and the company. Customers who have bad experiences often develop negative attitudes toward those products and companies. Once formed, attitudes are extremely difficult to change.

Customers' attitudes toward a company and its products can have a profound effect on the success of the company's marketing strategies. Customers who have negative attitudes about a company or its products usually do not buy the company's products or services. Insurance companies should identify areas in which they face unfavorable attitudes and then work either to change the factors causing negative attitudes or change the customer's perceptions of those factors from negative to positive. Such changes may be challenging for insurance companies because anxiety and other psychological factors can inhibit many customers from purchasing insurance because they don't want to think about the dangers associated with insurance—death or disability. Even when customers recognize and accept their need for insurance, they may delay purchasing products that will provide long-term economic security in favor of products that satisfy more immediate needs, such as a new car or better clothing.

Purchase Decision Process

The purchase decision process that most customers follow consists of five major stages: problem recognition, information search, evaluation of alternatives, purchase decision, and postpurchase evaluation. Figure 5.5 shows a simplified model of the purchase decision process. The specific activities included in each stage of the process vary depending on the type of product being purchased and the experience of the customer.

Generally, a consumer making a major new purchase will pass through all five stages and spend quite a bit of time in each stage, while a consumer making a minor rebuy purchase may skip some or all of these steps. Many customers progress through some of the stages and then decide not to make a purchase. Other customers may be dissatisfied after evaluating their purchase and may return the product and repeat the entire process.

Figure 5.5. Purchase Decision Process

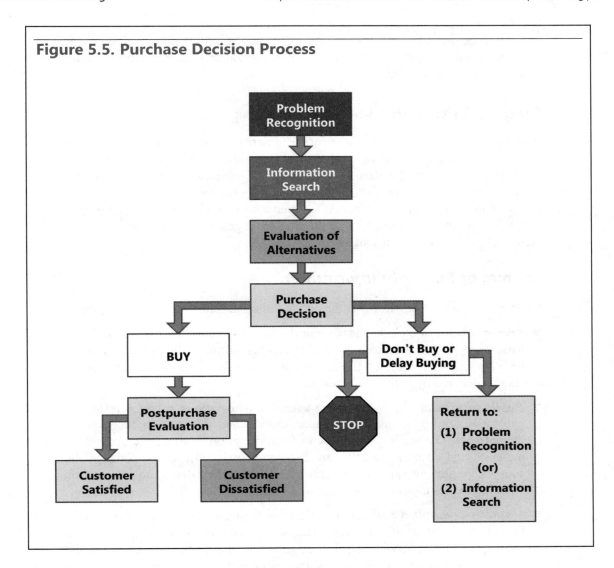

Stage 1: Problem Recognition

Problem recognition occurs when an individual or organization realizes that a difference exists between a desired state and the actual state. An unmet need or a potential opportunity can create this difference. Insurance and financial services companies sometimes use advertising that seeks to tell the customers they have a particular unrecognized need. For example, a single person with few assets and no dependents may not recognize a need for life insurance because he associates life insurance with providing income to help a family in the event a primary finacial provider dies. However, such a person may have a need for insurance to alleviate the financial burden of funeral and other final expenses from family members who may survive him.

As described previously, a variety of internal and external factors influence a customer's ability to recognize problems or opportunities that can be resolved by purchasing products or services. For example, consumers whose culture causes them to believe that it is their responsibility to provide financial security for their families may quickly recognize a need for insurance when a child is born into the family. Also, the attitudes of friends and family and events in a person's life can influence problem recognition. For organizations, problem recognition might occur when declining profits require that an organization seek ways to reduce the costs of employee benefits.

Stage 2: Information Search

Information searches provide a way for customers to evaluate various options for products or services that might solve their problems or meet their needs. How much information and how much time a customer spends gathering information varies depending on the customer, type of purchase decision and decision-making behavior involved, and the customer's experience with making that type of purchase. For organizations, the amount of time spent gathering information also depends on each organization's size and buying habits.

Sources of Purchase Information

Information sources generally can be divided into the following three categories:

- **Personal sources** include friends, family, and associates. Customers generally trust the opinions of these individuals. Personal sources often refer customers to other external sources. Consumers rely heavily on personal information sources when they purchase insurance.

- **Public sources** include government agencies, associations, product-testing organizations, magazine and newspaper articles, and information available on the Internet. Generally, customers view information from public sources as unbiased and accurate and, therefore, more valuable. However, some public sources, particularly magazines and newspapers, may distribute information on behalf of selling companies.

- **Marketer-dominated sources** include advertising, salespeople, sales promotion literature, point-of-purchase displays, Internet Web sites, and other outlets used by companies trying to sell their products or services to consumers and organizational buyers. Customers gather information about financial products primarily from marketer-dominated information sources.

Stage 3: Evaluation of Alternatives

At the end of their information search, customers usually have compiled a set of alternatives, called an *evoked set* of alternatives, from which to make a purchase decision. To evaluate their evoked set of alternatives, customers generally set some evaluative criteria and then rank those choices from best to worst. *Evaluative criteria* are those features, characteristics, or specifications that a customer considers when making a choice. Depending on the purchase decision, these criteria might include price, service, delivery, company or brand name, prestige, convenience of purchase, or any other characteristic that the customer desires or does not desire in the product. For example, a customer's evaluative criteria for a group of similar life insurance policies offered in the same face amount might include the premium amount, illustrated rate of return, cost comparison indexes, illustrated dividends (if any), reputation and financial strength of the issuing company, services offered by the issuing company, and the customer's attitude toward the producer. Whether a particular alternative is selected for purchase depends on how well it matches the customer's ranked criteria.

Recent studies have shown that the buying rate of prospects who receive recommendations from producers about what type and how much insurance to buy is higher than the buying rate of prospects who do not receive such recommendations. In large group insurance purchases, negotiations between the buyer and group representatives from each of the competing insurers also play a part in the evaluation process.

Stage 4: Purchase Decision

In this stage, the customer decides whether to buy a product. If more than one alternative meets the customer's evaluative criteria, or if none of the alternatives in the customer's evoked set is satisfactory, the customer can make no purchase, or delay the purchase and repeat one or more of the earlier stages in the process. For example, a customer who identifies one or more satisfactory alternatives may need more information to evaluate the acceptable products; a customer who does not identify any satisfactory alternatives may need to return to problem recognition and repeat the entire decision process.

A customer's decision also can be affected by factors other than their evaluative criteria, such as the product's availability, unexpectedly receiving adverse information about the product, the offer of a competitor, or the need to buy some other product. For example, a consumer who applies for life insurance might be assigned a substandard rating or be declined by the insurance company and would need to reconsider alternatives.

Stage 5: Postpurchase Evaluation

After customers make a purchase, they usually evaluate their choices by how well the product performs. If the performance meets expectations, the customer generally is satisfied. If the performance does not meet expectations, the customer is likely to be dissatisfied. Dissatisfied customers may

- Return products
- Complain about the product to other individuals, the supplier or distributor, and/or regulatory and other governmental authorities
- Take legal action

Customers who are generally dissatisfied with their purchase are often classified in one of two psychological states: buyer remorse or cognitive dissonance. *Buyer remorse* is a state that prompts customers to question whether they should have purchased the product at all, or whether they should have purchased an alternative brand or another product than the one they actually bought.

Cognitive dissonance is a state in which the customer determines that his purchase behavior is inconsistent with his self-image. Because he cannot change the behavior that created the dissonance, the customer redefines his perception of the behavior in terms that support rather than challenge his self-image.

Buyer remorse and cognitive dissonance are especially common when the purchase decision involves a large financial outlay, such as for insurance products. Insurance companies can lessen the effects of buyer remorse and cognitive dissonance through the following practices:

- Providing policyowners with a welcome kit that contains claim forms, instructions for obtaining service, and other materials

- Making follow-up calls to new customers and conducting annual reviews with established customers to assure them that products and services are performing as expected

- Providing toll-free numbers for customer service

- Encouraging producers to reinforce the need for the purchase during the policy delivery process and make follow-up calls to customers

- Informing policyowners of specific uses, in addition to insurance protection, for insurance products—for example, using the cash value of whole life insurance policies to pay college tuition, or assigning a cash value policy to obtain a loan

- Providing superior customer service and regular, ongoing, and meaningful communications

Customer Relationship Marketing

Customer behavior helps insurance marketers understand the types of purchase decisions customers make and how they make and evaluate those decisions. This information about behavior, while very valuable, will not help a company determine which products it should offer to which target market or what new products should be developed to address new needs, or how to grab a potential customer's attention in an advertisement or direct mail piece. In addition to gaining insights into how and why customers act the way they do, marketers must ask customers what they want in terms of products and services and carefully listen to and address their responses. Companies can then use this information to develop a relationship with the customer that ideally meets most of the customers' needs related to an insurance purchase and service after the sale.

Customer relationship marketing is the enterprise-wide business strategy that allows a company to create, maintain, and enhance relationships with customers and other stakeholders by creating customer value and satisfaction.[12] Customer relationship marketing involves listening to customers; learning what they value in products, services, distribution channels, and communication methods; and then using that information to match products and services to an individual customer's needs, provide customer satisfaction, and build customer loyalty.

The goal of customer relationship marketing is to increase customer satisfaction and build customer loyalty by learning from *every* interaction with a customer, using this information to anticipate the customer's needs, and offering customized products and services. Companies practice customer relationship marketing because the cost of acquiring a new customer is much higher than the cost of keeping a current customer. This cost difference is especially evident in the insurance industry, where finding prospects, educating them, earning their trust, and underwriting their policies is so expensive that many types of policies do not become profitable for at least seven years. Profitable companies target the right customers by identifying those who are valuable to the company and calculating the value of those customers over a lifetime of purchases.

Targeting the Right Customers

Customers have unique and different needs, and not all of those needs can be satisfied with the same products and marketing strategies. Companies with a customer relationship marketing focus need to make sure they target the right customers for their particular products and services.

Companies also recognize that some customers offer greater economic value to the company than other customers. Customers who only occasionally purchase a company's products or have needs that cannot be satisfied by a company's products, prices, or services are often referred to as *low-value customers*. The gap between what the customer wants and what the company can provide is described as the *customer sacrifice*. If this gap is large, the cost of attempting to satisfy the customer is probably high, and the company might be better off targeting other customer groups. When a company selects one target group over another, the decision becomes an *opportunity cost*—the benefit that is forfeited or given up in choosing one alternative over another.

High-value customers offer great economic value to a company. The high value of these customers is based on several characteristics, including their tendency to

- Desire the company's products

- Purchase multiple products

- Buy the more expensive and higher-margin products offered by the company

- Trust the company and its employees

- Be loyal to the company's products

- Recommend the company or its products to others

In most industries, including the insurance industry, high-value customers represent a much smaller percentage of the market than do low-value customers. Value, however, is not a matter of the number of customers a company has but of customer profitability. The idea that value depends on customer quality rather than customer quantity is illustrated in *Pareto's Principle*, also called the *80-20 Principle*, which states that 80 percent of a company's profits are generated by 20 percent of its customers. In the insurance industry, high-value customers often account for an even greater percentage of profits.

Companies that practice customer relationship marketing generally invest time and resources in customers in direct proportion to the estimated return they will provide to the company,[13] As a result, companies tend to invest more resources in high-value customers than low-value customers. High-value customers whose needs a company can satisfy effectively and efficiently and whose business is dependable and profitable often are referred to as *core customers*. Companies use many resources to identify valuable core customers.

Identifying Valuable Core Customers

Technological advances help companies identify their most valuable customers. Sophisticated database technology lets companies gather and maintain a wealth of information about current and potential customers. Each time a customer interacts with a company, the details of that interaction are entered into a database, giving the company an electronic record of important information, including the

- Date and purpose of the contact (product purchase, request for information, complaint, account updates, sales follow-ups)

- Company's response (mailing forms, making contract changes, transferring funds)

- Customer service efforts

- New business possibilities

- Customer satisfaction level

The more interactions a company has with a customer, the more information it can add to its customer database.

Using data mining, companies can develop comprehensive profiles of valuable customers based on common demographic, psychographic, and behavioristic characteristics, observed patterns in their purchase behavior, and product preferences. Figure 5.6 shows the types of information typically included in a comprehensive profile of a financial services customer.

By applying statistically-generated predictive techniques to the customer profiles created through data mining, companies attempt to predict future customer behavior. For example, companies can forecast the customers most likely to provide the greatest value over time, the products they are likely to purchase, and the prices, distribution systems, and promotion methods that are likely to produce the most positive results to attract these customers.

Using detailed customer information, companies can design marketing efforts that address current and future customer needs. For example, understanding customer expectations about the speed, accessibility, and quality of customer service can help a company determine the most effective service channel to use (for example, call center or online service center), the appropriate number and types of service personnel to employ, and the kind of training and information its service personnel should have.

Calculating Lifetime Customer Value

Using database systems, companies can now assign a monetary value to the profit potential a customer represents. *Lifetime customer value*, also known as *lifetime value*, is the economic benefit a company receives from its relationship with a customer calculated over time. Companies generally measure lifetime customer value by how much the profits a customer generates over time exceed the company's cost of acquiring, developing, serving, and retaining the customer.

Though specific calculations are beyond the scope of this text, lifetime customer value calculations typically include predictions of the types of products each customer will purchase, income likely to be generated by the customer, costs associated with marketing to and serving that customer in the future, and projected length of the relationship. The value assigned to a lifetime customer can be divided into the following three elements:

- *Historical value* is the value of all transactions to date between the company and the customer.

Figure 5.6. A Comprehensive Customer Profile

Purchases. All purchases from the company are recorded and stored. These records provide information about the number, type, and cost of each product the customer owns.

Non-sales interactions. Non-sales interactions, such as, for example, calls for product information and visits to the company's Web site, provide information about the types of services the company provides and the customer's satisfaction with those services.

Demographics. A customer's financial needs and the types and sizes of their purchases often are related to demographic characteristics. Tracking these demographics can help identify both current and future product development opportunities.

Psychographics. A customer's preferences for products, distribution channels, prices, and communication methods often are influenced by such factors as personality, social class, interests, and lifestyle. Knowing what those preferences are can help companies match marketing mixes to customer needs and preferences.

Risk Tolerance. The amount of financial risk a customer is willing and able to accept is often a determining factor in the types of products bought and the amount of service needed to maintain the desired level of comfort and satisfaction.

Household relationships. Financial services purchases often are decided jointly by multiple members of a household and based on household rather than individual needs. Tracking these relationships helps companies understand a customer's product needs and purchase behaviors.

Major life events. Major events in a customer's life, including births, marriage, divorce, death, college graduation, and retirement, often trigger new or revised financial needs, product preferences, and marketing opportunities.

Risk to the company. Each customer represents certain risks to companies marketing financial services products. For insurers, customer risk is associated with factors such as health, occupation, and lifestyle.

Purchase behavior. Identifying purchase behavior and predicting future behavior can help companies increase the effectiveness of their marketing campaigns and customer service strategies.

Satisfaction levels. Although satisfaction is difficult to determine at the individual customer level, it is an important predictor of future behavior. Satisfied customers typically remain customers; dissatisfied customers often defect and tell others about their dissatisfaction.

Profitability. Factors such as lifetime value or customer "wallet share" are important elements in designing marketing programs and allocating marketing resources.

- *Current value* is the present value of all expected transactions between the company and the customer, assuming the existing customer behavior pattern remains the same.

- *Potential value* is the value the company could realize if it can persuade the customer to increase future spending and/or reduce expenses by changing behavior patterns.[14]

Because customer relationship marketing focuses on managing the customer experience going forward, companies are more concerned about current and potential value than historical value. When customers have low current, but high potential, value, a company seeks to nurture and improve their profitability. A company may allocate new resources to unlock the potential of these customers or it may delay committing significant resources to these customers until the company determines their future contribution to profit. Customers who have current value but little potential value are unlikely to become more valuable to the company in the future. They are worth retaining, but the amount of future investment in these customers should be carefully weighed based on their low potential for future contributions to the company. Customers who represent current value and have significant potential value are a company's core business. Although they are relatively few in number, the profit they generate over the course of a lifetime of patronage can be substantial. Companies generally allocate significant resources to maintain and develop the profit potential of these valuable customers.

Developing Customer Relationship Marketing Strategies

Customer relationship marketing strategies typically emphasize retaining and developing current customers. *Customer retention* is the extent to which customers remain with a company. *Customer development* is the process a company undertakes to maximize customer value by expanding its products and services and more effectively satisfying customer needs. Whether a company adopts a retention or development strategy for its individual customer relationships depends in large part on the value of the customer and the relationship that customer has with the company.

Although customer retention and development strategies require unique approaches and different levels of resources, most customer relationship marketing strategies contain the following common elements: (1) self-service options, (2) cross-selling and up-selling, (3) mass customization, (4) tiered service, and (5) life event-oriented marketing.

Self-Service Options

In the traditional insurance customer/insurance company relationship, an insurance producer typically provides service to the customer. Technological advances, however, provide other methods for policyowners to develop relationships with a company. Today, insurers offer their customers a variety of self-service options, including toll-free telephone numbers, company Web sites, and e-mail.[15]

The Internet has become a primary self-service tool for customers of insurance companies. Web sites allow customers to gain helpful information whenever they want it. Customers appreciate this self-service option because it is available 24 hours a day, 7 days a week. Some of the reasons customers prefer to conduct self-service online include convenience, information availability, and time efficiencies.

The Internet also allows companies to improve relationships with customers by providing useful information about customer behavior. Companies can use Web site monitoring to study customer behavior and track how customers use a company Web site.

Cross-Selling and Up-Selling

The most successful companies do more than sell more or better products; they manage the customer's entire financial picture. Companies should know what products the customer has, what products the customer needs, and what other products would benefit the customer. A company that effectively manages its customers' needs is likely to build meaningful customer relationships. To improve customer relationships, companies often use cross-selling and up-selling strategies.

Cross-selling is the process of identifying an existing customer's needs for additional products while selling, or after selling, a primary product and then promoting products that complement that primary product to provide a more complete solution.

> **Example:** Assume that a customer contacts a producer about purchasing a fixed annuity. After talking with the customer, the producer realizes that the customer's need is for financial security after retirement. The producer provides the customer with information about annuity products as well as the benefits of a long-term care policy. The producer sells the customer the annuity contract and a long-term care policy.

Cross-selling benefits the company by increasing profitability and customer loyalty. The customer receives the benefits of the convenience of having one company manage multiple products and the peace of mind that comes from knowing that a legitimate need has been satisfied. Cross-selling also helps discourage customers from moving their business elsewhere. For example, a producer may discover a customer's need for life insurance while selling him an automobile policy. The more ties a customer has with a producer or a company, the more likely the customer is to remain with that producer or company.

Up-selling is a strategy similar to cross-selling except that it involves promoting a more powerful, more enhanced, or more profitable product than the one a customer originally considers purchasing.

> **Example 1:** A customer interested in purchasing a $100,000 life insurance policy might decide to purchase a $250,000 life insurance policy after a producer explains the difference in benefits and costs to the customer.
>
> **Example 2:** A producer offers a variable annuity with enhanced death benefits or enhanced living benefits to a customer inquiring about a traditional variable annuity.

Mass Customization

One of the most effective ways companies establish meaningful relationships with customers is by customizing or personalizing their products, services, and communications to the needs of individual customers. Customizing products and services allows financial services companies to sell products according to the customer's specific wants, needs, and preferences. This high-level personalizing of product offerings and service delivery on a large scale is sometimes referred to as *mass customization*.

The goal of mass customization is to understand customers and create a match between what individual customers in a market segment need and want with the products and services the company can provide. Mass customization presents a challenge for financial services companies because they must find a way to profitably customize financial products in mass markets. One approach that has shown promise is to provide customers with a menu of standardized options and allow them to build their own products. For example, insurance companies that sell variable annuities often offer customers a simple base product that offers standard benefits at a low fee plus an additional set of enhanced benefits that the customer can purchase at an additional cost.

Tiered Service

Customer relationship marketing encourages companies to treat customers differently based on the customer's current and potential value. *Tiered service* is a strategy under which the service level an individual customer receives reflects the customer's value to the company. Two ways in which companies offer tiered service are

- *Fee variance*, which involves offering a consistent level of service to each customer but varying the fees a customer pays for the service based on the customer's profitability to the company. In this situation, low-value customers pay more than high-value customers for the same level of service. A company's core customers may even receive some services at no cost. Regulatory restrictions in some industries may limit a company's ability to use this approach.

- *Service variance*, which involves varying the number and level of services a customer receives according to the customer's value to the company. Low-value customers generally receive basic services designed to meet basic needs. As a customer's value increases, the company increases the level of service for the customer. Core customers often receive additional services. By varying the levels of service, companies satisfy and retain their most valuable customers without sacrificing their lower-value, price-sensitive customers.

Some companies also provide tiered service by offering various combinations of fee and service variance for their more valuable customers.

Although tiered service often appeals to companies, offering some customers better services or better rates than other customers sometimes creates dissatisfaction among customers, especially those in the lowest tiers. Companies can minimize this potential customer dissatisfaction by ensuring that all customers receive an equal basic level of service and that all customers are treated with respect. Companies also can reduce customer frustration by ensuring that their products and services perform as advertised.

Life Event-Oriented Marketing

Life event-oriented marketing is the practice of timing sales and promotional efforts around significant events in customers' lives. This marketing strategy is designed to meet specific, definable customer needs as those needs arise. For example, insurers often target promotions around life events such as marriages, job promotions, changes in family size or composition, and retirement because these events may create a need for increased insurance protection. Other financial services companies also use life event-oriented marketing. For example, a bank that conducts a life event-oriented marketing campaign for automobile loans might target its efforts to a segment that consists of students who are graduating from college and about to enter the workforce.

Benefits of Customer Relationship Marketing

Customer relationship marketing benefits both the customer and the company. For the customer, the benefit of a relationship with a company is the value the customer receives in addition to the products or services the customer purchases. For the company, the benefit of a relationship with a customer is the ability to build customer satisfaction into customer retention, customer loyalty, and long-term profitability.

Value to the Customer

For a customer, the value of a relationship with a company is the difference between the total benefit the customer receives from the relationship and the customer's total costs. *Total customer benefit* includes all the services, personal attention, recognition, and image the customer gains from the relationship that develops through repeated interactions with a company. *Total customer cost* refers to the total of all the time, energy, and emotion a customer invests in a relationship with a company. These benefits and costs are in addition to the benefits and costs associated with the purchase of specific products and services.

Because it is based on perceptions, value does not mean the same thing to every customer. Differences in priorities or personalities can make a product or service seem trivial to one person and extremely important to another. The same is true for relationships. As a result, companies must concentrate their marketing efforts on the customers who value their products and services, and not attempt to satisfy customers who may never find value.

Value also is not constant. Customers frequently reassess the value of their relationship with a company just as they reassess the value of the products and services they own. If the value they perceive matches or exceeds their original expectations (and no other product or relationship offers greater value), customers usually remain satisfied. If the customer's reassessment produces a value that does not meet expectations, the customer may abandon the product and the company.

Value to the Company

Companies generally equate value with profitability and that value generally increases the longer a customer does business with the company. As a result, customer retention is an important factor in profitability, particularly for insurance companies. To retain a customer, a company must first satisfy the customer. To increase customer profitability, the company must build satisfaction into customer loyalty. By meeting and even exceeding its customers' expectations of value, a company creates customer satisfaction. *Customer satisfaction* can be defined as the state in which the customer perceives that a company's products and service meet or exceed expectations and satisfy needs. Satisfied customers generally are more likely to become loyal customers, who are typically profitable customers.

Customer Retention

Companies strive for more than just customer satisfaction; they also want to retain the customers who purchase their products. *Customer retention* is the ability to influence a customer to remain with a company. Most companies focus on customer retention more than customer satisfaction because even satisfied customers sometimes make changes in the products they choose to purchase.

> **Example:** Sarah Herzberg has been satisfied with the term life insurance policy she purchased two years ago from Bluebird Insurance Company. She recently learned, however, that Bestway Insurance Company offers a similar term life policy for a lower premium. Even though Ms. Herzberg has been a satisfied customer of Bluebird for two years, she decides to purchase the cheaper policy from Bestway.
>
> **Analysis:** If a competitor offers a satisfied customer a similar product or service for a better price, in a more convenient form, or in a better location than the customer's current company, the satisfied customer may begin purchasing from the competition.

The insurance industry has long believed in the value of customer retention, which it calls *persistency*. *Persistency* is the retention of business that occurs when an insurance policy remains in force as a result of the continued payment of the policy's renewal premiums. Insurance companies monitor persistency because retained customers generally are more profitable than new customers. Retained customers provide a steady stream of revenue and allow the insurer to spread customer acquisition costs over a longer period of time. In general, retained customers are also less price sensitive than new customers. Companies often need to offer discounts or other incentives to attract new customers, but these efforts usually are not necessary for existing customers. As a result, the company's profit margins on products they sell to existing customers tend to be higher than margins on products sold to new customers.

Measuring Customer Retention. Insurers measure the persistency of a block of insurance policies by determining the percentage of business that is in force at the beginning of a specified period and that remains in force at the end of the period, which is referred to as the ***persistency rate***. A block of policies is a group of policies issued to insured persons who are all the same age, same gender, and in the same risk classification. For example, an insurer may classify into one block all whole life policies issued to females age 30 whose health histories and medical tests are within certain limits.

To calculate persistency, most insurers first calculate the lapse rate. The ***lapse rate*** is the ratio of business in force that terminates for nonpayment of premium, whether by surrender or lapse, to the total business in force at the beginning of a specified period, as shown below:

$$\text{Lapse Rate} = \frac{\text{Business in force that terminates for nonpayment of premium}}{\text{Total business in force at the beginning of period}}$$

In the context of lapse rates, "business in force" refers to a specific block of policies, and a company can measure it by the number of policies, total premium, or total face amount of that block of polices. Lapse rates do not include terminations that result from the death of an insured or a policyowner, or a policy's expiration, term conversion, or reaching maturity. Persistency rates are calculated by subtracting the lapse rates from 100 percent.

> **Example:** Suppose 20 policies in a block of 100 policies lapse for nonpayment of premiums or are surrendered during a given period,
>
> The lapse rate for that period is: 20 percent (20 policies/100 policies = .20)
>
> The persistency rate is 80 percent (100 percent − 20 percent = 80 percent)

As a short-term measure of persistency, marketers usually focus on lapse rates based on the ***13-month lapse rate***, which is the proportion of new policies on which no part of any required second-year premium has been paid. Marketers use a 13-month lapse rate instead of a one-year rate to include lapses of annual premium policies; most lapses of such policies occur when the first renewal premium remains unpaid at the end of the policy's 13th month in force. The 13-month lapse rate for a particular product item is important for three reasons:

■ First-year policy lapses generally have a greater negative impact on a product's profitability than do lapses during later policy years, because it typically takes several years for a company to recover the costs of developing and marketing new products.

■ First-year lapse rates are usually an early and good indicator of whether quality business, which tends to persist, is being sold, because lapses are generally higher in the first year than in subsequent years.

■ First-year policy lapses alert the company to problems with the product or the distribution channel so that the company can rapidly take action to correct the problems.

Persistency rates differ from company to company depending on such factors as

- Customer characteristics, such as age, gender, income, and education
- Product characteristics such as type, quality, and pricing
- Type and quality of the distribution channels
- Quality of the customer service
- Efforts made to conserve existing policies
- Intensity of competition among companies

Evaluating persistency is both a science and an art. For example, a decline in persistency might indicate that the sales force is selling products that don't meet the needs of their customers. Perhaps the sales force is selling more expensive policies than the customers can truly afford. Management must be able to identify the underlying cause of declines or increases in persistency for such rates to have valuable meaning for a company.

Strategies to Improve Persistency. Companies can improve product persistency through customer relationship marketing efforts such as maintaining frequent contact with their customers through newsletters, e-mails, customer satisfaction surveys, and by acknowledging special dates such as birthdays and policy anniversaries. Companies can also help improve the persistency of their products through well-written business, product design, sales force incentives, conservation units, and internal replacements.

Well-Written Business. Well-written business helps ensure the persistency of an insurance policy. *Well-written business*, also called *quality business*, is a policy sale that has the following three characteristics:

- The company (or producer) identifies the specific needs of the customer, and the customer recognizes that those needs are important
- The insurance product actually meets those needs
- The customer is financially capable of paying the premiums

By selling well-written business, a company begins the process of conserving business at the time of sale and helps ensure that the business will remain in force.

Persistency also improves if customers understand and value the products they have purchased. Producers and companies need to completely explain policies before they are purchased, review them at the time of policy delivery, answer policyowner questions, and provide quality post-sale service.

Product Design. An insurance company can also improve persistency by keeping its products and product mix as attractive and competitive as possible. A well-designed product is less likely than a poorly designed product to be replaced. In addition, if a policyowner is contemplating replacement, then a competitive product mix increases the chance that a policyowner will replace existing business within the company, rather than with another company.

Insurers can reduce policy surrenders by building surrender charges into the product design of cash value life insurance policies and deferred annuities. A *surrender charge* is an expense charge imposed on some types of life insurance policies when the policyowner surrenders the policy. Surrender charges are generally highest in the policy's early years and usually decrease steadily until around the policy's 10th or 15th year, at which point the charges are usually eliminated.

Sales Force Incentives. Some companies offer producers incentives based on their persistency results. These incentives may take the form of a ***persistency bonus***—extra earnings for favorable persistency results—or a penalty for excessive lapses. Some companies charge back commissions for early lapses and count only commissions net of lapses when they establish production bonuses. Additionally, companies often vary the production bonus rate, improving it when persistency is above average and reducing it if persistency is below average. Companies may even cancel production bonuses when persistency is very poor.

Additional methods companies use to encourage the sales force to improve persistency include

- Establishing a persistency honor roll to focus attention on individual producers or field offices that consistently produce quality business

- Creating charts to show how favorable persistency can raise the earnings of producers or agency heads

- Providing field management with the records of producers whose business shows very favorable persistency and producers whose persistency experience has been unusually poor

- Basing field management compensation on the persistency of the business written by the producers they manage

- Showing on the commission statement of each producer the amount of commissions lost because of lapses

Conservation Units. Some companies have established special ***conservation units***, which are departments staffed with personnel specially trained to conserve—or keep in force—policies. If the conservation unit learns of an impending lapse, surrender, or replacement, a customer service specialist automatically contacts the policyowner to try to conserve the policy. In addition, the specialist usually notifies the policyowner's producer so that the producer can try to conserve the policy or determine if the policyowner has new insurance needs that require a new policy. Figure 5.7 lists ways conservation units attempt to preserve business.

Conservation units also help save the business of ***orphaned policyowners***—policyowners who do not currently have a relationship with a producer. The producer might have switched companies or left the business, leaving the policyowner without a personal contact. A policyowner who does not have a relationship with a producer is more likely to allow a policy to lapse than is a policyowner with a producer. To avoid such an occurrence, conservation units either assign these orphaned policyowners to new producers or handle the orphaned policyowners themselves.

Figure 5.7. Conservation Unit Strategies

Emphasize to the policyowner the advantages of keeping a policy in force. The most obvious advantage is continued life insurance protection, especially if the insured is now ineligible for a new policy or is eligible only at a higher premium rate.

Suggest alternative solutions to a policyowner in financial difficulty, such as
- Using the policy's cash value or accumulated dividends to pay the premiums.
- Converting the contract to a lower premium permanent plan—for example, converting a 20-payment life policy to a continuous premium whole life policy.
- Reducing the policy's face amount.
- Leaving the face amount of the policy unchanged but reducing the periodic premiums for the policy by changing the premium schedule.

Make late-remittance offers. A late-remittance offer informs the policyowner that the company will accept an overdue premium after the expiration of the grace period and will reinstate the policy without requiring the completion of a reinstatement application or the submission of evidence of insurability.

Offer to reinstate a lapsed policy. Reinstatement is the process of restoring a lapsed policy to premium-paying status in accordance with the conditions of the policy contract.

Internal Replacement. Occasionally, companies suggest that policyowners who are considering lapsing a policy opt instead for internal replacement. In simple terms, a *replacement* is the act of surrendering or lessening the value of one life insurance policy or annuity contract to buy another life insurance policy or annuity. The motivation for an internal replacement is that, if business is not replaced internally, it may be replaced by policies of other companies. Internal replacement allows the current company to retain premiums and cash values. This approach also provides the company with an opportunity to sell additional products to current policyowners.

One strategy U.S. companies frequently use to promote internal replacement is the *1035 exchange*, which is a tax-free replacement of an insurance policy for another insurance contract covering the same person that is performed in accordance with the conditions of Section 1035 of the Internal Revenue Code. A 1035 exchange is designed to help a policyowner avoid specified tax disadvantages that may occur with replacement. For example, when a policyowner surrenders a policy and receives its cash value in a lump sum, any portion of the sum that exceeds the premiums paid for the insurance policy is taxable as ordinary income.

Example: Assume that Clayton Powers surrenders a 15-year-old permanent life insurance policy after paying $14,000 in premiums. If the cash surrender value paid to Mr. Powers is $18,000, then Mr. Powers would realize a gain of $4,000 ($18,000 − $14,000 = $4,000), and the gain would be taxable. However, under the provisions of Section 1035, if Mr. Powers actually exchanges the existing life insurance policy for a new insurance contract for which his cost is $18,000, and does so in

> accordance with the section's requirements, Mr. Powers has no taxable gain, incurs no tax liability on the $4,000, and receives additional insurance coverage from the additional cost of the policy.

Companies must carefully consider the financial implications of any internal replacement programs they plan to adopt. A company must weigh its potential loss of business against the cost of developing and implementing a replacement program. For example, companies must consider how they will deal with the additional expenses associated with issuing and underwriting the replacement policy (in cases in which evidence of insurability is required) and paying first-year commissions on that policy. Companies must also comply with all applicable federal securities laws when implementing internal replacement programs.

Customer Loyalty

Companies that retain customers can begin to establish customer relationships and build customer loyalty. *Customer loyalty* is the commitment of a customer to remain a customer of, and to place repeat business with, a company, despite influences and marketing efforts of competing companies that may cause other customers to switch. Customer loyalty involves more than just retaining a customer and maintaining existing business. It involves generating new business and a greater share of customer purchases through repeat business over an extended period of time or gathering referrals that result in new business for the company.

Customer loyalty is good for business. Like retained customers, loyal customers contribute to profitability, generate new business through referrals, and provide feedback that companies can use to evaluate and improve their products and services. Though retained customers may only remain with the company until a better offer is presented to them, loyal customers provide continued repeat business, which usually leads to increased company profitability. Loyal customers also deliver additional benefits, such as opportunities to maximize customer value. Each product and service delivered to the customer and to the customer's satisfaction strengthens the relationship and makes the customer more open to additional purchases.

Customer loyalty also reduces customer defection. *Customer defection*, or *customer attrition*, is a customer's abandonment of a current company for a competing company. A customer who buys one or more products and then defects to another company may actually create losses. This is especially true in the financial services and insurance industry where policies and annuity contracts generally must stay in force for several years before the company can recover its costs of developing and marketing products. A high rate of attrition, particularly during a contract's early years, can lead to financial losses for the insurer.

A company rarely, if ever, achieves customer loyalty through any single aspect of its operations, such as price or product features. Instead, customer loyalty depends on how well a company understands and responds to its customers' needs and how effectively it delivers the value that customers expect—or better. Offering flexible products and pricing, multiple interaction channels, anytime-access to customer assistance, and many other features that empower customers to interact with the company on the customers' terms also help achieve loyalty.

Key Terms

customer-centric marketing
   approach
customer behavior
consumer
organizational buyer
problem-solving strategy
routine response strategy
low-involvement product
limited problem-solving strategy
high-involvement product
extensive problem-solving strategy
external factor
subculture
social class
reference group
primary group
secondary group
role
status
consumer socialization
buying center
customer relationship
internal factor
motivation
need
physiological need
psychological need
hierarchy of needs
want
perception
selective perception
preconceptions
selective distortion
selective retention
brand loyalty
problem recognition
personal source
public source
marketer-dominated source
evoked set

evaluative criteria
buyer remorse
cognitive dissonance
customer relationship marketing
low-value customer
customer sacrifice
opportunity cost
high-value customer
Pareto's Principle
core customer
lifetime customer value
historical value
current value
potential value
customer retention
customer development
cross-selling
up-selling
mass customization
tiered service
fee variance
service variance
life event-oriented marketing
total customer benefit
total customer cost
customer satisfaction
customer retention
persistency
persistency rate
lapse rate
13-month lapse rate
well-written business
surrender charge
persistency bonus
conservation unit
orphaned policyowner
replacement
1035 exchange
customer loyalty
customer defection

Endnotes

1. This paragraph's discussion of customer-centric orientation is adapted from Gene Stone, *Customer Relationship Management* [Atlanta: LOMA (Life Office Management Association, Inc.), ©2002]. Used with permission; all rights reserved.

2. Mark Adel, *Customer Contacts* [Atlanta: LOMA (Life Office Management Association, Inc.), ©2002], 25. Used with permission; all rights reserved.

3. KnowThis, "Customer Buying Behavior: Types of Consumer Purchase Decisions," *KnowThis.com*, http://www.knowthis.com/tutorials/principles-of-marketing/consumer-buying-behavior/types-of-purchase-decisions.htm (11 June 2009).

4. Jagdish N. Sheth, Banwari Mittal, and Bruce I. Newman, *Customer Behavior: Consumer Behavior and Beyond*, LOMA ed. (Fort Worth: Dryden Press, 2001), 374.

5. Stone, 6.

6. Karen Terry, *Finding New Customers: Who Is Buying Individual Life and Why?* (Windsor, CT: LIMRA International, 2005), 7, http://www.limra.com/members/abstracts/reports/4909.pdf (11 June 2009). Used with permission.

7. Sheth, Mittal and Newman, 41.

8. Frederick E. Webster, Jr., and Yoram Wind, "A General Model for Understanding Organizational Buying Behavior," *Marketing Management*, Winter/Spring 1996, 57.

9. Terry, 10.

10. Abraham H. Maslow, *Motivation and Personality*, 2nd ed. (New York: Harper & Row, 1970).

11. Mark Adel and Barbara Foxenberger Brown, *Foundations of Customer Service* [Atlanta: LOMA (Life Office Management Association, Inc.), ©2003], 104. Used with permission; all rights reserved.

12. Much of this chapter's discussion of customer relationship marketing is adapted from Patsy Leeuwenburg, *Financial Services Marketing* [Atlanta: LOMA (Life Office Management Association, Inc.), ©2005]. Used with permission; all rights reserved.

13. Nick Poulos, "Meeting Customer Needs," *CRM Magazine*, September 2000, http://www.destinationcrm.com/Articles/Older-Articles/Hot-Prospects/Meeting-Customer-Needs--46852.aspx (11 June 2009).

14. Valoris Abram Hawkes, T*he Heart of the Matter: The Challenge of Customer Lifetime Value,* white paper supplied by *CRM-Forum*, 2000, http://www.crm-forum.com/library/art/art-087/brandframe.html (30 November 2000).

15. Mary Art and Maria Dynia, *Policyowner Self-Service: Company Practices* (Windsor, CT: LIMRA International, 2005), 3, http://www.limra.com/members/abstracts/execsum/4815exec.pdf (11 June 2009). Used with permission.

Chapter 6

Basic Product Concepts

Objectives:

After studying this chapter, you should be able to

- ■ Identify the key differences between goods and services and describe the challenges companies face when marketing services

- ■ Distinguish among the four types of products in the consumer products classification system

- ■ Explain the concepts of product class, product line, product form, product item, and product mix

- ■ Describe the stages of the product life cycle and the marketing strategies associated with each

- ■ Identify ways in which companies use packaging, branding, product differentiation, and positioning as part of their overall marketing strategy

- ■ Describe six types of new products and distinguish among the three basic types of product development strategies

- ■ Describe the five steps in the product development process

Outline

The product is what the customer receives in the marketing exchange process. It is the most important variable in the marketing mix. Without products, a company has nothing to price, promote, or distribute to customers.

Some people think of a product in terms of its *generic characteristics*, which are the physical, technical, and functional characteristics that make a product what it is in its most basic or standard form. These characteristics might include technical specifications, blueprints, or a list of ingredients. The generic characteristics of a traditional whole life insurance policy might include the policy's life insurance benefits, cash value benefits, and standard policy provisions.

Customers, however, do not simply buy collections of generic characteristics; they seek ways to satisfy wants and needs. A customer who buys life insurance may want freedom from certain financial worries or an opportunity to express love, care, and responsibility for loved ones. From the customer's perspective, the product is everything he receives that helps provide a solution to a problem or the means to satisfy a want or need. The product the customer buys is the means to an end, not the end itself.

Classification of Products

Products may be divided in a variety of ways for marketing purposes. Some companies might divide their products into commercial products and consumer products with different pricing structures, advertising campaigns, and sales forces for each. The most basic classification system divides products into goods, services, and ideas, depending on the nature and characteristics of the product.

Goods, Services, and Ideas

A *good* is a product that has definite physical features. You can see, touch, and sometimes smell, hear, and taste goods. Automobiles, televisions, and candy bars are goods.

A *service* is an activity that one party performs for another. Services can be experienced only as they are performed, used, or consumed. Services have few, if any, physical aspects. Insurance and most other financial products are services.

An *idea* is a concept, philosophy, image, belief, or issue. Companies or organizations market ideas to convince people to alter their behavior or their perception in some way. For many years, the American Medical Association has marketed the idea that cigarette smoking is hazardous to people's health to convince them not to smoke. Companies also market ideas to provide a reason for customers to purchase or use their products. An insurance company may market the idea that retirement planning is important for younger people to help persuade them to purchase some of that insurer's products.

The Goods-Services Continuum

Although goods and services generally are distinguished by their degree of tangibility, few, if any, products are either purely goods or purely services. A car is primarily a tangible good. You can see it, touch it, and even smell it. However, when you buy a car, you also receive some valuable services. The manufacturer provides a warranty with the car and may also provide financing. The dealer might install some additional accessories you purchased, such as a high-end sound system. These elements of service you receive with the car can be quite valuable, even if you pay for them separately, and, in some cases, you might not even buy the car without them.

On the other hand, when you hire a plumber to fix a leak, the plumber primarily provides an intangible service. The plumber's labor and expertise enable him to fix the leak. However, to perform the repair work successfully, he must also provide some tangible materials such as washers and replacement piping. The goods you receive from the plumber are necessary for him to repair the leak, but you don't receive any benefit until he provides the actual service.

Other products, such as a meal you purchase in a restaurant, represent a more nearly equal combination of goods and services. The good is the food you eat. The service includes waiting on you, preparing and serving your food, cleaning up after the meal, providing background music or other entertainment, and all the other aspects that make up the total "product" of dining out.

Marketing professionals view most products as somewhere on a continuum between pure goods and pure services. This *goods-services continuum* recognizes that virtually all products contain varying degrees of both goods and services and categorizes a product accordingly. Figure 6.1 illustrates how some common products are classified along the goods-services continuum; as you can see, insurance and other financial products primarily are services.

Challenges in Marketing Services[1]

Companies that produce services face significant marketing challenges because of the following three characteristics that distinguish services from goods:

- Intangibility
- Perishability
- Heterogeneity

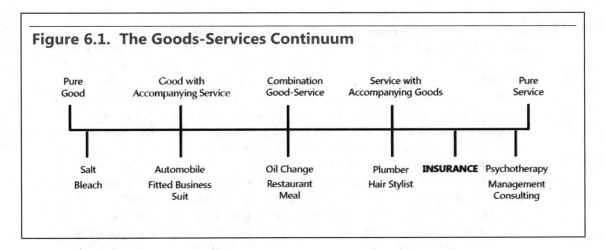

Figure 6.1. The Goods-Services Continuum

Intangibility refers to a lack of physical attributes that can be detected by the senses. The intangibility of services makes them more difficult to market than goods. Most goods can appeal to customers' physical senses; most services can't. Goods can be displayed in stores, pictured in advertisements, demonstrated to prospective customers, and tried in advance. Because people can experience goods through their senses, it's often easier to persuade customers to purchase goods than services.

Intangibility also makes it harder for customers to recognize the differences between one service and another. Customers can examine and try on different shirts to determine which one looks, feels, and fits best. It's not that easy to determine the differences between life insurance products. Insurance products are essentially promises to perform services in the future, such as paying benefits. The real test of an insurance product's quality occurs when customers require those services. Until customers actually need the benefits, which may be years in the future, they can't experience the services and decide which is best.

To overcome the problem of intangibility, insurers often try to give their products a sense of a tangible, physical presence. They develop advertising and promotional campaigns to associate their companies and products with familiar physical objects that suggest trust, protection, or reliability. Prudential gives its customers "a piece of the rock," Allstate customers are "in good hands," and, "like a good neighbor, State Farm is there" for its customers. In addition, insurance companies call their services "insurance products" rather than "insurance services" because *product* sounds much more tangible than *service*.

Some insurers also attempt to illustrate the benefits of insurance in a tangible form. Commercials for annuities and other retirement products feature senior citizens enjoying leisure activities. Advertisements for homeowners insurance contain photographs of a damaged house being rebuilt after a catastrophe. Insurers also might use testimonials from existing customers who describe how insurance benefits improved their lives by paying for needed medical treatment. These testimonials serve as both tangible demonstrations of an insurance product's benefit and recommendations of the insurer from satisfied customers.

Perishability. Although some goods such as milk or produce must be purchased and used soon after production, many other goods can be produced in large, economical quantities and then stored until needed for sale and consumption. An appliance store can keep refrigerators in its warehouse for months, if necessary, before selling them. Services, however, can't be stored. If a commercial airliner takes off with an unsold seat, that seat can't be sold later. A doctor who doesn't see any patients today can't transfer those unused hours to see more patients tomorrow. *Perishability* is the inability to stockpile performance of a service for use at a future date.

Perishability affects insurance in numerous ways. Producers often spend a lot of time with customers to sell certain products but have a limited number of hours each day in which to meet with those customers. Insurance companies can't prepare and store large quantities of completed address changes or other customer services until customers request them. Benefits can't be paid until a claim has been filed, investigated, and evaluated. Many policies can't be underwritten until the application has been completed.

Insurers can help manage the time that is available for personal selling by training their producers to identify, meet with, and sell products to customers in the most effective and efficient ways possible, and by providing producers with professionally prepared advertising and promotional materials. Companies can also reduce the amount of time sales representatives spend on prospecting by providing the names of qualified prospects to those representatives.

Companies also can manage perishability by maintaining an appropriate level of service capacity. Insurers lose money when they have idle service providers, but if they have too few service providers, customers may spend too much time on hold or experience other service delays. Insurance companies try to balance expected customer demand with the right level of underwriting, policyowner service, claim administration, and other customer support services.

Insurers increasingly use the Internet to maximize their sales and customer service capabilities. An insurer's or insurance producer's Web site is available 24 hours a day and can be accessed by large numbers of customers anywhere in the world at the same time. Customers also can view summaries of their accounts, make address changes, request policy loans or other withdrawals, request beneficiary changes, pay premiums, file claims, and obtain many other services online without the prior involvement of the insurer's customer service personnel.

A well-designed Web site is also a proven method of generating qualified prospects and can shorten the time required for personal selling considerably because customers can obtain detailed information about the company and its products before meeting with a producer. A growing number of insurers and producers also sell insurance products online. Although customers usually prefer contacting an insurance producer before purchasing complex products such as variable or universal life insurance, certain basic products such as term life, auto, and travel insurance are often sold directly over the Internet. Customers can obtain rate quotes and, in some cases, complete and sign the actual application form and pay the initial premium online.

Heterogeneity. Customers often base their primary attitudes toward goods on the performance of the product itself. Manufacturers of goods often can standardize their production processes so that one box of a particular detergent has the same contents and performs the same as the next. Customers often rely on this standardization and base their purchase decision on their previous experience with the same product.

However, customers frequently base their attitudes toward a service on the performance of the person providing the service. Each person who provides a particular service has a different personality, attitude, skill set, and degree of training. People don't always perform consistently, either; they may be ill, tired, or distracted. The quality of a service provided by an individual changes from day to day and from customer to customer. *Heterogeneity* is the variability or lack of consistency in the performance of a service.

To improve service quality and reduce inconsistency, companies need to (1) adopt consistent, job-related employee selection criteria; (2) standardize operating procedures whenever feasible; and (3) provide the best education, training, and motivation possible for their personnel. Insurers who sell their products through independent agents face an even greater challenge in overcoming heterogeneity than those who use career agents, because of the wider diversity in the education and training of independent agents. Another way of reducing heterogeneity is by taking full advantage of current technology, such as automated telephone systems or computerized policy issue systems.

In some ways, the lack of standardization of services, which results from their heterogeneity and their intangibility, can present a marketing advantage. As a result of mass-production processes, many goods are available only in a limited variety of sizes, colors, and feature packages. So, a customer may not be able to purchase the exact product she wants. However, services often can be customized to meet a customer's exact needs. A barber can cut as much or as little hair as the customer desires, or a babysitter can stay at the customer's home as long as needed.

An insurer's ability to sell a more customized product is a very desirable benefit for many customers. The exact range of products and features a particular insurer may provide is determined by the company's management, in accordance with legal requirements and actuarial principles. However, most insurers do offer a wide variety of optional features, benefits, and guarantees that can be added to many of their standard product offerings. A number of products, including universal and variable life insurance and variable annuities, are specifically designed to give the customer a considerable degree of control over basic product features—such as face and cash values, premium payments, and investment options—that the customer often can change repeatedly over the life of the product. A skilled, experienced insurance producer often is able to discuss with the customer the various features and options available and then prepare a product package that meets the customer's specific needs.

Consumer Products Classification System

A common way to classify products intended for use by customers and their households is based on (1) the reasons customers buy the product, (2) the amount of information customers need to buy the product, and (3) the shopping and purchase behaviors of customers toward the product. According to this system, products can be divided into the following four primary groups:

- Convenience products

- Shopping products

- Specialty products

- Unsought products

A *convenience product* is a relatively inexpensive product that requires a minimum of time, information gathering, and shopping effort on the part of most customers. Customers purchase convenience products frequently and those products are widely available from many outlets. Customers typically believe that any competing convenience products are similar in quality and performance, so brand and price are secondary considerations.

Many of the products bought from 24-hour supermarkets and vending machines are convenience products. Only a few specialized types of insurance, such as airline flight insurance, generally are considered convenience products.

Retailers seldom make much effort to promote particular convenience products. Manufacturers of convenience products focus on keeping customers aware of the products and making them available in as many outlets as possible.

A *shopping product* is a product for which consumers are willing to exert the time and effort needed to gather information and compare products before purchase. Shopping products are usually more expensive and less frequently purchased than convenience products. Shopping products can be divided into the following two categories

- A *homogeneous shopping product* is a product that customers view as similar in quality or features to other products but different enough in price to warrant comparison shopping. Homogeneous shopping products include household appliances, most hardware products, electric tools, and certain makes of automobiles. Many customers also consider basic bank loans and term life, automobile, and homeowners insurance to be homogeneous shopping products.

- A *heterogeneous shopping product* is a product that consumers view as different enough from other products to compare quality, style, or features as well as price. Furniture, clothing, and china are heterogeneous shopping products. Retailers of heterogeneous shopping products often offer an assortment of competing products so that customers can compare products without having to go to any other locations. Many service products, including most lines of insurance, are heterogeneous shopping products.

The retailer of shopping products usually is far more involved in the sales process than are convenience products retailers. Buyers of expensive heterogeneous shopping products often expect individualized service and well-trained sales personnel to provide needed information and advice. Companies that make shopping products usually assist the retailer by providing specialized product training and marketing materials.

Manufacturers of shopping products devote much of their marketing efforts toward convincing customers that their products are superior to those of their competitors, so that the ultimate purchase decision is not based merely on price. In practice, this can be difficult because most companies that produce a particular product soon learn just which features and benefits customers actually want in the product. They then modify their own products to provide those same features and benefits. As a result, the various competing brands become very similar, and customers often believe that all the brands and models are practically the same.

The process by which a product reaches a point in its development where it has no features that differentiate it from competitive products other than price is known as *commoditization*, and such a product is called a *commodity*. In many industries, commoditization can be a major problem leading to price wars and reduced profit margins.

To avoid commoditization, companies often try to show customers specific ways in which their products really are superior to the competitor's products, such as ease of use or reliability. Goods manufacturers may provide a product in a variety of sizes, shapes, and colors. Some companies will promote one or more features of their products that do differ from those of their competitors and try to convince customers that these features make their product superior to the competition. Insurers may emphasize specific options or guarantees available on particular products and provide those features with distinctive names.

In addition, when a company's product is similar to its competitor's product, the company may be able to differentiate its product by offering additional or superior services such as better financing, free installation or delivery, longer warranties, or user-friendly technical support. Providing superior customer service and access to an interactive Web site with an online benefit calculator are two ways an insurer can differentiate its products from those of its competitors.

A *specialty product* is a product that customers will make a special effort to obtain. Buyers of specialty products usually know exactly which brand of a product they want and are willing to search until they find it. Luxury cars, high-end photographic equipment, and designer clothing are specialty products. Specialty products are often expensive, but do not have to be. Many customers will only purchase particular brands of cereal, coffee, or ice cream.

Many specialty products essentially are pre-sold to customers before they begin the actual shopping process. The manufacturer's marketing convinces the customer to purchase that particular product; the retailer merely answers questions and assists the customer in obtaining the product. Specialty products often can be marketed successfully through fewer outlets than other products.

Personal services, especially those that the customer believes are important, often are specialty products. Many people, for example, will see the same doctor, dentist, or lawyer for many years. Sometimes, insurers or producers can convince customers of the personal nature and value of the services they provide. For example, customers might appreciate a producer who was able to cut through red tape with an insurer to get a claim expedited. If that happens, customers may view the insurance products being offered as specialty products. Those customers will be less likely to shop for better prices or features elsewhere when they renew or purchase a new policy, or to consider unsolicited offers or proposals from other insurers or producers.

An *unsought product* is a product that most customers are not actively seeking. Products are unsought because customers are unaware the product exists, unaware they may need or can use the product, or do not want to think about the product. Brand-new products sometimes are unsought products because the public is not aware of them. Many people don't like to think about death or illness, so they don't want to shop for products like cemetery plots or many types of insurance. In addition, some customers simply are unaware certain products, such as long-term care insurance, even exist.

The marketing of unsought products often requires special emphasis on educating customers through personal selling, sales promotion, and advertising. The marketer must first convince customers they have an actual need and then show how the unsought product will provide the solution. Marketers may need to use considerable tact and discretion in their efforts due to the nature of the product. Personal selling often becomes the most effective and efficient way to sell unsought products.

Different customers often exhibit different behavior when purchasing specific products. Many customers still view insurance, especially the more complex types of insurance, as a heterogeneous shopping product. They want to examine the features and benefits of various policies, such as guarantees, rates of return, and options. They research various insurers to determine their financial stability and reputation. They evaluate the insurance producer based on her knowledge, skill, and personality. However, increasing numbers of customers now think of insurance as a homogeneous shopping product. They may purchase basic lines such as auto or term life insurance over the Internet. For other lines, customers are only interested in obtaining and comparing price quotes from a number of insurers or producers.

Customer familiarity with particular types of insurance products often is a key factor in determining the proper marketing strategy for the product. Affluent Baby Boomers often are familiar with annuities and other retirement products, so insurers marketing to that segment might emphasize the particular product's special quality and features. On the other hand, other market segments are less familiar with such products, so insurers may need to adopt a strategy designed for unsought products with those customers.

Product Mix

The total assortment of products available from a company is called its ***product mix*** or *portfolio of products*. Companies often organize their product mix on the following levels:

- A ***product class*** is the entire group of products produced by a particular industry or industry sector. Life insurance, health insurance, and annuities are three product classes.

- A ***product line*** is a set of different products that are closely related because they (1) function similarly, (2) are marketed to the same target markets, (3) are priced about the same, or (4) are distributed through similar distribution systems. Individual life and group life insurance are separate product lines.

- A ***product form*** is a group of products within a product line that share certain basic characteristics. Whole life and term life are product forms within the individual life insurance line.

- A ***product item*** is a specific version of a specific product form within a product line. Each specific type of policy offered by an insurer is a product item.

Figure 6.2 illustrates various life insurance products that a particular company might offer organized according to class, line, form, and item.

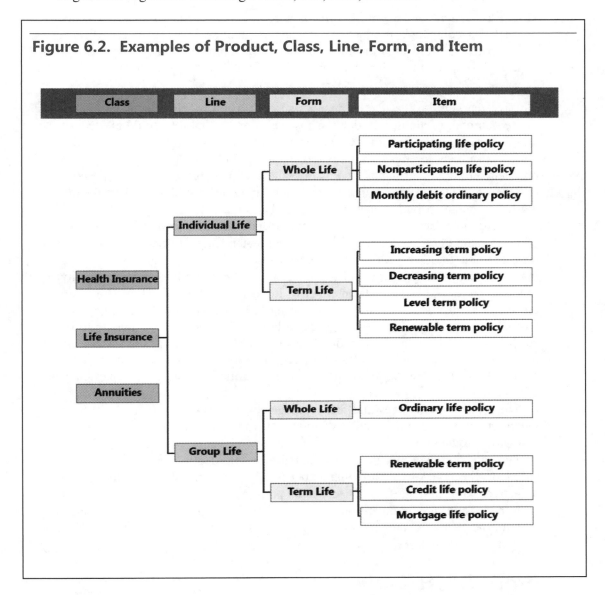

Figure 6.2. Examples of Product, Class, Line, Form, and Item

When a company compares its product mix to others in the same industry, it measures the mix according to width (wide or narrow), depth (deep or shallow) and consistency (consistent or inconsistent).

- The ***width of a product mix*** is a comparative measure of the number of different product lines or classes a company offers. An insurer that sells life insurance, health insurance, property/casualty insurance, and annuities has a wider product mix than one that sells only life insurance.

- The ***depth of a product mix*** is a comparative measure of the number of different product forms or product items that a company offers in each product line. An insurer that sells various types of term life, whole life, universal life, and variable life insurance policies has a deeper product mix than an insurer that only sells term life insurance.

- The *consistency of a product mix* is a comparative measure of how closely related a company's product classes and product lines are to each other. A company that sells only insurance products has a more consistent product mix than a company that sells insurance, mutual funds, mortgages, and IRAs.

A wide product mix offers a company multiple sources of revenue and multiple markets, so that the company's success is not overly dependent upon a limited number of similar products whose sales or profitability could all decline rapidly at the same time due to events beyond the company's control. It also allows customers to engage in one-stop shopping for a variety of the company's products. On the other hand, a company with a narrow product mix may find it easier to establish expertise in a more limited range of products, and its overall marketing and distribution costs usually will be lower as well.

A deep product mix allows companies to pursue different market segments with the same lines of products; allows for a greater range of prices, features and benefits; and frequently discourages competition. Customers also may believe that a company has greater expertise in a particular product line or better quality products because of the greater number of items it offers in that line. However, too many similar products may be confusing to customers, sales personnel, and customer service staff, and the sales volume of certain items may not be sufficient to justify their individual development, production, and marketing costs. On the other hand, a shallow product mix allows companies to concentrate their efforts on a few better-selling or more profitable items in any particular product line.

The relative advantages and disadvantages of a consistent, as opposed to an inconsistent, product mix generally are similar to those of a narrow, as opposed to a wide, product mix.

Typically, product mix decisions related to width, depth, and consistency are based on the company's particular expertise, its license, its overall marketing objectives and strategies, the needs and preferences of the company's target customers, and the competition's product mix. Companies must constantly monitor the changing marketing environment and modify their product mix when necessary.

Product Life Cycle

The *product life cycle (PLC)* describes the series of stages—introduction, growth, maturity, and decline—through which a product usually progresses, from its first appearance until its eventual withdrawal from the market. Companies use the PLC to determine the most appropriate marketing strategies to use for products during each stage of the cycle and to identify the best time to modify or discontinue existing products and develop new products.

During the *introduction stage*, sales are often low and companies concentrate on gaining market acceptance and stimulating demand for the new product. The company may actually lose money on the product in this stage due to high development and promotional costs. The company must monitor the product's performance carefully and address product weaknesses swiftly. The company may focus its marketing efforts on the market segment that shows the most interest in the product, so that the product can become profitable more quickly. Many products never become successful and are withdrawn from the market without ever leaving the introduction stage.

In the *growth stage*, sales and profits increase rapidly as the product gains acceptance and profit per unit peaks. New competitors enter the market, and companies often extend their product lines to fend off these competitors and appeal to a wider market segment. Advertising and promotion costs remain high, but the emphasis often shifts to building brand loyalty.

In a product's *maturity stage*, total sales continue to increase, but at a decreasing rate. The maturity stage usually is the longest stage in the product's life cycle. Most potential customers are already familiar with the product, so that the only way for a company to increase its own sales or market share usually is to take market share from competitors with similar products. To do this, companies often need to change the variables in the marketing mix, possibly by changing pricing structures or using different distribution channels. Customer satisfaction becomes a key marketing objective for sellers, because unsatisfied customers will switch to competitors.

Eventually, new technology, regulatory changes, shifting customer demands, demographic trends, or other environmental changes cause total industry sales for a product to decline. During the *decline stage*, companies withdraw their products from the market or maintain them with reduced promotion and distribution efforts. Those companies that still remain in the market may be able to maintain sales volume through increased market share and continue to make profits on the product until it is no longer offered for sale.

Figure 6.3 illustrates the general shape of the PLC for most products throughout the four stages.

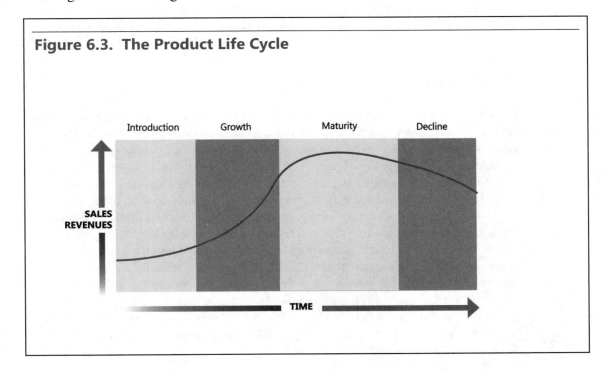

Figure 6.3. The Product Life Cycle

The amount of time a product stays in each stage and the rate of change in sales vary from one product to another. Fads like pet rocks may become popular, seemingly overnight, but disappear from the market in a matter of months. On the other hand, products like automobiles and refrigerators, that reflect current state-of-the-art technology, can remain in the maturity stage for decades. Product items and forms move through the PLC more rapidly than product lines or classes.

Insurance and other financial service products also move through the PLC as a result of environmental changes, such as changing demographics, technology, economic conditions, and regulation. For example, as Baby Boomers have aged into their 50s and 60s and life expectancy has increased, newer insurance products such as variable annuities and long-term care products have emerged and entered the growth stage. At the same time, with fewer younger adults starting families and buying their first homes, traditional insurance products such as individual whole life have entered the maturity stage.

Sometimes, an individual company's sales of a product may remain steady or actually increase, even though the overall market for that product is declining. Companies may be able to extend the growth or maturity stages of their own products considerably through effective marketing and may even reverse the cycle of a particular product that has entered the decline stage. This can occur if a company finds new uses or new markets for a product. For example, some insurance companies that face declining sales of traditional product lines can market their policies in developing countries with far lower levels of insurance penetration.

Companies must monitor their product mix to ensure that they have a variety of products at different stages in the PLC. The high start-up costs of introducing a new product can be offset by profits from established products in the growth and maturity stages. Companies that wait until too many of their products are declining before developing new ones may find themselves in financial difficulty as a result.

Packaging

Packaging serves a number of purposes for many products. Many tangible goods such as toothpaste are useless without a container in which to store, transport, and dispense them. However, a product's packaging also allows the manufacturer to deliver a message about the product to the potential customer. Familiar packaging like the Coca-Cola glass bottle or the Campbell's soup red-and-white label helps a customer identify and associate a product with a manufacturer. Packaging also can call attention to a product or create interest in a new product, sometimes merely by putting words like *new* or *improved* on the packaging itself.

For a service product, ***packaging*** consists of the tangible and intangible elements that surround the product. Although services usually do not require physical protection or storage, a service product's packaging can create or reinforce a customer's perception about the characteristics, quality, or value of the product and can form the basis for the customer's decision whether to purchase the product. The packaging of life and health insurance products and annuities includes the following elements:

- The appearance of the written and graphic materials related to the product, such as letters, applications, forms, brochures, proposals, buyer's guides, sales illustrations, and the policy itself. The design, grade of paper, choice of colors, quality of the printing, choice of words, and use of grammar are all parts of the packaging.

- The image and attitude of the person selling or providing service on the product—how her office looks and how she speaks, dresses, acts, responds to inquiries, handles technical matters, exhibits knowledge or expertise, shows concern for the customer, and understands the customer's needs.

- The image and credibility of the company offering the product—whether the company is large or small, well-known or less known, or single-line or multiline.

A service product's packaging can help a customer make a decision about the product's quality. Many customers observe the characteristics of the service company's personnel prior to a potential purchase and use them as an indicator of the company's likely performance after purchase. Customers want to do business with companies whose representatives will be reliable, responsive, competent, and empathetic, so they look for those same qualities, or the lack thereof, prior to making the purchase decision.

Customers also use the tangible elements of a service product's packaging as an indicator of the quality of the product and the company itself. For example, a customer's perception of a product that requires a large cash outlay may be negatively affected if the printed materials or other elements associated with the product are poorly prepared, contain grammatical errors, look cheap, or are in some way not consistent with the image of the product or the expected quality of its accompanying service. Conversely, overly extravagant promotional materials also may adversely affect a customer's perception of the product. Such perceptions of likely quality can influence whether the customer decides to buy or reject a particular product and even whether that customer continues to buy and use any products from that company.

Branding

Branding is the process a company uses to identify itself and its products and distinguish its products from those of its competitors. A **brand** is a name, number, term, sign, symbol, design, or combination of these elements used to identify a company or one or more of its products and to differentiate the company and its products from the competition.[2]

A brand may include a brand name and a brand mark. A **brand name** is a word, letter, or group of words or letters that can be vocalized. A **brand mark,** also known as a *logo*, is a symbol, design, distinctive coloring, unusual type style, or combination of these elements that can be recognized but can't be spoken. Allstate is a brand name, while the familiar cupped hands symbol is the brand mark. Together, the word *Allstate* and the cupped hands symbol make up the brand.

Advantages of Branding

Branding helps customers identify products and recognize which ones they do and do not want to buy. A customer who believes Hewlett-Packard makes high-quality products may buy a new computer on that basis alone, even if he has no other way to evaluate its quality. The very ownership of certain status brands such as Rolex watches or Mercedes-Benz automobiles provides psychological benefits for some people.

Branding provides a number of advantages for sellers as well. Companies can promote and advertise more effectively by establishing an appropriate brand image for the company rather than giving specific reasons to buy each individual product. A *brand image* is the perception of the brand by the customer, positive or negative. It can be an expression of the experience the customer thinks he will receive from the company. For service companies, establishing a favorable brand image can be extremely important because customers may have no other way of evaluating a company's products. Insurers usually try to establish an image of reliability, security, and caring, which often extends to their selection of brand names and logos. For example, the name *Prudential* suggests good judgment, while its Rock of Gibraltar logo suggests stability.

Companies often protect the value of their brands by registering them as trademarks or service marks. A *trademark* (used with goods) or *service mark* (used with services) is a word, phrase, symbol, design, or some combination that identifies and distinguishes the products of one party from those of others. In the United States, trademarks and service marks are registered with the U.S. Patent and Trademark Office. The registration process also helps companies avoid using a brand, symbol, or slogan that another company is already using.

Trademarking brand names helps maintain brand image. Trademarks belong exclusively to their owners, who have proprietary rights to use them. Competitors sometimes market inferior products that appear very similar to well-known brand-name products and easily could be mistaken by customers for the brand-name products. In addition to losing business, a company's brand image suffers if customers believe the inferior competitive products are actually its own brand-name products. A company often can bring legal action to prevent competitors from infringing upon a registered trademark with products that are overly similar in appearance and to recover monetary damages for any losses suffered as a result of infringement.

The most important goal of a company's branding strategy often is to establish, maintain, and strengthen brand loyalty. There are three degrees of brand loyalty, from weakest to strongest:

- *Brand awareness*, also known as *brand recognition*, means that buyers recognize the brand name and can associate it with the product in question. Brand awareness may seem like a very weak form of brand loyalty, but it is often the major focus of advertising campaigns for new products. Brand awareness usually means that customers can identify some of the characteristics of the product and would at least consider buying it. For a company with strong brand awareness like McDonalds, the mere sight of the Golden Arches logo reminds customers around the world of the restaurant and its products.

- *Brand preference* is the customer's choice of a particular product, when available, over competing products, but the willingness to accept a substitute product when the preferred product is not available. Brand preference is rarely absolute, but it can be strong or weak for particular customers, depending on the price differential the customer is willing to accept. Some customers prefer Pepsi to Coke at the same price but will buy Coke instead if it is on sale.

■ ***Brand insistence*** is the customer's unwillingness to accept any substitute for the preferred brand. Absolute brand insistence is fairly rare, but some customers are willing to go to considerable expense and difficulty to locate and purchase a particular product. Brand insistence often involves specialty products.

Customers frequently develop strong preferences for particular service companies. Brand loyalty is especially important for insurers, because loyal customers are far more likely to maintain and renew existing insurance policies and purchase new products from the company. Even if customers decide to purchase term life insurance primarily on the basis of price, they may still rely on a preferred insurer for complex products such as variable life insurance, whose features, guarantees, fund alternatives, and fees vary substantially from company to company. For unfamiliar lines of insurance such as long-term care, brand loyalty may determine whether a customer will even consider making any purchase at all.

Types of Brands

A ***manufacturer brand,*** or *proprietary brand*, is a brand created by, controlled by, and identified with the company that produces or manufactures a product. Manufacturer brands can be divided into two categories:

■ A ***family brand*** is a single brand that applies to all of a company's products, including, in some cases, very dissimilar products. American Express uses its family brand on credit cards, travel services, and consumer publications. Family branding allows marketers to take advantage of a brand's or a company's reputation and the recognition associated with the name. Advertising and promoting one product in a family brand may benefit all the other products in the family.

■ An ***individual brand*** is a separate brand name given to each product item or product line. Individual branding helps companies avoid confusing customers and compete better for limited retailer shelf space. ConAgra Foods has dozens of individual brands from Banquet chicken to Wesson oil. Companies also use individual branding to appeal to specific market segments, such as General Motors, which manufactures both Cadillacs and Chevrolets. Sometimes, a company may even acquire another company specifically to gain the rights to use a particular brand name.

Individual branding can be more expensive than family branding because separate promotional campaigns must be developed for each individually branded item. A company also may be unable to take advantage of a favorable overall image if it relies exclusively on individual branding. As a result, many companies combine the individual and family brand in association with each product, such as Kellogg's Rice Krispies.

A ***distributor brand***, sometimes referred to as a *private brand* or a *private label*, is a brand created by, controlled by, and identified with the company that distributes or sells a product. Kenmore and Craftsman are distributor brands for appliances and tools sold by Sears retail stores. Sears buys products manufactured by other companies, puts its own brand names on them, and then sells the products to consumers. Insurers sometimes put their own brand on products they distribute that are issued by other companies, such as mutual funds used to back variable products.

Product Differentiation

Companies must be able to distinguish their products, both from competitors' products and from other items in their own product mix. We introduced how companies use product differentiation, the practice of distinguishing a product from other products in terms of its form, style, quality, or some other characteristic, in chapter 1. Product differentiation is extremely important in markets such as insurance or financial services where a large number of similar products are available.

Branding, packaging, and pricing are three common methods companies use to differentiate their products. Branding is usually crucial to product differentiation, but, by itself, it is rarely sufficient. Many people are aware that Tide, Gain, and All are different detergents, but they may not know what the differences are or why they should buy one brand instead of another. Packaging also may make it easier to distinguish between products, but it often provides no indication which product is better. Price difference can be a reason to select one product over another, but most companies prefer to differentiate in some other way in order to avoid price wars that reduce profit margins.

Effective product differentiation often focuses on features or attributes that most customers want and can easily understand. Companies may rely on short slogans or catch phrases in their marketing. For example, Bounty paper towels are the "quicker picker upper," which is a short, easy-to-remember way of saying that Bounty towels absorb moisture and clean up spills more quickly than other paper towels do.

Many insurers offer products with similar features, benefits, and prices. Insurers usually can't reduce the actual differences among their various products to catch phrases, so they must rely on personal selling by trained producers to explain those differences and to convince customers to purchase a particular product. In fact, some marketing theorists believe that service companies can use three factors in their marketing environment to help them differentiate their products from competitors more effectively:

- *People*, which refers to all the people required to provide the services being offered to the consumer

- *Process,* which refers to the procedures and activities that support the services offered

- *Physical evidence* of the service which can include packaging, environment (claims office, agent's office, etc.), and ability to provide the services promised[3]

Insurers often attempt to differentiate their products based on the additional services they offer. Companies that effectively use the Internet, 24-hour call centers, and other state-of-the-art technologies to provide improved customer and claim service will have an advantage over their competitors. In fact, many customers simply think that an insurer's courteous and efficient handling of routine service requests is a good indication of a high-quality insurance product.

Positioning

Positioning is the process by which a company establishes and maintains in customers' minds a distinct place, or position, for itself and its products. Companies may attempt to position the company as a whole or various products individually. Positioning usually involves all aspects of the marketing mix, not just the product itself. Successful product positioning involves the following three elements:

- Selecting the target market

- Selecting the category in which the product will compete

- Determining the key benefit or benefits the product offers

No product can be all things to all people. Features or attributes that may be desirable for some customers may be unimportant or even undesirable for others. Some customers prefer low-fat foods because of their health benefits, while other customers dislike the taste too much to buy them. Companies usually attempt to position their products to appeal to their target customers or to position different products to appeal to different target markets.

Companies also select the category in which their products will compete. The product category a company selects determines the size of the market and the number and types of competitors the company will face. A larger market offers more sales opportunities, but usually it also has a greater number and variety of competitors. Stove Top Stuffing was positioned as a starchy side dish rather than a holiday stuffing alternative to compete in the much larger everyday food market rather than just the holiday market. On the other hand, 7-Up avoided competing with soft drink market giants Coke and Pepsi by successfully creating a new category for itself, which it called the Uncola.

Finally, a company must determine the key benefit a product offers. This is a benefit that is both important to target customers and something that the company's competitors can't or don't offer as effectively, efficiently, or economically. The key benefit can be based on product or company attributes, price/quality/service dimensions, distribution characteristics, or any other aspect of the marketing mix. Sometimes, a company may be able to offer a benefit that no one else does. For a number of years, Crest toothpaste was the only brand containing cavity preventative fluoride as an ingredient; Crest advertising emphasized that fact for decades. A product attribute that is not or cannot be offered by competitors is known as a *unique selling proposition (USP)*.

A company's target market, company/product category, and key benefit typically are summarized in a positioning statement such as:

> For [**target customers**], Company X or Product Y is the type of [**business/product category**] that offers [**key benefit**].

Positioning is particularly important in the financial services industry, where a large number of competitors offer similar products. However, the typical approach for an insurer is to position itself as a company rather than positioning individual products, which may be complex and difficult to differentiate in the context of a typical promotional campaign. For example, a company that targets its products to families might define itself as the insurer that "protects your family's financial future."

Product Development

Product development—the process of creating or modifying a product—is one of a company's essential marketing and profit-generating activities. Companies often need to develop new products or modify existing ones to remain competitive and meet customer needs. New products may result in considerable gains in revenues, market share, and customer satisfaction. However, if a new product does not meet customer needs, it is likely to fail, and the company's market position, distribution capacity, and corporate image may suffer as a result.

Although most people think of a new product as something totally different that has never been offered before, new products actually can take a variety of forms. Figure 6.4 shows six different types of new products with some insurance examples of each.

Usually, as the degree of novelty increases, so does the level of risk associated with the new product.

Product Development Strategy

Product development begins with an overall product development strategy which determines the company's general approach to product development and product marketing. The strategy may be revised later by company management. Companies also may adopt different strategies for different product lines or different markets. The three basic product development strategies are

- Product imitation
- Product improvement
- Product innovation

A ***product imitation strategy***, sometimes referred to as a *me-too strategy*, attempts to simulate, as closely as possible, another company's successful product. This strategy typically allows companies to reduce research and development, advertising, and promotion costs, and also minimizes the risk of customer rejection of the product. Companies with limited resources or those seeking to expand their product mixes often adopt a product imitation strategy.

Figure 6.4. Types of New Products

New Product	Description	Example
Major Innovation	A new product that has never been offered by any company and that meets needs not addressed by any other product	Long-term care insurance, when first introduced
Start-Up Product	A new product that has never been offered before but meets needs already served by existing products	Managed care plans, such as HMOs, PPOs, and POS plans, when first introduced
Product Mix Extension	A product that is new to a particular company's product mix but has been available from other sources for some time	A life and health insurance company adds automobile and homeowners insurance
Product Line Extension	A product that is (1) a new form in an existing product line or (2) a new version of an existing product form. A product line extension is an addition to the company's product portfolio	(1) A company that currently offers term life insurance adds return of premium (ROP) term insurance (2) A company adds universal life to its existing portfolio of individual life insurance products
Product Modification	Changing the characteristics of an existing product to give it a competitive advantage or to respond to market demands. A product modification usually replaces the original product in the company's portfolio	A company adds enhanced death benefits or enhanced living benefits to a variable annuity to be more competitive
Style Change	Altering the appearance or tangible aspects of a product, but leaving the product's basic features and benefits intact	A company develops new application form designs, new product logos or trademarks, or consolidated billing statements

Source: Adapted from Christopher H. Lovelock, "Developing and Implementing New Services," in *Developing New Services*, ed. William George and Claudia Marshall (Chicago: American Marketing Association, 1984), 45–46.

Companies that use a product imitation strategy usually want customers to believe that their product is essentially the same as the original product; therefore, they may design their product to be similar in appearance to the original product and may even give their product a similar brand name. To be competitive, these companies rely on other elements of the marketing mix—such as lower price, better promotion, or more effective means of distribution. Imitative products can be highly successful. In the 1950s, ballpoint pen sales were limited primarily to the high-end business and upscale markets until BIC introduced a low-cost, disposable model and quickly became the dominant leader in the industry.

There are risks involved with adopting a product imitation strategy. Customers often believe that imitative products—especially if they are less expensive—are inferior, and that belief may affect the company's reputation as well. For many companies, the only feasible way to compete using imitative products is through aggressively low pricing, which can result in a severe strain on the company's resources. In addition, the company that introduced the original product may have established considerable brand loyalty or other advantages, such as highly efficient distribution channels or patent rights, which make effective competition difficult.

A *product improvement strategy* seeks to introduce new versions of existing products with significant differences to better satisfy customer needs. These differences may include additional features, a different style or design, or changes in the production process. Adding riders for accelerated death benefits for terminal and chronic illness to life insurance policies or various guarantees to variable annuities are examples of product improvements. Companies may develop improved versions of their own products or a competitor's products. Product improvement is the most common type of product development strategy.

The costs involved with developing and marketing an improved product usually are higher than with an imitative product because of the need to inform customers and distributors of the improvements in the product; the risk of customer rejection of the product is higher as well. However, it often is much easier for companies to compete against existing products by developing products that offer distinct advantages to the customer rather than by merely offering imitative products. In addition, the development process for an improved product usually is less expensive and less time-consuming than for a completely new product.

A *product innovation strategy* involves developing products that provide completely new or different ways of satisfying customer needs. Some product innovations such as photocopiers required the development of new technology, while others like Post-it notes involved a new application of existing technology. The new product can better satisfy an existing need—for example, microwave ovens, which heated food faster than conventional ovens. The new product can even create a perceived need where none existed previously, like video game systems that created a new form of entertainment few people had imagined.

Product innovation offers the highest levels of both risk and reward of any product development strategy. Companies often must devote considerable time and resources toward the development and marketing of completely new products, and the failure rate can be high, because of either technological problems or customer rejection. Companies also face the risk that competitors may be able to develop and market their own versions of new products more quickly and less expensively.

However, the rewards of being the first to successfully introduce a new product are considerable. Although competitors may attempt to produce their own versions of successful products, the company that gets its product to the marketplace first usually has a considerable period of time in which it will be the exclusive provider, and its reputation and brand loyalty among customers can grow substantially as a result. It may also be able to obtain patent rights, more efficient distribution, or other advantages that serve as effective barriers to competition from imitators. As a result, a company that first markets a product successfully and can take advantage of that status will usually have the largest market share, even after competitors develop their own similar products.

Product Development Process

Following a defined process consistently typically improves a company's product development success rate and reduces development time and expense.[4] The product development process for a particular company may be based on the company's size, mission, objectives, culture, markets, current products, customers, competition, distribution systems, location, and employees. Many companies use a five-step product development process:

- Product planning
- Comprehensive business analysis
- Technical design
- Implementation
- Performance monitoring and review

Product Planning[5]

Most insurers today have dedicated product development teams with representatives from several departments who work primarily or exclusively on product planning and development. For companies that do not have their own product development department, the actuarial department often assumes primary responsibility for product development.

Product planning consists of three basic activities:

- Idea generation
- Screening
- Concept development and testing

Idea generation involves searching for new product ideas that are consistent with both the company's overall product development strategy and the needs of its target markets. New product ideas come from many sources both inside and outside an insurance company. Many of these ideas come from marketing, either from the sales force or from intelligence and research. Other sources include other managers and employees, customers, consultants, and consumer groups. Generating new product ideas is most successful when a company has both an ongoing, formal identification process and procedures that encourage employees and others to submit their own product ideas. Creativity is generally stressed during idea generation; the practical aspects of a product are examined during screening.

Screening is a weeding-out process designed to evaluate each new product idea quickly and inexpensively to select those that warrant further investigation. More new product ideas are rejected during the screening phase than any other phase of the development process.[6] Generally, any information required for screening either is already known by the screening team or can be easily obtained.

Because screening involves a quick and somewhat limited evaluation of the merits and feasibility of each new product idea, a company must be careful not to reject a good idea whose potential is underestimated, or, alternatively, pursue a deceptively attractive poor idea and waste company resources. Some companies have developed checklists of specific screening criteria that encourage employees to be consistent and systematic in their evaluation of new product ideas. Figure 6.5 lists some of the typical new product screening criteria used by insurance companies.

Companies often translate complex new product ideas into a product concept. A *product concept* is a verbal or pictorial version of a proposed product that includes its general form and a description of some of its features and benefits expressed in a manner consumers can understand.

> **Example:** Return of Premium (ROP) term insurance might be a new product idea for a particular insurer. The product concept expressed to the customer might be: "a term life insurance policy that, for a higher premium, pays a death benefit during the time period in which you may need it to support your family, but, if you are alive at the end of that time, returns all the premiums paid to you so you may use those funds to meet other needs, such as providing for your retirement."

Some companies use *concept testing,* which is a marketing research technique designed to measure the acceptability of new product ideas, new promotion campaigns, or other new marketing elements before entering production. During concept testing, one or more product ideas are described to distributors or customers to determine which new product might have the greatest appeal to a particular target market. Concept testing helps determine (1) how customers or distributors compare a new product idea to existing alternative products, (2) which sets of product benefits or attributes customers or distributors would prefer in a new product idea, (3) which new product ideas are unacceptable in the marketplace, and (4) which target market represents the greatest sales potential for a new product. The greater the degree of innovation involved in the new product, the greater the emphasis placed on concept testing.

Figure 6.5. Typical Criteria Used to Screen a New Product Idea

1. Is the product idea compatible with the company's overall goals and strategic objectives? Will the addition of the product enhance the company's image?

2. Does a real need exist for the product in the target markets in which the company operates? Will the product help the company maintain its current market position? Can the product build on the company's current customer base?

3. Can any products currently offered by the company be modified, packaged differently, or changed in some other way to meet the needs addressed by the product idea?

4. Will the new product generate additional sales or simply displace sales of an existing product? Or will the sales of an existing product be displaced by a competitor if the new product is not developed?

5. Based on initial impressions, does the market potential for the product appear large enough to generate whatever level of response, growth, return on investment, or contribution to surplus or profit that the company generally seeks from its products?

6. Can the product be marketed through the company's existing distribution systems? If not, can the company acquire, or quickly develop expertise in, the distribution systems required for the product? Is the market large enough to justify the expense of developing a new distribution system?

7. Will the product support a level of commissions that will motivate the sales force?

8. Will the company's current personnel and systems be able to handle the product's technical and service requirements?

9. Will the target markets for the product find it desirable and reasonably easy to understand?

10. Would this product be more attractive or profitable if offered through a separate affiliate or subsidiary?

Insurance companies often use senior management, field advisory councils, and focus groups for concept testing. A **field advisory council** is a group of producers designated to represent and provide feedback from the sales force in areas such as product design, rate setting, underwriting philosophy, and customer service.

Comprehensive Business Analysis

A company's most promising product ideas and concepts then undergo a **comprehensive business analysis**, which is an evaluation of all the factors that are likely to affect the design, production, pricing, marketing, and sales potential of the new product. Companies typically conduct a more extensive analysis for completely new products than for modified products.

The comprehensive business analysis typically consists of the following five elements:

■ A **market analysis**, which is a study, usually prepared by the marketing department, of all the environmental factors that might affect sales of a product, such as customer needs, the competition, and the distribution system.

■ The **product design objectives**, which specify an insurance product's basic characteristics, features, benefits, issue limits, age limits, commission and premium structure, underwriting classes, and operational and administrative requirements. Product design objectives are considerably more specific than the general product characteristics that may have been discussed during idea generation.

- A *feasibility study*, which is research designed to determine the operational and technical viability of producing and selling the product. The marketing department examines the sales aspects of the feasibility study. The screening criteria listed in Figure 6.5 are used again during the feasibility study, but in greater detail.

- A marketing plan, which includes specific, detailed, action-oriented activities related to the pricing, promotion, and distribution of a particular product or product line. The marketing department, with input from other departments, develops marketing plans for each individual product, which are then incorporated into the company's overall marketing plan. Companies also may develop an exit plan to determine what to do if a new product is unsuccessful.

- **Preliminary sales and financial forecasts.** Based on the marketing plan, the product development team, with input from the marketing department, estimates potential unit sales, revenues, costs, and profits for the proposed product. These forecasts help determine the financial viability of the new product. The team modifies these forecasts as additional information becomes available.

Example: Harmony Life Insurance Company is considering developing a Return of Premium (ROP) term insurance policy. Market analysis indicates that sales of Harmony's existing life policies have been below expectations and that a large number of customers in Harmony's target market—younger, middle income families—are postponing life insurance purchases. Also, some of Harmony's competitors already have successfully introduced similar ROP term policies, but the product's overall share of the target market is still rather low.

Analysis: Harmony's product development team concluded that its sales force is well positioned to sell ROP term policies. Harmony advertises itself as "your family's around-the-corner one-stop insurance shop," specializing in packages for younger families that include auto and homeowners policies offered through Harmony's affiliated property/casualty company. Harmony's producers usually are licensed to sell both life and property/casualty insurance, and they believe they easily can add an ROP term policy to the packages they offer customers. They also are enthusiastic about the prospect of higher commissions on a product they believe will be easier to sell than current term life policies. Concept testing also revealed that a large number of customers in Harmony's target market who had not yet purchased an individual life insurance policy had expressed an interest in purchasing the ROP term policy that was described to them; they also agreed with a statement that it would be "very important" to keep renewing the policy every year. Harmony's sales forecast indicates a significant increase in life insurance sales volume by adding the ROP term policy to its portfolio and an increase in persistency as well.

If the comprehensive business analysis indicates a product has good potential, the product development team incorporates these results into a formal product proposal and presents it to top management for approval. If approved, the product proposal serves as the overall guide for product design and development, testing, and introduction.

Technical Design

After management approves a new product proposal, the development team must formulate the detailed product design. This involves setting an insurance product's actuarial assumptions regarding interest, persistency, expenses, and mortality or morbidity; creating the necessary application forms and sales contracts; and establishing the product's rate structure, benefit levels, and issue and underwriting standards.[7]

Representatives from functional areas that might be affected by the proposed product's design or pricing, such as marketing, underwriting, legal, financial, systems, and claims, review the proposed new product and suggest changes based on their area's needs. The information systems department might be concerned that the company's existing systems would not be adequate to process transactions for the new product, or the actuarial department might be concerned that the premium rates are too low. The product design may also be reviewed by the field advisory council, selected producers or other distribution channel members, and the head of agency operations. The design is revised until the functional areas affected by the product reach a consensus.

The product development team also develops a schedule and budget for the product's implementation. In some cases, assigning additional resources to product development activities can speed up the expected completion date, so the team may develop some alternative budgets and the resulting schedules.

Finally, the product development team presents the product design and accompanying schedules and budgets to top management for approval. Management may approve the design, reject it entirely, or call for further refinements and revisions. Management also chooses the schedule and budget most appropriate for the product.

Implementation

After the new product's design and other details have been finalized, the company must take various steps before it can begin selling the product. *Implementation* involves establishing the administrative structures and processes needed to take a product to market. Implementation consists of three concurrent activities: (1) obtaining necessary regulatory approvals, (2) designing promotion and training materials, and (3) developing and putting in place all information systems and procedures necessary to market and administer the product.

Policy Filing. In the United States, insurers generally must obtain approval for any life insurance or annuity product from the state insurance department in each state in which the insurer intends to offer the product. *Policy filing* is the act of submitting a policy contract form and any other legally required forms and documents to the appropriate insurance department for approval. Variable life insurance and annuity products also must be registered with the Securities and Exchange Commission (SEC) before being offered for sale.

Most states impose a ***prior approval requirement***, under which a form must be filed with and approved by the state insurance department before it can be used in that state. A few states have a ***file and use requirement***, under which an insurer may use a policy form, without obtaining prior approval, after filing it with the insurance department. Although prior approval is not required, the department subsequently may review and possibly disapprove the form.

The state insurance department reviews policy forms to make sure they contain all provisions required under state law and may disapprove any filing if it does not comply with the state insurance code and regulations. In addition, the department usually will disapprove a policy form if it is unjust, unfair, inequitable, misleading, deceptive, illegible, or deemed contrary to public policy. Most states also require that insurance contracts meet certain ***readability requirements***, which are standards that limit sentence length, word length, and the amount of technical jargon and legal language in the contract form. The insurer must revise or withdraw any policy form that the state insurance department disapproves.

Since 2004, more than half of the states have become members of the ***Interstate Insurance Product Regulation Commission (IIPRC)***, a multi-state public entity that establishes uniform standards for certain insurance product lines, including life insurance, annuities, disability income insurance, and long-term care insurance, and provides for voluntary centralized electronic filing and expeditious review of products in those lines. States may opt out of particular product standards. Subject to any applicable opt-outs, approval of a product by the IIPRC is effective in any member state, although insurers still may elect to file separate applications for particular products in individual states.

Design of Promotion and Training Materials. Companies must educate and train producers so they understand the new product and can accurately present it to customers. This usually requires the marketing department to design a variety of promotion and training materials. Insurers that distribute their products directly to customers do not need to train producers. However, they do need to promote those products to the public and to train customer service and other sales support staff.

The marketing department chooses a product name, designs sales materials, and creates product-specific promotional and advertising materials for the general public. The department then prepares introductory sales kits and sample sales presentations for producers. Training materials provide producers and support personnel with information about (1) the features and benefits of the new product, (2) the intended market for the product, (3) sales ideas and approaches, (4) compensation for selling the product, (5) how to fill out and submit applications or transaction requests, (6) the types of services that will be needed to support the product, and (7) any regulations regarding the product.

Systems Activities. Because systems activities often require the greatest amount of time in the product development process, they should be started as early as possible. The information systems department may need to buy or develop new systems or modify current systems to support the new product. The systems department must then program and test the new systems and develop appropriate documentation, reports, internal procedures, and systems maintenance routines.

To speed up the implementation process, a growing number of companies are dividing implementation activities into two categories: Day 1 and Day 2. *Day 1* functionality refers to administrative and systems processes that must be in place and functioning before a product can be introduced to market. *Day 2* functionality refers to processes that are necessary at some future date to service and administer the product, but which can be implemented after the product has been introduced. Allowing a product to be introduced to market before all implementation processes have been completed can shorten time to market by an average of 12 to 17 weeks, depending on the product, according to a recent LIMRA study.[8]

Day 2 implementation can be risky; the company may suffer delays in other areas, additional expense, customer dissatisfaction, and loss of business if any processes can't be completed when first needed. These problems might even cause the new product to fail. As a result, some insurers insist that all implementation activities be completed prior to product launch. However, many insurers now allow certain activities, such as developing customer statements for the product, to be completed after the actual launch.

Product Launch. After the implementation activities are completed, the company is ready to begin selling the new product. At this time, any necessary information systems are brought online, and service and support personnel are allocated. In addition, the company starts promoting the product to the public, through specific advertising materials about the new product, media releases, and other publicity.

Also, at this time, the company trains producers and internal staff on the new product. Company representatives hold training sessions and distribute training, educational, and promotional materials to producers and other sales personnel. Underwriters, policy issue personnel, claims personnel, and customer service personnel must be trained to administer the new product. Customer service personnel, in particular, must be prepared to answer customers' questions about the product.

Careful planning and execution are critical for a successful product launch. If systems don't function properly, the company can't issue policies or administer the product. If advertising and publicity materials aren't in place, customers will not be aware of the new product. Producers and support personnel who are not properly trained can't provide adequate customer service or answer customer questions. First impressions are important; an insurer may never be able to overcome unfavorable customer opinions that are formed about a newly launched product.

Performance Monitoring and Review

The product development process does not end with the product launch. Following a product launch, the company reviews the product's early performance to identify any potential weaknesses and determine any necessary changes. Marketing's role in the review focuses primarily on sales. For example, the marketing department may find additional producer training is needed.[9] However, the results of the review process might also suggest other new products or modifications, or ways to improve the product development process itself.

After the product has been on the market for a period of time, the company determines how successful the product has become based on how well its sales, income, and profit goals have been met. Figure 6.6 shows some of the factors insurance companies consider in measuring the success of new products.

Figure 6.6. Factors Considered in New Insurance Product Performance Review

- Total face amount of insurance sold

- Number of policies sold

- Expected profits

- Amount of new annualized premium income generated

- Impact on other products

- Increase in the number of new policyowners

- Impact on the company's market share

- Increase in the value of the company

- Demographic characteristics of customers who purchased the product

- Policy lapse rates, loan rates, and claim experience

- Sales success of various distribution systems or methods

- Success of various advertising campaigns and sales promotions

---

Sometimes, the performance of new or existing products does not meet company expectations. If a product is not successful, the company must determine why the product is not meeting its objectives and whether to modify the product's marketing mix or withdraw the product from the market.

Product Modification. A product may fail to meet marketing objectives because of weaknesses in the product itself or in the way it is marketed. If a product did not satisfy the needs it was intended to meet, it may need to be redesigned or repositioned to meet a different need. If a product is not profitable enough, the company might need to tighten its underwriting requirements or reduce the costs of administering and marketing the product.

Companies also can address problems with other aspects of a product's marketing mix. The company might need to advertise more heavily or revise confusing or inadequate brochures. Similarly, the company might need to revise the commission or incentive structure to encourage producers to sell the product or reduce its price to make it more competitive.

The product modification process should be just as systematic as the product development process. Product modifications should be based on a careful evaluation of customer needs, environmental factors, company goals and objectives, product performance, and customer and producer feedback to ensure that the modified product is appropriately designed.

Product Withdrawal. A company that can't effectively or efficiently modify a poorly performing product may withdraw the product from the market. In general, withdrawal means no longer soliciting new product sales. However, existing insurance contracts often remain in force and must continue to be serviced, in some cases for decades after the product is withdrawn.

Decisions to discontinue a product can be difficult. A company's managers may view discontinuing the product as a sign of personal or organizational failure. Producers may lose a source of sales, and existing customers may lose a product they need. Withdrawing an unprofitable product at the wrong time or without offering an acceptable replacement can hurt sales of other products, give competitors too much of an advantage, or even damage a company's reputation. To prevent these adverse effects, a company may introduce a replacement product with higher projected profitability when the original product is withdrawn.

Some companies only withdraw a product after extensive unsuccessful efforts to modify the product or after the product has become a major financial burden. Instead, companies should review their product portfolio periodically, analyzing each product's historic sales and profits and projecting future sales, costs, and profits for the product or any potential modifications of the product. Those products that are not likely to be sufficiently profitable in the future typically are withdrawn.

Key Terms

generic characteristics
good
service
idea
intangibility
perishability
heterogeneity
convenience product
shopping product
homogeneous shopping product
heterogeneous shopping product
commoditization
commodity
specialty product
unsought product
product mix
product class
product line
product form
product item
width of a product mix
depth of a product mix
consistency of a product mix

product life cycle (PLC)
packaging
branding
brand
brand name
brand mark
brand image
trademark
service mark
brand awareness
brand preference
brand insistence
manufacturer brand
family brand
individual brand
distributor brand
positioning
unique selling proposition (USP)
product development
product imitation strategy
product improvement strategy
product innovation strategy
idea generation

screening

product concept

concept testing

field advisory council

comprehensive business analysis

market analysis

product design objectives

feasibility study

implementation

policy filing

prior approval requirement

file and use requirement

readability requirement

Interstate Insurance Product

   Regulation Commission (IIPRC)

Endnotes

1. Valarie A. Zeithaml, A. Parasuraman, and Leonard L. Berry, "Problems and Strategies in Services Marketing," *Journal of Marketing* (Spring 1985): 33–46.

2. This and other definitions in this section are adapted from Committee on Definitions of the American Marketing Association, *Marketing Definitions: A Glossary of Marketing Terms* (Chicago: American Marketing Association, 1960).

3. 12 Manage, "Explanation of Extended Marketing Mix (7-Ps) of Booms and Bitner," http://www.12manage.com/methods_booms_bitner_7Ps.html (11 June 2009).

4. Abbie Griffin, *PDMA Research on New Product Development Practices: Updating Trends and Benchmarking Best Practices* (Chicago: Product Development and Management Association and Abbie Griffin, 1997), 28–29.

5. Portions of this section are drawn from Nancy Muise, *Individual Life Product Development Process: The Need for Speed* (Windsor, CT: LIMRA International, 2007), http://www.limra.com/members/abstracts/reports/5870.pdf (12 June 2009). Used with permission.

6. William M. Pride and O. C. Ferrell, *Marketing Concepts and Strategies*, 10th Ed. (Boston: Houghton Mifflin, 1997), 231.

7. Portions of this section are drawn from Francois Genest, "Product Myopia," *Journal of the American Society of CLU* (July 1986): 67–68.

8. Muise, 23.

9. Genest, 68.

Pricing Insurance Products: A Marketing Perspective

Objectives:

After studying this chapter, you should be able to

- Explain how pricing affects product marketing, and describe three primary pricing objectives
- Describe how various factors such as costs, customers, demand, competition, regulatory requirements, and other marketing mix variables affect product pricing
- Explain the major differences between pricing insurance products and other products, and describe three different types of pricing strategies
- Explain specialized rate structures that relate to insurance pricing
- Identify the factors that insurers assess to evaluate their pricing decisions
- Explain the challenges of pricing product lines and product portfolios

Outline

Pricing Objectives
- Profit-Oriented Pricing Objectives
- Sales-Oriented Pricing Objectives
- Competition-Oriented Pricing Objectives

Primary Factors Affecting Pricing Decisions
- Cost
- Customers
- Demand
- Competition
- Regulatory Requirements
- Other Marketing Mix Variables

Pricing Strategies
- Cost-Driven Pricing Strategies
- Customer-Driven Pricing Strategies
- Competition-Driven Pricing Strategies

Rate Structures

Price Review

Product Line and Portfolio Pricing Considerations
- Pricing a Product Line
- Pricing a Product Portfolio

*P*ricing is the process a company uses to determine the amount to charge a customer for a product. In the insurance industry, pricing typically is called rate making, and prices are called premiums. To be successful, a company must set a price for its products so that the revenue the company earns will be greater than its total costs and the company will make a profit. An insurer's marketing department helps the actuarial department and other functional areas develop prices for insurance products.

Pricing Objectives

A *pricing objective* is a goal that a company wants to achieve when pricing a product. Companies must determine their pricing objectives before making other pricing decisions. Pricing objectives may be short-term or long-term and may vary from one product or product line to another. A company's pricing objectives should be stated in writing and specify the time period during which any pricing goals need to be achieved. Companies periodically review their progress toward meeting their pricing objectives within the appropriate time frame and then determine if any changes must be made.

A company's pricing objectives must be consistent with its overall corporate and marketing objectives. For example, if one of a company's overall objectives is to provide the best service in the industry, the company's product prices may have to be higher than those of competitors to cover its higher operating expenses.

Although pricing objectives vary widely, they can be grouped into three primary categories: profit-oriented, sales-oriented, and competition-oriented objectives.

Profit-Oriented Pricing Objectives

A *profit-oriented pricing objective* focuses on the absolute or relative return that a company wants a product to generate. Some companies establish the objective of profit maximization, or the largest profit possible. Although most businesses hope to maximize profits, as a practical matter, profit maximization can be very difficult for an insurance company to achieve. For example, an insurer might believe that its current customer service staff will be able to process the additional work volume resulting from the anticipated sales of a new product and set its prices accordingly. If, however, the insurer discovers it needs to increase its staff to process the additional work, then its actual costs will be higher and its actual profit lower than projected.

Profit maximization is even more difficult to achieve for companies that have a large number of products or product lines. Using the previous example, in projecting its customer service staffing costs, an insurer must consider the ability of its staff to process the total work volume resulting from all of its products, including any other new products being introduced as well as its existing products.

In addition, selling certain products for little profit may enable a company to sell other, related products at a higher profit. For example, to offer a comprehensive group health insurance package that is attractive to the customer, a company might include a group dental product that is marginally profitable along with the more profitable medical and disability products.

A *target return objective*, the most commonly used type of profit-oriented objective, typically sets a specific level of profit as an objective. Target return objectives can be established for an entire company, or for one or more product classes, product lines, or product items. For example, a company might set a target return objective of 10 percent profit on group health sales for the upcoming year and then establish a pricing structure designed to meet the target objective.

Sales-Oriented Pricing Objectives

A *sales-oriented pricing objective* focuses on a specific level of unit sales or dollar sales that the company wants a product to generate. A sales-oriented objective for a company might be to generate $40 million in premium through new sales of long-term care insurance in the upcoming year.

Increasing sales does not necessarily mean that a company is increasing its profits. If the increase in revenue is accompanied by an even greater increase in total cost, profits could decrease. Under some circumstances, though, a company is willing to forego immediate profits to achieve other objectives. By increasing sales in a particular market, a company may hope to enhance its status in that market and improve its appeal to customers, which will eventually lead to increased profits.

Competition-Oriented Pricing Objectives

Generally, a *competition-oriented pricing objective* involves maintaining or increasing a particular level of market share. *Market share* is the ratio of a company's sales of a product within a specified market at a particular point in time to the total industry sales for that type of product in that same market. Market share can be measured either by the quantity of a product sold, such as the total amount of coverage an insurer sells, or by the dollar value of a product's sales, such as an insurer's premium income. Increasing market share may not

184 | Chapter 7: Pricing Insurance Products: A Marketing Perspective

always result in an increase in overall sales volume for a product if industry sales as a whole are declining.

To achieve market share objectives, companies usually must base their own pricing decisions on competitors' and potential competitors' pricing. A company that already has a high market share might attempt to discourage competition. Such a company prices its products at levels low enough to make a profit but, at the same time, make it difficult for potential competitors with higher start-up costs to do the same. As a result, the company discourages potential new competitors from entering the market.

Companies that hope to establish a reputation quickly and gain market share in a competitive market might decide to beat the competition. These companies price their products lower than those of their competitors and focus their promotion efforts on highlighting their low prices. Companies that follow a policy of price competition must be willing and able to change their products' prices frequently to respond to competitive developments and typically must sell large volumes to meet profit goals.

Using price to beat the competition has major flaws. Competitive price advantages are often short-lived because most competitors in many industries can change their prices just as quickly as the company that initially set the lowest prices. Such pricing may actually encourage customers to postpone making purchases if they believe prices will continue to drop.

Insurers face additional problems if they attempt to use price to beat the competition. Prices of many products such as gasoline fluctuate regularly from week to week as companies react to their competitors' pricing decisions. However, state anti-discrimination laws require that all insureds in a particular risk category be charged the same rate for the same coverage. As a result, during product design, an insurer might examine the price of similar competing products and set its own price accordingly, but once the insurer establishes a price for the product, it cannot subsequently raise or lower that price merely to respond to competitive pressures. In addition, pricing insurance products too low can prevent a company from recovering its costs and result in significant financial losses. Because some insurance products remain in effect for many years, these losses can continue for decades.

Many companies, including insurers, set their prices at the general level their competitors establish, known as **status quo pricing** or *meeting the competition*, which then allows companies to compete on a nonprice basis. **Nonprice competition** exists when companies attempt to gain customers by using marketing mix factors other than price. An insurance company might choose to compete by promoting a product's distinctive benefits or features, the quality of its customer service and distribution systems, or some other nonprice factor that distinguishes that product from similar ones offered by competitors. A major advantage of nonprice competition is that customer loyalty usually is stronger when it is based on factors other than a product's price. When low price is the primary reason that customers buy a product, competitors often can lure customers away with similar, lower-priced products of their own.

Primary Factors Affecting Pricing Decisions

From a marketing perspective, companies must consider the following factors in making pricing decisions:

- Cost

- Customers

- Demand

- Competition

- Regulatory requirements

- Other marketing mix variables

Cost

Cost is a major factor that influences the pricing of products. A product's cost sets the lower limit for the product's price because no company can sell its products below cost for very long and expect to survive. Determining the cost of many products is relatively straightforward. If a company sells a car, most of the costs, such as labor, materials, advertising, and overhead, are already known or can be easily calculated.

Determining the cost and potential profitability of insurance products is much more complicated. For an insurance product to be profitable, the premiums the insurer receives plus the investment earnings the company makes by investing the premiums must be more than the payments it makes to policyowners and beneficiaries (policy claims, cash value disbursements, loans, dividends, and so on) plus operating costs (product development, distribution, administration and overhead, taxes, reinsurance, and so on).

Some of the revenue earned from and costs associated with a block of insurance policies may not occur for decades. The insurer's actuarial department must estimate these earnings and costs by relying on assumptions about several complex economic and actuarial factors, including mortality and morbidity rates, lapse rates, inflation, and interest rates. These assumptions may extend years into the future, and the estimated costs and earnings may differ significantly from what actually occurs. The actuarial department generally seeks input from all functional areas of the company that have relevant input—marketing, sales, investment, underwriting, claims, legal, and accounting—in making its assumptions. Too conservative an estimate of future costs and earnings may result in a premium that is too high to be competitive. Too optimistic an estimate of costs and earnings may lead to premiums that are too low for a company to make a profit.

Also, insurers must allocate their costs properly to specific products. To help make decisions about the proper allocation of costs easier, businesses typically classify costs as either direct or indirect and as either fixed or variable.

The costs associated with a company's products are classified as direct or indirect depending on their traceability to a particular product. A *direct cost* is any cost that is specifically traceable to or caused by a particular product. The cost of processing a death claim is a direct cost for that particular life insurance product. An *indirect cost* is a cost that is not directly traceable to any single product. Indirect costs often stem from a company's general operations, which are not directly related to a particular product or business segment. The salary of an insurer's CEO is an indirect cost.

Some company expenses may have both direct and indirect components. For example, an insurer's advertising department may use its staff and facilities to create brochures promoting a particular annuity. The department also creates other advertisements that seek to build the company's overall image, which benefits all products. The costs associated with creating and producing the materials promoting the annuity would be considered a direct cost for the annuity, while the costs associated with creating and producing advertisements promoting the company's image are indirect costs.

A *fixed cost* is a cost that remains constant regardless of the amount or volume of a product sold over some determined time period. The rent that an insurer pays each month for its office space is a fixed cost because it does not depend on how many products the insurer sells that month. A *variable cost* is a cost that varies directly with changes in the amount or volume of a product sold. Commissions that a company pays to its producers are an example of a variable cost. Producers generally earn a commission for each insurance product they sell, so the more of a particular product an insurer sells in a particular time period, the more it pays in commissions. Producers' commissions usually represent the largest variable cost for an insurance product for companies that rely on personal selling.

Figure 7.1 lists some examples of comparisons of insurers' direct and indirect, and fixed and variable costs.

Figure 7.1. Insurance Company Costs

Direct Costs	Indirect Costs	Fixed Costs	Variable Costs
Underwriting costs	Rent	Product development costs	Policy issue
Policy issue costs	Property taxes	Rent	Premium collections
Producers' commissions	Human resources department costs	Property taxes	Premium taxes
Claims processing costs	Mailroom costs	Underwriting salaries	Producers' commissions
			Medical examination fees
Product manager's salary	Company executives' salaries	Utilities	Product manager's salary

Customers

The way a customer perceives the value and cost of a product helps determine the price that a company can charge for the product. Just as a company usually will not sell a product if the cost to the company is more than the price it plans to charge for the product, a customer usually will not purchase a product if the customer perceives that the cost exceeds the product's value. Generally, the higher the value a customer places on a product, the more the customer is willing to pay for that product. Companies that charge too little for their products actually may sacrifice profits unnecessarily.[1]

The value of a product to a customer usually is measured by the benefits the customer receives from that product. Often, this can be very difficult for companies to quantify. However, a company's marketing efforts can significantly influence a customer's perception of a product's value. The same product's value also may vary from one market segment to another or one situation to another. Individuals with families may place a higher value on life insurance than would single individuals. Similarly, individuals may place a higher value on life insurance following the unexpected death of a friend or relative.

For some customers, the value they place on a product may be determined by the prevailing market price or the absolute lowest price available for similar products. *Price consciousness* is a measure of the importance a specific customer attaches to price and also the customer's awareness of particular prices. Most customers are aware of the prices of gasoline, food, and automobile insurance, because they buy these products frequently. However, most customers do not purchase central heating systems or life insurance nearly as frequently and generally are not as aware of the price differences among these products.

Typically, a company will need to vary its pricing strategy depending on the general level of price consciousness in a particular market segment. For customers who are acutely price conscious, a company may have difficulty pricing its products at any level above the competition. However, in a target market in which customers are not particularly price conscious, such as vacationers considering travel insurance, a company may have more leeway to vary its pricing.

Customers who are making a purchase decision will compare the value of a product to its cost. Customers view cost from a different perspective than companies do. To the customer, a product's cost represents everything of value that the customer gives up in exchange for the product. This cost often exceeds the purchase price of the product itself. For example, for some people the cost of going to the movies may include the costs of hiring a babysitter, parking fees, and the gas used to travel to the theater.

For the customer, the cost can include non-monetary components as well. For many people, the cost of refreshments in the movie theater includes the time required to stand in line to make the purchase. Such a customer might purchase popcorn if there is no line at the refreshment stand, but, if there is a line, the customer might decide that the value of the popcorn is not worth the additional inconvenience of standing in line. For a customer considering the purchase of an insurance product, the non-monetary costs can include the time spent evaluating the product, including the time spent with the producer; the effort required to complete the application and supply any needed documentation; the inconvenience of a medical examination; and the perceived difficulty of filing a claim or otherwise obtaining service.

Companies that can reduce their customers' perception of the non-monetary components of a product's cost may be able to sell more of that product at a particular price as a result. In the popcorn example, the theater owner might be able to increase sales by having additional employees working at the refreshment stand at certain peak times to reduce customers' waiting time. Similarly, insurance companies may be able to increase sales by finding ways to reduce the customers' non-monetary costs whenever feasible, such as by enabling customers to complete applications, file claims, or obtain other services online.

When purchasing a product, customers also consider the opportunity cost. For example, a customer who goes to the movies can't attend a concert scheduled at the same time. If the customer is on a tight budget, he might also need to forego dining out before the show. The opportunity cost often is a major consideration for customers in deciding whether to purchase a particular insurance product or other type of financial product, because the money a customer spends on insurance or annuity premiums will be unavailable for other potential investments or for day-to-day expenses.

A customer's purchasing power often affects that customer's perception of the opportunity cost of a particular product. All customers have limited resources—income, credit, and wealth—available to purchase products. *Purchasing power*, also called *buying power*, is the measure of the customer's ability to buy goods and services. A customer's purchasing power is strongly affected by general conditions in the economy, such as rates of inflation, taxes, and unemployment. Each time a customer buys a product, she uses some of her purchasing power. Because every customer's purchasing power is limited, each customer must allocate that purchasing power among the products desired. If a customer purchases certain products, she may, as a result, be unable to purchase others.

Whenever customers make a purchase decision, they determine whether the value they receive from the purchase is worth the opportunity cost that results from being unable to purchase other products. In general, the greater the impact a purchase has on a particular customer's purchasing power, the more consideration the customer is likely to give to the opportunity cost involved in making the purchase. For example, most people would not spend much time considering any opportunity cost that might result from buying a candy bar from a vending machine, but they would carefully consider any financial sacrifices that might result before deciding to purchase a new home. For some customers with substantial purchasing power, the opportunity cost involved in purchasing an insurance policy would not be a major factor. Other customers with less purchasing power might carefully consider what items they would have to forego if they decided to make such a purchase.

Demand

Demand is an economic term for the number of units of a product that a company can sell under given conditions. A variety of factors can affect demand for a product, including general economic conditions, product availability, substitute products, factors in the marketing mix, and the value customers place on the product. Changes in any of these factors may cause increases or decreases in the demand for a product.

In economic theory, the ***law of demand*** states that, as a general rule, the demand for a product is inversely related to the product's price. In other words, as the price increases, demand decreases, and as the price decreases, demand increases. This relationship between price and demand can be illustrated graphically by the demand curve, as shown in Figure 7.2.

Although demand for nearly all products increases as the price decreases (and vice versa), the amount by which the demand increases varies widely from product to product. For some products, such as big-screen televisions, a change in price can result in a much larger change in demand. For other products, such as water, demand remains fairly constant even if the price changes by a considerable amount.

The ***price elasticity of demand*** measures the percentage change in the quantity demanded of a product relative to a percentage change in the product's price. In other words,

Price Elasticity = Percentage Change in Quantity Demanded
Percentage Change in Price

A product is said to have ***elastic demand*** if a change in the product's price results in a greater-than-proportional change in the quantity demanded for that product. Products with elastic demand (like big-screen televisions) have a price elasticity greater than one (>1) and are referred to as *price elastic*. A product is said to have ***inelastic demand*** if a change in the product's price results in a less-than-proportional change in the quantity demanded for the product. Products with

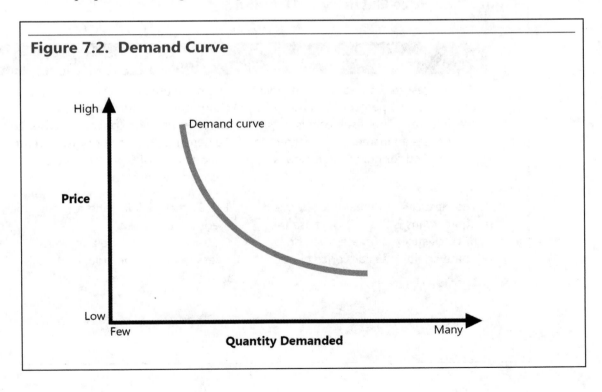

Figure 7.2. Demand Curve

inelastic demand (like water) have a price elasticity less than one (<1) and are referred to as *price inelastic*. A product whose price elasticity is exactly equal to one is referred to as *unit elastic*. Figure 7.3 illustrates the price elasticity of demand.

In general, demand for products that make up a small percentage of a customer's budget or are necessities—such as water—tends to be inelastic. On the other hand, demand for products that make up a large percentage of a customer's budget or are not necessities—such as big-screen televisions—tends to be elastic. Price elasticity normally applies to an entire product class. As a result, if an insurer's term life policy is price elastic, then, generally, all products in the life insurance class tend to be price elastic.

Because so many factors can affect the demand for a product, determining the price elasticity of demand for products is a difficult task. If companies are able to determine the price elasticity of their products, however, they can also determine whether offering lower prices is likely to result in a significant increase in sales. For example, people are not required by law to have long-term care (LTC) insurance on themselves, so it is not a necessity like auto insurance, which is required by law for all drivers in the United States. Further, the cost of LTC insurance premiums can be a very significant expense, especially for older individuals. This would suggest that the demand for LTC insurance is somewhat elastic, a finding which is supported by some recent studies.[2] Therefore, if the price of LTC insurance decreased, significantly more people would likely purchase it.

Figure 7.3. Price Elasticity of Demand

Elastic Demand	Inelastic Demand
The interest rate on home equity loans decreases by 4 percent from the previous rate. The result of this decrease is an increase of 8 percent in the demand for home equity loans.	The premium an insurance company charges for an individual medical expense insurance policy increases by 10 percent. The result of this increase is a decrease of 6 percent in the demand for coverage.
The elasticity of demand for home equity loans is 8/4 = 2. Because the price elasticity is greater than one, home equity loans are price elastic.	The elasticity of demand for individual medical policies is 6/10 = .6. Because the price elasticity is less than one, individual medical policies are price inelastic.

Competition

A company must consider its competitors when pricing its products. No company can offer the most competitive prices on every product in its portfolio, but competitive pricing can help make most products more appealing to target customers. Competitors' pricing strategies and their prices for similar products can strongly affect the latitude a company has in pricing its own products. When pricing a product, a company generally needs to consider the following factors regarding its competition:

- **Number of competitors and number of competing products.** In markets where competition is strong and products are easily substituted, price often becomes a way to establish a competitive advantage.

- **Level of costs for the company and its competitors.** Companies that have lower costs associated with a product may be able to obtain a competitive advantage by setting lower prices that competitors cannot meet profitably.

- **Expected reaction of each competitor to pricing decisions.** In some industries, competitors may respond to a company's price changes by making comparable price changes on their own products. Some insurers may introduce new products or withdraw other products in response to a competitor. Some insurers may modify their promotional efforts as a result of a competitor's pricing decisions, such as by increasing the emphasis on the company's superior customer service. Others may ignore competitive actions entirely.

- **Each competitor's overall strengths and weaknesses.** A competitor's business and product strengths and weaknesses may shape a company's pricing strategy. If the target market believes a competitor's products are of superior quality, a company might decide it needs to beat the competitor's prices, sometimes significantly, to gain a competitive advantage. On the other hand, a company may decide to set its prices above those of a competitor with an image of inferior quality.

Because insurance companies have less flexibility in changing established prices than do companies in many other industries, insurers must evaluate this type of information carefully to set proper price levels initially in relation to the competition's product prices.

Regulatory Requirements

Most jurisdictions in the United States do not directly regulate premium rates for life insurance. On the other hand, most states do require that insurers obtain approval of their premium rates for individual health insurance.

Although life insurance premium rates are not directly regulated, the requirements that insurers comply with all provisions of the state insurance code and regulations indirectly influence the premiums that insurers charge for their products. Insurers are legally required to maintain at all times certain minimum levels of surplus. An insurer's *surplus* is the amount of assets that the company has over and above its policy reserves and other obligations. *Policy reserves* are liability accounts that identify the amounts of money that the insurer estimates it needs to pay policy benefits as they come due. Regulators in the United States and Canada set the minimum amount of policy reserves that insurers must establish and levels of surplus they must maintain. Therefore, insurers must charge premiums high enough to generate sufficient revenue to enable them to maintain the assets needed to meet their legal surplus and reserve requirements. For that reason, these surplus and reserve requirements may effectively prevent insurers from using excessively low rates as a pricing strategy.

Other Marketing Mix Variables

Because a product's marketing mix variables are closely related, pricing affects and is affected by the other three elements of the mix. The type of promotional efforts, the form of distribution system, and the product itself—including its specific features, benefits, and level of service—affect a product's cost and, therefore, its price. For example, an insurance company must make it financially worthwhile for producers to sell its products, so the cost of commissions or other compensation must be included in the price structure.

The pricing of a product also influences the ways in which it is promoted and distributed. Advertisements for bargain-priced items often display the product's price prominently, while premium pricing is much less likely to be mentioned in advertisements. Companies also may need to use different distribution methods depending on a product's pricing. Products that have many options or complex pricing structures, such as many insurance products, may require intensive personal selling to explain the price, features, and benefits to the customer.

Pricing Strategies

A *pricing strategy* helps define the way a company establishes prices for its products. Pricing strategies fall into three broad categories:

- Cost-driven strategies
- Customer-driven strategies
- Competition-driven strategies

Cost-Driven Pricing Strategies

With a *cost-driven pricing strategy*, also called a *cost-plus strategy*, a company sets its prices to cover the costs incurred in creating, selling, and servicing a product and to allow for a predetermined level of profit. A cost-driven pricing strategy usually is the simplest strategy a company can adopt.

To set a cost-driven price for an insurance product, the insurer first must determine the total costs incurred by the company for the product. This includes all the direct costs as well as a portion of the company's overall indirect costs. Then, the company adds the target return, plus an additional margin to cover unexpected costs, and the result is the premium needed to meet the company's pricing objective. For example, if an insurer has a target return of 8 percent for one of its products, the company adds a margin of slightly over 8 percent to its costs to arrive at a premium that will cover costs and allow an 8 percent profit.

A cost-driven pricing strategy is most effective in markets in which the company using the strategy is the market leader or has significant brand or company loyalty. However, a strictly cost-driven strategy may be ineffective for companies in competitive market situations. For example, assume that the Starlight Insurance Company has designed a term life insurance product that has been priced to cover its costs and generate a 10 percent profit. However, the Benevolent Insurance Company offers a similar term life product at a lower price. If too many customers buy Benevolent's product instead of Starlight's because of the lower price, Starlight's strategy to cover costs and meet a target return objective will not be successful.

Customer-Driven Pricing Strategies

With a *customer-driven pricing strategy*, a company sets prices according to what customers are willing to pay for the value they receive. Because customer-driven pricing strategies focus on product value, they frequently are referred to as *value-based pricing strategies*. Selling products at auction is an example of a customer-driven pricing strategy. Each potential customer decides how much the product is worth to him, and the product is sold to the customer who places the highest value on it by bidding the most amount of money for it.

Insurance companies that use customer-driven pricing must determine what values customers place on different products and price their products accordingly. If the company charges more than the target market's perceived value of a product, the product is unlikely to sell.[3] Product value may not mean the same thing to every customer. For some customers, the value of an insurance product may be the presence of various guarantees or supplemental benefits; for others, the security provided by a financially strong company may be important.

Providing ongoing customer service and building relationships with customers also add value to a product. The more valuable the relationship with a company is to a customer, the more products that customer is likely to purchase and the more likely that customer will be to remain loyal over time. Companies in many industries use pricing to help build and maintain relationships with customers. For example, banks and other financial services companies may offer free checking or other discounts to preferred customers. Offering such discounts to repeat customers or those who purchase more than one product can be effective in keeping those customers and building loyalty. The practice of offering price reductions to customers who purchase multiple products from a company's product mix is referred to as *relationship pricing*.

Insurers are considerably more limited than other companies in the discounts they can offer to customers. However, relationship pricing is offered sometimes by multiple-line insurers that provide a variety of property and casualty products through affiliated companies in addition to life insurance products. These insurers might, for example, provide a discount on a package that includes automobile, homeowners, and term life insurance. Typically in such cases, the prices of the property and casualty insurance products are discounted rather than the price of the life insurance product.

Psychological pricing is a customer-driven pricing strategy based on the belief that customers find certain types of prices or price ranges more appealing than others. Some companies use *odd-even pricing*, which is the practice of ending the price at a combination of dollars and cents rather than at an even number of dollars. These companies believe that they will sell more of the product at $49.98 than at $50 because customers will think they are getting a bargain by paying "40-something" dollars rather than $50 for the product. Even pricing, on the other hand, may be used to project an enhanced image of quality for a product. For example, a restaurant that prices its steak dinners at $20 may be perceived as more upscale than one with similar meals priced at $19.95. *Prestige pricing* is a form of psychological pricing that involves setting intentionally high prices for a product to convey an image of high quality. Prestige pricing is often used for luxury items such as certain brands of automobiles, liquor, and perfume, and for professional service providers such as management consultants or financial advisors.

Psychological pricing strategies are most effective when customers are extremely price conscious or when customers' perceptions of a product's quality are strongly influenced by its price. Insurance companies use psychological pricing when quoting lower monthly premium rates for certain products, such as $100,000 of term life insurance for $40 a month, rather than an annual premium.

Promotional pricing is a customer-driven pricing strategy in which a company sets lower-than-normal prices on certain products in an attempt to stimulate sales of all of the company's products. The most frequently used type of promotional pricing involves price leaders. A *price leader* is a product whose price is set at an intentionally low level to attract customers who will purchase additional products at regular prices. Grocers often use price leaders by setting low prices on frequently purchased items such as milk or bread to attract customers into the store. To attract a customer base for future whole life product sales, some insurers use term insurance products as price leaders. When price leaders are priced below cost, they are known as *loss leaders*. Insurance companies do not use loss leaders, as a general rule, because the practice is actuarially unsound.

Competition-Driven Pricing Strategies

With a *competition-driven pricing strategy*, a company sets its prices relative to those charged by its competitors. For example, an insurance company that has a pricing objective of meeting the competition might set its premium rates at the average level of the rates that 10 of its closest competitors offer for a particular type of product. On the other hand, if a company has a pricing objective of beating the competition, it might set rates at a fixed amount less than those charged by the market leader. For example, if the market leader's rate for a term life policy for males of a particular age group is $5.00 per $1,000 of coverage, the competing company might decide to establish a rate that is $.20 per $1,000 lower than the market leader, resulting in a rate of $4.80 per $1,000 of coverage.

Competition-driven pricing strategies often take one of two forms: penetration pricing and flexible pricing. *Penetration pricing* is a competition-driven strategy in which a company charges a comparatively low price designed to build market share and to produce a large sales volume quickly. AOL (formerly America Online) adopted penetration pricing when it switched from an hourly fee for its

Internet subscription service to a flat monthly fee that was generally significantly lower than the fees charged by market leader CompuServe. AOL rapidly gained market share as a result and became the market leader. Later, AOL was able to increase its monthly fee gradually and still keep a substantial market share.

Flexible pricing, also called *variable pricing*, is a competition-driven pricing strategy in which the price a company charges for a product varies according to specific sales conditions. Most companies that sell group insurance products follow a flexible-price strategy by charging one price to an organization with a small number of employees and a lower price to an organization with a large number of employees.

Flexible pricing for group insurance products may take the form of competitive bidding or a negotiated contract. *Competitive bidding* is a process in which buyers ask potential suppliers to offer price quotations on a proposed contract. A *negotiated contract* is one in which the terms and prices of the contract are established through talks between the buyer and seller. The group insurance sales process often begins with competitive bidding and, as various contenders for the sale are rejected, ends with the customer entering into a negotiated contract with the successful bidder. Negotiated contracts generally are not available for individual insurance products.

Rate Structures

In addition to basic pricing strategies, insurance companies have developed some specific rate structures that can be used under certain conditions. These rate structures frequently take one of the following forms:

- *Preferred risk discounts* are reduced premium rates offered to individuals whose health and other lifestyle characteristics indicate that their mortality rate will be lower than average. For example, nonsmokers who participate in wellness programs may receive the preferred risk discount.

- *Quantity discounts* involve establishing premium rates graded by the size of the policy. Customers who purchase more insurance pay lower premium rates per unit of coverage. Insurers often use banding to establish quantity discounts. With *banding*, a company creates a number of contiguous bands based on the face amount of a policy and charges different premium rates for each band. For example, a company might charge one premium rate per $1,000 of coverage for term policies up to a face amount of $250,000, a lower premium rate per $1,000 of coverage for policies between $250,000 and $500,000, and a still lower premium rate per $1,000 of coverage for policies exceeding $500,000.

- Many insurers use the *policy fee system*, which charges a flat amount per policy to cover administrative expenses in addition to a specific rate per $1,000 of coverage. Using a policy fee system, a company might charge individuals of a certain age $5 per $1,000 of face amount plus a $40 policy fee for term life coverage. In this example, the premium for a $100,000 policy would be $540: $500 ($5 × 100) for the coverage plus the $40 policy fee. Insurers also use the policy fee system in conjunction with banded rates. The policy fee is intended to cover the fixed expense involved in administering any policy regardless of the premium amount.

■ *Gender-based pricing* involves charging different premium rates to males and females because of the difference between male and female mortality rates. Some insurers instead practice *unisex pricing* and charge the same premium rate to individuals in the same age and risk class regardless of their gender. Unisex pricing often results from regulatory restrictions that prohibit insurers from using gender-based pricing. Most insurance companies use unisex pricing for employer-sponsored pension plans and group life insurance plans.

■ *Market-by-market pricing*, also known as *market-specific pricing* or *channel-specific pricing*, occurs when a company charges different premium rates depending on the jurisdiction, geographical area, or target market in which a product is sold. For individual life insurance products, differences in rates for policies issued in different states usually reflect (1) differences in premium tax rates, (2) legislated product features that increase costs, or (3) higher reserve requirements. Market-by-market pricing is used frequently for health insurance products.

Price Review

Pricing is an ongoing process for insurance products. Companies must review their prices periodically to determine if the price they are charging for a product is too high or too low. Companies often use target return objectives to evaluate performance. To evaluate its pricing decisions, a company assesses (1) the price's impact on the company's financial performance, (2) the price's impact on the performance of producers and other distributors, (3) the reactions of both competitors and customers, and (4) how closely a product's actual experience matches the pricing assumptions made in setting the premium. Insurers monitor the following factors for each product:

■ The *investment margin*, which is the difference between the investment rate the insurer assumes when pricing the product and the investment rate the insurer actually earns

■ The *underwriting margin*, which is the difference between the benefit costs—such as the cost of death benefits or health benefits—that the insurer assumes in its pricing and the product's actual benefit costs

■ The *expense margin*, which is the difference between operating expenses assumed when the product was initially priced and the expenses actually experienced by the company

■ The difference between assumed lapse experience and actual lapse experience

■ The difference between the amount of taxes assumed in pricing and the actual taxes incurred

If actual performance deviates significantly from the expected results, then the insurer must determine the reasons for these deviations and, if possible, take corrective action. These corrective pricing actions can range from revising the product's dividend scale to revising the product's rate structure or using a different distribution system. In some cases, the company may even withdraw the product from the market.[4]

Product Line and Portfolio Pricing Considerations

Most companies market more than one product, and they usually do not determine pricing for any particular product on an isolated basis. Because costs, demand, customer perceptions, the level of competition, and other product factors are interrelated in a particular product line, a company often must consider its entire product line or product portfolio when pricing a product.

Pricing a Product Line

To price a product line, a company must rank each product item from the lowest-priced to the highest-priced and determine the price of each item in the line. The goal is to price all the products in a product line to cover the total cost and target return for the entire line. This includes covering the direct costs of every item in the product line plus a certain percentage of the company's indirect costs.

Because the lowest- and highest-priced items in a product line frame the entire range of prices in a line, they also help form a buyer's perception of the total product line. To maintain pricing consistency, the premium charged for each product should reflect the differences between the features and benefits offered by each item in a product line. For example, if a company introduces a disability income policy that pays benefits to age 65, the premiums charged for that policy should be lower than for a similar policy that provides benefits to age 70. Consistency is especially important when all the products in a product line are marketed to the same target market. The more price conscious customers are, the more important price consistency becomes.

If the cost difference between items in a product line is small, customers typically will buy the more expensive item, if they believe there is some value to the additional features it offers. For example, a waiver of premium for disability rider does not increase the cost of most life insurance policies covering younger insureds by a substantial percentage, so many such customers add that type of rider to their policies. On the other hand, if the price difference between items in a product line is substantial, customers are much less likely to purchase the more expensive product. The price difference between term and whole life insurance is substantial for many customers, and, as a result, they may be less likely to purchase whole life insurance than term insurance, even if they believe whole life insurance does provide significant added value.

In certain situations, companies may price some products in a product line low to meet competition. For example, most states require specified minimum levels of auto insurance coverage that all drivers must carry. To meet the competition, insurers often must set very low rates for policies offering merely the legally required coverages. If this approach is used, the company must price other products in the line higher to compensate for the lower profit margins earned on the low-priced products. Although higher prices may adversely affect these products' sales because of the effects of the price elasticity of demand, these higher prices may still increase a company's overall profit. As a result, for an auto insurer with low rates on basic coverage policies to meet costs for its entire product line and operate profitably, it must set appropriately higher premium rates for policies offering higher levels of coverage.

However, artificially pricing one product higher to compensate for lower profits on another product is a dangerous practice. The greater the cost difference between the products, the more difficult it will be to persuade customers that the higher priced product offers enough extra value to justify the added cost. In addition, unexpected conditions might cause serious revenue or cost problems in one or more products or in the entire line.

Pricing a Product Portfolio

A company also needs to ensure that the total rate structure for all its products is adequate. If a company chooses the risk and profit assumptions properly, all premiums for all products should be adequate. However, a decision to adjust one or more pricing factors may require that the company develop new prices for a number of products.

To establish or change prices for a portfolio, insurers often use mathematical models or simulations to forecast results based on a number of hypothetical situations. One such situation might consist of estimating a company's total forecasted sales for a particular product at various combinations of issue ages and face amounts so that the outcome will reflect the entire range of the product's sales. These models, which are referred to by a number of terms including model offices, pricing models, pro formas, or sensitivity analyses, can be created to generate forecasts for the entire company, for a particular branch office or other distribution channel, or for a particular product item or product line. The main use of such models is to determine the adequacy of the overall rate structure for a particular block or blocks of policies.

Key Terms

pricing
pricing objective
profit-oriented pricing objective
target return objective
sales-oriented pricing objective
competition-oriented pricing objective
market share
status-quo pricing
nonprice competition
direct cost
indirect cost
fixed cost
variable cost
price consciousness
purchasing power
demand
law of demand
price elasticity of demand
elastic demand
inelastic demand
surplus

policy reserves
pricing strategy
cost-driven pricing strategy
customer-driven pricing strategy
relationship pricing
psychological pricing
prestige pricing
promotional pricing
price leader
loss leader
competition-driven pricing strategy
penetration pricing
flexible pricing
competitive bidding
negotiated contract
preferred risk discount
quantity discount
banding
policy fee system
gender-based pricing
market-by-market pricing
investment margin
underwriting margin
expense margin

Endnotes

1.   Philip Kotler and Gary Armstrong, *Principles of Marketing*, 9th ed. (Upper Saddle River, NJ: Prentice-Hall, 2001), 380–381.

2.   Charles Courtemanche and Daifeng He, "Tax Incentives and the Decision to Purchase Long-Term Care Insurance" (Working Paper Series, Social Science Research Network, 31 October 2007), 19, http://www.ssrn.com/abstract=1012969 (12 June 2009).

3.   Kotler and Armstrong, 386–387.

4.   Frederick A. Randall, "Profit Margins: The Danger Zone," *Best's Review* (September 1987), 153.

Chapter 8

Distribution Systems and Strategies

Objectives:

After studying this chapter, you should be able to

- ◼ Distinguish among the three main categories of insurance distribution systems

- ◼ Describe the basic contents of an agency contract and an agency manager contract

- ◼ Explain the differences between affiliated agents and independent agents

- ◼ Describe the process under the Producer Licensing Model Act for licensing insurance producers

- ◼ Describe the purpose and characteristics of first-year commissions and renewal commissions

- ◼ Explain how insurers use financing plans, security benefits, bonuses, expense allowances, and support services in producer compensation schedules

- ◼ Identify the major components of agency manager compensation plans

- ◼ Explain the role of broker-dealers, banks, and other insurance companies in distributing insurance products

- ◼ Describe the role of the Securities and Exchange Commission (SEC) and the Financial Industry Regulatory Authority (FINRA) in regulating securities broker-dealers and their representatives

- ◼ Describe the three main direct response distribution channels used by insurers and explain how direct response distribution channels differ from other types of distribution channels

- ◼ Identify the factors a company considers when making decisions about which distribution systems and channels to use

- ◼ Describe three levels of distribution intensity and identify when each is used

- ◼ Distinguish between vertical and horizontal channel conflict and describe methods of managing channel conflict

Outline

Personal Selling Distribution Systems
- Sales Agents
- Financial Planners
- Licensing of Insurance Agents
- Compensation

Third-Party Distribution Systems
- Broker-Dealers
- Banks and Other Depository Institutions
- Other Insurance Companies

Direct Response Distribution Systems
- Direct Mail
- Telemarketing
- Internet

Distribution System Strategies
- Distribution Channel Characteristics
- Other Channel Selection Factors
- Distribution Intensity

Managing Distribution Channels
- Channel Conflict
- Managing Channel Conflict

After a company has developed and priced a product, it needs to decide how to sell the product to its customers. Insurers today use three primary types of systems to distribute products:

- ***Personal selling distribution systems***, in which commissioned or salaried sales representatives sell products through oral and written presentations made to prospective customers

- ***Third-party distribution systems***, in which financial institutions or other organizations distribute to their own customers insurance products issued by other companies

- ***Direct response distribution systems***, in which companies initiate or conduct the sales process by communicating directly with customers

Each of these broad distribution systems contains various distribution channels. A ***distribution channel*** consists of the specific people, institutions, or communication methods that are used to connect companies to their customers. Insurers frequently modify their distribution channels to meet changing customer demands. An insurance company's success often depends on how effectively it selects, manages, and integrates its distribution channels. Figure 8.1 shows the three main insurance distribution systems and various distribution channels within each system.

Personal Selling Distribution Systems

Until recently, personal selling distribution systems accounted for virtually all the individual life insurance sales and the vast majority of individual annuity sales in the United States. Personal selling remains the most widely used system for the distribution of insurance products. In 2006, about 90 percent of individual life insurance sales and nearly 60 percent of individual annuity sales in the United States, by premium volume, were made through personal selling distribution systems.[1]

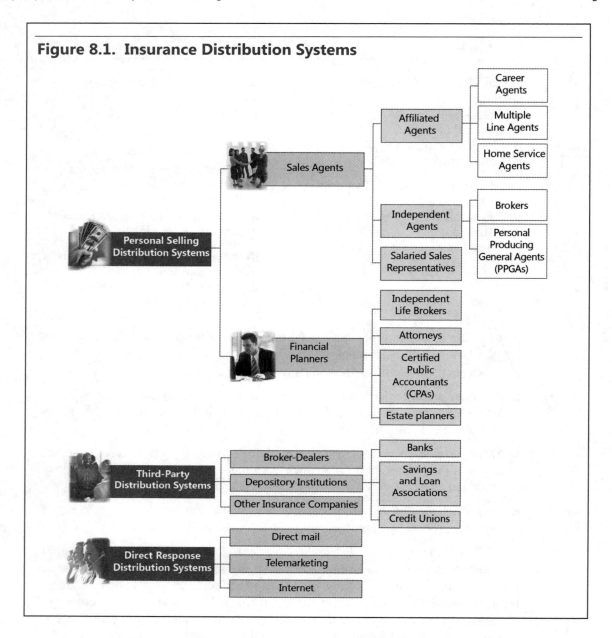

Figure 8.1. Insurance Distribution Systems

Personal selling distribution systems rely on sales representatives to identify and contact prospective customers, provide them with product information, and assist them in the purchase-decision process. Insurance companies use two basic channels in their personal selling distribution systems: sales agents, who account for most insurance sales, and financial planners.

Sales Agents

Although many insurers have expanded their distribution channels in recent years, most companies rely heavily on sales agents to distribute products to customers. In the insurance industry, an **_agent_** is an independent sales representative or company employee who is authorized under the terms of an agency contract to act on behalf of an issuing company, or **_principal_**, during interactions with customers. An *agency contract* is a written agreement between the agent and the principal that defines the agent's role and responsibilities and describes the agent's compensation. Although customers sometimes refer to the agent who sells and services their policies as "my agent," legally, an insurance agent is the representative of the insurer, not the customer.

The Agency Contract

Insurers typically enter into separate agency contracts either with each individual agent or with an agency manager, who, in turn, enters into agreements with individual agents. Most insurers who contract directly with agents use standard agency contracts drafted by the company's legal department in consultation with the marketing department. If the insurance agency enters into agreements with the agents, the agency develops the terms of the agreements. In some cases, a company or agency may develop a different, more personalized contract for a particular agent whose experience, expertise, or sales ability justifies such treatment.

The agency contract between an individual insurance agent and an insurance company or agency describes all aspects of the agreement between the parties. Although the exact terms of the agency contract vary from company to company, most contracts typically cover the following subjects:

- **Nature of the insurer/agent relationship**. Most insurance agents are independent contractors; however, some are company employees. The agency contract usually specifies whether the agent is an employee or an independent contractor. Unlike independent contractors, employees are subject to specific company direction in the performance of their work, such as requirements to spend certain amounts of time performing administrative work in the office. However, employees generally have more rights under various state and federal laws such as anti-discrimination or unemployment compensation laws than do independent contractors.

- **Authority of the agent to represent the insurer**. Most insurance companies authorize agents to solicit and accept applications, issue receipts, and collect initial premiums. However, agents generally are not authorized to bind the insurer to an insurance contract or collect renewal premiums. Many agency contracts also prohibit agents from changing premium rates, altering contracts, or incurring debts on the company's behalf.

- **Agent's duty to the insurer.** The agent owes certain duties to the insurer, including loyalty, acting in good faith, and adhering to company rules and governmental regulations. For example, producers have a duty to account for company funds, to adhere to timetables for remitting premium receipts or applications, to satisfy the company's reporting requirements, and to follow the company's operating policies.

- **Compensation**. Most companies compensate agents on a commission basis rather than by a salary. The agency contract usually contains a commission schedule and describes any other form of compensation the agent might receive, including reimbursement for expenses. Typically, an insurer that contracts directly with an agency pays commissions and other compensation to the agency, and the agency manager's contract with the producer determines what portion of the compensation the producer will receive. Most insurers reserve the right to revise the commission schedule or to reduce commission rates on policies that replace existing insurance coverage with the same insurer.

- **Production requirements**. Most agency contracts specify minimum production and persistency rates that agents must satisfy to remain associated with the company, or, in some cases, to receive benefits such as health insurance.

- **Termination.** An agency contract typically continues until terminated by either party to the contract or by specific circumstances. Most contracts specify the amount of notice the terminating party must give the other party. The contract also specifies the obligations of each party after termination, such as confidentiality and nondisclosure requirements and the agent's obligation to return company equipment and records, including customer files.

- **Termination for cause.** Most agency contracts list specific circumstances that allow the insurer to terminate the contract for cause. For example, an insurer usually may terminate a contract for cause if an agent violates specific terms of the agency contract or other company policies, has a license suspended or revoked, or is convicted of a crime. Under these circumstances the company may terminate the contract without advance notice and also may be relieved of various contractual obligations that would otherwise apply, such as the obligation to pay renewal commissions.

- **Errors and omissions insurance**. Insurance agents face a risk of customers suing them for various misrepresentations or mistakes, such as misrepresenting the potential return on a product or making mistakes in an application. Consequently, some agency contracts require agents to be protected by errors and omissions insurance coverage. ***Errors and omissions (E&O) insurance*** is insurance that protects an insurance producer against financial liability for any negligent acts or mistakes. E&O insurance will not cover a producer for intentional acts or wrongdoings.

The legal relationship between an insurer and an agency manager is far more complex than the one between the insurer and an individual agent. Agency managers, regardless of whether they are company employees or independent business people, do not merely represent the insurer by selling insurance products, but they also manage an ongoing business. In fact, due to their management responsibilities, many agency managers actually sell little or no insurance.

Insurers enter into a separate agency manager contract with each manager. This contract sets out the exact nature of the business and legal relationship between the parties. An agency manager and the insurance company often negotiate agency manager contracts individually. However, agency manager contracts generally cover certain standard subjects, which are described in Figure 8.2.

Figure 8.2. Standard Subject Matter of Agency Manager Contracts

■ Status as independent contractor or employee of the insurance company

■ Extent of authority to represent the company in specific marketing areas, appoint agents for the company, collect initial premiums from policyowners, and function as a sales agent

■ Responsibilities regarding agent supervision, agency planning, and cost control

■ Limitations on the manager's authority

■ Performance requirements such as increasing sales of the insurer's products, recruiting and developing career agents, and managing expenses for the insurer

■ Termination provisions, stating justifiable causes for termination and the length of time required for notice of termination by either the agency manager or the company

■ Compensation schedule outlining the rate of base salary, if any; commissions; overrides; bonuses; security benefits, if any; service fees; expense allowances; and other compensation

■ Whether the company pays agents' commissions and other compensation directly to the agency manager or to individual agents or second-line managers

■ Rights of the insurer to revise the compensation schedule

■ Vesting provisions, if any, on renewal and override commissions

Types of Agents

Depending on the terms of the agency contract, agents are usually divided into two main categories:

■ An *affiliated agent* is an agent who sells primarily the products of a single company. In general, insurers recruit and train affiliated agents and invest considerable time and money in establishing and maintaining agency offices. As a result, the insurer can exert a great deal of control over the activities of these agents.

■ An *independent agent* is an agent who does not have an exclusive contract with one company or obligations to sell one company's products exclusively and may submit insurance applications to any insurer with which the agent has an agreement. In general, insurers provide limited, if any, office support and do not train or finance independent agents, although they may provide training or promotional materials for specific products. Independent agents require a much smaller financial investment by insurers than do affiliated agents, but insurers have less control over the activities of these agents than they do over the activities of affiliated agents.

In the United States, the percentage of life insurance and annuity products that are sold through independent agents rather than through affiliated agents has increased steadily over the last few years. As recently as the early 1980s, affiliated agents generated approximately two-thirds of new individual life insurance premiums in the United States, but by 1997, premium sales by independent agents exceeded those of affiliated agents.[2]

Affiliated Agents. Most affiliated agents today are career agents. A *career agent*, also known as an *agency-building agent*, is under a full-time contract with one company and sells primarily that company's products. Previously, many career agents were referred to as *captive agents* or *exclusive agents* and were under contract with one company exclusively and not allowed to sell any products from other insurers. Now, however, many companies allow career agents to distribute the products of another insurer under certain circumstances.

For example, if an insurance applicant fails to meet an insurer's underwriting criteria, a career agent might be allowed to place this substandard business with another insurer. Similarly, an insurer that does not offer long-term care (LTC) insurance might allow a career agent to sell another company's LTC policy to an established customer in order to keep the customer from contacting another insurer's agent. An insurer's career agents are collectively known as its *field force*, and the offices in which career agents work are known as *field offices*.

Field offices traditionally have been divided into *branch offices*, headed by *branch managers* or *general managers*, and *general agencies*, headed by *general agents* (*GA*), although in recent years the distinctions between these types of offices have lessened. Branch offices are established and financed by the insurer itself, and the branch manager, supervisors, and support staff are employees of the insurer. General agencies are established and financed by the GA, who usually is an independent businessperson having an agency contract with the insurer. The GA is responsible for managing the office profitably, although the insurer may provide some assistance with expenses, depending on the terms of the agency contract. A general agency's support staff are employees of the agency, and the insurer's degree of control over the GA and any office activities is defined by the agency contract.

Branch managers and general agents are responsible for recruiting, training, and developing career agents and increasing sales of the insurer's products. The agents themselves are under contract to, and receive commissions from, the insurer and usually are considered to be independent contractors rather than employees.

A *multiple-line agent* is an agent who distributes life insurance, health insurance, annuities, and property/casualty insurance products for a group of financially interrelated or commonly managed insurance companies. Like career agents, multiple-line agents are considered independent contractors rather than employees of the insurer. However, multiple-line agents establish and maintain their own offices, known as *multiple-line agencies* (*MLA*) or *multiple-line exclusive agencies* (*MLEA*), and hire all necessary support staff, with little or no expense allowance from the insurer.

Multiple-line agents often have the ability to sell a larger number of products to customers than do career agents. Many customers prefer to use one agent to meet all their insurance needs, including life insurance and property/casualty insurance needs. Further, by learning more about a customer's needs from other transactions with the customer, an agent also has a greater opportunity to cross-sell products to that customer. For example, a customer who has recently purchased a homeowners policy for a new house may also be a good prospect for life insurance. The persistency rate for multiple-line agents often is higher than for career agents as well. The more products a customer purchases from an agent and the more satisfied the customer is with the services provided by the agent, the more likely the agent is to retain the customer.

A *home service agent*, also known as a *debit agent*, is a career agent who sells specified products, typically low-face-value whole life insurance with monthly premiums. Home service agents provide policyowner service in an assigned geographic territory and often are authorized to collect renewal premiums at customers' homes. Unlike most career agents, home service agents are considered employees of the insurer and are supervised by a district manager, who also is a company employee. Presently, only a few companies use home service agents to distribute their products.

Independent Agents. Traditionally, the primary type of independent agent has been the ***personal producing general agent (PPGA)***, a commissioned salesperson who is an independent contractor, is not housed in an insurer's field office, and engages primarily in personal production (sales of new policies). PPGAs typically are experienced salespeople who hold agency contracts with several insurance companies and who spend most of their time selling insurance rather than building and maintaining an agency. Because PPGAs often have minimal office expenses, some insurers use PPGAs as a less expensive alternative to general agencies in a particular geographic region.

PPGAs often place substantial amounts of business with only one or two insurers to maximize production bonuses and any support services they may receive. Insurers typically give PPGAs the option of recruiting and training full-time subagents, and PPGAs receive overriding commissions on products sold by their subagents. Some companies that use PPGAs set minimum production requirements that PPGAs must meet to maintain their contracts.

Since the 1980s, PPGAs have declined in number. Currently, most insurers who use independent agents market their products through a wider network of individuals known as brokers. Strictly speaking, a ***broker***, sometimes referred to as an *agent-broker*, is an agent who does not have an exclusive contract with any single insurer or specific obligations to sell a single insurer's products. Although brokers may have a primary insurer, they usually enter into separate agency contracts with each insurer with whom they place business. These contracts may be *single case agreements*, which cover only the one particular policy or contract that the agent is placing with the insurer, or they may give the agent the right to submit as much business to the insurer as the agent desires. Like PPGAs, brokers are responsible for their own office space and other expenses, but they rarely receive support services from any insurer. Brokers usually are experienced insurance salespersons who require little training other than on specific products.

As a result, insurers incur few, if any, costs in connection with brokers until commissions are due.

The primary difference between brokers and PPGAs usually is the compensation schedule. PPGAs receive a slightly higher commission scale and more incentive payments and support services than do brokers. In addition, PPGAs typically are permitted to use subagents, while brokers are not. PPGAs often submit substantially more business to an insurer over a considerable length of time than do brokers, who are subject to minimal, if any, production requirements. Insurers who use brokers as a distribution channel typically enter into contracts with considerably more agents in a particular geographic area than those who use PPGAs. In some cases, however, the difference between brokers and PPGAs is only a matter of the particular name or category the insurer assigns to the agent.

Some brokers and PPGAs join a **_producer group_**, which is an organization of independent insurance producers that negotiates compensation, product, and service agreements with insurance companies. An insurer may develop products to be sold exclusively by a particular producer group or may dedicate certain customer service staff to support the producer group exclusively. Producer groups generally focus on a specific segment of the insurance market, such as high-income individuals or small businesses.

Salaried Sales Representatives. In addition to commissioned agents, some companies use salaried sales representatives to distribute certain types of products. A **_salaried sales representative_**, also called a _salaried sales agent_, is a company employee who is paid a salary for making sales and providing sales support. Most insurers handle their group insurance and annuity sales through **_group representatives_**, who are salaried sales representatives specifically trained in the techniques of marketing and servicing group products. Group representatives promote their companies' group products to agents, benefits consultants, and organizational buyers of group products. They often assist agents in group sales by designing, negotiating, and helping to present group proposals. After completing a sale, group representatives usually assist at worksites by enrolling eligible employees in the plan and making regular service calls to answer employee questions and help keep eligible employees enrolled.

Financial Planners

Many individuals consult financial planners for assistance in making financial decisions for their future, which often include the purchase of various insurance products. A **_financial planner_** is a professional who analyzes a customer's personal financial circumstances and goals and prepares a plan, usually in writing, to meet the customer's financial goals, such as retirement planning or college savings. Many financial planners are professionals such as accountants, attorneys, estate planners, stock brokers, and tax consultants who also provide financial planning services to their customers. Financial planners often develop long-term, trusting relationships with their customers.

Some financial planners merely charge customers either an hourly or a flat fee for their services and do not sell products. Other planners also distribute insurance and other financial service products. Although most life insurance is still sold by sales agents, financial planners sold almost 20 percent of all individual annuities, by premium volume, in the United States in 2008.[3]

Professionals such as CPAs, attorneys, or insurance agents who serve as financial planners must comply with all the laws and ethical codes governing their profession. In addition, financial planners involved in product sales must adhere to all applicable governmental regulations regarding the type of product being sold. This includes licensing or registration requirements as well as regulations regarding advertising and customer privacy.

Some financial planners are insurance agents who enter into agency contracts with one or more insurers to distribute their products. Other financial planners serve as independent life brokers for their customers. An ***independent life broker***, also known as a *life broker*, is a salesperson who is licensed to sell insurance but is not under contract with any insurer. Unlike a broker, who represents a particular insurer in any given transaction with a customer, an independent life broker serves as the legal representative of the customer. Not all insurers and producers adhere to the same definitions, however, so some of them may refer to any independent producer simply as a "broker," regardless of the capacity in which the producer functions. Legally, however, it is the contractual relationship between the parties—not the title used by a particular insurer or producer—that determines whether the producer is a representative of the insurer or the customer.

Independent life brokers enter into sales agreements rather than agency contracts with insurers. The sales agreement specifies the conditions under which the independent life broker can submit applications to the insurer and the compensation to be received from the insurer. Independent life brokers earn commissions on sales, and these commissions usually are higher than commissions for affiliated agents. Some insurers provide independent life brokers with incentives such as bonuses or limited support services as well. Independent life brokers typically do not have minimum production requirements.

Licensing of Insurance Agents

In the United States, the individual states primarily are responsible for regulating the insurance industry. Because customers rely on the knowledge and integrity of their insurance agents, the states have imposed licensing requirements on agents and other sales representatives to ensure that they are individuals with a good history and background and are knowledgeable about the products they sell.

In most states, laws governing agent licensing are based on the ***Producer Licensing Model Act***, which is a model law that specifies the requirements an individual must meet to be licensed as an insurance producer. Under this Act, an insurance producer is defined as an individual who sells insurance products, solicits sales, or negotiates insurance contracts in any state. Producers must be licensed in each state in which they do business. States distinguish between ***resident producers***, who reside or maintain their principal place of business within the state and are issued a *resident license*, and ***nonresident producers***, who reside or maintain their principal place of business in another state and are issued a *nonresident license*.

To obtain a resident license, an individual must be at least 18 years of age, submit a written application using the state's approved form, complete any required insurance-related education, pass the applicable exams, and pay the applicable licensing fees. The application indicates the lines of insurance the applicant wishes to sell. In most states, a life insurance license covers the sale of annuities. However, various types of property and casualty insurance, health insurance, and variable products, including variable annuities, usually are considered separate lines of insurance and require separate applications. Some states also accept online applications for resident licenses, while nearly all states accept online applications for nonresident licenses.

Applicants must pass a written examination for each line of insurance for which they have applied. In many states, applicants must complete a specified amount of insurance-related education before taking the written examination. Many states waive examinations for applicants for nonresident licenses, as long as they have a resident license and have passed similar examinations in their home state.

Once an applicant submits an application to the state insurance department, the insurance department may conduct whatever investigation it deems necessary into the applicant's character, experience, background, and fitness for a license before acting on that application. In most cases, states issue licenses upon completion of the investigation. Occasionally, however, the insurance department may find that an applicant is not qualified to hold an insurance license. The Producer Licensing Model Act lists a number of acts an applicant may have committed that would authorize the insurance department to deny a license. Most of these acts involve either fraud or dishonesty in the license application process, misappropriation or conversion of funds, or fraudulent or dishonest behavior in conducting the business of insurance. Similarly, the state insurance department might discover that an applicant had been convicted of a felony or had a license revoked in another state. Under such circumstances, the insurance department typically will deny the license application.

In many states, a producer's license remains valid indefinitely, as long as required renewal fees are paid. Most states require producers to complete a specified number of hours of continuing insurance education courses annually to maintain their licenses.

Compensation

The compensation that insurers pay agents, other producers, and agency managers is the largest component of many companies' overall distribution costs and an integral part of their marketing strategy. For insurers using a career agency system, an insurer pays over 70 percent of its distribution expenditures to producers or managers in the form of compensation or benefits.[4]

Producer Compensation

Companies design compensation schedules for their producers to (1) attract and retain successful insurance producers and (2) help focus producers' attention on key company and marketing objectives. For example, if a company wants to emphasize the sale of well-written business, it may reward writing business that has a high persistency rate.

Compensation schedules on insurance products vary considerably from one company to another and from one product to another due to differences in product costs, competing products, sales goals, distribution systems, and other factors. For example, a company may decide to pay a higher commission on a particular new product to encourage producers to promote that product to customers. Similarly, independent agents have more options available when recommending insurance to their customers than do affiliated agents. As a result, an insurer may need to pay a higher commission to independent agents to persuade them to sell that insurer's products rather than those of competitors.

Typically, the general terms of a compensation schedule are described in the body of a producer's contract. The actual commission rates, bonus rates, and other specific terms usually are attached as addenda to a producer's contract so they can be amended more easily. Most sales compensation programs are based on a commission system, which provides greater incentive to producers than does a salary system.

In some cases, state insurance laws restrict the amount of compensation that insurers can pay to producers. The most notable example of such statutory limits is Section 4228 of the Insurance Code of the State of New York, which places significant limitations on how insurers compensate producers. For example, under Section 4228, the first-year commission paid to a producer generally must not exceed 55 percent of the policy's first-year premium. These limitations apply to all insurers doing business in New York, and to those insurers' life insurance and annuity operations in all other states as well as New York. Many life insurance companies that want to do business in New York but do not want their business in other states to be governed by these limitations establish a subsidiary company that is domiciled in New York and operates only in New York. In that case, only the subsidiary is required to comply with the requirements of Section 4228; the insurer's other operations are exempt.[5]

Commissions and Bonuses. Commissions are the largest single component of producers' compensation. Most commission schedules vary according to whether the commission is a first-year or a renewal commission. A *first-year commission* is a commission equal to a stated percentage of the amount of premium the insurer receives during the first policy year. A *renewal commission* is a commission on policies that remain in force that is equal to a stated percentage of each premium paid for a specified number of years after the first policy year. First-year commissions are designed to give a producer an incentive to make new sales. Renewal commissions, usually significantly lower than first-year commissions, are designed to encourage producers to sell quality business, reward loyalty to the company, and, especially, to promote persistency by encouraging the producer to provide ongoing service to policyowners.

Typically, first-year commission rates for life insurance products range from 40 to 90 percent of the first-year premium. For some products with variable premium payments, such as universal life and variable life policies, insurers may pay a lower commission rate on the amount of the premium payment that exceeds a particular figure known as the *target amount*. Some insurers also pay higher commissions for policies covering younger individuals than for those covering older individuals.

First-year commissions are frequently *annualized*, which means the insurance company calculates and pays the first-year commission due the producer in a lump sum, as if the entire year's premium had already been paid, regardless of the actual mode of payment applicant chooses.

> **Example:** If an insured purchases a policy with a first-year premium of $1,000, paid quarterly, and the producer's first-year commission rate is 50 percent, the producer ordinarily would receive $125 [($1,000 ÷ 4 = $250) x 0.5] each quarter upon payment of the quarterly premium. If the producer's commissions are annualized, the producer would receive the entire first-year commission of $500 upon receipt of the initial premium payment. If the policy lapses or is cancelled during the first policy year, the commission on any unpaid premium amount generally is charged back to the producer and deducted from the producer's commission account.

Renewal commission rates are usually between 2 and 5 percent of premiums received. Renewal commissions can be vested, nonvested, or conditionally vested.[6] A *vested commission* is one that is guaranteed payable to a producer whether or not she represents the company when the commission becomes due, even if she resigns or is terminated immediately after making the sale. A *nonvested commission* is one that is payable to a producer only if the producer still represents the company when the commission becomes due. A *conditionally vested commission* is one that becomes vested after the producer reaches a certain age or number of years of service with the company.

Few companies provide fully vested renewal commissions without restrictions. Some companies require producers to exceed certain minimum performance requirements to qualify for vesting or, alternatively, provide for more accelerated vesting for producers with high sales or persistency. Affiliated agent contracts often provide for vesting of certain renewal commissions in the event of the producer's death, disability, or retirement. From the producer's standpoint, vesting is important because it gives the producer equity in the business that he generates, provides additional protection for the producer's dependents in case of his death, and serves as a start of a retirement plan.

Some companies pay service fees, which are similar in some respects to renewal commissions. A *service fee* is a small percentage, such as 1 or 2 percent, of the premiums payable after the renewal commissions have ceased, usually for providing ongoing policyowner service. The company pays the service fee to the producer who services the policy, even if that producer did not sell the policy originally. Service fees help ensure that policyowners will receive proper service after the producer who sold the policy leaves the company.

Annuity commission schedules are somewhat different from those of most life insurance products. Many life insurance policies feature premiums that either remain the same or gradually increase while the policy remains in effect. Annuities, however, often feature large initial premiums with considerably smaller, if any, subsequent premiums.[7] As a result, annuity commission schedules generally do not distinguish between first-year and renewal commissions and instead offer a considerably lower commission rate—typically 4 to 7 percent of any premium. Many commission schedules also provide for chargebacks of part or all of the commission paid if an annuity is surrendered within the first year of issue.

Life insurance commissions typically are paid to producers according to a **deposit-based commission schedule** in which commission percentages are based only on new premium payments. As an alternative to deposit-based commissions, insurers sometimes pay annuity commissions on an **asset-based commission schedule**, also known as a *trail commission schedule*, in which commission percentages payable on sales are based on the accumulated value and growth of a product's funds. Under an asset-based commission schedule, commissions paid after the purchase of the annuity are known as *trail commissions*. Asset-based commission schedules are designed to improve persistency, conserve annuity assets, and persuade producers to provide better service to annuity contract holders.

Few insurers today pay annuity commissions exclusively according to an asset-based schedule. Instead, they provide for a combination of an up-front deposit-based commission and a trail commission. Under a combination of a deposit-based and an asset-based schedule, the insurer might pay a 2 percent up-front deposit-based commission on premium payments plus a 1 percent trail commission on the accumulated contract value, starting in the second contract year.

> **Example:** If a customer purchased a $100,000 deferred annuity that earned 5 percent interest in the first year, the producer would receive an up-front commission of $2,000 ($100,000 × .02), a trail commission in the second year of $1,050 ($105,000 × .01), and future trail commissions for subsequent years that would be calculated in the same manner.

Insurers pay trail commissions far more frequently on deferred annuities than on immediate annuities, because persistency is not an issue with immediate annuities, and there is little servicing of immediate annuities by producers. Trail commissions typically start during the second contract year, although, for contracts with three- or four-year surrender charge periods, trail commissions may begin after the surrender charge period expires. Up-front commissions are significantly lower on products that pay trail commissions, and, as a result, insurers often offer producers a choice between receiving either their entire commission up front or a lower up-front commission with one or more trail commission options. For annuities held for a number of years, producers usually receive a higher total commission under a schedule that includes trail commissions rather than under a schedule with up-front commissions alone.

In addition to commissions, many producers can receive bonuses for selling certain products or as a reward for exceptional performance. Most bonuses are structured to require both high production and good persistency rates. Most companies pay bonuses annually or quarterly and calculate them as a percentage of overall premiums or commissions earned. Bonuses also may be calculated based on the premiums of a particular product or product line. Persistency is included in bonus calculations by requiring certain persistency rates to qualify for a bonus, by paying a higher bonus to producers with higher persistency rates, or both.

Bonuses can also take the form of cash or merchandise awards for sales contest winners. In addition, companies frequently sponsor incentive conferences, which often are held in popular vacation destinations. These conferences reward producers who meet qualifying production requirements by providing them with an all-expenses-paid vacation as well as valuable education, training, and networking opportunities. Sales contests and conferences are an especially effective form of motivation for independent agents, who frequently are eligible for more than one contest or conference with different insurers. The choice of which incentive programs an independent agent actively pursues will influence which insurers' products the agent promotes more heavily.

Financing Plans. Retaining qualified producers is a major concern for many insurers. Insurers seldom recover the expense of recruiting and training career agents who leave the company after a short period of time. Many producers leave an insurer because they can't earn an adequate income during their first years with the company. To help producers through this difficult period, insurers generally assist them with financing plans which provide a cash flow while the producer develops customers and eventually transitions to being compensated by straight commissions.

There are three main elements of most financing plans, each of which can be used alone or in various combinations.[8]

■ An *advance* is a loan made to a producer in anticipation of future commission earnings. The company or agency deducts reimbursement for advances from the producer's commissions as they are earned. Advances are used primarily with experienced producers who have recently joined a company or an agency. Some companies do not require the producer to repay all or part of the loan if the producer exceeds certain production requirements.

■ A subsidy plan increases the amount of commissions a producer earns in a predetermined manner. A *fixed subsidy plan* is a financing plan that pays the producer a predetermined flat dollar amount in addition to commissions earned during a specified period. If a producer earns $500 in commissions in one month and the insurer provides a subsidy of $2,000 a month, the producer would receive total compensation of $2,500 for the month. A *variable subsidy plan* multiplies a producer's commission by a predetermined percentage to determine the producer's compensation. If a producer earns $1,500 in commissions one month and the insurer offers a 100 percent subsidy, the producer would receive an additional $1,500 subsidy, resulting in total compensation of $3,000 for that month. Most financing plans offered today are variable subsidy plans.[9]

■ A *salary plan* pays a producer a pre-established monetary amount for work performed during a specified period of time in lieu of part or all of the commissions actually earned during that period. An insurer might guarantee a new producer a monthly salary of $2,500, with the understanding that the company will retain the producer's earned commissions, up to $2,500. Commissions in excess of $2,500 would be payable to the producer.

In most cases financing is highest in a producer's first year and ceases entirely after three or four years. As part of the financing agreement, the insurance company can require producers who receive assistance to attend training classes and other business meetings or to make a certain number of documented sales calls. In most cases, producers must meet certain production requirements to continue qualifying for financing or to avoid termination of their contracts.

Security Benefits. Another major component of any compensation package is the availability of security benefits such as group life and health insurance, disability income insurance, savings plans, deferred compensation programs, and retirement plans. Many employees view these benefits, especially health insurance, as more important than a higher salary level.

Although many affiliated agents are independent contractors rather than employees, most insurers in the United States provide various security benefits to affiliated agents as part of their agent compensation programs. These benefits vary from company to company and are usually not the same as those received by an insurer's home office employees. Producers usually assume some or all of the cost of a particular benefit. In addition, most insurers have minimum production requirements that producers must maintain to be entitled to security benefits. Producers who fail to meet the production requirements for benefits may lose their eligibility for security benefits entirely, or they may have to pay all or a larger percentage of the benefit cost. Most independent agents receive security benefits, if any, through their agency rather than through an insurer, although some insurers offer deferred compensation plans to independent agents.

Other Benefits. Some companies provide affiliated agents with an ***expense allowance***, which is reimbursement for certain business expenses such as advertising and computer purchases. Some insurers also reimburse agents for the cost of Chartered Life Underwriter (CLU), Chartered Financial Consultant (ChFC), Certified Financial Planner (CFP), or Fellow, Life Management Institute (FLMI) courses or similar educational expenses. Expense allowances usually are subject to minimum production requirements and may be limited to a certain percentage of premium sales or commissions. Expense allowances usually are paid monthly.

Insurers also provide a wide variety of support services to producers, such as

- Administrative/clerical support

- Education and training, including holding seminars and classes that qualify for producer continuing education or other professional education credits and ongoing training on new and existing products

- Prospect/lead development and referral programs

- Toll-free telephone and computer lines to the home office from the producer's office

- Software programs to aid in prospect and customer contact management, product illustration, needs analysis, financial planning, and advanced underwriting

- Computer support training

A number of companies are adopting the concept of *segmented service*, which means the level of support services a producer receives varies according to the producer's productivity. Segmented service allows insurers to allocate limited support resources primarily to producers who can use them most effectively, and also serves as motivation for producers.

Agency Manager Compensation

Agency managers have a wide variety of responsibilities other than personally selling insurance. In fact, many agency managers do not sell any policies themselves. Insurers must structure their contracts with agency managers so that the manager's compensation fairly reflects his contribution to sales and profitability and is commensurate with what he might expect to receive in other industries. Managers' compensation schedules vary as a result of the insurer's overall marketing strategy and whether the manager is a company employee or an independent businessperson.

Some agency managers are insurance company employees, whose responsibility is managing the company's operations at the particular agency. In such cases, the company assumes direct responsibility for overhead expenses such as rent, advertising costs, and staff salaries, and the managers' compensation only reflects the value of their services to the company. Other agency managers are independent business people. To operate their agencies profitably, they must receive sufficient additional compensation to cover the agencies' operating expenses.

Salary. Some insurers pay managers who are company employees a base salary, which compensates the manager for performing job functions that do not fit well under an incentive compensation plan. In some cases, this salary is nominal, but, in other cases, the salary may represent a significant portion of the manager's income.

New managers and managers of newly established offices often receive a higher base salary than experienced managers receive. These managers undergo a transition period, during which the incentive-based components of the managers' compensation increase, sometimes gradually, while the base salary decreases. This transition period typically is longer for managers of newly opened agencies than for managers assigned to mature agencies.

Insurance companies rarely offer agents who own their own agencies a salary as part of their compensation schedule, but those who have just started an agency may receive a temporary salary or other financing arrangements from the insurer.

Commissions and Bonuses. Insurers generally pay their agency managers the usual producer's commissions on business personally sold by the managers.[10] Personal sales are a substantial part of overall agency sales for many managers who are independent businesspersons. Most companies, however, expect their managers who are company employees to devote more time to developing the agency than to personal production. At these agencies, the managers typically sell insurance products only when assisting new producers and, in such cases, may get a share of the new producer's commission.

The largest component of most agency managers' compensation consists of overriding commissions and bonuses. An *overriding commission*, also called an *override*, is a commission on the new and renewal business generated by a particular field office or group of agents. Usually, the higher a base salary the insurer pays the agency manager, the lower an override percentage the company will pay. First-year overrides, which encourage new sales, typically are expressed as a percentage of the total amount of first-year commissions or first-year premiums the agency generates. Renewal overrides may last for the duration of the contract or terminate after a few years, and they may also decrease over time.[11]

Bonuses are paid to agency managers to reward specific kinds of performance, based on factors such as agent productivity, new agent development (recruitment, training, and retention), agency persistency; and agency growth.[12] The portion of the manager's compensation based on each of these factors usually depends on the manager's control over and accountability for each factor and the emphasis that the insurer places on each factor. In newer agencies, for example, the company initially may place more emphasis on successful recruitment than on sales.

Security Benefits. Most companies offer their agency managers some form of security benefits in addition to their other forms of compensation. Managers who are company employees generally receive the same types of security benefits as other company employees, such as group life and health insurance, disability income insurance, savings plans, stock purchase plans, and retirement plans. Some companies also offer managers who own their agencies group life and health insurance and, in some cases, retirement benefits, and usually pay some or all of the cost of the benefits as well.

Expense Allowances. Traditionally, managers who owned their agencies paid all of their agencies' expenses from the total revenue they received from salary, personal commissions, overrides, service fees, and bonuses. The manager had to decide how to allocate that revenue between personal income and payment of expenses.

Now, however, most insurers pay some of those expenses themselves, either directly or, in some cases, by giving the manager a specific expense allowance. Insurers may decide to assume certain expenses such as rent, utilities, support staff salaries, computer equipment, and software because it is economically or administratively advantageous to do so, or to ensure that expenditures remain within company guidelines. In such cases, the company may reward or penalize the agency manager depending on whether the agency meets certain pre-established expense standards.

Second-Line Manager Compensation

Larger insurance agencies need a staff of second-line managers to perform basic agency management functions such as recruiting, training, and producer supervision, to allow the agency manager to devote more time to overall administration and business planning. In addition, second-line managers can obtain on-the-job training and experience that will enable them to be promoted to agency manager or home office management positions.[13]

Many agencies have **unit supervisors**, who are sales managers responsible for recruiting, training, and supervising some or all of the agency's producers. Some unit supervisors only supervise new agents, while others supervise and provide additional training for veteran agents as well. Other agencies rely on assistant or associate managers, who have more general management responsibilities instead of merely supervising a unit of agents.

These second-line managers may receive a base salary, but their compensation usually includes first-year overrides, new-agent development bonuses, agent retention bonuses, production bonuses, and security benefits. Second-line managers may receive renewal overrides as well. For some second-line managers, personal production also represents a significant portion of their compensation. Because the transition from a full-time sales position to a full-time management position often can disrupt a successful producer's income flow, many agencies provide financing plans for new second-line managers.

Group Representative Compensation

Group representatives usually receive a salary plus incentive compensation based on factors such as overall sales, group operations profitability, persistency, and in-force premium growth. Companies that pay a lower base salary offer the possibility of earning a larger bonus, while companies that pay a more substantial base salary offer smaller bonuses. Some companies, also pay group representatives a nominal override based on the commissions paid to the producers with whom the group representative has worked. Most companies pay group representatives' travel expenses, and some companies provide them with automobiles.

Third-Party Distribution Systems

An increasing number of insurers are contracting with third parties to distribute their insurance products. These third-party distributors usually are other financial institutions such as securities firms, banks, and other insurance companies, that distribute the insurer's products in addition to their own financial products.

Some insurers use wholesalers to help manage their third-party distribution systems. A *wholesaler* is a sales intermediary appointed by an insurer to promote the insurer's products to third-party distributors and support market development. An *intermediary* is a person or entity who sells and services financial products on behalf of a financial services company. Unlike agents, wholesalers typically do not sell an insurer's products directly to customers. Instead, they serve as a liaison between the insurer and the third-party distributors.

Wholesalers meet regularly with the third-party distributor's sales force to present product information, supply sales materials, provide sales training, and explain how to do business with the issuing company. In some cases, wholesalers also recruit agents on behalf of the issuing company. The insurer's marketing department helps the wholesaler answer questions from the distributor's sales personnel and provides product information. Wholesalers sometimes represent more than one insurance company.

Broker-Dealers

In the United States, variable life insurance and annuity products—in which value varies according to changes in market performance and the owner assumes some or all of the product's financial risk—are classified as securities as well as insurance. A *security* is a document or certificate representing either an ownership interest in a business or an obligation of indebtedness owed by a business, government, or agency. Stocks, bonds, and mutual funds are well known types of securities. Securities can only be distributed through broker-dealers registered with the *Securities and Exchange Commission (SEC)*, which is the federal agency that has oversight authority over the securities industry, including the governance of the sales of securities.

A *broker-dealer* is a type of financial institution that buys and sells securities either for itself or for its customers and provides information and advice to customers regarding the purchase and sale of securities. Strictly speaking, a *securities broker* is any entity engaged in the business of buying or selling securities for the account of another, and a *securities dealer* is an entity engaged in the business of buying or selling securities for its own account. However, because most brokers and dealers conduct business for both themselves and other clients, they are usually referred to as broker-dealers.

Most insurers who use an affiliated agency force to market their products distribute their variable products directly by establishing an *insurance company broker-dealer,* sometimes referred to as an *insurance brokerage,* which is a registered insurance company or a registered subsidiary of an insurance company that sells variable insurance products and securities and typically also provides specialized financial planning and investment services. Other insurers usually enter into distribution agreements with existing broker-dealer firms to market their variable products.

Broker-dealers distribute variable products at their retail branch offices through registered sales representatives. Broker-dealers distribute both *proprietary products*, which are products developed and managed by the company itself, and *nonproprietary products*, which are products developed by another company. Sales representatives who distribute variable life insurance and annuity products also must be licensed by the state as insurance producers and often sell fixed annuities and other insurance products in addition to variable life insurance and annuities.

In the United States, the SEC is responsible for regulating the activities of broker-dealers and the individuals who sell and distribute securities, including variable life insurance products and variable annuities. The SEC has delegated much of this authority to the *Financial Industry Regulatory Authority (FINRA),* which is a nongovernmental self-regulatory organization empowered by the SEC to license, investigate, and regulate securities dealers and their representatives.

To be allowed to distribute variable life insurance and annuity products or any other securities, broker-dealers must become members of FINRA in addition to registering with the SEC. The broker-dealer must submit extensive background information about the individuals who control its securities business and a detailed statement of its financial condition. An individual who is associated with a broker-dealer and engages in transactions involving variable life insurance, variable annuities, or any other securities must also register with FINRA. This requirement applies to officers, directors, salespersons, and managers, but not to a broker-dealer's clerical and ministerial personnel.

FINRA provides for two levels of registration: registered representative and registered principal. A *registered representative* is a business associate of a FINRA member who is engaged in the investment banking or securities business, including soliciting the sale of securities or training securities salespeople. A *registered principal* is any registered representative who is an owner, partner, officer, manager, or director of a FINRA member and is actively engaged in the management of the member's investment banking or securities business, including solicitation, conduct of business, or the supervision of registered representatives or other principals. Registered representatives and registered principals are referred to collectively as *registered persons*.

The broker-dealer is responsible for registering all representatives and principals with FINRA and for notifying FINRA of the termination of any registered person. Anyone applying for FINRA registration must complete an appropriate application, undergo a detailed background check, and pass a specified examination administered by FINRA. Registered principals must pass both a representative's and a separate principal's examination. There are several categories of registered representatives, each requiring a different examination, depending on the types of securities an individual intends to sell. There are also several categories of registered principals, depending on the type of business the individual manages or supervises. An insurance producer who sells variable life insurance or variable annuity products must be registered with FINRA as either a Limited Securities Representative—Investment Company and Variable Contracts Products (Series 6 Representative), a General Securities Representative (Series 7 Representative), or an appropriate Registered Principal.

In the United States, producers who are registered representatives also need errors and omissions coverage. However, because of the increased risk associated with selling equity-based products, coverage for registered representatives usually has a higher premium and deductible than does coverage for other producers.

Banks and Other Depository Institutions

In many parts of the world, banks are one of the primary distribution channels for insurance products. However, until recently, regulatory requirements in the United States prevented most affiliations between banks and insurance companies, which made it difficult for banks to distribute insurance products effectively. The ***Gramm-Leach-Bliley (GLB) Act*** of 1999, also known as the *Financial Services Modernization Act (FSMA)*, removed many of the regulatory barriers among various financial institutions such as banks, broker-dealers, and insurance companies. Banks and other depository institutions such as savings and loan associations and credit unions still are not authorized to issue insurance, but they may enter into agreements with insurers to distribute insurance products.[14] The distribution of insurance products to bank customers through a bank-affiliated insurer or insurance agency is referred to as ***bank insurance*** in the United States or as *bancassurance* in some other countries.

A *depository institution* is a financial institution that engages in the retail banking activities of accepting deposits from individuals and businesses and making loans. In many parts of the world, banks are the only type of depository institution available to most customers. In the United States, however, other depository institutions such as savings and loan associations and credit unions compete with banks in a number of areas. These other institutions also market insurance products to their customers in much the same manner as banks do. Some credit unions, in particular, have become very active in marketing insurance products to their members. Any reference to "banks" in this text in connection with marketing of insurance products generally applies to other depository institutions as well.

Banks in the United States primarily rely on financial consultants to sell life insurance and annuities. *Financial consultants* are full-time bank employees whose primary function is to sell various investments, including securities, annuities, and traditional bank products such as certificates of deposit. They are licensed to sell life insurance and annuities and are also registered representatives of broker-dealers. Financial consultants also may be called account executives, investment advisors, brokers, or similar titles. Because they have established relationships with their customers and are familiar with their customers' financial matters and other investments, they often are in a position to recommend life insurance and annuity products.

Banks often distribute insurance products through multiple channels, including the use of platform employees or direct response distribution channels such as direct mail or the Internet. A **platform employee** is a front-line bank employee whose primary function is to handle customer service issues and sell traditional bank products such as checking and savings accounts, but who is also licensed and trained to sell insurance. Platform employees usually sell simple life insurance products such as term life and refer more complex opportunities to financial consultants.

In the United States, banks have had far more success selling annuities than life insurance products. According to recent LIMRA studies, banks accounted for 16% of annuity sales by premium volume in the United States in 2007 but less than 2% of individual life insurance sales.[15] Financial consultants generally are able to present annuities to customers successfully as an investment option. However, more than 60% of customers in the United States are unaware that they can purchase life insurance through banks, although many customers in other parts of the world believe banks to be a trusted and reliable source for all types of financial products, including life insurance. [16]

Insurance companies typically pay banks commissions and other compensation for products sold, and the banks then decide how to compensate their employees for the sales. Some bank insurance producers receive a commission for insurance and annuity sales. Others receive a salary plus some type of incentive instead, because many banks do not want producers using aggressive sales tactics on customers.[17]

Only bank employees who are licensed producers may receive commissions for the sale of insurance. To motivate unlicensed bank employees to refer customers to licensed bank insurance producers, banks are allowed under U.S. federal laws and laws in most states to pay unlicensed bank employees a nominal fee for making such referrals as long as the fee is not based on whether the referral actually results in an insurance sale.

Other Insurance Companies

Although insurance companies focus on sales of proprietary insurance products, they also have become distribution channels for a wide range of nonproprietary products including disability income, individual health, and small-group health.[18] By distributing these nonproprietary products, insurance companies provide their sales force and their customers with a full range of financial products and increase both sales-force and customer satisfaction.

Insurers use three primary arrangements to distribute nonproprietary products:

■ A *home-office-to-home-office arrangement*, in which an insurance company enters into an agreement with another insurance company to distribute specific products or product lines issued by that company.

■ A *brokerage general agency arrangement*, in which an insurance company enters into an agreement for its affiliated agents to sell products offered through an independent general agent, known as a *brokerage general agent (BGA)*, who is under contract to a number of insurers. BGAs can provide a wider selection of products than can be provided under a home-office-to-home-office arrangement. Brokers also enter into agreements with BGAs, who provide administrative, marketing, and other support services in addition to offering an assortment of products from various insurers.

■ An *in-house brokerage agency arrangement*, in which a company establishes its own brokerage agency—rather than using an outside agency—to solicit distribution agreements with other insurers to sell those insurers' products.

Direct Response Distribution Systems

Direct response distribution systems connect insurance companies with their customers through direct communication channels, such as the mail, telephone, or Internet, instead of through sales representatives. Although pure direct response distribution systems do not involve any face-to-face contact between the customer and a sales representative, most insurance companies give customers access to customer service representatives or sales agents who can answer questions or assist customers in making purchases. Most insurers use direct response systems in conjunction with other distribution systems.

Direct Mail

Direct mail is a communication channel that uses a mail service to distribute sales materials directly to a mailing list of prospective customers in an identified target market. There are two main types of direct mail communications. An *invitation to contract* is a direct mail communication designed to solicit and close a sale. An *invitation to inquire* is a direct mail communication designed to generate interest in a product or service and provide prospective customers with a way, such as a toll-free telephone number or postcard, to request and receive additional information.

The package of sales materials that customers receive via direct mail is called a *mail kit*. Mail kits typically include an introductory letter and some promotional material such as an advertisement, product brochure, or information sheet. An invitation to contract usually contains, in addition, pricing information and a response device such as an insurance application with a business reply envelope.

Insurers draw names of prospective customers for direct mail campaigns from one of three types of mailing lists:

■ A *house list* is a company-owned list that includes names of people who have shown interest in the company's products or who have been referred by the company's current customers. A company's own house list is usually the most productive type of list for obtaining responses.

- A *response list* is a list obtained from another company that includes names of people who have purchased products from the other company through direct response marketing. Response lists usually are the second most productive types of lists.

- A *compiled list* is a list of names and addresses derived from sources such as directories, newspapers, trade show registrations, property tax rolls, voter lists, and other rosters. Companies often purchase compiled lists from third parties who perform the research from which the lists are derived. People on compiled lists generally have no particular direct response buying history.

Each mailing list has a certain profile based on the geographic, demographic, psychographic, or other characteristics of the people who are on the list. When choosing a list, companies attempt to match the list's profile to the target customer profile of the product being sold.

A customer who responds to an invitation to contract or an invitation to inquire generally receives a *fulfillment kit*, which is a package of materials designed to address or fulfill the customer's request. Customers who request information usually receive product information and an application for coverage in the fulfillment kit. Customers who respond to an invitation to contract may receive the policy, insurance service materials (such as claim forms and policy change forms), and billing for the first premium.

Telemarketing

Telemarketing is the use of the telephone to produce sales. Direct response distribution channels use two types of telemarketing:

- *Outbound telemarketing* occurs when a company representative or mechanized system telephones customers in the company's target markets with the intent to generate sales. Insurers use outbound telemarketing to initiate contacts with prospects, solicit sales after contact has been established, promote new or increased coverages to existing customers, and follow up on direct mail offers. In the United States, the use of outbound telemarketing has been limited by the establishment of national and regional "do not call" lists. Customers who do not want to receive sales solicitations over the telephone can have their phone numbers removed from calling lists used for marketing purposes.

- *Inbound telemarketing* occurs when a company provides customers with a toll-free number to use when inquiring about products or placing orders. In a direct response distribution system, inbound telemarketing is mainly used to handle customer responses to invitations to inquire. It also can be used in conjunction with print, broadcast, or Internet advertisements that encourage customers to call a toll-free number for information or a quote.

Internet

One of the most significant developments in marketing in the last decade has been the rapid growth of the Internet as a distribution channel for a wide variety of products. The United States Census Bureau reported that total online retail spending in the United States in 2006 exceeded $100 billion.[19] Electronic commerce has forged a path for companies to more easily and quickly perform business transactions, and deliver products and services to their customers.

The insurance industry also has turned to the Internet as a means of generating sales. Most insurers and many distributors have established Web sites that provide information about the various products and services they offer. These sites also allow customers to contact the company by telephone or e-mail to ask questions or to speak with a customer service representative or sales agent.

Insurers and distributors use a variety of techniques to generate leads via the Internet, most of which are designed to persuade customers either to visit a company's Web site or to e-mail the company for additional information. These techniques include

- **Targeted e-mail marketing**. E-mail is a very inexpensive and virtually instantaneous method of contacting large numbers of prospects. Insurers compile lists of current policyholders and prospects and send them messages designed to elicit a response. The most successful types of targeted e-mails are newsletters, either about the company itself or more general insurance or financial topics. The e-mail may contain the contents of the newsletter, or it may allow the recipient to access a portion of the company's Web site containing the newsletter content. Other targeted e-mails resemble direct mail invitations to inquire about specific policies or more general offers to save money on various types of insurance. Many companies use outside agencies to help develop e-mail campaigns.

- **Search engine marketing (SEM)**. Many people use online search engines such as Google and Yahoo! to help them find information about particular topics. *Search engine marketing (SEM)* is the practice of advertising and marketing Web sites by means of search engines. A *search engine* is a Web site that allows visitors to search for content on the Internet by inputting key words or topics and obtaining a numbered list of sites containing those words or pertaining to those topics. For example, a customer interested in finding information about life insurance might input a phrase such as "life insurance," "affordable life insurance," or "term insurance" and be provided with a list of sites including insurer Web pages, agency Web pages, and general business and financial sites that discuss insurance. The customer can click on any site on the list and be sent to that Web page.

Search engines use automated programs that periodically search the Internet and retrieve data from millions of Web pages, then rank each Web page they encounter for relevance for particular key words according to certain predetermined criteria. Sites that appear at the top of a search list have been determined by the search engine program to be the most relevant regarding those particular key words.

A search for a common phrase such as "life insurance" typically produces thousands—or even millions—of results from a search engine. Most people do not want to visit a large number of Web sites to obtain information on a topic, so they may only visit a few of the sites near the top of the results list. To increase traffic to their Web sites, many companies use a technique called search engine optimization. ***Search engine optimization (SEO)*** is a method of designing Web pages so that they meet search engine criteria for relevance for various common key words and phrases and thus rank as high as possible in search results for targeted key words. Some companies use their own information technology personnel for search engine optimization. Others use outside consultants.

Another common method of search engine marketing is the use of ***sponsored links***, by which a company pays a search engine a fee to be listed at the top of the search results page for certain keywords. For example, a search for "term insurance" might produce a results page containing a number of sponsored links to insurer and distributor Web sites. Most search engines highlight sponsored links in some way and clearly identify sponsored links as such so that search engine users understand that a company has paid for the Web site they are visiting to be listed on the results page and that it is not necessarily the most relevant site in regard to the key words.

- **Web advertising**. Many companies advertise their products and services on other Web sites using paid advertisements. For example, insurers and other financial service companies often advertise on the Web sites of various business or financial publications, much the same as they might run print advertisements in the publication itself. However, the Web advertisement allows the customer to click on the advertisement and automatically be directed to the insurer's Web site. Some Web sites charge for advertisements on a periodic basis, usually monthly. Other sites charge advertisers based on the number of visits to the advertiser's Web site that the ad generates.

- **Aggregators**. As an alternative or in addition to establishing their own Internet sales channels, some insurers and distributors use an ***aggregator***, a term used in the United States to describe an intermediary that lists products from several different companies on a single Web site. Some aggregators provide product and price information and then direct customers to individual company or distributor Web sites or contact numbers. Other aggregators allow customers to initiate the application process online with the insurer and pay the initial premium online by credit card or bank draft authorization. The aggregator typically receives a fee from an insurer in return for each submitted application or qualified lead.

Companies typically determine the success of these lead generation techniques by the ***click-through rate (CTR)***, which is a measurement of the number of people who visit the company's Web site directly by means of the particular lead generation technique. The CTR usually is expressed as the percentage of the total number of times that an advertisement, targeted e-mail, or other Web marketing material is seen that directly results in a visit to the advertiser's Web site. For example, if a Web page containing an advertisement is viewed 100,000 times and there are 5,000 visits to the advertiser's Web site as a result, then the advertisement has a 5 percent CTR (5,000 visits ÷ 100,000 viewings).

Many insurers only use the Internet to provide information to customers or to generate leads. However, a growing number of insurers also are using Web sites to complete sales. In some cases, the customer may initiate a sale by taking steps such as requesting a quote or completing an application. In other cases, the customer can complete the entire sales transaction online, including payment of the initial premium and receipt of issued policy documents. According to a recent LIMRA study, more than 70% of online consumers considered it likely that they would use the Internet in some capacity in connection with future life insurance or annuity purchases, and more than 30% said it was likely that they would actually apply or pay for insurance online.[20]

Distribution System Strategies

Companies face distribution system decisions throughout the marketing process. A company needs to make distribution system decisions when it develops a new product or product line or identifies a new target market for an existing product. In addition, changes in a company's marketing environment may lead the company to reconsider its distribution system decisions. A company's distribution system strategy will determine the number and types of distribution channels it uses in a particular market as well as how it manages any potential conflicts that may arise among the various channels.

Distribution Channel Characteristics

Few companies can use all of the distribution systems or all of the channel options that are available in any market. Each distribution channel has its own strengths and weaknesses, which insurers must consider in deciding which channels to use. The channel characteristics that have the greatest impact on an insurer's channel decisions fall into three categories: channel control, channel expertise, and channel cost. Figure 8.3 summarizes the differences among commonly used distribution channels in each of these categories.

Channel Control

Channel control refers to the amount of influence a company has over a particular channel's distribution activities, the types of products it emphasizes, and the information that customers receive. Insurers typically have the greatest level of control over affiliated agents and direct response distribution channels. Affiliated agents may be contractually obligated to sell the insurer's products and to act on the insurer's behalf in all customer interactions. In direct response channels, the insurer implements marketing activities directly and therefore has complete control over the products and messages that it delivers to customers.

Insurers have less control over other personal selling channels and third-party distribution channels. Independent agents and financial planners are not obligated to emphasize any one product or company over another or to offer the same products to all of their customers. Insurers who use third-party distributors have no influence over the types of products on which sales personnel focus their

Figure 8.3. Distribution Channel Control, Expertise, and Cost

Channel	Channel Control	Channel Expertise	Channel Cost
Affiliated Agents	High level of control over marketing activities	High level of sales expertise Significant cross-selling and up-selling opportunities High familiarity with single company's products	High cost Insurers provide commissions, other financial support, training, and administrative support
Independent Agents	Moderate control over marketing activities; level depends on specifics of contract or sales agreement	High level of sales expertise Cross-selling and up-selling not limited to products of a single company May have limited familiarity with particular company's products	Moderate cost Insurers provide compensation, but few support services
Financial Planners	Low level of control over marketing activities	Knowledgeable about customers and products May have limited sales experience Cross-selling and up-selling not limited to products of a single company	Low cost Insurers may provide commissions, but offer few, if any, support services
Third-Party Distribution Channels (banks, broker-dealers, other insurance companies)	Limited control over marketing activities	May have high level of product and sales expertise May have wide variety of competing financial products available for sale	Low cost Insurers compensate distributors but often offer few, if any, support services
Direct Response Channels (direct mail, telemarketing, Internet)	High level of control over marketing activities	Few, if any, cross-selling or up-selling opportunities Channel limits ability of insurer to convey product and company information to customers	Overall low cost; initial investment high, but quickly recovered Marketing costs low percentage of total product costs

marketing efforts and no direct control over the supervision, training, evaluation, or conduct of third-party sales staff.

A company can gain a greater degree of control over its distributors by providing for certain measures of control under the terms of its contractual agreement with the distributor. For example, an insurer might require in its contract with a distributor that the distributor's sales personnel attend periodic product training sessions conducted by the insurer. Such measures do not give the insurer as much control as it has over affiliated agents or direct response channels, but they may be relatively inexpensive and easy to implement.

Channel Expertise

When selecting a distribution channel, insurers must consider a channel's sales expertise and its knowledge about insurers and the products they offer. Affiliated agents and independent agents have a high degree of sales expertise and general knowledge of insurance products. They also recognize the importance of cross-selling and up-selling to increase their earnings. However, affiliated agents offer insurers a distinct advantage over independent agents because they are more familiar with their particular insurer's product portfolio. Independent agents may have only limited knowledge of a particular company and are under no obligation to sell its products.

Financial planners have extensive knowledge about their customers but may lack expertise about particular products or companies. Their primary concern usually is helping the customer achieve overall financial goals rather than selling any particular insurance or other financial service product. In some cases, financial planners also may lack extensive sales experience.

Third-party distributors vary widely in terms of sales experience, product knowledge, and company knowledge. Although third-party distributors generally encourage multiple sales as a way to ensure customer retention and asset growth, they usually offer a wide variety of financial products, and insurers have no control over which products they actively promote or eventually sell. Direct response channels offer little, if any, human interaction with customers, and the insurer often cannot effectively convey all the necessary information about its product portfolio to customers due to the limitations on the nature and amount of information that can be provided to the customer through the direct response channel. In addition, direct response channels offer very limited opportunities for cross-selling or up-selling.

Channel Cost

Some distribution channels are considerably more expensive for insurers to establish and maintain than others. Affiliated agent channels are the most expensive to develop and maintain. In addition to paying commissions to agents for sales, insurers usually are responsible, directly or indirectly, for recruiting and training agents, paying the salaries of field office staff, and covering the general overhead expenses of the field offices. Newer or smaller insurance companies may not have adequate financial resources or expertise to develop an affiliated agency force and, therefore, may need to use independent distributors such as independent agents, financial planners, or third-party distributors. Other insurers may use independent distributors to reduce costs or to avoid ongoing active management responsibilities.

Independent distributor channels usually require fewer resources than do affiliated agent channels. Although insurers pay commissions to independent agents and provide them with product training and some administrative support, they typically do not provide general sales training, education, or financing. Financial planners receive even fewer support services. Insurers that contract with third-party distributors compensate those distributors, who, in turn, train and compensate their sales representatives. The insurer typically provides no direct services to third-party sales representatives.

Direct response channels often require a substantial up-front investment to set up facilities and equipment, hire and train support staff, and develop sales materials. However, insurers usually can recover this investment fairly quickly. Because they reduce the company's reliance on salaried or commissioned sales representatives, the overall staffing and training costs of direct response channels generally are considerably lower than for other distribution channels. Over the long run, therefore, direct response channels have the lowest direct costs of all distribution channels used by insurers. The actual marketing expenses for a product distributed through direct distribution channels become a very small component of the product's costs.

Distribution channel decisions often involve long-term contractual commitments that are difficult and costly to change. Starting a new distribution channel can take several years and substantial resources. If a company believes its existing channels are not effective or sufficient for its needs, it may be quicker and more cost-effective for the company to modify an existing channel. For example, providing more extensive product training and a more lucrative commission schedule to an existing network of independent agents may improve product sales much more quickly than starting a network of affiliated agents.

Other Channel Selection Factors

In addition to the differences among the distribution channels themselves, companies must consider the following factors in determining which channels to use:

■ **Customers**. A company's choice of distribution channels is influenced by the background and needs of customers in the insurer's target markets. What are their demographic (particular age or economic group or general population) and geographic (local, regional, or national) characteristics? Do they prefer to purchase insurance products through sales representatives or directly from the insurer? Do they comparison shop or prefer buying from the same agent or company? How much help do they need to understand the product or complete the sale? How often do they shop for insurance? Do they buy all types of products or just those that meet specific needs such as retirement planning?

If most of a company's customers have the same needs, it may be able to establish a single distribution channel. If, however, there are significant numbers of different types of customers in a target market, the company may decide to use multiple distribution channels to satisfy various customer buying preferences.

■ **Products**. Some products lend themselves more to one type of channel than another. For example, complex insurance products such as universal life policies are difficult for many customers to understand. As a result, these products, are more likely to require personal selling through an agent or financial planner than are less complex products, such as term policies, which can be distributed through direct response systems.

■ **Company.** A company's mission, goals, objectives, company culture, and marketing philosophy influence its channel choices. In addition, to attract and retain distributors, a company must provide the compensation, technological support, customer service, product quality, and sales training they need. The type and amount of resources that a company is able to offer in each of these areas affects its channel choices.

For companies considering developing new distribution channels, the more similar a new channel is to one that a company already uses, the more its existing expertise can be carried over to the new channel. A company would probably have more difficulty adapting to a system or channel that is significantly different from its existing channels. For example, a company that has extensive expertise in direct mail marketing might find it easier to use the Internet to market its products than would a company that has relied exclusively on an agency force.

- **The Marketing Environment.** As economic conditions fluctuate, technology improves, competitive forces intensify, and social and legal conditions change, the relative benefits and drawbacks of various distribution channels change. For example, the passage of the GLB Act made it possible for insurers to enter into third-party distribution agreements with banks and other depository institutions. As a result, these institutions have become a significant source of sales for certain insurance products. Similarly, widespread public use and acceptance of the Internet as a source of information and a means of purchasing products has resulted in the creation of an entirely new insurance distribution channel within the last 15 years.

Distribution Intensity

An insurer must determine the level of *distribution intensity,* which is the number of distribution channels the insurer uses in a market. Distribution intensity determines the degree of market coverage a product receives. Ideally, an insurer uses as many channels as are necessary to make the company's products easily accessible to customers. If the insurer has too few distribution channels available, customers will be unable or unwilling to make the effort necessary to purchase the product. If the insurer has too many channels, it has wasted its resources by increasing its total cost of marketing without any increase in sales.[21]

Companies typically can choose from the following three levels of distribution intensity:

- *Intensive distribution* involves using as many distribution channels as possible to sell products within a given market. Although the use of intensive distribution is most common for manufactured products such as soft drinks and chewing gum, its use for insurance and other financial products is growing. An insurance company that sells its products through affiliated agents, independent agents, financial planners, banks, direct mail, and the Internet is using intensive distribution.

- *Selective distribution* involves the use of only a few distribution channels relative to the number of prospects within a given market. An insurer that uses only affiliated and independent agents to sell its life insurance products is using selective distribution.

- *Exclusive distribution* involves the use of one distribution channel to sell products within a given market. Exclusive distribution is used primarily for products that are purchased infrequently, used over a long period of time, and require specific sales or service expertise. Insurers often use exclusive distribution for their most complex products. For example, an insurer might enter into an exclusive distribution agreement with a particular agency for group health insurance products in a given market.

Managing Distribution Channels

Many insurers use multiple distribution channels to reach different target markets or to market different products in the same market. For example, a company might market universal and variable life insurance products through its agents and term insurance products through direct response. However, using too many or the wrong combination of channels can cause problems for an insurer. To make multiple channels work effectively, insurers must carefully manage their relationships with distributors and the relationships distributors have with one another.

Channel Conflict

One of the primary reasons for managing distribution channels is to deter channel conflict. ***Channel conflict*** is the friction or disagreement within or between channels that results when the goals and behavior of one channel or channel member are at odds with the goals and behavior of another channel or channel member. Channel conflict can occur between different channels, between an issuing company and a channel, or between members of a single channel. Channel conflict often occurs when channels or channel members do not have the same goals or they do not understand or accept their roles. Channel conflict can result in ***channel cannibalism***, which occurs when sales from a new distribution channel displace sales from an existing channel.

There are two types of channel conflict:

- ***Horizontal conflict*** is the friction between two or more channels or between two or more channel members at the same level in a single channel. Horizontal conflict can occur when there is ***dual distribution***, which is the use of multiple distribution channels to distribute the same product to the same target market. A company is practicing dual distribution if it sells immediate annuities to retirees through its affiliated agents, through third-party distributors such as banks, and through the Internet. Horizontal conflict stems primarily from competition between channel participants and the fear of channel cannibalism. Horizontal channel conflict can also result when there are different compensation structures for different channels.

- ***Vertical conflict*** is the friction between an issuing company and members of its distribution channels. Vertical conflict is the most frequent and usually the most severe form of channel conflict. It often arises when actions that may be good for an issuing company may not benefit a current distribution channel that faces increased competition as a result. For example, the increasing use of the Internet by insurers to generate sales may result in a conflict with agents who fear a substantial loss of income as a result.

Managing Channel Conflict

The most effective means for insurers to manage channel conflict usually is to avoid it. For example, an insurer might use different distribution channels to market to different market segments.[22] A company with an agency system might use its direct mail efforts to target customers who are not being actively targeted by its existing distributors—for example, by offering older customers low-premium or guaranteed-issue products. Similarly, a company might develop new products exclusively for new distribution channels, such as products to be sold exclusively over the Internet. The insurer might then assign customers who purchased the Internet-only products to its agents for service, which enables the agents to collect service fees and gives them the opportunity for future sales to those customers.

Increasingly, though, insurers are managing potential channel conflict by integrating multiple distribution channels. For example, insurers that sell products through banks often use company-affiliated wholesalers or salaried sales representatives to assist bank personnel in sales of traditional insurance products. For complex, broad-based financial needs, bank professionals generally manage sales transactions and the insurer's sales personnel manage customer relationships and provide administrative support. By using such an approach, credit for sales is shared by members of both channels.

Key Terms

personal selling distribution system
third-party distribution system
direct response distribution system
distribution channel
agent
principal
agency contract
errors and omissions (E&O)
   insurance
affiliated agent
independent agent
career agent
field force
field office
multiple-line agent
home service agent
personal producing general agent
   (PPGA)
broker
producer group
salaried sales representative
group representative
financial planner
independent life broker
Producer Licensing Model Act

resident producer
nonresident producer
first-year commission
renewal commission
annualized
vested commission
nonvested commission
conditionally vested commission
service fee
deposit-based commission schedule
asset-based commission schedule
advance
fixed subsidy plan
variable subsidy plan
salary plan
expense allowance
overriding commission
unit supervisor
wholesaler
intermediary
security
Securities and Exchange
   Commission (SEC)
broker-dealer
securities broker

securities dealer
insurance company broker-dealer
proprietary product
nonproprietary product
Financial Industry Regulatory
  Authority (FINRA)
registered representative
registered principal
Gramm-Leach-Bliley (GLB) Act
bank insurance
platform employee
home-office-to-home-office
  arrangement
brokerage general agency
  arrangement
brokerage general agent (BGA)
in-house brokerage agency
  arrangement
direct mail
invitation to contract
invitation to inquire
mail kit

house list
response list
compiled list
fulfillment kit
telemarketing
outbound telemarketing
inbound telemarketing
search engine marketing (SEM)
search engine
search engine optimization (SEO)
sponsored link
aggregator
click-through rate (CTR)
distribution intensity
intensive distribution
selective distribution
exclusive distribution
channel conflict
channel cannibalism
horizontal conflict
dual distribution
vertical conflict

Endnotes

1. Thomas Rosendale, *Individual Life and Annuity Distribution: Two Sectors Take Different Paths*, Special Report, 22 January 2007 (Oldwick, NJ: A.M. Best Company, 2007), 2-3, http://www.ambest.com.

2. LIMRA International, *Census of U.S. Life Insurance Sales Personnel* (Hartford, CT: LIMRA International, 1999), 2. Used with permission.

3. Dan Q. Beatrice, *U.S. Individual Annuities: Fourth Quarter 2008 Report,* Executive Summary (Windsor, CT: LIMRA International, 2009), 3, http://www.limra.com/members/abstracts/execsum/9082exec.pdf (15 June 2009). Used with permission.

4. Kathleen Krozel, *U.S. Agency-Building Distribution System Costs Study* (Windsor, CT: LIMRA International, 2007), 2, http://www.limra.com/members/abstracts/execsum/5693exec.pdf (15 June 2009). Used with permission.

5. Much of the information in this paragraph is from NY Code, Chapter 28, Section 4228, and James MacDonald, "Section 4228 of the New York State Insurance Law," *Marketing for Actuaries: Individual Life, Health, and Annuities*, 2000 ed. (Hartford, CT: LIMRA International, 2000), VIII-1–VIII-11. Used with permission.

6. This section is based in part on Paul D. Laporte, "Traditional Distribution Systems," *Marketing for Actuaries: Individual Life, Health, and Annuities*, 2000 ed. (Hartford, CT: LIMRA International, 2000), IV-6–IV-7. Used with permission.

7. This section is based in part on Daniel Landsberg and Joseph Montminy, *Compensation Practices for Deferred Variable Annuities* (Windsor, CT: LIMRA International, 2005), http://www.limra.com/members/abstracts/reports/5005.pdf (15 June 2009). Used with permission.

8. Laporte, IV-16-IV-17.

9. Margaret S. Honan and Lucian J. Lombardi, *Fundamentals of Developing New Agents* (Windsor, CT: LIMRA International 2005), 28, http://www.limra.com/members/abstracts/reports/4845.pdf (15 June 2009). Used with permission.

10. Laporte, IV-25-IV-26.

11. Ibid., IV-26.

12. Ibid., IV-28.

13. Much of the information in this section is from Kathleen Krozel, *U.S. Agency-Building Distribution System Costs Study*, Executive Summary (Windsor, CT: LIMRA International, 2007), http://www.limra.com/members/abstracts/execsum/5693exec.pdf (15 June 2009). Used with permission.

14. In general, laws prohibit banks from issuing insurance products. However, laws in Connecticut, Massachusetts, and New York have allowed mutual savings banks to issue life insurance policies on residents of those states for many years.

15. Dan Q. Beatrice, *U.S. Individual Annuities: Fourth Quarter 2007 Report: Industry Highlights*, Executive Summary. (Windsor, CT: LIMRA International, 2008), 3, http://www.limra.com/members/abstracts/execsum/5981exec.pdf (15 June 2009); Polly P. Eggers, *Banks Offer Life Insurance: Who Knew?* (Windsor, CT: LIMRA International, 2008), 11, http://www.limra.com/members/abstracts/reports/7007.pdf (15 June 2009). Used with permission.

16. Eggers, 7.

17. Paul D. Laporte, "Nontraditional and Emerging Distribution Systems," *Marketing for Actuaries: Individual Life, Health, and Annuities*, 2000 ed. (Hartford, CT: LIMRA International, 2000), V-7. Used with permission.

18. Ron Neyer, *Company Practices for Manufacturer/Distributor Arrangements*, MarketScan, (Hartford, CT: LIMRA International, 2001) http://www.limra.com/abstracts/3497.aspx (23 July 2001). Used with permission.

19. U. S. Bureau of the Census, "Table 1016. Online Retail Spending, 2001 to 2007, and Projections, 2008," *Statistical Abstract of the United States: 2009*, (Washington, DC: GPO, 2009), http://www.census.gov/compendia/statab/tables/09s1016.pdf (15 June 2009).

20. Mary M. Art, *Optimizing Opportunities with Online Customers: Consumer Internet Use for Insurance Information and Practice* (Windsor, CT: LIMRA International, 2007), 30; http://www.limra.com/members/abstracts/reports/5675.pdf (15 June 2009). Used with permission.

21. E. Jerome McCarthy and William D. Perreault, Jr., *Basic Marketing: A Managerial Approach,* 9th ed. (Homewood, IL: Richard D. Irwin, 1987), 286–287.

22. Mike Kryza, "Operating in a Multi-Distribution Channel Environment," presentation, Strategic Research Institute's Product Development & Multi-Channel Distribution Conference, Chicago, 19 July 2000.

<table>
<tr><td>

Chapter

9

</td><td>

Marketing Communications: Engaging the Customer

</td></tr>
</table>

Objectives:

After studying this chapter, you should be able to

- Describe the communication process
- Describe the purpose of integrated marketing communications (IMC) and the methods companies use to accomplish IMC
- Describe the four types of promotion tools companies use to convey messages to customers
- Identify three strategic objectives that promotions are designed to achieve
- Distinguish between push and pull promotion strategies and describe a combination promotion strategy
- Identify the major factors that affect a company's promotion mix choices and describe how each factor can affect the promotion mix decisions
- Describe four methods companies commonly use to establish promotion budgets

Outline

Coordinating Promotion Efforts

Promotion Tools
- Personal Selling
- Sales Promotion
- Advertising
- Publicity

Developing a Promotion Strategy
- Defining a Strategic Objective
- Selecting a Strategic Approach

Creating an Effective Promotion Mix
- Company Goals and Strategies
- Corporate Culture
- Distribution Channel Characteristics
- Target Market Characteristics
- Product Characteristics
- External Environment

Creating the Promotion Budget
- Percentage of Sales Method
- Competitive Parity Method
- All-You-Can-Afford Method
- Objective and Task Method

Promotion—the main link between a company and its customers—includes all the methods that companies use to influence customers to buy and distributors to sell products. It involves (1) informing customers about a product, its price, and how it can be purchased, (2) persuading customers to buy a product, and (3) reminding customers about the value they receive by doing business with a company.

Promotion could not occur without effective communication. **Communication** is the exchange of information with others. Although information exchanges can take many forms, all exchanges require the following four basic elements:

- A **sender**, which is the creator or source of a communication. The sender, or source, of a marketing message might be a company, marketing manager, producer, spokesperson, or some other conveyor of a message.

- A **message**, which is the information a sender wishes to deliver to an audience. Marketing messages can be advertisements, sales presentations, news releases, displays, ideas, proposals, posts to an Internet blog, or other concepts.

- A **communication channel**, which is the method by which a sender delivers its message to its intended audience. Communication channels for marketing messages might be insurance intermediaries, publications, broadcast media, direct mail, telemarketing, Internet Web sites, blogs, podcasts, conferences, events, or some methods of delivering messages.

- A **receiver**, who is the person or group for whom a message is intended. The receiver of a marketing message might be current or former customers, producers, business owners, corporate managers, broadcast audiences, consumer groups, investors, regulators, or society in general.

Communication begins when the sender translates ideas into words or symbols through a process known as **encoding** and then sends the message through a communication channel to the receiver. The receiver then decodes the message. **Decoding** is the process of translating the words and symbols in a message into meaningful ideas. If the receiver sends a response, or **feedback**, to the sender, the process reverses. Distractions or distortions of any sort that interfere with the steps of the communication process are called ***noise***. Figure 9.1 illustrates the communication process.

Companies consider with great care each part of this process when they develop and put into practice their promotions. They also watch carefully for noise or any other potential breakdowns in the communication process. This process may seem rather basic, but it is critical for the creation of successful messages. Think about the following example. An insurance marketing manager spends thousands of dollars working with an ad agency to design an advertising campaign for major regional newspapers. During the campaign, an advertisement for another company's product appears on the page facing the insurer's ad. The other advertisement is so compelling that it creates noise in the communication process and the insurance company's target audience never notices the intended advertisement.

Coordinating Promotion Efforts

To communicate effectively, a company must determine which promotion tools best suit the purpose of the communication, the company's products, and its intended receivers. Also, the company's promotion strategies should allow it to deliver the appropriate message in the proper form to the targeted audience using the appropriate channel for that audience. Because a company has an opportunity to leave a lasting impression about itself, its products, and services each time it communicates with its customers, a company's marketing communications must work together to present a consistent and cohesive message. A company that

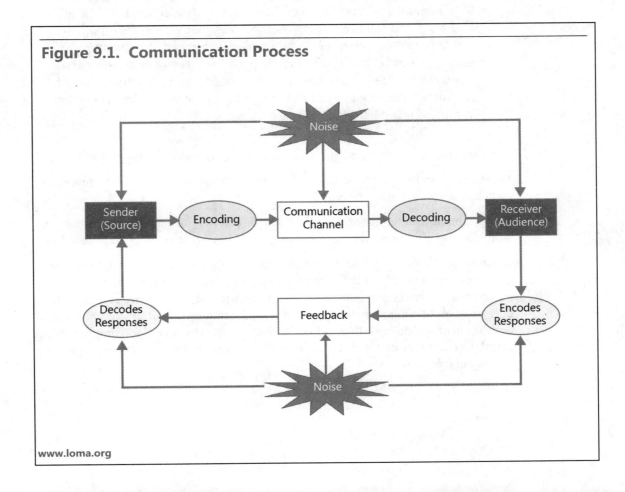

Figure 9.1. Communication Process

coordinates all its communications to deliver a clear, consistent message about the company and its products is using an approach called ***integrated marketing communications (IMC).***[1] The purpose of IMC is to provide a connection between each of a company's promotion campaigns and service interactions so that all messages a company sends support or build on previous messages and fit with the company's marketing mission and goals.

Although many companies are adopting an IMC approach, not all companies choose to follow or have the resources to implement this communication strategy. To implement a good IMC program, a company must often spend a large amount of time and resources to coordinate communications and responses. It is also not easy to effectively coordinate communications.

> **Example:** Suppose a company that traditionally has marketed only health insurance products decides to introduce and promote a deferred annuity. This expansion requires that the company change all of its communications and not just add the annuity message to its existing messages. Producers need to know that the company has decided to reposition itself as a financial services company rather than as only a health insurance provider. Customers need to know that buying health insurance and annuities from the same company makes sense; both products are a way of providing living benefits. To accomplish this task, producers will need to update their sales presentations and other materials they give to potential customers. The company's advertisements will have to reflect the company's expansion of its product line. Any news releases the company prepares will have to communicate that the company is a provider of both health insurance and deferred annuities. And, the method of delivering the message to intended customers may also need to change. For example, if the company has largely used the Internet and Web-based resources to reach its markets, it may need to use another type of communication channel to reach early-retirement adults who would be interested in a deferred annuity.

Companies can adopt an IMC approach in one of the following ways:

- Assign responsibility for developing promotions to a centralized marketing communications department

- Appoint a marketing communications director who ensures consistency by reviewing all promotion messages and campaigns that product areas develop

Either method will allow a company to provide its customers with one clear, consistent message about the company and its products. To ease the workload of its centralized marketing communications department, a company can provide to everyone involved an overview of its IMC strategy and the communication development guidelines that reflect the strategy. However, a company must maintain oversight of the IMC initiative to ensure that communications remain consistent over time.

Promotion Tools

Companies use four promotion tools to help them convey their messages to customers: personal selling, sales promotion, advertising, and publicity. Each promotion tool has strengths and weaknesses, and each is more suited to particular tasks than other tasks. Figure 9.2 summarizes these strengths and weaknesses.

Personal Selling

Personal selling is a promotion tool that relies on presenting information during face-to-face or telephone meetings between a company or its representative and one or more prospective customers. Many insurance companies use personal selling as one of their primary tools for promotion. Personal selling allows a company or its representatives to

- Communicate information about complex financial products

- Provide immediate responses to customer questions

- Tailor the sales presentation to the specific needs of potential customers

Cost is the major disadvantage of personal selling. A company spends more money to reach each potential customer using personal selling than using other tools such as advertising, sales promotion, or publicity.

Sales Promotion

Sales promotion includes incentive programs—usually monetary—designed to encourage distribution channel members to sell a product, or customers to purchase a product. Sales promotion aimed at distribution channel members is called *trade sales promotion*. Sales promotion aimed at consumers or organizational buyers is called *consumer sales promotion.* Although sales promotion can be an effective method of encouraging customers to try new products and remind them of existing products, insurance companies seldom use consumer sales promotion. Regulations in many states and jurisdictions limit or prohibit offering gifts or prizes because they might be considered an illegal inducement to buy a particular insurer's product unless they are offered to everyone. However, insurance companies do use trade sales promotion to encourage distribution channel members to increase their sales efforts. Most sales promotion efforts are short term and intended to spur sales during a defined period.

Advertising

Advertising is any paid form of nonpersonal communication or promotion about a company or its products or services that an identified sponsor generates and the media transmits. Media for advertising include television, radio, direct mail, the Internet, magazines, newspapers, and outdoor media such as billboards, signs, and posters.

Figure 9.2. Strengths and Weaknesses of Promotion Tools

Promotion Tool	Strengths	Weaknesses
Personal Selling	Interactive	High cost
	Messages can be tailored to specific buyer needs	Risk of losing account if salesperson leaves company
	Can deliver complex messages	Limited to one-to-one or one-to-few interactions
	Allows immediate response to customer objections/questions	Customers equate the sales agent's performance or behavior with the company. For example, an agent who leaves a negative impression will reflect poorly not only on the sales agent but also on the company the agent represents.
Sales Promotion	Effective in encouraging product trial and sales	Little impact on long-term sales or profitability
	Produces measurable short-term results	Tends to encourage product-oriented rather than needs-oriented marketing
Advertising	Economical for reaching large audiences	May not be effective in reaching narrowly targeted audiences
	Company maintains control over message	Cannot deliver complex messages
Publicity	Fast	Company has little control over exposure or message
	Economical	Company may experience negative publicity
	High credibility	

In general, advertising is more economical than personal selling because it reaches large numbers of potential customers. However, the costs associated with different media and the audiences they are designed to reach vary significantly. Companies should use only those media that will reach their target audience effectively and efficiently. Advertising that reaches audiences outside the target market typically is wasted; advertising that is too narrowly focused may not reach all of a company's potential customers.

Publicity

Publicity is any non-paid-for communication of information that is intended to bring a person, place, thing, or cause to the notice or attention of the public. Companies frequently provide information to the media—often in the form of news releases—but companies do not pay the media to present the information. The media decide if they wish to air the information and determine the amount of information to transmit about the company, including how they present the information.

Traditionally, news releases have been intended for print publications and contained words only. An expansion of the traditional news release is the multimedia news release. Multimedia news releases incorporate text with multiple media elements, such as digital video clips, high-resolution photographs, audio, graphics-enriched brochures, and Web page links, to deliver a message to the intended audience typically via a Web site or e-mail.[2] Marketers use multimedia news releases (MNRs) not only to provide information in a news format but also to capture the attention and interest of an intended audience. MNRs may include options for a customer or other audience member to sign up for a Web event, such as a podcast, watch product or service demonstrations, or click on links to complete transactions. The MNR provides a forum for the company to provide information to an audience and establishes ways for customers or other viewers to interact with the company and possibly establish a relationship.

Publicity is one of the most economical means of getting new product information to an audience largely because the company pays no direct costs for this form of promotion. In addition, audiences generally consider publicity to be more credible than paid advertisements because product information is presented in a news format. On the other hand, a company that wants to gain media exposure cannot guarantee that its efforts will result in any exposure at all. If the media do not consider the company's message newsworthy, then they will ignore it. An *exposure* is created when a news release, feature story, photograph, or other information is published or broadcast in the media during a given period of time. Also, the company has no control over the messages the media convey to the audience or the timing of those messages. For example, if a company releases information about an innovative new product on the same day that a national disaster strikes, the company's news is not likely to be publicized, because the media will report on the bigger news event. Also, because a company has little or no control over publicity, it sometimes results in the spread of misinformation or negative publicity. Negative publicity can occur at any time, and when it does, the company must take steps to recover its image.

Developing a Promotion Strategy

Promotion truly begins when a company develops its promotion strategy. A company can develop a strategy to support its overall corporate promotion efforts or a single promotion campaign. A *promotion campaign* is usually a short-term marketing program intended to achieve one primary goal. That goal might be to introduce a new product to the market, increase an existing product's market share, or establish or reinforce an image of the company itself. Although companies make a number of strategic decisions with respect to promotion, the three most important relate to the company's strategic objective, strategic approach, and promotion mix.

Defining a Strategic Objective

Customers need a reason to buy a specific product or service. The reason may be that

- The product includes more features, offers better benefits, or sells for a lower price than other products.

- The product or company has a strong brand image or reputation.

- The product satisfies a need that is not addressed by other products on the market.

Promotion supplies customers with reasons to buy products and services. Unfortunately, few promotions can present all of the reasons why consumers and organizational buyers should purchase a particular product from a particular company. As a result, companies design most promotions to achieve one of three strategic objectives: (1) to increase product sales, (2) to define a company's or product's position in the market, or (3) to create a strong image of a company or product.

Increasing Sales

One very common strategic objective for promotion is to increase sales. However, not all customers are ready to make a purchase. Some customers may not even know about a company or product and others may not recognize a need for that product for themselves. Promotion helps bridge these gaps. When exposed to promotions, customers typically move through a sequence of possible responses. This sequence of responses is referred to as a *response hierarchy*. One of the most commonly used hierarchies is the *AIDA model*, which defines four possible responses customers may display as a result of exposure to promotion: (1) attention, or awareness, (2) interest, (3) desire, and (4) action. Figure 9.3 shows which promotion tools most effectively generate the responses described by the AIDA model.

Because customers' responses to promotion are linked directly to their level of buyer readiness, a company must first identify the buyer-readiness stage of the target audience of the promotion. If customers are not yet aware of a product, promotion designed to stimulate demand would be ineffective. Similarly, a promotion that a company designs to stimulate awareness would be wasted on an audience ready to take action and buy the product.

Figure 9.3. Promotion Tools Most Effective for Each AIDA Response

AIDA Response	Most Effective Tools
Attention	Advertising, Publicity
Interest	Advertising, Publicity
Desire	Advertising, Personal selling
Action	Personal selling, Sales promotion

Positioning

Promotion allows a company to communicate a product's position—the distinct place a product has in customers' minds. Promotion also helps differentiate one company's or product's position from another. In markets, such as the market for term life insurance, where a large number of competitors offer similar, easily substituted products, differentiation is an extremely important activity. The key benefit—price, service, reputation, or some other distinguishing benefit—that a company promotes can give distributors a reason to sell the product or customers a reason to buy the product.

> **Example:** A life insurance provider markets its term life insurance product specifically to senior citizens. This insurer tries to differentiate its product from the competition based on the product's price, by emphasizing the product's reasonable premium rates.

Personal selling can aid a company's efforts to differentiate its products from competitors by having producers promote products' key benefits.

Image Building

An image consists of the beliefs or impressions that people hold about a particular company or product. Images can be based on what a company does or on what customers think the company values. For example, in recent years many companies have tried to demonstrate their environmental responsibility by publicizing their efforts to make their office buildings more energy efficient, reducing paper waste by encouraging customers to opt for online statements instead of paper, and other efforts. If a customer is aware of these initiatives he may form an opinion that the company values environmental responsibility, which may lead him to form a more favorable opinion of the company overall. The reverse is also true; a company that publicizes its environmental responsibility but that does not follow through in a consistent way with such efforts may be viewed as not valuing environmental responsibility, which may lead some consumers to develop an overall negative opinion of the company. Sometimes images reflect reality; sometimes they don't. In all cases, images influence the way consumers and organizational buyers respond to companies and products. Branding helps cultivate images in a customer's mind by associating a product or family of products with recognizable features such as names, symbols, or terms. Recall the slogans, "You're In Good Hands With Allstate®," and "Like a good neighbor, State Farm is there®." And, consider the solidity and stability represented in Prudential's brand symbol—the Rock of Gibraltar. Promotion plays a major role in maintaining a particular brand or image in the minds of customers.

Companies frequently design ***image-building promotion campaigns*** to shape customer beliefs about the company or its products. In general, image-building campaigns are part of a company's corporate promotion strategy and all of a company's promotion messages should reflect and build on that image. For example, if a company has built its reputation on its excellent financial stability, then its promotion campaigns can focus on that stability. Other aspects that insurance and financial services companies stress in image-building campaigns include reliability, good customer service, responsiveness to individual needs, and social responsibility.

Selecting a Strategic Approach

Promotion strategies can be divided into three basic categories: push strategies, pull strategies, and combination strategies.

Push Strategies

A *push strategy* is a promotion strategy designed to provide distributors with an incentive to sell a product, in effect, moving or "pushing" the product through the channel to customers. Companies that use personal selling distribution systems often use push strategies to keep their distributors motivated and interested in building sales. Figure 9.4 illustrates an advertising concept an insurance company might use as part of a push strategy directed to distributors. Companies also encourage sales by providing product information, sales aids, illustrations, and other sales support to intermediaries.

Push strategies also use sales promotion, such as contests and special incentives, to motivate distributors. An insurance company that uses a personal selling distribution system that includes brokers may reimburse those brokers for some advertising expenses related to a particular product promotion if the broker achieves a predetermined sales goal for that particular product. A company that uses personal selling distribution systems may also hold a sales contest to promote a new product and reward the top sales agents with trips.

If a company focuses its promotion solely on its distributors, it gives up its control over the messages that potential customers receive about the company. Companies can provide information to their distributors to pass on to the customer, but the way the distributor passes that information on can vary widely among distributors. For this reason, most insurers use both push and pull strategies to some degree.

Pull Strategies

A *pull strategy* is a promotion strategy designed to stimulate customer demand by giving customers an incentive to purchase a product, in effect "pulling" the product through the channel. A producer for an insurance company might send pre-screened prospects an e-mail that contains information describing an individual health insurance policy. The message should also motivate the customer to purchase a product or contact a company or its distributor to obtain more information about the product. Figure 9.5 shows a pull strategy print advertisement that encourages customers to contact the company for more information.

Unlike a push strategy, a pull strategy allows a company to retain more control over how the company presents its products to customers. The more control a company retains over its communications, the more easily it can develop a uniform corporate image.

Figure 9.4. An Advertising Concept for a Push Strategy

Are you looking for a way to open the door to the young professional market but just don't seem to have the right products to offer them? Put your brainstorming pad away and call Penfield Insurance Company today.

Penfield, a well-known provider in the life and health insurance industry for over 50 years, now offers a line of flexible premium deferred annuity products specifically targeted to young professionals. Penfield's annuity program provides agents with support materials, a commitment to national consumer advertising, Internet prospecting supported by Penfield's updated Web site, competitive compensation, and much more. Selling to this market is easy with Penfield's focus-group-tested sales materials.

To find out more about Penfield's new annuity product line, call 1-800-555-8527 or visit us at http://www.pnfld.insco.com.

 Penfield Insurance Company

Figure 9.5. An Advertising Concept for a Pull Strategy

You probably don't have a lot of free time, so when you make a list of all the things you should do, saving for retirement probably doesn't head the list. But you know you need to save, and you don't want to have to sweat over funds.

Acme, the company that covers your medical costs for unexpected illnesses and accidents, wants to help you cross retirement planning off your "To Do" list, so you can spend your free time doing "important" things.

Take care of your errands, and let Acme help you plan for your retirement. Visit us at our Web site (http://www.acme.insco.com) or call 1-800-555-8256 to find out more about our new line of retirement products.

Acme Financial Services

Combination Strategies

A promotion strategy that uses elements of both push and pull strategies to create both distributor and customer demand for a company's product or service is called a ***combination strategy***. For example, a company might launch both a sales contest for producers to encourage distributors to sell a product and an advertising campaign directed at consumers and organizational buyers to prompt them to seek more information by calling an insurance agent or insurance company call center for an insurance quote.

Creating an Effective Promotion Mix

To support its promotion strategies, a company must decide on its ***promotion mix***—the specific blend or combination of promotion tools a company uses to promote its products and services. The promotion mix should allow a company to promote its products and services efficiently and effectively by using the most appropriate promotion tools in the right amount and the right combination to achieve its purpose. For example, neither publicity nor sales promotion is very effective on its own, so companies often use these tools to support advertising and personal selling.

A number of factors affect a company's promotion mix decisions. The most important of these factors are shown in Figure 9.6.

Figure 9.6. Factors that Affect Promotion Mix Choices

Company goals and strategies

Company culture

Distribution channel

Product characteristics

Target market characteristics

External environment including competitors' actions and regulatory restrictions

Because looking at any one of these factors in isolation will not provide enough information to support promotion mix decisions, companies consider all relevant factors together when they plan their promotion mix.

Company Goals and Strategies

A company's goals and strategies greatly influence the decisions it makes regarding which promotion tools to use, the amount of money it spends on promotion, and how and to what degree it responds to competitors' actions related to promotion mix changes. For example, if a company's goal is to increase sales by 15 percent, then it will develop a very different promotion mix from a company that is trying to increase profitability by 15 percent.

Corporate Culture

A company's corporate culture affects promotion mix decisions in the same way that it affects other marketing decisions. For example, a company that has relied heavily on personal selling in the past may be slow to shift its promotion dollars to advertising. In addition, companies that lack experience with certain promotion tools may not use them. As a result, a company's promotion mix may remain the same for long periods of time.

Distribution Channel Characteristics

Each of the three main distribution systems that insurance companies use—personal selling distribution systems, third-party distribution systems, and direct response distribution systems—requires a different promotion mix. For example, for personal selling distribution systems companies often provide sales and service support to the producers in the system. The promotion mix for personal selling systems will include many tools and services to support personal selling, such as mailing lists and other lead sources, product information, sales illustrations, monetary support to share the cost of advertising, and customer service. This mix will probably also include advertising and sales promotion to generate awareness and interest and to encourage customers and intermediaries to move products through the channel. A direct response distribution system generally uses advertising as its main promotion tool with little or no sales promotion or personal selling needed.

Target Market Characteristics

Three major components related to the target market affect promotion mix decisions: (1) the target market's buyer readiness, (2) the size of the market and how geographically dispersed it is, and (3) the target market composition.

Buyer Readiness

As mentioned earlier most customers go through a sequence of buyer readiness stages, beginning with simple awareness of a product and then moving to interest in the product, product trial, and adoption of a product for regular use. The AIDA model can help a company identify the types of promotion tools that are most likely to generate the desired response in the target market. In general, advertising and publicity are most effective at grabbing a customer's attention or interest. Personal selling is the best at stimulating desire. Personal selling and sales promotion are most effective for prompting a customer to take action. For example, if a target market largely consists of customers who have no awareness of a product, a company may choose to run advertisements to capture attention or interest. The company could then follow that advertising with personal selling to create desire or acknowledge need for the product.

Size and Location of the Market

From a cost perspective, personal selling generally is more effective than advertising for reaching customers in smaller, more geographically concentrated markets. Advertising is more effective than personal selling in larger, more geographically dispersed markets. However, cost is not the only factor that affects the promotion mix. Other factors, such as type of product, customer traits, or media characteristics, may override cost in determining which form of promotion a company selects. For example, an insurer may use advertising targeted through special-interest media for small, concentrated target markets. *Special-interest media* are media targeted to customers with an interest in a particular topic such as homes and home improvement, money or retirement issues, and sports and recreation. In the same way an insurer may use personal selling for large, geographically dispersed markets if complex product offerings require significant customer education.

Composition of the Target Market

The type of members—consumers or organizational buyers—in a company's target market affect the promotion tools it selects. Companies that market products to consumers may rely on advertising and sales promotion to generate awareness, interest, and desire, and then use personal selling to close the sale. Companies that market to organizational buyers may use advertising only to generate awareness and then focus on personal selling to build interest and generate sales.

Product Characteristics

The nature of the product, its stage in the product life cycle, and the amount of post-purchase service it requires affects the kind of promotion mix that will be most effective in reaching the product's target customers.

Nature of the Product

How complex a product is, its price, and how frequently it is purchased all have a strong influence over the types of promotion a company uses in its promotion mix. In general, promotion mixes for products that are complex, high-priced, or infrequently purchased rely more heavily on personal selling than do the promotion mixes for products that are simple, inexpensive, or frequently purchased. For example, customers expect more detailed, personalized information and service when committing a large amount of money toward the purchase of a complex product such as most types of insurance. Personal selling is usually more effective than most other promotion tools in meeting these expectations. In contrast, a company can promote convenience items that require little personalized information and attention most effectively and economically using advertising and sales promotion. In fact, it would waste resources to use personal selling to promote low-cost, easy-to-use products—such as soft drinks, laundry detergents, and toothpaste.

Product Life Cycle Stage

The blend of promotion tools that a company includes in its promotion mix for a product reflects a product's position in the traditional product life cycle. For example, promotions for a product in the introduction stage of the product life cycle focus on creating awareness of or interest in the product. Although advertising and publicity are the most effective tools to generate awareness, companies often use all four primary promotion tools to generate awareness and interest in the introduction stage of the product life cycle. A company will use personal selling, advertising, publicity, and sales promotion to customers and distributors, as appropriate. During the growth stage, as competition increases and product differentiation becomes important, the promotion mix often uses advertising and personal selling as a way to remind customers of the product's features and benefits. For products in the maturity stage, companies focus on sales promotion directed to consumers and intermediaries as a way to maintain product interest and sales. As a product moves into the decline stage, the company is likely to spend much less time and money promoting it.

Post-purchase Service Requirements

For products that require a large amount of post-purchase service, or for products that require a continuing financial commitment on the part of the customer, personal selling can be a key tool to reinforce the purchase decision. For example, regular contact from an insurance producer can greatly improve the persistency of life insurance products. A company can also use product advertising and ongoing communications from the company to affect a customer's post-purchase view of the company. Product advertising that reinforces the company's reputation and stability or stresses its excellent customer service may reinforce the customer's purchase decision and help build a more lasting relationship with the customer.

External Environment

The external environment greatly influences a company's promotion mix decisions. Regulations, economic environment, competitor's actions, and even public perceptions of the industry affect the promotion mix a company chooses. The two strongest influencers in the external environment on the promotion mix are regulatory considerations and competitors' actions.

Not only do regulations affect how a product is developed, but they also affect how a product is promoted. Regulations may restrict the use of certain types of promotion for certain types of insurance and financial products, require the use of more supporting sales literature for complex products, and otherwise influence the choices a company makes in determining its promotion mix.

Competitors' marketing activities can also affect a company's promotion mix decisions.

> **Example:** Suppose a competitor begins offering a deferred annuity product similar to one a company is promoting, but the competitor's product offers a better interest rate guarantee. If the company cannot modify its deferred annuity product to remain competitive on the interest rate guarantee, then it may need to refocus its promotion activities to stress another benefit such as the importance of financial security or the company's long-term strong financial ratings.

Competitors' promotion efforts also affect a company's promotion mix. For example, if a competitor begins running a very effective trade sales promotion campaign, a company may need to initiate its own trade sales promotion to maintain distributor loyalty, product sales, and market share. Similarly, if a company's advertising budget is below its competitors' budgets and it is losing market share, the company may need to increase advertising spending to regain its position.

Creating the Promotion Budget

The promotion budget covers a company's expenses for developing, producing, and distributing promotion materials, contracting for media time and space, and monitoring promotion performance. For many functions in a company, setting budgets is simply a matter of weighing costs against the anticipated revenues that will result from the expenditures. Setting promotion budgets is more difficult. First, a company cannot easily measure or quantify the results of promotion campaigns which makes it difficult to tie costs to revenues or results. For example, in an image-building campaign, images generally develop over time. While a company may be able to determine whether an image-building campaign changed customer perceptions of the company, the results may not be available until long after the campaign money has been spent. Second, it may not be possible to measure exactly how much customer perceptions changed. Linking changes in image to changes in sales is even more difficult.

Despite these challenges, companies must budget for promotion expenses. Four methods companies frequently use to create promotion budgets are the percentage of sales method, competitive parity method, all-you-can-afford method, and objective and task method.

Percentage of Sales Method

The *percentage of sales method* is a method that bases the promotion budget on a specified percentage of past or projected sales. Insurance companies that use the percentage of sales method frequently base their promotion budgets on a percentage of past or projected first-year premiums. For example, if an insurer sets its promotion budget for a new life insurance product at 1 percent of first-year premiums and estimates that first-year premiums for the product will be $100 million, then the total promotion budget for the product would be $1 million as shown below:

$$\$100,000,000 \times .01 = \$1,000,000$$

The advantages of the percentage of sales method are that it is easy to use and simple to calculate. One major disadvantage of this method is that it assumes a direct, unchanging relationship between promotion and sales. In fact, changes in the company's price or profit goals, promotion spending, complexity of the product, or marketing environment can cause the relationship to change over time. In addition, the percentage of sales method may trigger the wrong spending decision. For example, basing a promotion budget on a percentage of sales during a sales slump would most likely lead to lower spending the following year. The way to break a sales slump, however, may be to spend more on promotion, not less.

Competitive Parity Method

A company that uses the *competitive parity method* bases its promotion budget on the budgets one or more of its competitors has established. Companies can apply the competitive parity method in three ways: (1) by budgeting the same dollar amount for promotion as a competitor does, (2) by using the same percentage of sales as a competitor who also uses that method, or (3) by using the average ratio of promotional costs to sales for the industry, based on cost and sales figures from an industry trade association or publication. An insurer may find it difficult to obtain information about the dollar amount a competitor spends on promotion or the percentage of sales a competitor uses to determine its promotion budget; however, industry publications often include information that would allow a company to determine a competitor's average ratio of promotional costs to sales.

Although keeping up with the competition is a fairly simple approach to budgeting, the competitive parity method has drawbacks. For example, the competitive parity method

- Assumes that the relationship between promotion spending and sales does not change.

- Allows competitors to exert influence over a company's business. Simply following a competitor's budget does not address a company's unique marketing goals. If the company's marketing activities differ from its competitor's activities, simply mimicking the competitor's budget will not result in an appropriate budget for the company.

- Fails to consider present or future conditions. Competitive parity budgets are based on a competitor's past budgets. Sudden changes in the competitor's promotion spending can affect how adequate the company's budget and sales are.

- Fails to consider different methods of classifying promotion spending. Unless the company knows exactly what the competitor's classifications mean, it may be basing its promotion budget on misunderstood information.

All-You-Can-Afford Method

Companies that use the *all-you-can-afford method* base their promotion budgets on available funds. If the company is performing well, it allocates more money to marketing communications. If the company is performing poorly, the company spends less on promotion.

Although the all-you-can-afford method is easy to apply, it does not attempt to establish any relationship between spending and sales levels. When sales are high, the need for promotion generally decreases. When sales are low, the need for promotion to build revenues usually increases. Companies that use this method run the risks that (1) promotion dollars will be wasted if too much money is spent or (2) the company may miss marketing opportunities if too little money is spent.

Objective and Task Method

Often considered the best approach for allocating dollars for promotion, the *objective and task method* establishes a promotion budget based on promotion objectives and the cost of meeting those objectives. Specifically, this method requires a company to (1) target specific goals to achieve through promotion, (2) determine the types and costs of the promotion activities needed to accomplish each goal, and (3) set the budget to meet the identified costs. Because this method requires a company to first decide exactly what activities are necessary to meet its objectives, the company usually creates the budget after developing its promotion campaign, rather than before. Typically, many different functional areas of a company participate in determining the promotion objectives and activities for this approach and actually help develop the promotion budget. Key selling partners, such as distributors, may also participate in budgeting using this method.

The advantage of the objective and task method is that it recognizes promotion has a purpose and achieving that purpose requires a certain commitment of time and resources. If the amount of time and resources required is too high, then perhaps the goals are too ambitious and should be cut back. If the goals are important, then the company must be willing to commit the additional time and resources needed to reach those goals. The major disadvantage of the objective and task method is that it is a complex process, especially when it is used to set the annual promotion budget for an entire company or product line for the entire year ahead. Companies must allocate enough funds in their annual budget so that they can adapt and respond to unexpected market opportunities or unanticipated challenges or problems.

Key Terms

communication
sender
message
communication channel
receiver
encoding
decoding
feedback
noise
integrated marketing
    communications (IMC)
personal selling
sales promotion
trade sales promotion
consumer sales promotion
advertising

publicity
exposure
promotion campaign
response hierarchy
AIDA model
image-building promotion campaign
push strategy
pull strategy
combination strategy
promotion mix
special-interest media
percentage of sales method
competitive parity method
all-you-can-afford method
objective and task method

Endnotes

1. Philip Kotler and Gary Armstrong, *Principles of Marketing*, 9th ed. (Upper Saddle River, NJ: Prentice-Hall, 2001), 515.

2. Tim Bahr, "From Audience to Interested Potential Customer," *MarketingPower*, http://www.marketingpower.com/content-printer-friendly.php?&Item_ID=361219 (23 January 2008).

Chapter 10

Promotion Tools

Objectives:

After studying this chapter, you should be able to

- Identify the major steps in the personal selling process
- Describe the purpose of trade sales promotion and identify three important types of trade sales promotions
- Explain the purpose of consumer sales promotion, and identify some of the types of sales promotions companies use for customers
- Explain how advertisements can vary depending on their purpose, the scope of the selected market, and the target audience
- Differentiate between product and institutional advertising and describe two types of product advertising and four types of institutional advertising
- Describe the five-step process used to develop an advertising campaign
- Identify two types of objectives of advertising campaigns
- Describe the factors that influence the budget for effective advertising
- Identify the advantages and disadvantages associated with different types of advertising media
- Describe the importance of frequency and timing of advertisements in scheduling media
- Describe how insurers use pretesting and post-testing to measure the effectiveness of advertising
- Describe the three primary objectives of publicity
- Identify the factors that determine the newsworthiness of publicity items and the effectiveness of publicity

Outline

Personal Selling
- Why Companies use Personal Selling
- The Personal Selling Process

Sales Promotion
- Trade Sales Promotion
- Consumer Sales Promotion

Advertising
- Advertising Purpose
- Advertising Scope
- Advertising Audience

- Developing an Advertising Campaign
- Evaluating Advertising Effectiveness

Publicity
- Publicity Objectives
- Getting Publicity Information to the Public
- Evaluating the Effectiveness of Publicity

An insurance company's goal in promoting its products is to maximize the impact of the company's message while controlling overall promotion costs. How successful a company is in achieving this goal depends on how effectively the insurer uses personal selling, sales promotion, advertising, and publicity.

Personal Selling

For many insurers, personal selling accounts for the largest percentage of the company's promotion budget as well as the largest percentage of overall product sales. Consequently, an insurance company's overall success often depends on the effectiveness of its personal selling efforts.

Why Companies Use Personal Selling

For insurance companies, one major advantage of personal selling over most other forms of promotion is that it establishes an interactive connection between the company and its prospective or current customers. This link between customer and company, by means of its producers, allows a company to (1) educate customers about insurance products, (2) build public relations, and (3) lay the groundwork for building lasting relationships with customers.

Educating Customers

Insurance products and the ways they can be used to meet a customer's needs can be complicated. Although some customers are willing to gather and sort through detailed information about insurance and other financial services products, many prefer to consult with a knowledgeable insurance producer who can provide both information and expert guidance.

The producer can listen to a customer to find out exactly what the customer needs and wants; the customer, in turn, can pose questions about any aspects of the product that he doesn't understand and can obtain simple, clear answers from the producer. By interacting with a customer one-on-one and providing personalized information and answers to his questions or concerns, a producer provides a valuable service to both the company and its customers.

Building Public Relations

Producers represent the company to its customers and the customers to the company. The impact the producer's personal selling efforts can have on a company's—or even an entire industry's—reputation is enormous. Producers who present a professional image and conduct themselves ethically not only further their own professional growth, but also enhance the image of the insurance company they represent.

Building Customer Relationships

Producers talk to customers in their communities every day. They hear firsthand about problems that current and potential customers have with the company and its products and about the company's general image in the marketplace. Producers also hear about customers' product and service needs. As a result of this contact, producers can provide insurance companies with a great deal of marketing and customer service information.

Companies can use this information to make customer-focused marketing decisions. For example, if a producer reports that several prospects express a desire for more easily obtainable information about the current value of their insurance investments, the company may decide to establish a computerized telephone system or Web site to allow customers to obtain account information 24 hours a day, 7 days a week. Companies also can use information they gather during regular meetings with their sales force to develop and promote new products.

By taking time to learn about a potential customer's needs and then responding to those needs, producers and companies can earn their customers' trust and establish long-lasting business relationships. Satisfied customers who have purchased life insurance from a trusted producer working on behalf of a trusted company will be more approachable for sales of additional products that meet their other insurance and financial needs. They also are likely to make referrals and speak positively about the producer and the company. Long-term customer relationships build value for the company by generating a stream of income that continues over time.

The Personal Selling Process

Personal selling is the one form of promotion that has a noticeable connection with product sales. Figure 10.1 briefly describes the six major steps in the personal selling process used to promote insurance and other financial services products.

Depending on the company and the situation, one person may perform every step in the process, or different people may be assigned to perform different steps. In addition, some producers may condense the process by combining prospecting and needs analysis or proposal generation and sales presentation.

Figure 10.1. Major Steps in the Personal Selling Process

Prospecting

The process producers use to identify, contact, and qualify potential customers is known as *prospecting*. Potential customers are referred to as *prospects*. The name of a well-qualified prospect that a customer gives to a salesperson is called a *referred lead* or *referral*.

Analyzing Needs

Producers perform a needs analysis to help them determine the nature and extent of a prospect's needs and identify the number and types of products that can best serve those needs. Producers usually perform the needs analysis to determine the prospect's current financial situation, current insurance products owned, and financial priorities.

Generating Proposals

Using information gathered during the needs analysis, producers calculate the prospect's current and future financial needs and prepare a proposal that outlines the products and services that will best meet those needs.

Making Sales Presentations

A *sales presentation* is the promotional message a producer delivers to a prospect to explain the product or products recommended in the proposal, stimulate the prospect's interest in those products, and motivate the prospect to purchase the products.

Handling Objections and Closing the Sale

Prospects typically ask questions or raise objections several times during sales presentations. To make a sale, a producer must answer questions and handle objections each time they arise.

Providing Follow-Up Service

Follow-up service helps ensure the customer remains satisfied with the purchase by providing the producer with an opportunity to reaffirm the importance of the customer's purchase, generate future sales by reminding the prospect of unmet needs insurance products could fill, and reinforce the producer's and company's commitment to quality service.

Sales Promotion

Sales promotion includes trade sales promotion, which is directed toward producers as part of a push strategy, and consumer sales promotion, which is directed toward consumers and organizational buyers as part of a pull strategy.

Trade Sales Promotion

Because sales of insurance products rely heavily on the personal selling efforts of sales agents, brokers, and other producers, insurance companies devote considerable time and resources to supporting their producers through trade sales promotions. Three important types of trade sales promotions are sales aids, incentive programs, and recognition programs.

Sales Aids

One of the most difficult tasks for an insurance producer is explaining to prospects how insurance products can meet their needs. Insurance products can be complex, and verbal descriptions often cannot adequately explain how the products work under current conditions or how they are likely to work under changing conditions. To help producers with this task, insurance companies have developed *sales aids*, which are sales promotion materials that can be used in conjunction with a sales presentation. Examples of sales aids include

- Brochures and other sales literature that explain various products or policy benefits

- Audiovisual aids that can be used in sales presentations

- Computer-generated individualized sales illustrations that give year-by-year descriptions of a policy's premiums, cash values, and other features

- Financial planning software programs that show customers how various products help achieve financial planning goals

Companies can provide sales aids to producers free of charge, or the companies can charge a small amount for the materials to cover development and production costs. To retain control over both the wording and mathematical values involved, insurers typically generate sales illustrations on their home office computers as needed and then provide them to producers.

Sales aids are not attached to the insurance policy, so they are not part of the contract between the insurer and the policyowner; however, insurers must make sure that sales aids used during a sales presentation accurately describe policy benefits and are not misleading. To meet this goal, insurers carefully design sales aids that clearly explain both a policy's benefits and any restrictions on those benefits. A company's legal department typically reviews all brochures, sales kits, audiovisual aids, and other sales materials that producers will use to ensure that the information in those sales aids is not misleading or unclear and that it is in compliance with any applicable regulations. An insurance company may have to submit sales aids for certain products to appropriate regulatory agencies for their review.

Incentive Programs

Insurance companies often sponsor sales incentive programs for producers to spur product sales. Incentive programs frequently take the form of sales contests, which offer producers rewards or prizes for their production. Figure 10.2 shows an advertisement for a sales contest sponsored by a financial services company. Contests can offer winners cash, prizes, or merchandise not available in stores, such as clothing with the company's logo.

Figure 10.2. Using Sales Contests to Boost Sales

Slip into some sand, sun, and water in
BERMUDA!

Enter the Askaway United Insurance
May-to-September Sales Contest to
Win a free trip to Bermuda.

Askaway United Insurance's sales contest is open to brokers only. Winners will be selected based on achieving a stated increase in first-year target premiums for the period from May 1, 2010 – September 30, 2011. Winners will receive free airfare and will stay at an all-inclusive resort near the capital city of Hamilton. For more information on this contest or to learn how you can become a broker for Askaway, call us toll-free at 1-888-555-1212.

Incentive programs can focus on increasing sales of a particular product or on boosting overall production. The table below shows the two major types of incentive programs and their best uses.

Type of Incentive Program	Uses
Product-based sales promotions	Effective for new product promotion campaigns
	Less effective for established products
Total-production sales promotions	Tends to increase sales of all of a company's products
	More appropriate for a needs-oriented marketing approach than product-based promotions

To give all producers an equal chance of winning and to encourage the entire sales force to participate in sales campaigns, companies typically set different target sales levels for producers with varying levels of experience. For example, target sales levels for experienced producers may be set higher than target levels for new producers.

Sales campaigns usually last at least one year. To maintain producers' interest and enthusiasm during the campaign, companies may offer periodic incentives as well. For example, a company might sponsor a "fast start" contest during the first two months of the campaign, a "customer service month" during the campaign's middle months to encourage producers to contact current customers to review their coverage and needs, and a "fast finish" contest at the end of the campaign.

Recognition Programs

In addition to boosting product sales, trade sales promotions can also recognize, motivate, and educate the sales force. Two tools commonly used for this purpose are company publications and sales conferences.

Most insurance companies produce monthly publications, targeted to producers, designed to recognize outstanding performance. These publications can recognize producers who have achieved outstanding sales volume and persistency levels; received industry awards such as the National Quality Award (NQA), the DALBAR Award for outstanding customer service, or membership in the Million Dollar Round Table (MDRT); or earned professional designations such as Chartered Life Underwriter (CLU), Chartered Financial Consultant (ChFC), Certified Financial Planner (CFP), and Fellow, Life Management Institute (FLMI). Company publications also include articles written by sales staff and home office personnel.

Sales conferences and meetings also provide a forum to educate a company's sales force about products, product applications, and sales and marketing practices. In many cases, producers are geographically dispersed and have few opportunities to meet with one another to exchange ideas or discuss concerns. Sales conferences can serve an important communication need. In addition, because producers often place a high level of trust in the experience of individuals who have served in the field, producers are more likely to welcome their peers' ideas about sales methods and product applications rather than ideas from company management.

In addition, most insurance companies sponsor annual company, regional, and national meetings specifically for producers. The purpose of these meetings is to publicly acknowledge producer accomplishments. The specific meeting that an individual producer is invited to attend depends on the person's sales volume. Generally, the highest sales volume is required for an invitation to the meeting with the most prestige and the best location. An opportunity to attend a local or national sales conference in an attractive location may motivate a producer to increase sales efforts.

Consumer Sales Promotion

Consumer sales promotions give customers a special reason to buy a particular product or to do business with a particular company. Although insurance companies rarely use promotions such as coupons, sampling, and sweepstakes—which are common among packaged goods companies—some do use point-of-purchase materials, specialty advertising, and event sponsorship to encourage insurance purchases and reinforce their advertising and sales messages.

Point-of-purchase materials are promotional materials provided to customers where products are purchased. For insurance companies, these materials include display racks containing product brochures and advertisements or other exhibits placed in high-traffic sales areas. For example, an insurer that uses a celebrity to promote its products on television also may use displays featuring that celebrity in its sales locations or on kiosks. Insurance companies mainly use point-of-purchase materials to promote life and disability insurance sales through banks and credit unions.

As an alternative to traditional sales promotions, insurers often use specialty advertising and sponsorship of special events to reinforce their advertising and sales messages. *Specialty advertising* is a form of sales promotion that uses objects or articles imprinted with a company name or logo, address, phone number, and sometimes a slogan or sales message to promote a company, its producers, or its products. These imprinted items typically include calendars, coffee mugs, computer mouse pads, pens, and road atlases.

Insurance companies can provide specialty advertising items to customers directly or through their producers. Producers and sales agencies also may develop and distribute their own specialty advertising items to promote their business to customers.

> **Example:** An insurance producer who telephones a prospect to discuss retirement planning options might follow up that call by sending information to the prospect along with a business-card-size calendar imprinted with the producer's name, company logo, and phone number.

Another way insurers increase company and producer name recognition is through sponsorship of special events, such as professional or collegiate sports events, educational programs, arts and entertainment programs, community development projects, and celebrity appearances. As part of its sponsorship, an insurer may receive free event tickets that it can distribute to current and prospective customers or it may conduct on- and off-site event-related promotion activities. On-site activities may include distributing specialty advertising items, staffing display booths, or selling raffle tickets that qualify purchasers for prizes. Off-site activities include hosting event-related clinics or charitable fund-raising parties attended by event participants and local celebrities. In return for its sponsorship, the insurer receives regional and/or national advertising exposure for the company and its products.

Unlike most forms of sales promotion, specialty advertising and event sponsorship are not necessarily short term in nature and are not necessarily designed to spur immediate action. Instead, they are designed to allow insurance companies and their producers to get their names out to potential customers and to generate leads for future sales.

Advertising

When many people think of promotion, they think of advertising. Advertising is the most noticeable element of many companies' promotion activities, and often the most expensive as well. In 2006, total worldwide spending on advertising exceeded $600 billion.[1] Insurance companies in particular are rapidly expanding their advertising budgets, more than doubling the amount spent on advertisements between 2003 and 2007.[2]

Today's rapidly expanding and increasingly sophisticated methods of communication offer companies a wider variety of advertising choices than ever before. In determining what advertisements to use, a company must consider the (1) intended purpose of the advertising, (2) scope of the markets reached by the advertising, and (3) intended target audience for the advertising.

Advertising Purpose

Most advertising is designed to serve one of two primary purposes: (1) to promote specific products and services, or (2) to promote the companies that produce products and services. Advertising designed to promote or focus on particular products and services is referred to as ***product advertising***. Advertising designed to focus on a company, industry, or point of view is called ***institutional advertising***.

Product Advertising

The two primary types of product advertising are direct response advertising and product awareness advertising. ***Direct response advertising*** is designed to encourage customers to take action immediately, either by purchasing a product or requesting additional information about a particular product. This type of advertising is popular among insurers. Insurance company customers are often encouraged to respond to direct response advertising by contacting a producer, completing an application included in a direct mail package, returning a postcard or coupon to a company or a producer, visiting a company Web site, or calling a toll-free telephone number.

Product awareness advertising seeks to stimulate demand for a product or service over time. Typically, product awareness advertising is used to attract attention to the features and benefits of a specific product, arouse customer or distributor interest in a product, increase use of a product by its current customers, and help counteract the effects of advertising by competitors. The primary forms of product awareness advertising include

- ***Informative product advertising***, which provides information about a product. It can be used to announce and describe new products, publicize price changes, explain product uses, tell customers where to obtain products, and describe specific product features and benefits. Financial services companies devote a significant amount of advertising resources to informative product advertising.

- ***Persuasive product advertising***, which attempts to build customer preference and increase sales for a specific product by supporting or changing existing beliefs about the product. Sometimes persuasive advertising takes the form of ***comparative advertising***, or *competitive advertising*, which directly compares a product to a competing product on the basis of one or more product attributes. Because of the complexity of most insurance products, comparative advertising generally is used only for term insurance.

■ *Reminder product advertising*, which is used to reinforce customers' buying habits and a company's earlier promotion efforts by keeping the name of a mature product in customers' minds. For insurance products, reminder product advertising helps deter replacement and lapse by reassuring customers that they made a good purchase decision.

Institutional Advertising

Most insurers rely heavily on institutional advertising to promote themselves, their sales force, and their industry. Typically, institutional advertising takes one of the following four distinct forms:

■ *Image-building advertising* is intended to increase customer confidence in an industry or in a specific company by emphasizing the industry's or company's history, stability, experience, and progressive attitudes. Examples of this type of institutional advertising include advertisements announcing a company's rating by a major rating agency or publicizing specific recognition by trade association magazines or organizations. Image-building advertising can also be used to recruit insurance producers, motivate producers and employees, or counter negative publicity.

■ *Advocacy advertising* presents the position of an industry, company, or organization on an issue important to the public. Insurers might use advocacy advertising to state their position on proposed legislation concerning health care or to support safe driving programs.

■ *Informative institutional advertising* makes special announcements about a company such as mergers, acquisitions, relocation of offices, or new ventures. Informative institutional advertising is often targeted to company shareholders and potential investors, but consumers can also benefit from this type of advertising since they are interested in how mergers and acquisitions may affect their relationship with a company.

■ *Competitive institutional advertising* promotes one product category over a competing product category. For example, insurers sometimes use competitive institutional advertising to promote their fixed interest annuity crediting rates, term life insurance rates, and mutual fund performance compared to the industry as a whole or certain identified competitors.

Advertising Scope

Advertisements also differ according to the scope of the market the advertising is intended to reach. Advertising can be local, regional, national, or even international in nature.

Local and regional advertising are designed to reach limited geographic areas within a country, ranging from a single neighborhood to a large region. Companies that organize their marketing operations on a geographic basis may use advertising that corresponds to the same geographic divisions. Companies that want to promote products or services that are only available or significantly more popular in a particular geographic area also use regional or local advertising. Similarly, companies might use local advertising to deliver a customized message to a particular audience, such as by having a local celebrity endorse a product.

In the insurance industry, local and regional advertising is often used to promote local agencies or their producers, and advertisements typically include specific information about the person a customer should contact to purchase company products. Media for local and regional advertising include local newspapers and neighborhood newsletters, individual radio and television stations, billboards, and regional editions of national magazines.

National advertising is designed to reach the total market of a given country. For insurers, advertising on a national scope is generally used to promote a company's image or position on an issue, to introduce a new product or program, or to promote an existing product or program. National advertising typically uses magazines and newspapers with national circulations, national radio and television spots, and the Internet.

International advertising is designed to promote products, companies, and ideas throughout many countries. Although international advertising offers companies the greatest amount of exposure for their products, differences in language, culture, and legal restrictions can make advertising in international markets challenging. In fact, some companies find it necessary to change the names of their products when they market those products internationally because the names have different meanings in foreign markets than in domestic markets.

Advertising Audience

Advertisements are generally targeted toward particular customers or distributors. Advertising directed at individuals and organizations is referred to as *consumer advertising* and includes advertisements that appear on television and radio, in general-interest and business magazines, on billboards, and on Web sites. Consumer advertising is often used as part of an image-building promotion campaign.

Advertising directed toward distributors is referred to as *trade advertising*. Trade advertisements are often highly technical and describe the benefits to distributors of selling a company's products as well as the benefits to the customer of purchasing the company's products. Trade advertising is often used as part of a company's efforts to attract distributors. Most companies use specialty publications that target specific industries or occupations for trade advertisements.

Developing an Advertising Campaign

Companies rarely, if ever, use a single advertisement to promote their products or points of view. Instead, they develop an *advertising campaign*, which is a coordinated series of advertisements designed to promote a product, product line, or the company itself. Each advertisement plays a specific role in achieving the objectives of the overall advertising campaign.

Companies can develop advertising campaigns in-house, using the company's internal advertising staff, or they can use an advertising agency to perform some of these activities. An *advertising agency* is an organization that provides its clients with a variety of advertising-related services including development of advertising themes; selection of appropriate media; and creation, production, and placement of advertisements. Companies typically follow five main steps in developing an advertising campaign:

■ Establishing advertising objectives

■ Setting the advertising budget

■ Developing a media plan

■ Creating and producing advertisements

■ Evaluating advertising effectiveness

Establishing Advertising Objectives

The specific results a company hopes to achieve through an advertising campaign are referred to as its *advertising objectives*. These objectives typically focus on either sales or communication. A **sales-oriented advertising objective** usually describes desired results in terms of an increase in sales or market share. For example, a sales-oriented objective for an insurance company advertising campaign might be to increase new premium income for a term life insurance product by 10 percent over a six-month period. A **communication-oriented advertising objective** seeks to increase customer interest in and awareness and knowledge of a product or company. A communication-oriented objective might be to achieve a 10 percent improvement in the company's name recognition among members of the target market over a six-month period.

A company's advertising objectives will influence its decisions in a number of areas, including

■ **Type of advertising**. Companies need to decide the specific type of advertising they will use to achieve their objectives. Direct response and persuasive product advertising typically are effective in achieving specific sales objectives; institutional advertising and informative product advertising are more effective for achieving communication-oriented objectives.

■ **Type and amount of information to be included in advertisements**. If the purpose of the advertising is to create awareness or stimulate action, then the advertisements often include less information than do those designed to educate customers or change perceptions.

■ **Type of appeal advertisements will use**. Advertisements designed to create awareness and stimulate action often rely on emotional appeals while those designed to build interest or change perceptions usually require a logical or rational appeal.

■ **Length of time the advertising campaign will last**. To generate awareness, advertising usually must be presented frequently over a short period of time—for example, daily over a period of 30 days. Educating and motivating customers to take action often requires exposures over a longer period of time, such as weekly for several months.

Setting the Advertising Budget

In general, a company's advertising budget specifies how much of its overall promotion budget will be required to meet its advertising objectives during a certain time period. Advertising budgets vary considerably depending upon the type of business, the purpose and duration of the advertising campaign, the number of competitors, and the availability of financial resources. Determining the ideal amount to spend on advertising is difficult because, in most cases, a company cannot predict the exact results of spending a specific amount of money. The following factors typically influence the amount of money needed for effective advertising:

■ **Product characteristics**. New products typically require heavy spending for advertising to build awareness and gain market share. Mature products may require only occasional reminder advertising. Product differentiation is also important. Products that are similar to other products often require heavy spending on advertising to point out the product's unique aspects to customers.

■ **Media costs**. In addition to the costs of developing and producing advertisements, companies incur costs for placing these advertisements in specific media. These costs vary widely. For example, the costs of television advertising are generally higher than for other media. However, because television reaches large numbers of people, it can sometimes be more cost-effective than other media. For this reason, companies typically evaluate media costs of an advertisement in terms of the cost per thousand persons reached (CPM).[3]

■ **Market characteristics**. New or highly competitive target markets typically require larger advertising allocations than do established or less competitive market segments. Similarly, international and national markets typically require larger allocations for effective advertising than do regional or local markets.

Developing a Media Plan

After a company has determined its advertising objectives and budget, it then develops a media plan. A ***media plan*** is a document that specifies the types of media (television, radio, newspapers, magazines, outdoor, direct mail or Internet) in which advertisements will appear, the specific vehicles (television program, magazine, newspaper, or Web site) in which advertisements will run, and the schedule (number and pattern of exposures) for the advertisements. Because of the complexities involved with media planning, most companies work with an advertising agency to make these decisions.

Selecting the Appropriate Media Type

Most advertising messages can be communicated through a variety of media, including television, radio, magazines, newspapers, billboards, and the Internet. To determine which types of media are appropriate in a particular advertising campaign, companies need to gather information about the communication needs and preferences of potential customers. For example, companies can determine whether customers prefer to receive product information through personal selling, direct mail, broadcast advertising, or Internet sources. They can also determine which television programs and radio stations individuals in the target market prefer, which magazines and newspapers they read, and how many of them subscribe to online computer services. Companies also need to consider the marketing message they want to communicate to their customers. Typically, television advertising is a good way to communicate the visual or emotional aspects of products and services, illustrate how products and services work, or build images in the minds of customers. When the marketing message includes technical language and information or detailed company performance data, print media is more effective than television.

Companies also consider various media characteristics when selecting types of media for advertising. Three of the most important characteristics that affect media choices are reach, frequency, and waste. In an advertising context, **reach** refers to the total number of people exposed to an advertisement in a given medium. For example, a commercial on a popular television program may reach more than 25 million viewers. **Frequency** refers to the number of times the same people in a target market are exposed to a particular advertisement in a given medium in a given time period. For example, if a commercial appears on the same television program every week for 10 weeks, audiences will be exposed to the advertisement 10 times during the 10-week period. **Waste** refers to the number of non-target market people exposed to an advertisement in a given medium. For example, a television advertisement targeting middle-aged purchasers of deferred annuities will also be seen by seniors and younger age groups. The number of seniors and young people in the audience represents waste. By evaluating the reach, frequency, and waste associated with various options, companies can determine the combination of media and vehicles that will communicate the company's message most effectively to customers.

In addition, each type of media has its own advantages and disadvantages that can affect its suitability for a particular advertising campaign.

Television. National network, local, syndicated, cable, and specialty network television programming accounts for a large percentage of advertising spending in most countries. In the United States, television accounts for nearly 60 percent of all advertising spending.[4]

A number of factors contribute to the popularity of television as an advertising medium. Television allows companies to combine visual images, color, sound, and movement to create a wide variety of inviting and memorable messages. Television advertising also has tremendous reach; a single advertisement can be seen by millions of people. As a result, the cost per person reached for television advertisements is relatively low. Companies also are able to place advertisements on particular programs or at particular times to target select demographic markets.

Television also has disadvantages. For example, television generates considerable waste because it reaches noncustomers as well as customers. Companies can overcome this disadvantage to some extent by sponsoring television programs targeted to specific audiences or by using narrowcasting to reach their potential customers. **Narrowcasting** involves selecting media that reach only a well-defined audience segment, thereby reducing wasted exposure. When applied to television advertising, narrowcasting typically entails placing advertisements on local cable television or specialized networks. Another disadvantage associated with television advertising is cost. Although the cost per person reached is low, television's absolute costs, both to produce and to place advertisements, are high. These costs can be particularly high for an advertisement placed during a popular show, prime viewing hours, or especially during special events such as the Super Bowl or the Olympics.

Television advertising also has a life cycle of only a few months; after that, advertisements often become stale and ineffective from overuse. Companies need to produce fresh, new commercials on a regular basis to hold their customers' interest. New commercials increase advertising expenses and often require long lead times to develop. In addition, television advertising has a very short shelf life—that is, after a commercial has appeared, it is gone and customers no longer have it for reference when they are ready to make a purchase.

A final disadvantage of television is clutter. A typical television program breaks for advertising every 7 to 10 minutes, and these breaks may contain as many as 8 to 10 advertisements. Many customers perceive these advertisements as distracting interruptions and take steps to avoid or skip them. For example, many viewers now use devices such as TiVo, which allow them to record television shows and then watch them later while skipping over commercials that are broadcast during the show.

Magazines. Magazines have been the second most popular media vehicle for advertising spending in the United States for several decades.[5] One reason for the popularity of magazine advertising is its ability to overcome many of the disadvantages of television. Unlike television, magazines offer high credibility because readers generally consider magazines to be a trustworthy source of information. Also unlike television, magazines offer advertisements with a fairly long shelf life, quality image reproduction, and the ability for pass-along readership.

Perhaps the most important advantage of magazine advertising is that companies usually can find special-interest magazines whose readers closely match the demographics of the companies' target markets. For example, companies trying to reach people interested in financial products can advertise in consumer magazines such as *Money* or *Fortune* that are read by people interested in financial products. Companies can use trade magazines, including *Best's Review* and *National Underwriter*, to reach audiences in organizational markets. Using special-interest magazines helps companies more accurately target messages to their intended audience and reduce costly waste. Companies also can vary advertising across regional versions of magazines and share more complex information about products than would be possible using television.

A disadvantage of using magazines as an advertising medium is the high cost associated with advertisement development and placement. Another disadvantage is that most magazine advertising deadlines are several months in advance of the magazine's issue date, which means that magazine advertising has long lead times. Therefore, magazines typically are not a good choice for timely advertisements or messages.

Newspapers. Traditionally, newspapers have been a popular advertising medium. Newspapers are similar to magazines in that they are perceived to have high credibility as a source of important information. Newspapers also offer other advantages, including

■ Relatively low cost for producing and placing advertisements

■ Penetration of local markets

■ Long shelf life (advertisements or coupons in newspapers can be cut out and saved by readers)

■ Flexible sizes for advertisements

■ Short lead times because of publishing frequency, enabling messages to be updated quickly and easily

Newspapers also have disadvantages. For example, the quality of print reproduction in newspapers can be poor, so advertisements generally do not appear as crisp or appealing as advertisements in magazines or on television. Also, advertising in newspapers does not provide good *audience selectivity*, which is the ability of an advertisement to reach an intended target market. Although newspapers can provide some geographic segmentation, demographic selection is usually very limited.

Another disadvantage of newspapers as an advertising medium is the one-day life span of a newspaper. Most readers throw newspapers away or recycle them after they are finished reading, so newspapers typically offer very little, if any, pass-along readership. Also, in recent years, the number of people reading newspapers has declined as people increasingly use other media vehicles as sources of information. Finally, advertisements in newspapers must compete with a large number of other advertisements for the reader's attention in the short period of time the newspaper is read or kept.

Radio. Radio advertising offers relatively low production and media costs and short lead times, which enable companies to change advertising messages quickly if necessary. In addition, radio stations typically are programmed for a specific audience segment, and this segmentation helps companies reach select targeted audiences. Also, many companies appreciate the high frequency rate of radio advertisements, which means their advertising message will often be repeated.

However, radio is not an ideal medium in every situation. For example, like television, radio generally is not an effective medium for conveying complex or abstract information to consumers and is usually limited to advertising basic products or increasing company awareness. Radio advertisements also have a short shelf life, because they cannot be kept for reference or passed along, and companies need to create new advertisements periodically to maintain customer interest.

In addition, because many people engage in other activities—such as driving or working—while listening to the radio, they do not always have their attention fully focused on the radio message. There are also no visual images to remember with radio advertising. To be effective, radio advertisements must be short messages that are frequently aired so that the audience will remember the message. A radio advertisement might run every day during morning and evening drive time to ensure that the same listeners will hear the advertisement several times.

Direct Mail. As an advertising medium, direct mail offers companies a number of advantages. Unlike television and radio advertisements, direct mail gives companies the space necessary for presenting large amounts of complicated and detailed product information. Typically, direct mail also offers companies consistent reproduction quality for advertising materials.

In addition, direct mail also includes a high degree of audience selectivity, which reduces or even eliminates waste. Using the appropriate mailing list, companies can select a narrow market segment and create a message tailored specifically for that segment. Results of direct mail advertising are also easy to measure because of the high degree of audience selectivity. Low development and production costs and a low cost-per-person ratio make direct mail cost effective and attractive.

The disadvantages of direct mail include low response rates and uncontrolled exposure. Typical response rates for direct mail range from 0.5 percent to 3 percent. As a result, companies must send massive quantities of mail to get an acceptable number of responses. Given the rising cost of postage, conducting a direct mail advertising campaign can become quite costly, in spite of other cost-saving characteristics. In addition, although companies can be reasonably sure that members of the target audience receive direct mail advertisements, they can't guarantee that the audience will read the material. Some customers view direct mail as "junk mail" and discard it unopened. Also, companies may experience difficulties in obtaining accurate and updated mailing lists. Finally, developing and producing effective direct mail advertisements can involve long lead times, preventing companies from quickly beginning a new advertising campaign or changing information in a current campaign.

Internet. The financial services industry spent $2.54 billion in Internet advertising in 2006.[6] In the United States, Internet advertising in all industries increased 27 percent in 2007 with expenditures of almost $25 billion.[7] In its beginning stages, Internet advertising consisted primarily of company Web sites and e-mail advertisements. More recently, however, companies are finding innovative ways of advertising on the Internet, including the use of blogs and e-mail newsletters.

The various types of Internet advertising combine many of the advantages of other media. For example, like direct mail advertisements, Internet advertising can include large amounts of complicated information on company Web sites. However, Internet advertising is also similar to television in that it has the ability to offer sophisticated graphics and streaming video. Other advantages of Internet advertising include availability and a long shelf life. A customer with Internet access can visit a company Web site for information at any convenient time for as long as the company maintains the material on the Web site. Messages on the Internet also can be updated easily, which is a positive feature for companies that frequently need to change product or service information.

A disadvantage of Internet advertising is that the market covered by the Internet is limited to customers who have Internet access. Companies also find that some customers view e-mail advertisements as another form of junk mail and often ignore the company's messages in this advertising form. Some consumers are even afraid to open e-mail advertisements because of the possibility that they might contain a computer virus. The growth of Internet advertising also means that companies must compete with many other advertisements from a variety of other companies and industries for the attention of consumers.

Other Media. Companies also have a number of alternate forms of advertising available. For example, many companies use directories, such as the telephone yellow pages. Directories can be inexpensive compared with other types of advertising and can also reach a large number of customers who shop for products in specific categories, including insurance.

Companies can also use outdoor advertising, which takes a variety of forms. Product advertisements often appear on the sides of buses and subway cars; roadside billboards promote products, companies, and causes; highway signs urge us to take the next exit to enjoy some food or see the local sights; and outdoor or in-stadium sports events display information about companies or products. These and other forms of outdoor advertising can be effective in attracting attention and providing reminders of products to consumers through repeated exposure to the advertisement.

These other media also have some disadvantages. For example, a roadside billboard offers poor audience selectivity even though geographic selectivity may be strong. Outdoor and directory advertisements are limited in the amount of information that can be provided to the audience. In addition, consumers typically have a very short exposure time to advertisements as they travel past a billboard or read the side of a bus as it drives away.

Figure 10.3 provides a summary of the advantages and disadvantages of each type of advertising media.

Selecting a Media Vehicle

A company's choice of specific television programs, magazines, newspapers, or other media vehicles depends on the following four factors:

- Match between the demographic characteristics of the vehicle's target audience and those of the product's target market

- Size of the vehicle's target audience

- Vehicle frequency (Is a particular magazine published weekly, monthly, or quarterly? Is a particular television program aired daily, weekly, or once only?)

- Cost of advertising in the particular vehicle

The goal of advertising is to match the characteristics of the audience, product, and vehicle as closely as possible. For example, a magazine such as *Kiplinger's*, which is read by people interested in protecting their financial assets, would offer a good demographic match for the target audience of an insurer promoting a long-term care product. Similarly, a company that needs to provide repeated exposures during a particular time period to introduce a new product is not likely to select a vehicle with low frequency.

Scheduling Media

Scheduling media involves determining the frequency and timing of advertisements. Generally, customers must see or hear an advertisement a number of times to retain the intended message. How many times an advertisement should run to be effective depends on buyer turnover, purchase frequency, and customers' forgetting rate. **Buyer turnover** indicates how often new customers enter the market to purchase a product; markets with high buyer turnover typically require frequent advertising. **Purchase frequency** refers to the number of times a product is typically purchased; products purchased frequently generally require less advertising than do infrequently purchased products. Customers' **forgetting rate** is how fast customers forget a product or brand if no advertising is run; if the forgetting rate for a particular product is high, more advertising will be needed to maintain product awareness in the market.

Timing refers to the pattern in which exposure to advertisements occurs. Companies can use one of two basic patterns for timing advertisements:

- A **steady timing pattern** distributes advertisements evenly throughout a specified period of time. For example, a company may schedule a particular advertisement once a week on a specific television program for 26 weeks.

Figure 10.3. Advantages and Disadvantages of Major Types of Advertising Media

Type of Media	Advantages	Disadvantages
Television	*Lively and colorful—uses movement, sight and sound *Flexibility in getting consumers' attention *Can reach large audiences *Some demographic selection available *Relatively low cost per person	*Large amount of waste—difficult to target customers *High total cost *Long lead time required to develop and place ads *Need for production specialists *Short life cycle—new ads must be created periodically to maintain interest *Short shelf life—ads can't be saved for later reference *High clutter
Magazines	*Excellent geographic and demographic selectivity *High prestige and credibility among readers *Good reproduction quality *Long shelf life *Good pass-along readership	*Possibly high design and production costs *Long lead time required to develop and place ads *Often high total costs compared to other media
Newspapers	*High credibility as source of news and information *Relatively low cost *Short lead time *Flexible ad size *Penetration of local markets *Frequency of publication *Ability to update or change messages quickly and easily *Potentially long shelf-life—ads or coupons can be cut out and saved	*Inconsistent reproduction *Typically a one-day life span *Little pass-along readership *Lack of movement and sound *High degree of competition from other ads *Poor audience selectivity (other than geographic) *Limited demographics *Fewer readers each year

continued on next page

Figure 10.3. (*continued*) Advantages and Disadvantages of Major Types of Advertising Media

Type of Media	Advantages	Disadvantages
Radio	*Relatively low cost compared with other media *Short lead time *Can change or update messages quickly and easily *High frequency *Good geographic and demographic selectivity	*Restrictive message length—ads can't contain much information *Limited to sound only—no visual or print component *Need for repetition *Competition from other ads and other activities *Short life cycle—new ads must be created periodically to maintain interest *Short shelf life—messages not easily saved *Short recall factor
Direct Mail	*Can convey large amounts of information—length unlimited *Consistent reproduction *Excellent geographic and demographic selectivity *High personalization *Low development and production costs *Easily measurable results	*Long lead time *Low response rate *Expensive compared to other media *Potential rejection and negative reaction as junk mail *Difficulty of obtaining good mailing lists
Internet	*Can convey large amounts of information *Lively and colorful appearance using graphics and video *Users can access available messages at any time *Can change messages quickly and easily *Long shelf life	*High degree of competition from other ads *Often considered "junk mail;" negative reaction *Limited to customers with Internet access
Outdoor and Other Media	*Ease of attracting attention *Inexpensive cost compared to other media *Repetition of exposure to customers *Can reach large numbers of consumers	*Poor audience selectivity *Can't convey much information *Often short exposure time

- A ***pulsing pattern,*** also called a *bursting pattern*, distributes advertisements unevenly throughout a specified period of time. Companies that use pulsing patterns may schedule a large number of advertisements at the beginning of an advertising campaign and then reduce the number of advertisements as the campaign progresses. For example, a company might schedule an advertisement on different television programs every single day for two weeks, and then once a week on a specific program for the next six months. Alternatively, companies may concentrate advertisements during specific time periods during the year or specific parts of the day. Pulsing patterns are ideal for seasonal buying, special sales promotions, or new product introductions.

Because of the importance of providing repeat exposures over a short period of time, pulsing patterns currently are used more frequently than steady timing patterns.

Creating and Producing Advertisements

Effective advertisements can gain the attention of potential customers and persuade them to purchase a company's product or service. However, the task of creating and producing advertisements can be difficult. For its advertisements to be effective, a company must be able to (1) combine copy, art, and audio to develop a message that the audience will remember, (2) create the appropriate appeal or tone for the advertisement, and (3) select an appropriate execution style.

Developing a Memorable Message

Advertising campaigns are most effective when they convey a message that is remembered by consumers within the target market. Memorable advertising messages are the result of a combination of three basic elements:

- *Copy* is any spoken or printed words in an advertisement. Copy is an element of most advertisements in all types of media.

- *Art*, also called *graphics*, is any visual element in an advertisement, such as photographs, moving pictures, drawings, charts or graphs, the typefaces used for the copy, and even "white space"—the area in an advertisement that contains no words or pictures. Art is an important component of print, television, and Internet advertisements.

- *Audio* is the element in an advertisement that involves sound, including music, sound effects, and voices. Audio is typically used in radio, television, and Internet advertisements.

A variety of factors influence the way these three elements are combined in an advertisement's design. For example, the intended goal of an advertisement influences the amount of copy and art the advertisement includes. Advertisements intended to stimulate immediate action or change attitudes need to provide enough information for customers to make a decision or form an opinion. As a result, these advertisements typically include a large amount of copy and minimal art. Advertisements intended to capture attention or build an image usually include very little copy and rely heavily on graphic elements.

The advertising purpose often affects the size of advertisements. Product advertisements are usually relatively small. Research studies have shown that halving the size of an advertisement does not halve the number of people who read the ad. Therefore, several small ads may net more audience exposure for the same cost as one large advertisement. Because customers tend to associate a company's strength and stability with its size, institutional advertisements typically are large. The graphic elements included in institutional advertising—such as photographs, headlines, and white space—are bold and strong.

The intended audience also affects advertisement design. Trade advertisements usually contain more copy than do consumer advertisements. Trade advertisements also are more technical and rely less on visual elements to attract and hold attention.

Creating an Appeal

The advertising appeal is the basic tone a company uses to communicate its message to the audience. An advertisement's appeal can be humorous, informational, or emotional—that is, it can make audience members laugh, increase their knowledge or understanding of a product or company, or stimulate fear, happiness, desire, relief, or some other emotional response. For example, to create a humorous appeal, some insurers use talking animals or cartoon characters in their advertisements in an attempt to make people laugh and feel good when they think about the company. Other insurers might create an appeal based on fear by focusing their advertisements on a tragedy, such as a devastating storm or natural disaster. After describing the loss experienced by the people in this situation, the company describes how it takes care of its policyowners who endure such tragedies. Advertising is more successful when companies select an appeal that matches the advertising message and needs of the target market audience.

Selecting an Execution Style

The *execution style* of an advertisement is the specific form of presentation used to transform the advertisement's appeal into a message. An execution style can be used alone or in combination with another style. Some of the commonly used execution styles for insurance advertisements are:

■ **Storyline**. A storyline is a short scenario presenting a factual or hypothetical situation or a problem and showing the product being used to resolve the problem. For example, a young woman might explain that her father's decision to buy life insurance made it possible for the family business—and the family—to continue without him.

■ **Testimonial**. A testimonial shows customers, company representatives, or well-known personalities endorsing a product. For example, an insurer might use the star of a popular television program as a spokesperson in a campaign designed to boost the company's image and increase investor confidence.

■ **Mood**. These advertisements create a favorable impression about a product or company by suggesting a certain feeling, conveying a certain tone, or featuring a positive image. For example, an advertisement might show images from the past merging into the present to emphasize an insurer's long history as part of customers' everyday lives.

■ **Association**. An analogy is drawn between the advertised product or company and a person, a situation, or an activity that has a positive image among members of the target market. For example, suppose a life insurance company sponsors a television program about financial matters on a news network. Viewers' respect for the insight and integrity of the program's reporters and commentators can extend, by association, to the sponsoring company.

Evaluating Advertising Effectiveness

Companies can measure the effectiveness of their advertising through pretesting and post-testing. *Pre-testing* measures how well an advertisement performs on a limited basis before the company runs the advertisement in a full-scale campaign. *Post-testing* measures an advertisement's performance during or after its use in a campaign.

One common pretesting method is the direct comparison test. A *direct comparison test* involves showing members of the target market several advertisements and asking them to rate each advertisement according to how well it captures attention, creates interest in a product, conveys the intended message, changes beliefs about a product or organization, or motivates a purchase. Companies can use the results of these tests to determine which type of message, appeal, or execution style works best among members of a target market.

Another common pretesting method is a *pre-rollout test,* which involves showing an advertisement in a real-life context to a specific segment of the target audience and then asking audience members to evaluate the advertisement's effectiveness. For example, a company might place a single advertisement in a local newspaper and ask subscribers for their reactions. Companies can use the results of pre-rollout tests to predict how an advertisement will perform when introduced on a large scale.

Companies typically use the following post-testing methods to evaluate an advertisement's actual performance during or after use in a full-scale campaign:

■ A *recall test* measures how well customers remember advertisements. Recall tests can be aided or unaided. In an *aided recall test*, customers who do not recall a particular advertisement may be given information to jog their memories ("Do you remember any commercials from last night's program? Do you remember seeing an insurance commercial? What do you remember about it?"). An *unaided recall test* establishes whether and how well an audience member exposed to a particular advertisement remembers the advertisement without prompting or clues ("Do you remember any commercials from last night's program? What do you remember about them?").

■ A *recognition test* involves showing members of the target market actual advertisements to which they previously have been exposed and then asking them whether they remember the advertisements.

■ An *attitude test* measures and compares customers' views and beliefs before and after their exposure to an advertisement. Attitude tests help a company determine whether a campaign has accomplished its objectives of improving or changing customer beliefs or attitudes about the company or its products.

■ An *inquiry test* measures the number of responses or inquiries generated by an advertisement that invites customers to call or write for additional information about a product or that offers customers responding to the ad a free sample of the product or some other gift.

Publicity

Sometimes publicity about a company or its products is generated by sources outside the company such as a newspaper article or a television news story. More often, companies craft their own publicity in the form of news releases, news conferences, or public service announcements. Some companies use their marketing department to generate publicity; others have a separate public relations or communications department that oversees the company's general communication with the public. In either situation, publicity efforts must be coordinated with the company's other promotions so that their objectives and results are complementary.

Publicity Objectives

Company-generated publicity is designed to meet three primary objectives: (1) to effectively present information to the public, (2) to create favorable attitudes about a company, and (3) to counter negative publicity and improve a company's image.

Presenting Information

Companies use publicity to provide a wide variety of information to the public about themselves, their products, and their activities, to build a strong reputation for themselves and help generate sales. Insurers often use publicity to provide the following types of information:

■ **New initiatives**. This could include activities such as developing new products, adopting new distribution channels, expanding to new markets, opening new offices, entering into new ventures, and adopting new corporate policies or procedures.

■ **Information about the company**. This could include financial data about sales or profits, personnel changes and promotions, reports on directors or stockholder meetings, favorable legal developments such as resolution of lawsuits, awards or recognition the company or its personnel have received, significant new or renewed contracts, and historical information about the company and its products.

■ **Community service activities**. This might include sponsorship of sports, entertainment, or community events; philanthropic efforts; public service or educational programs; and presentations to school groups or service organizations.

Earlier we discussed how many people accept information presented in a news format more willingly than they accept the same information directly from a company and generally consider publicity a more credible method of communication than advertising. In addition, publicity can reach people who typically avoid advertisements.

Creating Favorable Attitudes

Publicity can be extremely effective in creating a favorable image for a company or even an entire industry. To project a good image, companies often donate time and money to charities; sponsor athletic, cultural, and academic programs; produce educational materials; and support community projects. News stories about these activities create awareness of the company and give the public the impression that the company is a positive, responsible corporate citizen.

Countering Negative Publicity

Publicity is not always positive. Sometimes media attention conveys an unflattering image or negative information about a specific company or its products. When negative publicity occurs, the company's reputation and the relationships it has established with the public can be severely damaged because people tend to accept negative information more readily than positive information. Companies, therefore, must understand how and when to counter negative publicity.

In general, companies should try to be cooperative with the media, even when discussing bad news. Companies that "stonewall" or otherwise respond poorly to unfavorable publicity risk losing goodwill that may have taken years to establish. Companies that respond quickly and openly during a crisis can lessen the impact of bad publicity. For example, if media reports allege unfair business practices by an insurer, the company could invite industry regulators into its business to conduct a market conduct examination, thereby demonstrating to the public that it has nothing to hide and is conducting business according to fair and ethical standards.

Getting Publicity Information to the Public

Although most companies work hard to create positive publicity for themselves and their products, the media decides whether the public will actually see the publicity. The media do not always respond to a company's news releases or invitations to cover news conferences and special events. Nor do the media accept public service announcements that are considered too self-serving or too commercial. The following factors usually determine whether the media will consider publicity items sufficiently newsworthy: (1) the audience appeal, (2) the reputation of the media specialist, (3) the quality of the release, and (4) the competition for news time and space.

Audience Appeal

A medium is more likely to accept publicity items that are relevant or appeal to its target audience than would other media. For example, the general public may not consider an announcement about a new insurance product to be particularly newsworthy, so details about the product are more likely to appear if the announcement is released to an industry trade publication than to a general consumer publication. Similarly, the opening of an insurance company's new regional office probably would be considered important to residents of the city where the office is located, but not to customers in other cities. Due to the regional nature of the announcement, the city's local newspapers and television stations would be better media to use than a national publication or a television station covering a different geographic region. Conversely, announcing a merger of insurance companies that will affect policyowners nationwide would be communicated more effectively through national publications and broadcast networks. Media specialists should recognize the appeal of certain publicity to a specific target audience and send news releases and feature stories only to appropriate media.

Reputation of the Media Specialist

News releases include the name of a contact person (usually the media specialist), who can provide additional information to a news editor or reporter. Journalists are more likely to respond favorably to publicity activities if they are familiar with and have respect for the media specialist responsible for the release. To attain such respect and familiarity, a company's media specialist must establish good working relationships with the editors and reporters who regularly receive the company's news releases. By maintaining ties with members of the media, media specialists also can anticipate the types of information that editors and reporters will find useful.

Quality of the Release

The media reject a large amount of publicity material simply because it is poorly prepared. A well-written, properly formatted news release may find its way into print; a poorly prepared offering is often ignored. In addition, a news release or feature story that includes good quality photographs or professionally produced video footage often receives more attention than comparable releases that do not.

All news releases and feature stories should follow the style and format the particular medium uses, and the writing should be clear and concise. An editor will not use items that require a great deal of editing, that are obviously promotional pieces, or that include exaggerated claims. On the other hand, editors are more likely to accept for publication a news release that closely resembles a news story.

Competing News Stories

Publicity items often compete with a wide variety of other news stories for the limited space or time available in any medium. Sometimes, major unpredictable events like natural disasters may occur that take media attention away from a company's releases. Other major news events, however, are easier to predict and may even be scheduled in advance. Media specialists can increase the likelihood that publicity items are accepted by scheduling news releases and other publicity activities for periods during which their items are less likely to compete with previously scheduled major news events. For example, a good media specialist probably would not schedule a local publicity event at the same time that an annual industry event such as a national conference is being held because the trade press would be concentrating its efforts on covering the conference.

Evaluating the Effectiveness of Publicity

In general, a company evaluates the effectiveness of its publicity by the number of exposures it receives in the media. Advertising agencies and public relations firms often keep track of their client companies' exposures by clipping printed publicity materials from newspapers and magazines and sending copies to their clients. These firms also keep track of the publicity their clients receive on television, radio, and the Internet. Companies can also hire private organizations to monitor their exposures in various media.

Tracking exposures can tell a company when and where its messages appeared and how many readers or viewers potentially saw, read, or heard each item. However, these measures cannot tell the company how many people actually saw, read, or heard the information or whether it changed their attitudes. For some publicity campaigns—such as those attempting to change public attitudes and build a company's or product's image—measuring results is both difficult and expensive. Separating the effects of publicity from the effects generated by other, concurrent promotion activities is also difficult. Whether such measurement is worth the extra time and cost depends on the particular marketing situation.

Key Terms

prospecting	media plan
prospect	reach
referred lead	frequency
sales presentation	waste
sales aid	narrowcasting
point-of-purchase materials	audience selectivity
specialty advertising	buyer turnover
product advertising	purchase frequency
institutional advertising	forgetting rate
direct response advertising	steady timing pattern
product awareness advertising	pulsing pattern
informative product advertising	copy
persuasive product advertising	art
comparative advertising	audio
reminder product advertising	execution style
image-building advertising	pre-testing
advocacy advertising	post-testing
informative institutional advertising	direct comparison test
competitive institutional advertising	pre-rollout test
consumer advertising	recall test
trade advertising	aided recall test
advertising campaign	unaided recall test
advertising agency	recognition test
sales-oriented advertising objective	attitude test
communication-oriented advertising objective	inquiry test

Endnotes

1. Stuart Elliott, "Another Trim in Spending for '07," *New York Times*, 27 June 2007, http://www.nytimes.com/2007/06/27/business/media/27adco.html (12 June 2009).

2. Jon Swallen, "Behind the Numbers: Who's Spending What, With Whom, and in What Channels?" speech, 2007 Insurance Marketing and Advertising Summit, The Hilton, New York City, 8 November 2007.

3. The "M" in "CPM" is derived from the Roman numeral for 1,000.

4. Bradley Johnson, "TV Still Rules, But the Net is Showing Gains," *Advertising Age*, 25 June 2007, http://adage.com/images/random/historicmediatrends.pdf (12 June 2009).

5. Ibid.

6. Lisa Phillips, "Insurance Marketing Online: Meeting Customer Expectations?" Summary, August 2007, *eMarketer*, http://www.emarketer.com/Reports/All/Emarketer _2000424.aspx (12 June 2009).

7. "U. S. Internet Ad Spending Grows in 2007," *Silicon Valley/San Jose Business Journal*, 11 February 2008, http://sanjose.bizjournals.com/sanjose/stories/2008/02/11/daily8.html (12 June 2009).

Chapter 11

Regulation of Life and Health Insurance Marketing

Objectives:

After studying this chapter, you should be able to

- Explain the regulatory system states use to regulate the insurance industry and the role of the National Association of Insurance Commissioners (NAIC)

- Identify the most commonly required provisions in life insurance contracts

- Describe the registration process for variable insurance products, including the use of the registration statement and the prospectus

- Describe insurer practices that are prohibited as unfair trade practices

- Identify specific standards that the NAIC Advertisements Model Regulations and the Financial Industry Regulatory Authority (FINRA) Advertisement Rule impose on insurance product advertisements

- Explain the Life Insurance Disclosure Model Regulation requirements for providing prospective life insurance purchasers with a standardized buyer's guide and a policy summary

- Describe four types of fraudulent, misleading, or unethical sales activities that insurance producers are prohibited from engaging in

- Describe transactions to which the NAIC Life Insurance and Annuities Replacement Model Regulation (Model Replacement Regulation) apply and the general procedures that insurers follow to comply with replacement regulations

- Explain how suitability requirements such as FINRA Conduct Rule 2821 affect producers' actions during the sales process

- Describe a market conduct examination and distinguish between a comprehensive and a target examination

- Describe the limits the Gramm-Leach-Bliley (GLB) Act places on financial institutions with regard to customer privacy and how the GLB Act regulates bank insurance

- Describe the role of the Insurance Marketplace Standards Association (IMSA) in defining acceptable marketing practices

Outline

Regulation of Insurance Marketing in the United States
- Regulation of Products
- Regulation of Promotion
- Regulation of Distribution
- Market Conduct Examinations

United States Regulation of Other Insurance-Related Activities
- Privacy Requirements
- Regulation of Bank Insurance

Insurer Self-Regulation

For many people, insurance provides the only protection they and their families have against financial hardship or potential catastrophic losses resulting from death or illness. Insurance can also provide people with an important means of accumulating assets. For these reasons, policyowners want to be certain insurers will remain in business and be able to meet their obligations, and that insurers and distributors will treat them fairly and ethically.

To ensure the financial well-being and business conduct of insurers and distributors and to maintain public confidence in the insurance industry, governments across the world regulate various aspects of their insurance industries. Two broad categories of regulation of insurance companies and products are:

- *Solvency regulation*, which addresses the need for insurance companies to be financially stable and capable of paying debts and disbursing insurance benefits and annuity proceeds when they are due.

- *Market conduct regulation*, which is designed to ensure that insurance companies conduct business fairly and ethically. Governments regulate a range of company operations, including company management, marketing, advertising, underwriting, claims, customer service, and complaint handling.

Most international insurance regulation is solvency regulation, which is referred to as **prudential regulation** in many countries. Each nation establishes the minimum criteria that insurers must meet to be able to conduct the business of insurance in that country. Most countries impose minimum capital requirements as a prerequisite to an insurer's obtaining a license to transact insurance; a company that is financially unsound is not permitted to receive a license. In the United States, insurers must obtain a **certificate of authority**, or *license*, which is a document that is issued by each state in which the insurer wishes to do business and that grants the company the right to conduct insurance business in that state. In addition, regulatory authorities in most countries continue to monitor and assess the solvency of all licensed insurers on an ongoing basis.

Solvency laws do affect the marketing of insurance in certain areas; for example, laws that establish minimum surplus and reserve requirements are a factor in the pricing of insurance policies. However, most laws that affect the marketing of insurance are market conduct laws. The market conduct laws in many countries contain similar provisions to those found in market conduct laws in the United States, which has the most extensive market conduct regulation in the world. Generally, as the insurance industry in a country matures, the degree of market conduct regulation increases as well.

Regulation of Insurance Marketing in the United States

In the United States, the various states are primarily responsible for regulating the insurance industry. Each state has its own laws, usually referred to as the *state insurance code*, that regulate the business of insurance in that state. Each state also has an administrative agency, typically known as the *state insurance department*, that is responsible for issuing certificates of authority and otherwise administering the state insurance code. The state insurance department operates under the direction of the *insurance commissioner*, known in some states as the *insurance superintendent* or *director of insurance*. The state insurance department also administers the state insurance code by issuing *regulations*, which are rules or orders that explain or help implement the provisions of the code. These regulations have the same force and effect as laws.

Although each state has its own set of laws and regulations governing insurance, these laws and regulations are similar throughout the various states in many instances because they are based on models developed by the National Association of Insurance Commissioners. The *National Association of Insurance Commissioners (NAIC)* is a private, nonprofit association of the insurance commissioners of all 50 states, the District of Columbia, and the four U.S. territories that promotes uniformity of state regulation by developing model laws and regulations as guidelines for the states. *Model laws* and *model regulations* are sample laws and regulations offered by the NAIC that the states are encouraged to use as a basis for their laws and regulations. The *Producer Licensing Model Act* is one example of an NAIC model law. Each state can enact model laws and regulations as written, use them as a basis for developing its own laws and regulations, or ignore them completely.

The federal government also regulates some aspects of the insurance industry. Variable life insurance and variable annuities are considered securities under federal law, and these products and the companies and individuals who distribute them are subject to federal securities regulation as well as state insurance regulation. Federal securities regulation is designed to protect investors. To achieve this protection, companies and individuals engaged in issuing and selling securities are required to conduct business fairly and in accordance with regulatory requirements. Such companies and individuals must also provide consumers with specific types of information to enable them to make informed decisions.

Most regulation of insurance marketing occurs in three primary areas:

- Products
- Promotion
- Distribution

Regulation of Products

To protect the public interest, the insurance laws of all states require that certain mandatory provisions favorable to policyowners be included in all insurance policies. Figure 11.1 includes a summary of the most commonly required life insurance contract provisions.

State insurance laws impose a number of restrictions on insurance contracts as well. Most state insurance codes contain **unfair discrimination provisions**, which are provisions designed to ensure that all individuals in the same underwriting classification are treated alike. These provisions prohibit insurers from unfairly discriminating between individuals of the same class and life expectancy in rates charged or benefits payable or any other term or condition of an insurance or annuity contract. Insurers specifically are prohibited from refusing to insure individuals or limiting the amount of coverage available because of their sex, marital status, race, religion, national origin, or, in many states, sexual orientation.

Figure 11.1. Required Life Insurance Contract Provisions

State insurance laws generally require life insurance contracts to contain the following provisions:

- An **entire contract provision** stating that the entire contract consists of the life insurance policy; the application, if it is attached to the policy; and any attached riders and endorsements.

- A **free-look provision** giving the policyowner a specified period, usually 10 to 30 days, within which to cancel the policy and receive a full refund of all premiums paid. This period may be extended for certain types of policies. Most states require the free-look provision to be included on the policy's front page.

- A **misstatement of age provision** stating that if the insured's age was misstated on the application, then the amount of benefits payable will be adjusted to the amount that premiums paid would have purchased for a person of the correct age. The misstatement of age provision usually also provides for the adjustment of benefits if the insured's sex was misstated; in these cases, the provision is known as the *misstatement of age and sex provision*.

- A **grace period provision** granting the policyowner the right to pay any required premium within a specified period, usually 30 or 31 days, after the premium due date. The policy remains in force throughout the grace period regardless of whether the premium is paid, although, if a claim arises during the grace period, the amount of the required premium may be deducted from the benefits due.

- An **incontestability provision** stating that the policy will be incontestable, other than for nonpayment of premiums, after it has been in force during the lifetime of the insured for a certain period of time after issue, usually one or two years.

- A **reinstatement provision** giving the policyowner the right to reinstate the contract to fully paid-up status within a certain period of time after the policy has expired by paying all unpaid and outstanding premiums plus interest and satisfying any other requirements specified in the provision. For example, reinstatement usually is conditioned upon the insured's supplying evidence of insurability and does not apply to policies surrendered for the cash surrender value.

- A **nonforfeiture provision** stating the amount of benefits that the insurer will pay if the policyowner stops making required premium payments on or surrenders a policy that has a cash value. The provision states how those benefits are calculated, and what options the policyowner has regarding the types of benefits available. This provision usually is based on state laws derived from the NAIC **Standard Nonforfeiture Law for Life Insurance**, which requires most individual life insurance policies to provide specified minimum nonforfeiture values.

Federal securities law is concerned primarily with requiring the disclosure of full and accurate information needed by an investor to make a decision about whether to buy a variable insurance product or any other security. Federal law also requires that each security and each company that issues securities be registered with the Securities and Exchange Commission (SEC), which allows the SEC to exercise oversight authority over the governance of the sale of securities. Recall from Chapter 8 that insurers must distribute their variable products through a broker-dealer that is registered with the SEC.

The SEC's primary function in the registration process is to ensure that all required information has been filed in accordance with the applicable laws so that potential investors can make an informed decision. The SEC does not supervise a company's investment decisions, judge the merits of any investments, or verify the accuracy of any information contained in the filing. In addition, registration does *not* indicate the SEC's approval of the product. In fact, representing a security as having SEC approval or endorsement is unlawful and subject to criminal and civil penalties.

To ensure that potential purchasers of variable insurance products have access to complete and accurate information about an insurer, the SEC's registration process requires the company to disclose specific information about its financial condition, its investment policies, and the variable products it intends to issue. Insurance companies comply with the SEC's registration requirements not by registering the company as a whole but, instead, by registering the separate account used by the insurer to fund benefits for variable annuities or variable life insurance products.[1]

An insurer's separate account is maintained apart from the insurer's general assets and consists of a number of subaccounts, each containing different types of assets. For example, an insurer might have several subaccounts containing various types of corporate stocks, another subaccount containing United States Treasury bills and notes, and another subaccount containing corporate bonds. Premiums that policyowners pay for variable insurance products are used to purchase shares in various subaccounts that the policyowner selects, and the value of a variable life insurance policy or variable annuity will vary according to the performance of the owner's selected subaccount investments.

To register a variable insurance product with the SEC, the insurer files a registration statement, accompanied by any required fees. The ***registration statement*** is a document that contains detailed information about the variable product and the insurer, including specified financial statements. The purpose of the registration statement is to require the company to disclose information about its structure, operations, and investment objectives, as well as information about the variable product it intends to issue.

Certain key information in the registration statement is contained in the ***prospectus***, which is a written document that describes specific aspects of a security, variable life insurance product, or variable annuity being offered for sale. SEC rules specify the information that must be included in a prospectus and require that the prospectus be provided as part of any sales offer to potential purchasers of variable insurance products, along with any other disclosure information that may be required by state law. In addition to the information included in any prospectus to potential new purchasers, companies that issue variable insurance products are required by the SEC to provide existing policyowners with periodic reports of financial information and account performance.

Figure 11.2 lists some of the information typically included in a prospectus.

Figure 11.2. Information Contained in a Prospectus

A prospectus for a variable insurance product typically includes the following items:

- A cover page with the name of the insurer, name and type of the separate account, types of variable products being offered, and date of the prospectus

- A table of fees, detailing the various expenses, followed by a hypothetical example showing the total amount of expenses incurred over time on a specific investment

- A table showing performance over time of each subaccount offered

- Background information about the issuing company's management and investment strategy, including the types of securities to be included in the portfolio

- A description of the variable insurance products and the policyowner's policy rights and invest-ment rights

- A description of the procedures for purchasing a policy and the method by which payments are credited

- Specified financial statements certified by an independent public accountant

---

To further its goal of full and fair disclosure to prospective purchasers of securities, the SEC has adopted a "Plain English Rule" that requires the cover page and other key sections of the prospectus be written in clearly understandable language. The rule requires issuers to use short sentences; definite, concrete and everyday language; active voice; no legal or business jargon; and no multiple negatives. A company should present all information in a prospectus in a clear, concise, and understandable manner. The use of graphs, tables, and charts is encouraged as long as they are not misleading.

Regulation of Promotion

Because insurance is an intangible product that people cannot examine or experience prior to purchase, customers often rely heavily on insurance promotion in making their purchase decisions. State and federal insurance laws and regulations contain a number of requirements and restrictions designed to ensure that the promotional information that insurers and producers provide to customers is fair, accurate, and complete.

Unfair Trade Practices

All states have provisions in their insurance codes that prohibit unfair methods of competition and unfair or deceptive trade practices. Many of these statutes are based on the NAIC *Unfair Trade Practices Act*, which identifies a number of general insurer practices that are prohibited if committed (1) flagrantly, in conscious disregard of the law, or (2) so frequently as to indicate a general business practice. The Unfair Trade Practices Act and other state laws regulating trade practices usually do not try to identify every activity that is considered to be unfair. Instead, they contain broad prohibitions against specified types of unfair practices, and, as a result, many states have adopted regulations that supplement and clarify these laws.

Many of the acts that constitute unfair trade practices, especially in regard to the promotion of insurance products, involve *misrepresentations,* which are false or misleading statements. The Unfair Trade Practices Act prohibits making any statement concerning insurance policies or annuity contracts that misrepresents

- The benefits, advantages, conditions, or terms of the policy

- The financial condition of any insurer

- The dividends or surplus share to be received or that has previously been paid on any policy

- The true nature of a product or class of products by the use of any misleading name or title

- Premium rates for the purpose of inducing the purchase, lapse, forfeiture, exchange, conversion, or surrender of any policy

- Any policy as being shares of stock

Other statements about the business of insurance are prohibited if they are

- Public statements or advertisements containing any representations with respect to the business of insurance or any insurer that are untrue, deceptive, or misleading

- False or maliciously critical or derogatory statements regarding the financial condition of any insurer that are calculated to injure the insurer

- Knowingly false statements of material fact regarding an insurer's own financial condition

- Advertisements or promotional materials that would cause a reasonable person to mistakenly believe that the state or federal government is responsible for or stands behind any particular insurance activity of any entity, guarantees any return on any insurance product, or is a source of payment of any insurance obligation

Advertising and Sales Promotion Materials

Although state unfair trade practices acts prohibit a number of deceptive and misleading promotional practices, most states have adopted specific regulatory requirements regarding the advertising of insurance and annuities by insurers and insurance producers. In many states, advertising requirements are based on the NAIC *Advertisements of Life Insurance and Annuities Model Regulation* and the NAIC *Advertisements of Accident and Sickness Insurance Model Regulation*, which establish minimum standards of accuracy and fairness while requiring insurers to disclose to the public all relevant information in advertisements for life and health insurance and annuities.

The Model Regulations define an advertisement quite broadly as material designed to create public interest in insurance or annuities or in an insurer or insurance producer; or to induce the public to purchase, increase, modify, reinstate, borrow on, surrender, replace, or retain a policy. The following materials are considered to be advertisements under this definition:

■ Printed or audiovisual material used in direct mail, newspapers, magazines, radio and television scripts, and on billboards and the Internet

■ Descriptive literature and sales aids of all kinds, including Web pages

■ Prepared sales talks, presentations, and materials for use by insurance producers

Ultimately, the insurer must ensure that all advertisements for its products comply with applicable regulatory requirements, regardless of who created the advertisement. Both Model Regulations require the insurer to establish and maintain procedures to control the content, form, and method of dissemination of all advertisements. For this reason, insurers require producers to submit any advertising materials to them for approval prior to use. While most state laws do not require an insurer to file advertisements with the state insurance department for approval unless the insurer's advertisements were previously found to be deceptive, the insurer is required to keep copies of all advertisements on file for a specified period of time.

The Model Regulations take a twofold approach to regulating the content of insurance and annuity advertisements. First, they set forth a series of general requirements of accuracy and fairness that all advertisements must meet. For example, the Model Regulations require that advertisements

■ Must be truthful and complete and clear enough to avoid deception

■ May not be misleading or deceptive to a person of average education or intelligence

■ May not omit material information if the omission would mislead or deceive purchasers

■ May not minimize, obscure, or hide required disclosures within the text of the advertisement

■ Must clearly identify the insurer and type of policy being advertised

■ May not make unfair or incomplete comparisons with policies, benefits, or rates of other insurers

■ May not disparage other insurers, producers, policies, services, or marketing methods

■ May not include statements, pictures, or illustrations that are false or misleading with respect to the financial condition, age, insurance in force, or ranking of the insurer

Second, the Model Regulations identify certain specific content, techniques, strategies, and methods as being actually or potentially deceptive and prohibit or restrict their use in advertisements. In addition, the Model Regulations require the disclosure of certain specific policy information in advertisements to ensure that potential customers have all the information needed to make their purchase decision. Figure 11.3 describes some of the specific advertising practices prohibited or required by the Advertisements of Life Insurance and Annuity Model Regulation. Figure 11.4 describes similar prohibitions or requirements included in the Advertisements of Accident and Sickness Insurance Model

Figure 11.3. Prohibited and Required Life Insurance and Annuity Advertising Practices

Under the Advertisements of Life Insurance and Annuities Model Regulation, advertisements for life insurance or annuities

- **CANNOT** use terms such as *investment, investment plan, charter plan, deposit, profit, profit sharing, interest plan, savings, savings plan,* or *retirement plan,* if the advertisement would tend to mislead consumers into believing they will receive something other than an insurance policy or annuity

- **CANNOT** refer to an annuity as a *CD annuity* or deceptively compare an annuity to a certificate of deposit

- **CANNOT** falsely state or imply that potential purchasers of a particular policy will become members of a special class or group and enjoy special rates or privileges

- **CANNOT** falsely state or imply that a policy is an introductory or special offer or that applicants will receive substantial advantages not available at a later date

- **CANNOT** use words such as *inexpensive, low cost,* or similar terms for guaranteed issue policies

- **CANNOT** falsely state or imply that, because there is no insurance producer or commission involved, there will be a cost saving to prospective purchasers of a policy marketed by direct response techniques

- **CANNOT** use words or symbols that might mislead prospective purchasers into believing that the solicitation is in some way connected with a governmental program or agency

- **MUST** use the words *life insurance* or *annuity* in the name of a product unless other language clearly indicates the product is a life insurance policy or annuity

- **MUST** prominently describe any premium changes for life insurance policies with non-level premiums

- **MUST** prominently disclose in any advertisement, whenever applicable, if an insurer reserves the right to change the amount of the premium during the policy term

- **MUST** prominently display any limitation of benefits for policies with graded or modified benefits

Source: Adapted from NAIC, *Advertisements of Life Insurance and Annuities Model Regulation,* (2000). Reprinted with permission from the National Association of Insurance Commissioners; further distribution is strictly prohibited.

Regulation.

Figure 11.4. Prohibited and Required Accident and Sickness Insurance Advertising Practices

Under the Advertisements of Accident and Sickness Insurance Model Regulation, advertisements for health insurance

- **CANNOT** employ devices that are designed to create undue fear or anxiety, such as images that emphasize persons in obvious pain in hospital beds or persons being evicted from their homes due to unpaid medical bills

- **CANNOT** describe policy limitations, exceptions, or reductions in a positive manner so as to imply they are benefits, such as "even pre-existing conditions are covered after two years"

- **CANNOT** describe premiums as *low*, *low cost*, *budget*, or use similar terms or state that premiums are *only* or *just* a particular amount for policies with modest premiums due to limited coverage or benefits

- **CANNOT** falsely state or imply that premiums may not be changed in the future

- **CANNOT** imply that a common type of policy or common benefit combination is *new*, *unique*, *bonus*, *breakthrough*, or otherwise unusual

- **CANNOT** imply coverage beyond the terms of the policy for a policy covering only one disease or a list of specified diseases

- **CANNOT** imply that the maximum payable benefit limits will be paid when less benefits are paid in an average claim

- **MUST** identify an accident and sickness policy as an insurance policy

- **MUST** indicate daily benefit limits if the advertisement emphasizes total maximum benefits available

- **MUST** prominently disclose if any described benefits vary by age

- **MUST** disclose in any invitation to contract the amounts of any deductibles or coinsurance and all exceptions, reductions, and limitations that affect the basic policy provisions without the use of deceptive terms such as *only, just, merely, minimum,* or *necessary* to describe the exceptions, reductions, and limitations

- **MUST** disclose any waiting or elimination period for specific benefits

- **MUST** clearly and conspicuously in prominent type state the limited nature of any policy providing benefits for specified illnesses or accidents or other limited benefits with language such as "THIS IS A LIMITED POLICY" or "THIS IS A CANCER-ONLY POLICY"

- **MUST** state, if applicable, that a particular policy is cancellable or renewable at the option of the insurer or that the insurer has the right to increase policy rates

Source: Adapted from NAIC, *Advertisements of Accident and Sickness Insurance Model Regulation*, (1999). Reprinted with permission from the National Association of Insurance Commissioners; further distribution is strictly prohibited.

The Financial Industry Regulatory Authority (FINRA) *Advertisement Rule (FINRA Conduct Rule 2210)* imposes similar requirements on advertisements and sales literature for securities, including variable products. As defined in the rule, advertisements and sales literature encompass a wide range of materials, including Web sites, billboards, news releases, form letters, mass e-mails, business cards, and letterhead stationery. In general, advertising materials must be fair and balanced and must provide a sound basis for evaluating the facts in regard to any particular security or type of security. The following are some of the specific standards imposed by the rule:

- FINRA members may not publish, circulate, or distribute any public communication that the member knows or has reason to know is false, misleading, or contains any untrue statement of a material fact

- Members may not make false, exaggerated, unwarranted, or misleading statements or claims in any communication to the public or omit any material fact if the omission would cause the communication to be misleading

- Materials must contain the name of the registered broker-dealer

- Materials must not contain any promises of specific investment results, any exaggerations, or any opinions for which there is no reasonable basis

- Materials must not imply that any state or federal regulatory body has endorsed or approved a product or a registered broker-dealer, principal, or representative

- Investment results cannot be predicted or projected

- Comparisons in advertisements or sales literature between investments must disclose all material differences between them

The Advertisement Rule requires members to submit advertisements and sales materials to FINRA for review and broker-dealers to keep all such materials on file for at least three years after every use.

FINRA also has issued specific guidelines to be considered in preparing advertisements and sales literature about variable insurance products. The guidelines require that all communications must clearly describe a product as a variable life insurance policy or variable annuity and may not represent or imply that the product or its underlying account is a mutual fund or a short-term, liquid investment. Advertisements cannot overly emphasize guarantees such as minimum death benefits or imply that such a guarantee applies to investment results or the separate account. Advertisements cannot imply that an insurer's financial rating applies to the separate account. Advertisements for variable life insurance policies in general must provide a balanced discussion of the insurance and investment features of the policy.

Disclosure

To ensure that consumers receive truthful and accurate information that enables them to make informed decisions about life insurance and annuity purchases, some states have imposed additional disclosure requirements in connection with the marketing of life insurance and annuities. A number of states have adopted regulations based on the NAIC *Life Insurance Disclosure Model Regulation*, which requires insurers to provide prospective purchasers of most individual life insurance policies with information to help them select an appropriate policy. The NAIC *Annuity Disclosure Model Regulation* imposes similar disclosure requirements for specified types of annuities.

The Life Insurance Disclosure Model Regulation requires the insurer to provide each prospective life insurance purchaser with a standardized buyer's guide and a policy summary. The *Life Insurance Buyer's Guide* describes in general language the basic types of life insurance and the costs and benefits involved with each type, how to determine the amount of life insurance needed, and the other factors to be considered before purchasing a life insurance policy.

A *policy summary* is a document that contains detailed information about the specific policy being considered for purchase. The policy summary must include the generic name of the policy and each rider; the name and address of the insurance producer and the insurer; and the date the summary was prepared. In addition, for the first five policy years and some selected years thereafter, including the maturity date, the summary must indicate the annual premium for the policy and each rider, the amount of basic death benefits and any added benefits from any applicable rider, and the total cash surrender benefits for the basic policy and any riders.

Regulation of Distribution

To safeguard the public interest, many state insurance laws regulate the sales activities of licensed producers as well as those of insurers. Similarly, FINRA has adopted a number of rules that regulate the conduct of registered persons. These laws and rules are designed to ensure that producers treat customers honestly and fairly and that they adequately protect their customers' interests.

Unfair Sales Practices

State unfair trade practices acts and other state insurance laws prohibit producers from making the same types of misrepresentations regarding insurance policies or the business of insurance as insurers are prohibited from making. Insurance producers also are prohibited from engaging in fraudulent, misleading, and unethical sales activities. The following actions by insurance producers are considered unfair trade practices:

- Misappropriation and commingling of funds
- Rebating
- Twisting and churning
- Unfair financial planning practices

Insurance producers often handle money belonging to customers or insurers. For example, producers typically accept initial premiums from customers at the time of application. Producers also may distribute dividend checks or surrender and loan funds to contract owners. Such actions are allowable as long as the producer has the authority under his contract to do so and he does not misappropriate or commingle funds. *Misappropriation* is the illegal misuse of a customer's or an insurer's money, even if the use is on a temporary basis. The *commingling of funds*, which is the practice of combining monies belonging to others with a producer's own funds, even on a temporary basis, is also prohibited in most cases.

Rebating is a sales practice in which an insurer or insurance producer offers a prospect an inducement to purchase an insurance policy or annuity, and the inducement is not offered to all applicants in similar situations and is not stated in the policy itself. The rebate usually is made in the form of a portion of the insurance producer's commission. Rebating generally is considered to be a type of unfair discrimination and is prohibited under the laws of all states except California and Florida.

Certain unfair trade practices may occur when an insurance producer advises customers to surrender one life insurance policy or annuity and replace it with another policy. Replacements can benefit the customer in some cases. For example, the policyowner's health may have improved significantly since the original policy was issued so that he now qualifies for better rates under a new policy. However, in other cases, replacement benefits the insurance producer who earns a high first-year commission more than it benefits the customer whose policy is replaced, especially when all the costs involved with surrendering the old policy and purchasing a new one are taken into consideration.

Twisting is a prohibited trade practice that occurs when an insurance producer misrepresents the features of a policy to induce a customer to replace an existing policy. For example, if a producer persuades a customer to replace a life insurance policy that has a significant cash value with a larger policy at the same premium, but fails to mention that the reason for the larger policy's lower premium is because the cash value of the original policy is being applied to the premium cost, the producer's action would be an example of twisting. *Churning* is a similar prohibited practice that occurs when the insurance producer induces the customer to replace one policy with another multiple times so that the producer can earn a series of high first-year commissions on the replacements. If a producer convinces a customer to replace one annuity with another whenever interest rates rise, supposedly to lock in the higher rate, without mentioning that the customer's account is being subjected to repeated surrender charges that offset any increase in value due to the rise in the interest rate, the producer's actions would constitute churning.

Many individuals who seek financial planning assistance consult insurance producers. State unfair trade practices acts or other state laws often include provisions designed to ensure that insurance producers accurately represent themselves to their clients in financial planning matters. According to such provisions, insurance producers are prohibited from holding themselves out to the public as financial planners, consultants, investment advisers, or any other specialist in financial planning if they are, in fact, only engaged in the commission-based sale of policies.

Insurance producers who are certified or designated financial planners may identify themselves as such, but they must disclose in advance of any product sale or solicitation that they are also insurance producers and that they will receive a commission for the sale of the policy in addition to fees for financial planning. Any agreement for financial planning service fees with an insurance producer must be in writing, signed by the client, and must include a statement that the client is not obligated to purchase any insurance product through the insurance producer.

If the state insurance department determines that an insurance producer has violated the unfair trade practices act or any other provision of the state insurance laws or regulations, the department has the authority to suspend or revoke the producer's license. Usually a suspension or revocation occurs only after the department has conducted an administrative hearing at which the producer is given the opportunity to present evidence.

In addition to suspending or revoking an insurance producer's license, the insurance department may impose a monetary fine. The insurance department generally has no authority to prosecute insurance producers for criminal offenses such as theft, but the department may refer any relevant information it has to the appropriate governmental authority for prosecution.

At the federal level, FINRA has issued a number of rules regulating the conduct of broker-dealers and registered persons, including the following rules:

- FINRA Conduct Rule 2110 requires members to "observe high standards of commercial honor and just and equitable principles of trade."

- FINRA Conduct Rule 2120 prohibits the use of any manipulative, deceptive, or fraudulent device or contrivance to induce the purchase or sale of any security. This rule prohibits twisting, churning, and other unfair or deceptive sales practices.

- FINRA Conduct Rule 2330 prohibits a member from making improper use of a customer's funds or guaranteeing a customer against loss in any transaction.

As part of its regulatory responsibility, FINRA conducts periodic compliance inspections of all broker-dealers. These inspections include a review of the broker-dealer's accounting books and records, sales practices, and financial condition. FINRA may also conduct investigations in response to customer complaints. Such investigations are intended to determine whether any rules or regulations have been violated and, if so, whether disciplinary action is necessary.

FINRA is empowered to take disciplinary action against member companies or registered persons who violate its rules. Individuals and firms accused of rule violations are entitled to a hearing at which they may present evidence on their behalves. Disciplinary sanctions may include fines, suspensions or revocations of registration or membership, or permanent bars from association with any member.

Supervision

FINRA requires broker-dealers to actively supervise their sales personnel to ensure their compliance with FINRA rules and securities laws. FINRA's **Supervisory Rule (FINRA Conduct Rule 3010)** requires broker-dealers to establish and maintain, in accordance with written procedures, a system for supervising the activities of their registered representatives and registered principals. Each member must designate at least one principal as the chief compliance officer, with responsibility for establishing and maintaining the supervisory system. The chief compliance officer must submit detailed written reports on the system to senior management at least once a year.[2] In addition, principals must directly supervise the actions of each registered representative to ensure that the representative understands how to conduct business in accordance with regulatory requirements and must meet with each registered representative at least once a year to discuss regulatory and compliance issues.

Insurance Replacement

Life insurance or annuity replacements that are made for the benefit of the producer, which are typically associated with twisting and churning, are prohibited as unfair trade practices. On the other hand, most states do permit replacements that are in the customer's interest rather than the producer's, as long as they satisfy certain regulatory requirements. In most states, regulations that govern replacement requirements are based on various versions of the NAIC *Life Insurance and Annuities Replacement Model Regulation (Model Replacement Regulation)*, which was developed to ensure that insurers and insurance producers provide consumers with fair and accurate information about policies so that consumers can make purchase decisions that are in their own best interests.

The Model Replacement Regulation applies to any transaction in which an individual annuity or life insurance policy is to be purchased and the salesperson, or insurer if there is no salesperson, knows or should know that, as a result of the transaction, an existing annuity or life insurance policy will be

- Used in a *financed purchase*, which is the purchase of a new policy for which the owner intends to pay premiums using funds taken from another policy

- Lapsed, forfeited, surrendered, or otherwise terminated

- Converted or otherwise reduced in value by the use of nonforfeiture benefits or other policy values

- Amended so that the benefits or term for which coverage remains in force is lessened

- Reissued with any reduction in cash value

State laws based on the Model Replacement Regulation typically require that the producer and applicant for any individual life insurance policy or annuity complete and sign a replacement statement that lists all of the applicant's existing life insurance policies and annuity contracts, if any, that will be replaced by the new contract. If replacements are involved, the insurance producer must give the applicant a written Notice Regarding Replacement providing general information about the potential effect of a replacement and advising the applicant to review all relevant information before making a final decision. The insurance producer then verifies that the information on the replacement statement is complete and submits it to the insurer. The producer also must give the applicant a copy of the replacement statement and all sales materials used in any presentation.

The insurer is responsible for supervising and monitoring the activities of all its producers to ensure their compliance with regulatory requirements. In cases in which applications are initiated as a result of direct response solicitation, the insurer must obtain the required replacement statement directly from the applicant. Usually, the insurer also must notify the existing insurer of the possible replacement so that the existing insurer has the opportunity to present its own information to the applicant. The applicant is best able to make an informed decision when both insurers involved have the opportunity to provide the applicant with information about the policies involved and the effects of any replacement.

Some states have imposed more extensive disclosure requirements on insurance producers and insurers before replacement of an existing life insurance policy or annuity can be made. The most comprehensive disclosure requirements are those mandated by Regulation 60 of the State of New York, which applies to life insurance policies or annuity contracts purchased and delivered or issued for delivery in New York. Under Regulation 60, the producer must provide the customer with a detailed disclosure statement comparing the features and benefits of the existing policy and the proposed replacement policy, and the insured then has 60 days to cancel the replacement policy and obtain a full refund of all premiums paid. If the original policy was issued by a company subject to New York insurance laws, the insured may also reinstate the original policy without a new contestable or suicide period and without having to provide evidence of insurability.

Suitability

One of the major developments in the regulation of insurance marketing in recent years has been the increasing imposition of suitability requirements in connection with the sale of annuities and other life insurance products. A *suitability requirement* is one that imposes a duty on producers to have reasonable grounds on which to believe that a specific product is suitable for a particular customer's needs. This requirement goes considerably beyond the prohibitions against fraudulent or misleading actions or statements contained in unfair trade practices acts. If no producer is involved in the marketing of the product, as with direct response products, the suitability requirement is imposed directly upon the insurer.

In 2006, the NAIC adopted the *Suitability in Annuity Transactions Model Regulation,* which requires producers to take specific measures to ensure the suitability of any purchase or exchange of an annuity contract that results in another insurance transaction, such as using the surrender value of an annuity to purchase another annuity or a paid-up life insurance policy. A majority of the states have adopted annuity suitability requirements based either on this model regulation or an earlier version of the regulation, the Senior Protection in Annuity Transactions Model Regulation, which imposed the same suitability determination requirements but applies only to transactions involving individuals 65 years of age or older.

Annuity transactions involving senior citizens often are the focus of regulatory concern. Many features of certain annuities, such as their surrender charges and lengthy accumulation periods, may make them inappropriate investment choices for senior citizens who typically have fewer sources of income, a more limited number of other resources, shorter life expectancy, and greater need for liquid assets for emergency purposes than do younger individuals. In addition to imposing suitability requirements, some states also have enacted additional laws designed to give senior citizens greater protection in regard to annuity transactions, such as by limiting surrender charges on annuities sold to senior citizens.

State suitability regulations based on the NAIC Suitability Model Regulation typically require that, before making a recommendation to a consumer to purchase or exchange an annuity, an insurance producer or insurer must have reasonable grounds for believing that the transaction is suitable for the consumer on the basis of facts disclosed by the consumer. The insurance producer or insurer is specifically required to make reasonable efforts to obtain information concerning the consumer's

- Financial status

- Tax status

- Investment objectives

- Current investment and insurance products

Insurance producers and insurers are also expected to obtain any other information considered reasonable by the producer or insurer and to use all known information in making a recommendation. The producer or insurer typically is exempt from suitability requirements if the consumer fails or refuses to provide requested information. Insurers are also required to establish and maintain a system of supervising recommendations to ensure compliance with applicable state suitability requirements.

FINRA conduct rules also address the suitability of investment recommendations to customers. The ***Suitability Rule (FINRA Conduct Rule 2310)*** requires members to have reasonable grounds for making an investment recommendation to a customer based on the facts disclosed by the customer as to his other security holdings, financial situation, and needs. The member is required to make reasonable efforts to obtain the following customer information:

- Customer's financial status

- Customer's tax status

- Customer's investment objectives

- Such other information considered to be reasonable in making recommendations to the customer

The general suitability requirements contained in the Suitability Rule apply to all securities. However, because of the number of enforcement actions brought against sales representatives in recent years based on inappropriate or unsuitable sales or exchanges of variable annuities, FINRA now imposes specific sales practice standards and supervisory requirements for transactions in deferred variable annuities.

FINRA Conduct Rule 2821, which became effective in 2008, considerably expands the requirements of the Suitability Rule by specifying criteria to be taken into consideration in making a suitability determination for the purchase or exchange of a deferred variable annuity. In particular, a FINRA member must have a reasonable basis to believe

- The customer has been informed of various features of deferred variable annuities such as surrender periods and charges, possible tax consequences, specific fees and charges, and the market risk

- The customer would benefit from specific features of a deferred variable annuity such as tax-deferred growth, annuitization, or death benefits

- The specific features of the particular annuity are suitable for the particular customer based on information obtained from the customer

■ Any surrender charges, new surrender period, increased fees and charges, loss of existing benefits, as well as any possible benefit from product enhancement or improvement, have been taken into account in determining the suitability of a policy exchange

The suitability determination required by Rule 2821 must be documented and signed by the person recommending the transaction. In addition, a registered principal must review, approve, and sign the suitability determination before the application is sent to the insurer for processing. Rule 2821 also imposes more comprehensive and detailed requirements for information to be obtained from a customer prior to recommending the purchase or exchange of a deferred variable annuity.

Market Conduct Examinations

The state insurance department uses the market conduct examination as one of its primary means of determining whether insurers are in compliance with the state's market conduct laws. A *market conduct examination* is a formal investigation of an insurer conducted by one or more state insurance departments that is designed to determine whether the insurer's market conduct complies with applicable laws and regulations. Market conduct examinations are authorized by and required under the insurance laws of all states.

The insurance department may conduct both comprehensive and target examinations. A *comprehensive examination* is a full-scope examination of all nonfinancial aspects of an insurer's operations. Many states require their insurance departments to conduct periodic comprehensive market conduct examinations of insurers operating in the state. Most market conduct examinations today, however, are *target examinations*, which are limited-scope examinations of one or more lines of business or specific areas of an insurer's nonfinancial operations, such as its advertising materials. Target examinations often arise as a result of customer complaints or recent changes in applicable regulations and may be conducted whenever the insurance department believes them necessary. An insurer's marketing activities frequently are the focus of a target examination.

To assist the insurance department in conducting examinations, state laws require insurers to maintain various business records for specified periods of time and to cooperate with the examiners in providing any requested materials. After the market conduct examination is completed, the insurance department files a written report and may issue an order to an insurer indicating any corrective action the insurer is required to take as a result of the examination findings.

If the market conduct examination reveals that an insurer has violated any applicable state insurance laws, or if the insurer fails to take any required corrective action, the insurance department may sanction the insurer. The insurance department may also impose sanctions based on any other evidence that gives the department reasonable cause to believe such violations have occurred. Sanctions usually may be imposed only after an insurer has been given notice and an opportunity to present evidence on its behalf at a hearing; sanctions also are subject to judicial review. Sanctions generally can include both a fine and a *cease and desist order*, which is a legally enforceable declaration by the insurance department that the offender must stop engaging in the prohibited conduct. In the case of severe violations, the insurance department is authorized to suspend or revoke the insurer's certificate of authority.

United States Regulation of Other Insurance-Related Activities

The Gramm-Leach-Bliley (GLB) Act has had a significant effect on the regulation of insurance-related activities in the United States. In addition to removing the regulatory barriers preventing the affiliation of insurance companies, banks, and other financial institutions, the GLB Act includes a number of safeguards designed to protect the public interest. These safeguards focus on maintaining the privacy of customers' personal financial information and properly regulating the insurance activities of banks and other financial institutions.

Privacy Requirements

During the course of their business relationships with insurance companies and other financial institutions, customers often provide a considerable amount of personal and financial information that generally is intended solely for the use of those particular institutions. This information can be valuable for marketing purposes, but many people do not want it to be disclosed to third parties.

The GLB Act places limits on the ability of financial institutions to disclose *nonpublic personal information*, which is defined as personally identifiable financial information that a consumer provides to a financial institution, including banks and insurance companies, which is not publicly available. The GLB Act requires financial service institutions to provide a privacy notice to customers at the time the customer enters into a contractual relationship with the financial institution and once a year thereafter. The privacy notice must describe what information the company collects about the individual, with whom it shares the information, and how it protects and safeguards the information. Individuals who have provided information to a financial institution but did not enter into a contract with that institution, such as applicants for an insurance policy who never actually purchased a policy, must be provided with a privacy notice only if the institution actually intends to disclose the information to a nonaffiliated third party. In either case, the individual usually must be given an opportunity to *opt out*—that is, to refuse to allow the financial institution to disclose the information to a nonaffiliated third party.

The GLB Act does not prevent financial institutions from sharing information with affiliated financial service companies; however, another federal law, the *Fair Credit Reporting Act*, does enable customers to opt out of allowing financial institutions to share credit reports and application information with affiliated companies. In addition, the GLB Act allows states the option of giving customers even greater privacy rights. For example, some states prohibit financial institutions from sharing a customer's nonpublic personal information in most cases, unless the customer specifically authorizes it in advance.

Regulation of Bank Insurance

The GLB Act provides that the insurance activities of any entity, including banks, shall be subject to functional regulation by the states. *Functional regulation* is the principle that a single regulatory body—in this case, the state insurance departments—should oversee similar financial activities, regardless of which type of financial institution engages in the activity. However, the GLB Act also provides that states may not use their regulatory authority to effectively prevent banks or other financial institutions from marketing insurance products, including annuities. In addition, state insurance laws, in general, may not have a discriminatory effect against banks or other financial institutions. As a result, for example, state producer licensing laws apply to bank personnel the same way that those laws apply to any other individuals wishing to sell insurance. Similarly, state unfair trade practices laws prohibiting fraud or misrepresentation in the sale of insurance also apply to a bank's insurance related activities.

The GLB Act did establish a number of *safe harbors*, which were specific areas in which states were expressly permitted to restrict a bank or other financial institution's insurance activities. No state is required to include these safe harbors in its insurance laws, but many states have done so. In particular, state insurance laws may

- Prohibit banks from requiring customers to purchase an insurance product from bank-affiliated personnel if the insurance is required in connection with a loan or extension of credit, or from charging additional fees if customers obtain the required insurance from non-bank-affiliated personnel.

- Require banks to disclose in writing that, if insurance is required in connection with a loan or extension of credit, the customer's choice of insurer or insurance provider will not affect the credit decision or credit terms.

- Prohibit banks from using health information obtained from a customer's insurance records for any purpose other than that for which it was originally obtained without express authorization.

- Prohibit banks from refusing to extend credit or provide any other product or service to a customer unless the customer also purchases an insurance product from the bank. This is a form of *tying arrangement*, which occurs when an organization conditions the sale of one product or service on the sale of one or more of the organization's other products or services. Many tying arrangements involving the sale of insurance by banks also are prohibited under federal banking laws.

- Require banks to disclose in writing prior to the sale of any insurance product by the bank that the product is not a deposit, not insured by the Federal Deposit Insurance Corporation (FDIC), and not guaranteed by the bank. When appropriate, banks must also disclose that the insurance product is subject to investment risk and possible loss of principal.

- Require banks that conduct both credit and insurance transactions with a single customer to complete the credit and insurance transactions through separate documents.

■ Prohibit banks that conduct both credit and insurance transactions with a single customer from including the expense of insurance premiums in the primary credit transaction without the express written consent of the customer.

Insurer Self-Regulation

The insurance industry in the United States realizes the importance of market conduct issues such as those addressed in this chapter and is working to improve market conduct through a variety of self-regulatory activities. Many companies now have a separate compliance department and have emphasized training in ethics for all employees and insurance producers. In addition, the American Council of Life Insurers (ACLI), a national insurance trade association, has established the ***Insurance Marketplace Standards Association (IMSA)***, a voluntary association of insurers designed to enable life insurance companies to monitor their own compliance with regulatory requirements and to promote high ethical standards in the sale of life insurance, long-term care insurance, and annuity products.

To qualify for membership in IMSA, insurers must first adopt IMSA's Principles and Code of Ethical Market Conduct. Figure 11.5 lists these principles, which are designed to help insurers develop strategies for market conduct compliance programs. Insurers then must create and apply practices that ensure company-wide compliance with the IMSA principles. Insurers also conduct an extensive self-assessment followed by a second independent assessment to determine their degree of compliance with IMSA principles. Upon completion of the assessment process, insurers become IMSA members for a three-year term; after that period they must undergo the assessment process again to continue their membership. IMSA membership demonstrates an insurer's commitment to conduct its business in an ethical manner and in compliance with applicable regulatory requirements.

Figure 11.5. Six Principles of Ethical Market Conduct

Central to the IMSA Program are its Six Principles of Ethical Market Conduct:

1. To conduct business according to high standards of honesty and fairness and to render that service to its customers which, in the same circumstances, it would apply to or demand for itself

2. To provide competent and customer-focused sales and service

3. To engage in active and fair competition

4. To provide advertising and sales materials that are clear as to purpose and honest and fair as to content

5. To provide for fair and expeditious handling of customer complaints and disputes

6. To maintain a system of supervision and review that is reasonably designed to achieve compliance with these Principles of Ethical Market Conduct

Source: Adapted from Insurance Marketplace Standards Association (IMSA), "Principles and Codes," http://www.imsaethics.org/Content/PrinciplesandCodes_44.aspx (16 June 2009). Used with permission.

Key Terms

prudential regulation
certificate of authority
state insurance code
state insurance department
insurance commissioner
regulations
National Association of Insurance
    Commissioners (NAIC)
model law
model regulation
unfair discrimination provision
entire contract provision
free-look provision
misstatement of age provision
grace period provision
incontestability provision
reinstatement provision
nonforfeiture provision
Standard Nonforfeiture Law for Life
    Insurance
registration statement
prospectus
Unfair Trade Practices Act
misrepresentation
Advertisements of Life Insurance
    and Annuities Model Regulation
Advertisements of Accident and
    Sickness Insurance Model
    Regulation
Advertisement Rule (FINRA
    Conduct Rule 2210)

Life Insurance Disclosure Model
    Regulation
Annuity Disclosure Model
    Regulation
Life Insurance Buyer's Guide
policy summary
misappropriation
commingling of funds
rebating
twisting
churning
Supervisory Rule (FINRA Conduct
    Rule 3010)
Life Insurance and Annuities
    Replacement Model Regulation
    (Model Replacement Regulation)
financed purchase
suitability requirement
Suitability in Annuity Transactions
    Model Regulation
Suitability Rule (FINRA Conduct
    Rule 2310)
FINRA Conduct Rule 2821
market conduct examination
comprehensive examination
target examination
cease and desist order
nonpublic personal information
functional regulation
tying arrangement
Insurance Marketplace Standards
    Association (IMSA)

Endnotes

1. Variable annuities used to fund qualified group retirement plans have been exempted from SEC registration requirements.

2. The requirement that broker-dealers appoint a chief compliance officer who files an annual written report with senior management was added by FINRA Conduct Rule 3012, which became effective in 2005.

Glossary

13-month lapse rate. A lapse rate based on the proportion of new policies on which no part of any required second-year premium has been paid. [5]

80-20 Principle. *See* **Pareto's Principle**.

1035 exchange. In the United States, a tax-free replacement of an insurance policy for another insurance contract covering the same person that is performed in accordance with the conditions of Section 1035 of the Internal Revenue Code. [5]

advance. A loan made to a producer in anticipation of future commission earnings. [8]

Advertisement Rule (FINRA Conduct Rule 2210). A FINRA rule that imposes a number of requirements on advertisements and sales literature pertaining to securities, including variable products, that are used to communicate with the public. [11]

Advertisements of Accident and Sickness Insurance Model Regulation. An NAIC model regulation which establish minimum standards of accuracy and fairness while requiring insurers to disclose to the public all relevant information in advertisements for health insurance. [11]

Advertisements of Life Insurance and Annuities Model Regulation. An NAIC model regulation which establish minimum standards of accuracy and fairness while requiring insurers to disclose to the public all relevant information in advertisements for life insurance and annuities. [11]

advertising. Any paid form of nonpersonal communication or promotion about a company or its products or services that an identified sponsor generates and the media transmits. [9]

advertising agency. An organization that provides its clients with a variety of advertising-related services including developing advertising themes, selecting appropriate media, and creating, producing, and placing advertisements. [10]

advertising campaign. A coordinated series of advertisements designed to promote a product, product line, or the company itself. [10]

advocacy advertising. A form of institutional advertising that presents an industry's, company's, or organization's position on an issue important to the public. [10]

affiliated agent. An agent who sells primarily the products of a single company. [8]

affinity group. A group formed when individuals with common needs, interests, and characteristics communicate regularly with each other. [3]

age distribution. The proportion of people in certain age ranges in a given population. [1]

agency contract. A written agreement between the agent and the principal that defines the agent's role and responsibilities and describes the agent's compensation. Referred to in Canada as a *producer agreement*. [8]

agent. An independent sales representative or company employee who is authorized under the terms of an agency contract to act on behalf of an issuing insurance company. [8]

agent-broker. *See* **broker**.

aggregator. An Internet intermediary that lists products from several different companies on a single Web site. [8]

AIDA model. A commonly used response hierarchy which defines four possible responses customers may display as a result of exposure to promotion: (1) attention, or awareness, (2) interest, (3) desire, and (4) action. [9]

aided recall test. A type of recall test in which customers are given information to jog their memories, or recall, of a particular advertisement. [10]

all-you-can-afford method. A method of establishing a promotion budget in which the budget is based on the amount of available funds. [9]

annualized. A method of calculating and paying first-year commissions that a company owes a producer in a lump sum, as if the entire year's premium had already been paid, regardless of the actual mode of payment the applicant has chosen. [8]

Annuity Disclosure Model Regulation. An NAIC model regulation which requires insurers to provide prospective purchasers of specified types of annuities with information to help them select an appropriate annuity. [11]

art. Any visual element in an advertisement, such as photographs, moving pictures, drawings, charts or graphs, typefaces used for copy, and even "white space"—the area in an advertisement that contains no words or pictures. Also known as *graphics*. [10]

asset-based commission schedule. A commission schedule in which commission percentages payable on sales are based on the accumulated value and growth of a product's funds. Also known as a *trail commission schedule*. [8]

attitude. A learned predisposition to respond to an idea, an object, or a class or group of objects in a consistent manner. [4]

attitude test. A post-testing method that measures and compares customers' views and beliefs before and after their exposure to an advertisement. [10]

attitudinal research. Marketing research designed to collect information about a person or group's attitudes. [4]

audience selectivity. The ability of an advertisement to reach an intended target market. [10]

audio. The element in an advertisement that involves sound, including music, sound effects, and vocal tones. [10]

bancassurance. *See* **bank insurance**.

banding. A method of providing quantity discounts in which a company creates a number of contiguous bands based on the face amount of a policy and charges different premium rates for each band. [7]

bank insurance. The distribution of insurance products to bank customers through a bank-affiliated insurer or insurance agency. Also known as *bancassurance* in other countries. [8]

barrier to entry. A business practice or condition in a market that hinders new companies from entering the market. [1]

behavioristic segmentation. A method of dividing the total market for a product according to consumers' behavior toward a product or company. [3]

benchmarking. A method of planning and implementing tactical/action programs that consists of (1) identifying the best outcomes that other companies have achieved for a specific marketing activity and what practices they used to cause those outcomes and (2) copying the best practices to equal or surpass the best outcomes. [2]

benefit segmentation. A type of behavioristic segmentation in which the benefits that prospective consumers seek are used to segment markets. [3]

BGA. *See* **brokerage general agent.**

BI. *See* **business intelligence.**

birthrate. The number of babies born per 1,000 people in the population. [1]

blog. A Web site or a Web site portion that provides news or commentary on a particular subject with the entries displayed in reverse chronological order, beginning with the most recent entry, and often allows site visitors to post comments there about the blog content. Also known as a *Web log*. [1]

bottom-up approach to budgeting. A method for developing a marketing budget in which marketing managers communicate to senior management the amount of resources that they will need to execute a marketing plan and when those resources will be needed. Senior managers then allocate funds to cover the various activities. [2]

brand. A name, number, term, sign, symbol, design, or combination of these elements used to identify a company or one or more of a company's products and to differentiate the company and its products from its competitors. [6]

brand awareness. The recognition of a brand or brand name by potential buyers and the ability to associate it with the product in question. Also known as *brand recognition*. [6]

brand image. The positive or negative perception of a brand by a customer. [6]

brand insistence. A customer's unwillingness to accept any substitute for the preferred brand. [6]

brand loyalty. A purchase behavior that is exhibited when a customer has a favorable attitude toward a specific brand that usually leads to consistent and habitual purchases of the same product over an extended period of time. [5]

brand mark. A symbol, design, distinctive coloring, unusual type style, or combination of these elements that can be recognized but can't be spoken. Also known as a *logo*. [6]

brand name. A word, letter, or group of words or letters that can be vocalized. [6]

brand preference. A customer's choice of a particular product, when available, over competing products, but the willingness to accept a substitute product when the preferred product is not available. [6]

brand recognition. *See* **brand awareness.**

branding. The process a company uses to identify itself and its products and distinguish its products from those of its competitors. [6]

broker. An independent agent who does not have an exclusive contract with any single insurer or any specific obligation to sell a single insurer's products. Sometimes referred to as an *agent-broker*.[8]

broker-dealer. A type of financial institution that buys and sells securities either for itself or for its customers and provides information and advice to customers regarding the purchase and sale of securities. [8]

brokerage general agency arrangement. An arrangement to distribute nonproprietary products in which an insurance company enters into an agreement to allow its affiliated agents to sell products offered through an independent general agent, known as a *brokerage general agent*. [8]

brokerage general agent (BGA). An independent general agent who is under contract to a number of insurers. [8]

build strategy. A type of marketing strategy under which a company seeks to increase a business unit's market share. This strategy usually requires that a company sacrifice immediate earnings to fund the growth required to improve a business unit's market position. [2]

bursting pattern. *See* **pulsing pattern.**

business cycle. A recurring pattern of fluctuations in economic activity of a nation that is characterized as expansion, peak, contraction, and trough and measured by a nation's gross domestic product and other macroeconomic variables over a specified period of time, generally a year or more. [1]

business intelligence (BI). An organized collection of procedures, software, databases, and devices that support problem-specific decision making. Formerly known as *decision support systems (DSS)*. [4]

business portfolio analysis. A process that allows a company to analyze the strengths and weaknesses of its separate business units to find out what contribution each unit can make to the company, based on current market trends. [2]

buyer behavior. *See* **customer behavior.**

buyer remorse. A psychological state in which customers question whether they should have purchased a product at all, or whether they should have purchased an alternative brand or another product rather than the one they actually bought. [5]

buyer turnover. A measure of how often new customers enter the market to purchase a product. [10]

buying center. An informal, cross-departmental decision unit whose main goal is to acquire, spread, and process information pertaining to purchase decisions. [5]

buying power. *See* **purchasing power.**

captive agent. *See* **career agent.**

career agent. An agent who is under a full-time contract with one company and sells primarily that company's products. Also known as an *agency-building agent*. Formerly known as a *captive agent* or *exclusive agent*.

cash cow. A business unit or product line on the market share/market growth matrix that has a high market share in a low-growth market. [2]

causal research. Primary research used to identify factors or variables that affect the values of other variables. [4]

cease and desist order. A legally enforceable declaration by a state insurance department that an offender must stop engaging in prohibited conduct. [11]

certificate of authority. In the United States, a document issued by a state insurance department that grants a company the right to conduct insurance business in that state. Also known as a *license.* [11]

channel cannibalism. A situation in which sales from a new distribution channel displace sales from an existing distribution channel. [8]

channel conflict. The friction or disagreement within or between channels that results when the goals and behavior of one channel or channel member are at odds with the goals and behavior of another channel or channel member. [8]

channel-specific pricing. *See* **market-by-market pricing.**

churning. An unfair trade practice that occurs when a producer induces a customer to replace one policy with another multiple times so that the producer can earn a series of high first-year commissions on the replacements. [11]

click-through rate (CTR). A measure of the number of people who visit a company's Web site by means of a particular lead generation technique, which is usually expressed as the percentage of the total number of times that an advertisement, targeted e-mail, or other Web marketing material is seen that directly results in a visit to the advertiser's Web site. [8]

cognitive dissonance. A psychological state in which a customer determines that his purchase behavior is inconsistent with his self-image and, because he cannot change the behavior that created the dissonance, redefines his perception of the behavior in terms that support rather than challenge his self-image. [5]

combination strategy. A promotion strategy that uses elements of both push and pull strategies to create both distributor and customer demand for a company's product or service. [9]

commingling of funds. An unfair trade practice that occurs when a producer combines monies belonging to others with her own funds, even on a temporary basis. [11]

commoditization. The process by which a product reaches a point in its development where it has no features that differentiate it from competitive products other than price. [6]

commodity. A product that has reached a point in its development where it has no features that differentiate it from competitive products other than price. [6]

communication. The exchange of information with others. [9]

communication channel. The method by which a sender delivers its message to its intended audience. [9]

communication-oriented advertising objective. An advertising objective that seeks to increase customer interest in and awareness and knowledge of a product or company. [10]

company mission statement. A statement of a company's fundamental purpose or reason for existence. [2]

comparative advertising. Persuasive product advertising that directly compares a product to a competing product on the basis of one or more product attributes. Also known as *competitive advertising*. [10]

competition-driven pricing strategy. A pricing strategy in which a company sets its prices relative to those charged by its competitors. [7]

competition-oriented pricing objective. A pricing objective related to maintaining or increasing a particular level of market share. [7]

competitive advertising. *See* **comparative advertising**.

competitive bidding. A process in which buyers ask potential suppliers to offer price quotations on a proposed contract. [7]

competitive institutional advertising. A form of institutional advertising that promotes one product or product category over a competing product or product category. [10]

competitive intelligence. *See* **marketing intelligence**.

competitive parity method. A method of establishing a promotion budget in which the budget is based on the budgets established by one or more of a company's competitors. [9]

compiled list. For direct mail or other marketing purposes, a list of names and addresses derived from sources such as directories, newspapers, trade show registrations, property tax rolls, voter lists, and other rosters. [8]

comprehensive business analysis. An evaluation of all the factors that are likely to affect the design, production, pricing, marketing, and sales potential of a new product. [6]

comprehensive examination. A full-scope examination of all nonfinancial aspects of an insurer's operations conducted by a state insurance department. [11]

concentrated marketing. A target marketing strategy that involves focusing all of a company's marketing resources on satisfying the needs of one segment of the total market for a particular type of product. [3]

concept testing. A sales marketing research technique designed to measure the acceptability of new product ideas, new promotion campaigns, or other new marketing elements before entering production. [6]

conditionally vested commission. A commission that becomes vested after the producer attains a certain age or number of years of service with the company. [8]

conservation unit. A department in an insurance company that is staffed with personnel specially trained to conserve—or keep in force—policies. [5]

consistency of a product mix. A comparative measure of how closely related a company's product classes and product lines are to each other. [6]

constraint. A environmental factor that limits a company's activities. [1]

consumer. An individual who purchases products and services for personal or household use. [5]

consumer advertising. Advertising directed to individuals and organizations. [10]

consumer market. A market that consists of individuals who buy products or services for personal or family use. [3]

Consumer Price Index (CPI). A number that results from comparing the average price of a "market basket" of goods and services at a specified point in time to the average price of the same market basket items at a different point in time. [1]

consumer sales promotion. Sales promotion efforts aimed at consumers or organizational buyers. [9]

consumer socialization. The process by which young people develop the skills, knowledge, and attitudes they need to function as consumers in the marketplace. [5]

controllable marketing variable. A marketing element, such as market selection, product, price, promotion method, or distribution system, that a company can define and manage itself. [1]

convenience product. A relatively inexpensive product that requires a minimum of time, information gathering, and shopping effort on the part of most consumers. [6]

convergence. The creation of a single financial institution being able to serve all of a customer's banking, securities, and insurance needs. [1]

copy. Any spoken or printed words in an advertisement. [10]

core customer. A high-value customer whose needs a company can satisfy effectively and efficiently and whose business is dependable and profitable. [5]

corporate culture. The attitudes, values, perceptions, beliefs, and experiences shared by a company's employees and instilled in new employees when they join the company. [1]

cost accounting system. An expense analysis tool that accumulates expense data to keep track of the expenses a company incurs to develop, market, and sell a product, and thereby effectively monitors and controls costs. [2]

cost-driven pricing strategy. A pricing strategy in which a company sets its prices to cover the company's costs incurred in creating, selling, and servicing a product and to allow for a predetermined level of profit. Also known as a *cost-plus strategy*. [7]

cost-plus strategy. *See* **cost-driven pricing strategy.**

CPI. *See* **Consumer Price Index.**

cross-functional team. In a matrix organizational structure, a group made up of employees from various functional areas who work together on a common assignment led by a project manager. [2]

cross-selling. The process of identifying an existing customer's needs for additional products while selling, or after selling, a primary product and then promoting products that complement that primary product to provide a more complete solution to the customer's needs. [5]

current value. With respect to lifetime customer value, the present value of all expected transactions between the company and the customer, assuming the existing customer behavior pattern remains the same. [5]

custom research firm. A firm that provides a full range of marketing research services to client companies on a customized, special-project basis. [4]

customer. A person or an organization that purchases a company's products. [1]

customer attrition. *See* **customer defection.**

customer behavior. All the mental, emotional, and physical activities that people engage in when they choose, purchase, and use products and services. Also known as *buyer behavior*. [5]

customer-centric marketing approach. A business philosophy in which a company bases all its plans and actions on customer wants and needs, and fulfilling those needs, to establish relationships with customers. [5]

customer defection. A customer's abandonment of a current company for a competing company. Also known as *customer attrition*. [5]

customer development. The process a company undertakes to maximize customer value by expanding its products and services and more effectively satisfying customer needs. [5]

customer-driven pricing strategy. A pricing strategy in which a company sets prices according to what customers are willing to pay for the value they receive. Also referred to as *value-based pricing strategy*. [7]

customer loyalty. The commitment of a customer to remain a customer of and to place repeat business with a company, despite influences and marketing efforts of competing companies that may cause other customers to switch. [5]

customer relationship. A mutual bond that forms as a result of all interactions between a customer and a business organization. [5]

customer relationship marketing. The enterprise-wide business strategy that allows a company to create, maintain, and enhance relationships with customers and other stakeholders by creating customer value and satisfaction. [5]

customer retention. The extent to which a customer remains with a company. [5]

customer sacrifice. The gap between what the customer wants and what the company can provide. If this gap is large, the cost of attempting to satisfy the customer is likely to be high, and the company might be better off targeting other customer groups. [5]

customer satisfaction. The state in which the customer perceives that a company's products and service meet or exceed the customer's expectations and satisfy the customer's needs. [5]

data mining. The process of analyzing the variables in a database or data warehouse to discover patterns and relationships. [4]

data warehouse. An integrated, subject-oriented database (or set of databases), often designed to support the functions performed by business intelligence. [4]

debtor-creditor group. A group that consists of lending institutions, such as banks, credit unions, savings and loan associations, finance companies, retail merchants, and credit card companies, and their debtors. [3]

decision support systems (DSS). *See* **business intelligence.**

decoding. The step in the communication process in which a receiver of a message translates the words and symbols in the message into meaningful ideas. [9]

demand. An economic term for the number of units of a product that a company can sell under given conditions. [7]

demographics. Measurable traits, such as age, gender, marital status, household size and composition, income and earnings, life-cycle stage, income and earnings, life-cycle stage, birth and death rates, race, nationality, education, and occupation, that describe or define a given population. [1]

demographic segmentation. A method of dividing the total market for a product based on the personal characteristics of people in the market. [3]

dependent variable. A marketing variable that reacts to or is influenced by another variable (for example, changes in independent variables). [4]

deposit-based commission schedule. A commission schedule in which commission percentages paid to producers are based only on new premium payments. [8]

depth of a product mix. A comparative measure of the number of different product forms or product items that a company offers in each product line. [6]

descriptive research. Primary research that provides a picture of or describes the nature of a market or a marketing problem or opportunity. [4]

differentiated marketing. A target marketing strategy that aims to satisfy the needs of a large part of the total market for a particular type of product by offering a number of products and marketing mixes designed to appeal to different segments of the total market. [3]

direct comparison test. A pretesting method in which target market members are shown several advertisements and then asked to rate each advertisement on how well it captures attention, creates interest in a product, conveys the intended message, changes beliefs about a product or organization, or motivates a purchase. [10]

direct cost. A cost that is specifically traceable to or caused by a particular product. [7]

direct mail. A communication channel that uses a mail service to distribute sales materials directly to a mailing list of prospective customers in an identified target market. [8]

direct response advertising. A type of product advertising designed to encourage customers to take action immediately, either by purchasing a product or requesting additional information about a particular product or service. [10]

direct response distribution system. A type of distribution system in which companies communicate directly with customers to initiate or conduct the sales process. [8]

director of insurance. *See* **insurance commissioner**.

distribution. The activities involved in making products available for customers to buy. [1]

distribution channel. A network that consists of the specific people, institutions, or communication methods that are used to connect companies to their customers. [8]

distribution intensity. The number of distribution channels an insurer uses in a particular target market. [8]

distributor brand. A brand created by, controlled by, and identified with the company that distributes or sells a product. Also referred to as a *private brand* or a *private label*. [6]

division. *See* **strategic business unit.**

dog. A business unit or product line on the market share/market growth matrix that has a low market share in a low-growth market. [2]

DSS. *See* **decision support systems.**

dual distribution. The use of multiple distribution channels to distribute the same product to the same target market. [8]

E&O insurance. *See* **errors and omissions insurance.**

e-commerce. *See* **electronic commerce**.

economic environment. All the parts of an economy that affect how products and services are produced, distributed, and used. [1]

economies of scale. A barrier to entry that exists when the unit costs of producing, selling, distributing, and promoting a product decrease as the number of units of the product sold increases. [1]

effective marketing exchange. In the marketing process, an exchange that achieves a company's goals. [2]

efficient marketing exchange. In the marketing process, an exchange that uses the least amount of resources to achieve a company's goals. [2]

elastic demand. A state that exists when a change in a product's price results in a greater-than-proportional change in quantity demanded for that product. [7]

electronic commerce. The use of computer networks to perform business transactions and help with the delivery of products and services to customers. Also known as *e-commerce*, *e-business*, or *"B to B"(business to business)*. [1]

empirical data. Information gathered through observation or experiment that confirms or disproves a research hypothesis. [4]

encoding. The step in the communication process in which a sender of a message translates ideas into words or symbols. [9]

enterprise dashboard. A visual representation that allows an at-a-glance overview of company health and monitoring of key performance indicators. [4]

entire contract provision. A provision stating that the entire contract consists of the life insurance policy; the application, if it is attached to the policy; and any attached riders and endorsements. [11]

environmental analysis. An ongoing examination of events and relationships outside the company that can influence strategic and tactical decision making and help companies identify potential opportunities for or specific threats to the company. [2]

environmental forecast. A prediction about major environmental trends that will affect a company's future business activities. [2]

errors and omissions (E&O) insurance. Insurance that protects an insurance producer against financial liability for any negligent acts or mistakes but does not cover a producer for intentional acts or wrongdoings. [8]

ethnographic research. A form of qualitative research that combines ethnography with observational research to deliver insights into a person's or group's attitudes, beliefs, motivations, and values that may affect their decisions or actions. [4]

ethnography. The process by which a researcher observes how people act in their natural environments. [4]

evaluative criteria. Those features, characteristics, or specifications that a customer considers when making a choice. [5]

evoked set. The set of alternatives customers are left with at the end of the information search and from which they make a purchase decision. [5]

exchange. A transaction in which one party gives something of value to another party to receive something of value in return. [1]

exclusive agent. *See* **career agent.**

exclusive distribution. The level of distribution intensity that involves the use of one distribution channel to sell products within a given market. [8]

execution style. The specific form of presentation used to transform an advertisement's appeal into a message. [10]

executive summary. A section in a company's marketing plan that briefly states the plan's purpose and recommendations. [2]

expense allowance. A reimbursement that some companies provide to affiliated agents for certain business expenses, such as advertising and computer purchases. [8]

expense analysis. The process of determining which marketing costs are associated with which marketing activities to help managers evaluate if a cost is worth the value the activity provides. [2]

expense margin. The difference between operating expenses assumed when a product was initially priced and the expenses actually experienced by the company. [7]

expense ratios. Mathematical comparisons that are derived by dividing the amount of expenses by a certain unit of measure, such as level of sales. [2]

expert system. A knowledge-based computer system designed to provide expert consultation to information users for solving specialized and complex problems. [4]

exploratory research. Primary research intended to provide insight into the general nature of a problem and to identify the variables that need to be considered in addressing the problem. [4]

exposure. Any news release, feature story, photograph, or other information that is published or broadcast in the media during a given period of time. [9]

extensive problem-solving strategy. A problem-solving strategy in which customers typically gather a lot of information before making a purchase and may use several criteria to evaluate alternative brand choices. [5]

external environment. Environmental factors that exist outside the company and are not under the company's control. [1]

external factor. In customer behavior, an influence on purchase decisions that exists apart from an individual or organization and can be measured and observed. [5]

external standard. A performance standard based on outside information such as published industry-wide averages or best practices. [2]

family brand. A single brand that applies to all of a company's products. [6]

feasibility study. In a comprehensive business analysis, research designed to determine the operational and technical viability of producing and selling a product. [6]

fee variance. One of the ways a company offers tiered service to a customer that involves offering a consistent level of service to each customer but varying the fees a customer pays for the service based on the customer's profitability to the company. [5]

feedback. In the communications process, the response a receiver of a message sends back to the sender of a message. [9]

field advisory council. A group of producers designated to represent and provide feedback from the sales force in areas such as product design, rate setting, underwriting philosophy, and customer service. [6]

field force. The collective term for an insurer's career agents. [8]

field office. An office in which career agents work. [8]

file and use requirement. A state requirement under which an insurer may use a policy form, without obtaining prior approval, after filing the form with the insurance department. [6]

financed purchase. The purchase of a new policy for which the owner intends to pay premiums using funds taken from another policy. [11]

Financial Industry Regulatory Authority (FINRA). A nongovernmental self-regulatory organization empowered by the SEC to license, investigate, and regulate securities dealers and their representatives. [8]

financial planner. A professional who analyzes a customer's personal financial-circumstances and goals and prepares a program, usually in writing, to meet the customer's financial goals, such as retirement planning or college savings. [8]

Financial Services Modernization Act. *See* **Gramm-Leach-Bliley Act.**

FINRA. *See* **Financial Industry Regulatory Authority.**

FINRA Conduct Rule 2210. *See* **Advertisement Rule.**

FINRA Conduct Rule 2310. *See* **Suitability Rule.**

FINRA Conduct Rule 2821. A FINRA rule that considerably expands the requirements of the Suitability Rule by specifying criteria to be taken into consideration in making a suitability determination for the purchase or exchange of a deferred variable annuity. [11]

FINRA Conduct Rule 3010. *See* **Supervisory Rule.**

first-year commission. A sales commission equal to a stated percentage of the amount of the premium the insurer receives during the first policy year. [8]

fixed cost. A cost that remains constant regardless of the amount or volume of a product sold over some determined time period. [7]

fixed subsidy plan. A financing plan that pays the producer a predetermined flat dollar amount in addition to commissions earned during a specified period. [8]

flexible pricing. A competition-driven pricing strategy in which the price a company charges for a product varies according to specific sales conditions. Also known as *variable pricing*. [7]

focus group. A marketing research data collection method that consists of an informal session during which a small group of people, usually no more than eight to ten individuals, are led through guided discussion and asked to discuss their opinions or feelings about a given topic, product, or service. [4]

forgetting rate. The rate at which customers forget a product or brand if no advertising is run. [10]

free-look provision. A provision in a life insurance contract that gives a policyowner a specified period, usually 10 to 30 days, within which to cancel the policy and receive a full refund of all premiums paid. [11]

frequency. In media advertising, the number of times the same people in a target market are exposed to a particular advertisement in a given medium in a given time period. [10]

FSMA. *See* **Financial Services Modernization Act.**

fulfillment kit. A package of materials designed to address or fulfill a customer's request when the customer responds to either an invitation to inquire or an invitation to contract. [8]

functional regulation. The principle that a single regulatory body should oversee similar financial activities, regardless of which type of financial institution engages in the activity. [11]

GDP. *See* **gross domestic product.**

gender-based pricing. A rate structure that involves charging different premium rates to males and females because of the difference between male and female mortality rates. [7]

generic characteristics. The physical, technical, and functional characteristics that make a product what it is in its most basic or standard form. [6]

geodemographic segmentation. A method of dividing the total market for a product by classifying people with similar demographic characteristics into geographically defined clusters. [3]

geographic segmentation. A method of dividing the total market for a product based on the needs and desires of populations in different jurisdictions or physical locations. [3]

GLB Act. *See* **Gramm-Leach-Bliley Act.**

good. A product that has definite physical features. [6]

grace period provision. A provision in a life insurance contract that grants a contract owner the right to pay any required premium within a specified period, usually 30 or 31 days, after the premium due date. [11]

Gramm-Leach-Bliley (GLB) Act. A law enacted by the U. S. Congress in 1999 that removed many of the regulatory barriers among various financial institutions, such as banks, broker-dealers, and insurance companies. Also known as the *Financial Services Modernization Act (FSMA)*. [8]

graphics. *See* **art.**

gross domestic product (GDP). The total output of goods and services produced by labor and property located within a country, valued at adjusted market prices. [1]

group representative. A salaried sales representative specifically trained in the techniques of marketing and servicing group products. [8]

hard research. *See* **quantitative research.**

harvest strategy. A type of marketing strategy under which a company seeks to maximize a business unit's short-term earnings and cash flow usually by reducing the amount of resources it expends on the business unit and allowing its market share to decline. [2]

heterogeneity. The variability or lack of consistency in the performance of a service. [6]

heterogeneous shopping product. A product that consumers view as different enough from other products to compare quality, style, or features as well as price. [6]

hierarchy of needs. A concept developed by psychologist Abraham Maslow that classifies needs into five hierarchical categories: (1) physiological needs, (2) security or safety needs, (3) social needs, (4) esteem needs, and (5) self-actualization needs. [5]

high-involvement product. A product that is bought infrequently, is in an unfamiliar product category, and requires a large cash outlay. [5]

high-value customer. A customer that offers great economic value to a company because the individual often purchases a company's products or has needs that a company's products, prices, or services can satisfy. [5]

historical value. With respect to lifetime customer value, the value of all transactions to date between a company and a customer. [5]

hold strategy. A type of marketing strategy under which a company tries to maintain a business unit's market position. The company generally invests only enough money to hold promotional activities and customer services constant. [2]

home-office-to-home-office arrangement. An arrangement to distribute nonproprietary products in which an insurance company enters into an agreement with another insurance company to distribute specific products or product lines issued by that company. [8]

home service agent. A career agent who sells specified products, typically low-face-value whole life insurance with monthly premiums, and provides policyowner service in an assigned geographic territory. Also known as a *debit agent.* [8]

homogeneous shopping product. A product that customers view as similar in quality or features to other products but different enough in price to warrant comparison shopping. [6]

horizontal conflict. A form of channel conflict evidenced by the friction between two or more channels or between two or more channel members at the same level in a single channel. [8]

household. In demographic terms, any single person who lives alone or any group of people, related or not, who share the same residence. [1]

house list. For direct mail and other promotion purposes, a company-owned list that includes names of people who have shown interest in the company's products or who have been referred by the company's current customers. [8]

hypothesis. An informed guess or assumption about a problem or a set of circumstances that can be accepted or rejected based on empirical data. [4]

IAIS. *See* **International Association of Insurance Supervisors.**

idea. A concept, philosophy, image, belief, or issue. [6]

idea generation. The step in the product development process that involves searching for new product ideas that are consistent with both the company's overall product development strategy and the needs of its target markets. [6]

IIPRC. *See* **Interstate Insurance Product Regulation Commission.**

image-building advertising. A form of institutional advertising that is intended to increase customer confidence in an industry or in a specific company by emphasizing the industry's or company's history, stability, experience, and progressive attitudes. [10]

image-building promotion campaign. A type of promotion campaign intended to shape customer beliefs about a company or its products. [9]

IMC. *See* **integrated marketing communications.**

IMSA. *See* **Insurance Marketplace Standards Association.**

implementation. The step in the product development process which involves establishing the administrative structures and processes needed to take a product to market. [6]

inbound telemarketing. Telemarketing that occurs when a company provides customers with a toll-free number to use when inquiring about products or placing orders. [8]

incontestability provision. A provision in a life insurance policy that states that a policy will be incontestable, other than for nonpayment of premiums, after it has been in force during the lifetime of the insured for a certain period of time after issue, usually one or two years. [11]

independent agent. An agent who does not have an exclusive contract with one company or obligations to sell one company's products exclusively and may submit insurance applications to any insurer with which the agent has an agreement. [8]

independent life broker. A salesperson who is licensed to sell insurance but is not under contract with any insurer. Also known as a *life broker*. [8]

independent variable. In marketing research, a marketing variable that influences the behavior of another variable and is not itself affected by changes in other variables. [4]

in-depth interview. A qualitative research data collection method in which a researcher interviews individual study participants to collect information about their attitudes, experiences, or expertise. Also known as a *one-on-one interview*. [4]

indirect cost. A cost that is not directly traceable to any single product. [7]

individual brand. A separate brand name given to each product item or product line. [6]

inelastic demand. A state that exists when a change in a product's price results in a less-than-proportional change in quantity demanded for that product. [7]

inflation. A prolonged rise in the average level of prices in an economy. [1]

information dashboard. A visual representation, usually in the form of graphs or charts, of key information managers need to make decisions. [4]

informative institutional advertising. A form of institutional advertising that makes special announcements about a company such as mergers, acquisitions, relocation of offices, or new ventures a company is involved in. [10]

informative product advertising. A form of product awareness advertising that provides information about a product. [10]

in-house brokerage agency arrangement. An arrangement to distribute non-proprietary products in which a company establishes its own brokerage agency—rather than using an outside agency—to solicit distribution agreements with other insurers to sell those insurers' products. [8]

inquiry test. A post-testing method that measures the number of responses or inquiries generated by an advertisement that invites customers to call or write for additional information about a product or that offers customers responding to an ad a free sample of the product or some other gift. [10]

institutional advertising. Advertising designed to promote a company, an industry, or a point of view. [10]

insurance brokerage. *See* **insurance company broker-dealer**. [8]

insurance commissioner. In the United States, the individual who directs the operation of a state insurance department. Also known as *director of insurance* or *insurance superintendent*. [11]

insurance company broker-dealer. A registered insurance company or a registered subsidiary of an insurance company that sells variable insurance products and securities and typically also provides specialized financial planning and investment services. Also known as an *insurance brokerage*. [8]

Insurance Marketplace Standards Association (IMSA). A voluntary association of insurers designed to enable life insurance companies to monitor their own compliance with regulatory requirements and to promote high ethical standards in the sale of life insurance, long-term care, and annuity products. [11]

insurance producer. An individual, including agency managers and salaried insurer or agency staff, licensed to sell insurance products, solicit sales, or negotiate insurance contracts in a state. Also known as a *producer*. [1]

insurance superintendent. *See* **insurance commissioner.**

intangibility. The lack of physical attributes which make services incapable of being perceived by the senses. [6]

integrated marketing communications (IMC). The coordination of all of a company's communications to deliver a clear, consistent message about the company and its products. [9]

intensive distribution. The level of distribution intensity that involves a company using as many distribution channels as possible to sell products within a given market. [8]

intermediary. A person or entity who sells and services financial products on behalf of a financial services company. [8]

internal assessment. An examination of a company's current activities, strengths and weaknesses, and ability to respond to potential threats and opportunities in the environment, called a SWOT analysis. [2]

internal database. A stored, computerized central source of information created from internal records and reports meant to be shared by many users throughout a company. [4]

internal environment. All the elements that come from within a company and over which the company has control. [1]

internal factor. In customer behavior, an influence on purchase decisions that operates within the minds of consumers or organizational buyers and affects their behavior. Also known as a *psychological factor*. [5]

internal standard. A performance standard that is developed by a company and based on the company's historical performance. [2]

International Association of Insurance Supervisors (IAIS). An organization created to develop international principles and standards for insurance supervision and improve supervisory systems for the insurance industry. [1]

Interstate Insurance Product Regulation Commission (IIPRC). A multi-state public entity that establishes uniform standards for certain insurance product lines, including life insurance, annuities, disability income insurance, and long-term care insurance, and provides for voluntary centralized electronic filing and expedited review of products in those lines. [6]

investment margin. The difference between the investment rate the insurer assumes when pricing a product and the investment rate the insurer actually earns. [7]

invitation to contract. A direct mail communication designed to solicit and close a sale. [8]

invitation to inquire. A direct mail communication designed to generate interest in a product or service and provide prospective customers with a way, such as a toll-free telephone number or postcard, to request and receive additional information. [8]

lapse rate. The ratio of business in force that terminates for nonpayment of premium, whether by surrender or lapse, to the total business in force at the beginning of a specified period. [5]

law of demand. In economic theory, a principle which states that all other factors remaining the same, as the price for a product increases, demand decreases and as the price for a product decreases, demand increases. [7]

legacy system. A combination of computer hardware and software that a company has used for a long time to perform specific tasks. [4]

legal form. The way a company is legally set up to allow it to operate in a particular state or other jurisdiction. [1]

license. *See* **certificate of authority**.

life broker. *See* **independent life broker**.

life event-oriented marketing. The practice of timing sales and promotional efforts around significant events in customers' lives. [5]

Life Insurance and Annuities Replacement Model Regulation (Model Replacement Regulation). An NAIC model regulation developed to ensure that insurers and insurance producers provide consumers with fair and accurate information about policies so that consumers can make purchase decisions that are in their own best interests. [11]

Life Insurance Buyer's Guide. A standardized buyer's guide that describes in general language the basic types of life insurance and the costs and benefits involved with each type, how to determine the amount of life insurance needed, and the other factors to be considered before purchasing a life insurance policy. [11]

Life Insurance Disclosure Model Regulation. An NAIC model regulation that requires insurers to provide prospective purchasers of most individual life insurance policies with information to help them select an appropriate policy. [11]

lifetime customer value. The economic benefit a company receives from its relationship with a customer calculated over time; generally measured by the extent to which the profits a customer generates over time exceed the company's cost of acquiring, developing, serving, and retaining the customer. Also known as *lifetime value*. [5]

lifetime value. *See* **lifetime customer value**.

limited problem-solving strategy. A problem-solving strategy that customers use for products they purchase only occasionally or when they need to acquire and use information to evaluate product alternatives before making a purchase decision. [5]

limited services research firm. A marketing research firm that offers limited services marketing research, often specializing in one area of research, for example, providing centers for telephone surveys. [4]

line of business. *See* **strategic business unit**.

logo. *See* **brand mark**.

loss leader. A price leader that is priced below cost. [7]

low-involvement product. A low-priced, frequently purchased product that requires little information for a customer to decide to purchase. [5]

low-value customer. A customer that has very little value to a company because the individual only occasionally purchases a company's products or has needs that cannot be satisfied by a company's products, prices, or services. [5]

mail kit. A direct mail package of sales materials that customers receive. [8]

management by exception. A performance management technique in which a manager investigates only performance that falls outside an established, acceptable performance range. [2]

manufacturer brand. A brand created by, controlled by, and identified with the company that produces or manufactures a product. Some companies refer to a manufacturer brand as a *proprietary brand*. [6]

market analysis. A study, usually prepared by a company's marketing department, of all the environmental factors that might affect sales of a product. [6]

market attractiveness/business strength matrix. An approach to business portfolio analysis developed by General Electric and McKinsey and Company in which business units or product lines are placed into one or more of nine matrix cells based on (1) the attractiveness of the market in which the business unit operates and (2) the unit's business strengths. [2]

market-by-market pricing. A rate structure a company uses when it charges different premium rates depending on the jurisdiction, geographical area, or target market in which a product is sold. Also known as *market-specific pricing* or *channel-specific pricing*. [7]

market conduct examination. A formal investigation of an insurer conducted by one or more state insurance departments that is designed to determine whether the insurer's market conduct complies with applicable laws and regulations. [11]

market penetration strategy. A corporate growth strategy that focuses on increasing sales of current products to current markets. [2]

market segment. A submarket or group of customers with similar needs and preferences. [3]

market segmentation. The process of dividing large, diverse markets into smaller, submarkets that are more alike and need relatively similar product or marketing mixes. [3]

market share. The ratio of a company's sales of a product within a specified market at a given point in time to the total industry sales for that type of product in that same market. [7]

market share/market growth matrix. An approach to business portfolio analysis, developed by the Boston Consulting Group, that places each business unit or product line in one of four quadrants on a matrix based on (1) the growth rate of the market in which the business unit competes and (2) the business unit's relative share of that market as compared with its largest competitor. [2]

market-specific pricing. *See* **market-by-market pricing**.

marketer-dominated source. An external source of purchase information that includes advertising, salespeople, sales promotion literature, point-of-purchase displays, Internet Web sites, and other outlets companies use to sell their products or services to consumers and organizational buyers. [5]

marketing. The activity, set of institutions, and processes for creating, communicating, delivering, and exchanging offerings that have value for customers, clients, partners, and society at large. [1]

marketing audit. A systematic examination and appraisal of a company's or SBU's marketing environment, goals, strategies, tactical/action programs, organizational structure, and personnel on a very broad basis. [2]

marketing control. The process by which companies monitor the results of their marketing plans and take corrective action as needed to ensure that marketing goals are reached. Marketing control consists of evaluating performance and reporting results. [2]

marketing goal. A specific written objective or goal a company wants to achieve using marketing efforts and activities. [2]

marketing implementation. The process of translating marketing plans and strategies into action. [2]

marketing information system. An interactive system of people, software and equipment, and procedures designed to provide managers with a continuous flow of information to help them manage marketing activities. [4]

marketing intelligence. The systematic collection and analysis of publicly available information about competitors and ongoing developments in the marketing environment. Also known as *competitive intelligence*. [4]

marketing management. The process companies use to plan, organize, implement, and control their marketing activities to create effective and efficient exchanges. [2]

marketing mix. The four main variables—product, price, place, and promotion, known as *the Four Ps*—that companies manage to fulfill marketing's broad role. [1]

marketing model. A statistical or management science tool that describes the mathematical relationships between certain variables (such as price, cost, or demand) that affect marketing decisions. [4]

marketing opportunity. A combination of circumstances that allows a company to use its strengths or capabilities to take advantage of current trends in the marketing environment or expand its activities. [1]

marketing plan. A written document that specifies the marketing goals for a particular product or product line and describes the strategies and the implementation and control efforts the company intends to use to achieve these goals. [2]

marketing planning. The process of setting goals and strategies for producing, distributing, promoting and pricing the products and services of a specific company and determining the resources the company will need to support these activities. [2]

marketing research. The discipline that focuses on collecting, analyzing, interpreting, and reporting information related to specific marketing problems or opportunities. [4]

marketing strategy. A specific plan designed to achieve a marketing goal. [2]

mass customization. A high-level personalizing of product offerings and service delivery on a large scale. [5]

mass marketing. *See* **undifferentiated marketing**.

matrix organizational structure. An organizational form in which a company assigns individuals from various functional areas to form a cross-functional team, and these team members report to both their functional managers and the project manager while a project is in process. As a result, this organizational form has vertical and horizontal lines of authority flowing down and across the organizational chart. [2]

media plan. A document that specifies the types of media in which advertisements will appear, the specific media vehicles in which advertisements will run, and the number and pattern of exposures for the advertisements. [10]

meeting the competition. *See* **status quo pricing**.

message. The information a sender wishes to deliver to an audience. [9]

me-too strategy. *See* **product imitation strategy**.

MEWA. *See* **multiple-employer welfare arrangement**.

micro-insurance. Protection against insurable risks of assets and lives of target populations such as micro entrepreneurs, small farmers, the landless, women, and low-income earners through formal, semi-formal or informal institutions. [3]

micromarketing. *See* **one-to-one marketing**.

misappropriation. The illegal misuse of a customer's or an insurer's money, even if the use is on a temporary basis. [11]

misrepresentation. A false or misleading statement. [11]

misstatement of age provision. A provision in a life insurance contract stating that if the insured's age was misstated on the application, then the amount of benefits payable will be adjusted to the amount premiums paid would have purchased for a person of the correct age. [11]

mobile marketing. The use of wireless technology to deliver advertising messages in a particular place, such as an airport, concert venue, or sports arena, usually with the intended receiver's consent. [1]

model law. A sample law offered by the NAIC that the states are encouraged to use as a basis for their laws. [11]

model regulation. A sample regulation offered by the NAIC that the states are encouraged to use as a basis for their regulations. [11]

Model Replacement Regulation. *See* **Life Insurance and Annuities Replacement Model Regulation**.

monopolistic competition. A market structure characterized by a large number of competitors, each selling similar but differentiated products and each accounting for a small percentage of the total market's sales. [1]

motivation. In customer behavior, the internal force that drives people to exhibit certain behavior or to take certain actions to reach a purchase decision. [5]

multiple-employer group. A group that consists of the employees of: (1) two or more employers in the same industry, (2) or more labor unions, or (3) one or more employers and one or more labor unions. [3]

multiple-employer welfare arrangement (MEWA). A multiple-employer group formed when small employers band together to offer group insurance and other benefits to their employees. [3]

multiple-line agent. An agent who distributes life insurance, health insurance, annuities, and property/casualty insurance products for a group of financially interrelated or commonly managed insurance companies. [8]

multivariable segmentation. A method of segmenting a market using a combination of variables to determine a segment. [3]

mystery shopper. An observational research tool in which a researcher disguised as a customer (1) investigates what happens during an actual interaction between a customer and a salesperson or customer service representative and (2) records such observations on a standardized response form. [4]

NAIC. *See* **National Association of Insurance Commissioners.**

NAICS. *See* **North American Industry Classification System.**

narrowcasting. A method of reducing advertising waste by selecting media that reach only a well-defined audience segment. [10]

National Association of Insurance Commissioners (NAIC). A private, non-profit association of the insurance commissioners of all 50 states, the District of Columbia, and the four U.S. territories that promotes uniformity of state regulation by developing model laws and regulations as guidelines for the states. [11]

need. In customer behavior, an unsatisfactory condition within a customer that leads to a specific action to improve the customer's condition. [5]

negotiated contract. A contract in which the terms and prices of the contract are established through talks between the buyer and the seller. [7]

negotiated trusteeship. A multiple-employer group that results from a collective-bargaining agreement between one of more unions and employers of union members. Also known as a *Taft-Hartley Group.* [3]

niche marketing. A form of concentrated marketing in which companies target small, narrowly defined subgroups within a segment that attract only one or a few competitors. [3]

noise. Any distractions or distortions that interfere with the steps of the communication process. [9]

nonforfeiture provision. A provision in a life insurance contract stating the amount of benefits that the insurer will pay if the policyowner stops making required premium payments on or surrenders a policy that has a cash value, how those benefits are calculated, and what options the policyowner has regarding the types of benefits available. [11]

nonprice competition. A type of competition that exists when companies attempt to gain customers by using marketing mix factors other than price. [7]

nonproprietary product. A product developed by another insurance company. [8]

nonpublic personal information. Personally identifiable financial information that a consumer provides to a financial institution, including banks and insurance companies, which is not publicly available. [11]

nonresident producer. An insurance producer who resides or maintains his principal place of business in another state and is issued a nonresident license by the state licensing authority. [8]

nonvested commission. A sales commission that is payable to a producer only if the producer still represents the company when the commission becomes due. [8]

North American Industry Classification System (NAICS). The official system used in North America to categorize businesses according to the type of economic or business activity in which they are involved. [3]

objective and task method. A method of establishing a promotion budget in which the budget is based on promotion objectives and the cost of meeting those objectives. [9]

observational research. A qualitative marketing research method that involves the study of the activities and behaviors of research participants with or without their knowledge, in natural or artificial settings, and through the use of human observers or mechanical devices. [4]

omnibus survey. In marketing research, a survey conducted regularly by a research company with a given target population. [4]

one-on-one interview. *See* **in-depth interview.**

one-to-few marketing. A type of target marketing strategy in which the marketing mix is tailored to a particular group of customers with similar characteristics, needs, or past purchase behavior and personalized to some extent. Also known as *one- to-some marketing*. [3]

one-to-one marketing. A type of target marketing strategy in which the marketing mix is customized for each individual consumer or consumers in a specific location. Also known as *micromarketing*. [3]

one-to-some marketing. *See* **one-to-few marketing.**

opportunity cost. A benefit that is forfeited or given up in choosing one decision alternative over another. [5]

organizational buyer. An individual who purchases products and services for business purposes. [5]

organization chart. A visual representation of an organization's established structure. [2]

organizational market. A market that consists of individuals or formal organizations that purchase products and services for business purposes. [3]

organizing. In marketing management, the process of lining up corporate resources to put company plans into action effectively and efficiently. [2]

orphaned policyowner. A policyowner who does not currently have a relationship with a producer. [5]

outbound telemarketing. Telemarketing that occurs when a company representative or mechanized system telephones customers in the company's target markets with the intent to generate sales. [8]

override. *See* **overriding commission.**

overriding commission. A sales commission on the new and renewal business generated by a particular field office or group of agents. Also known as an *override.* [8]

packaging. From a services marketing standpoint, the tangible and intangible elements that surround a product, including product literature and applications, the salesperson's image and attitude, and the image and credibility of the company offering the product. [6]

Pareto's Principle. A principle of customer profitability that states that 80 percent of a company's profits are generated by 20 percent of its customers. Also called the *80-20 Principle.* [5]

penetration pricing. A competition-driven pricing strategy in which a company charges a comparatively low price designed to build market share and to produce a large sales volume quickly. [7]

percentage of sales method. A method of establishing a promotion budget in which the budget is based on a specified percentage of past or projected sales. [9]

perception. The process by which people select, organize, and interpret information to give it meaning. [5]

performance standard. An established, ideal level of performance against which actual performance is measured. [2]

perishability. The inability to stockpile performance of a service for use at some future date. [6]

persistency. The retention of business that occurs when an insurance policy remains in force as a result of the continued payment of the policy's renewal premiums. [5]

persistency bonus. Extra earnings that a company may offer to producers for favorable persistency results that serve as a sales force incentive. [5]

persistency rate. A measurement of the persistency of a block of insurance policies determined by the percentage of business in force at the beginning of a specified period that remains in force at the end of the period. [5]

persona. A model created by a company's marketing staff that is used to represent a particular demographic portion of a market segment to better understand the habits, needs, and motivations of consumers in that segment. [3]

personal-producing general agent (PPGA). A commissioned salesperson who is an independent contractor, is not housed in an insurer's field office, and engages primarily in personal production (sales of new policies). [8]

personal selling. A promotion tool that relies on presenting information during face-to-face or telephone meetings with one or more prospective customers. [9]

personal selling distribution system. A type of distribution system in which commissioned or salaried sales representatives sell products through oral and written presentations made to prospective customers. [8]

personal source. An external source of purchase information that includes friends, family, and associates. [5]

persuasive product advertising. A form of product awareness advertising that attempts to build customer preference and increase sales for a specific product by supporting or changing existing beliefs about the product. [10]

PEST analysis. A business measurement instrument used to assess the current external business environment, evaluate a company's current position related to the business environment, and predict future environmental trends for marketing. Also known as the *STEP analysis method*. [2]

physiological need. A need that is physically or biologically determined, such as the need for food, shelter, sex, and clothing. [5]

place. In the context of the marketing mix, how and where customers purchase products. [1]

planning. A systematic process of evaluating opportunities, assessing resources, setting goals, and creating strategies for action and control. [2]

platform employee. A front-line bank employee whose primary function is to handle customer service issues and sell traditional bank products such as checking and savings accounts, but who is also licensed and trained to sell insurance. [8]

PLC. *See* **product life cycle.**

podcast. An audio or video broadcast about a particular subject or topic that is sent to a user's computer via an audio or video file in a format that can be played on or transferred to portable digital media devices, such as the iPod™ and Zune™. [1]

point-of-purchase material. Promotional material provided to customers where products are purchased. [10]

policy fee system. A method of providing quantity discounts in which a company charges a flat amount per policy to cover administrative expenses plus a specific rate per thousand dollars of coverage. [7]

policy filing. The act of submitting a policy contract form and any other legally required forms and documents to the appropriate insurance department for approval. [6]

policy reserves. Liability accounts that identify the amounts of money that an insurer estimates it needs to pay policy benefits as they come due. [7]

policy summary. A document that the NAIC Life Insurance Disclosure Model Regulation requires insurers to give prospective customers and that contains detailed information about the specific policy being considered for purchase. [11]

population. For marketing research purposes, the total group of individuals or organizations who are relevant to the research question and about whom a researcher wants to draw a conclusion. [4]

portfolio of products. *See* **product mix.**

positioning. The process by which a company establishes and maintains in customers' minds a distinct place, or position, for itself and its products. [6]

post-testing. Various tests a company can use to measure an advertisement's performance during or after its use in a campaign. [10]

potential value. With respect to lifetime customer value, the value a company could realize if it could persuade a customer to increase future spending and/or reduce expenses by changing behavior patterns. [5]

PPGA. *See* **personal-producing general agent.**

preconception. A preconceived or fixed idea that a person develops over time about what is reality based on their own needs, values, attitudes, beliefs, learning, and previous experiences. [5]

preferred risk discount. A rate structure in which reduced premium rates are offered to individuals whose health and other lifestyle characteristics indicate that their mortality rate will be lower than average. [7]

pre-rollout test. A pretesting method in which a specific segment of the target audience is exposed to a print or broadcast advertisement in a real-life context and then asked to evaluate the advertisement's effectiveness. [10]

prestige pricing. A form of psychological pricing that involves setting intentionally high prices for a product to convey an image of high quality. [7]

pre-testing. Various tests a company can use to measure how well an advertisement performs on a limited basis before the company runs the advertisement in a full-scale campaign. [10]

price. The monetary value of whatever the customer exchanges for a product. [1]

price consciousness. A measure of the importance a specific customer attaches to price and the customer's overall awareness of price. [7]

price elasticity of demand. A microeconomic concept that measures the percentage change in the quantity demanded of a product relative to a percentage change in the product's price. [7]

price leader. A product whose price is set at an intentionally low level to attract customers who will purchase additional products at regular prices. [7]

pricing. The process a company uses to determine the amount to charge a customer for a product. [7]

pricing objective. A goal that a company wants to achieve when pricing a product. [7]

pricing strategy. A strategy that helps define the way a company establishes prices for its products. [7]

primary group. A reference group that is small enough to allow group members to interact with one another face to face. [5]

primary research. Original market research that a company or vendor engages in to answer the current research question. [4]

principal. An insurance company or other party that has authorized an agent to act on its behalf. [8]

prior approval requirement. A requirement, mandated by a state, under which a form must be filed with and approved by the state insurance department before the form can be used in that state. [6]

private brand. *See* **distributor brand.**

private label. *See* **distributor brand.**

proactive organization. An organization that anticipates changes in the environment, pioneers innovative activities, and encourages new approaches and new ideas. [1]

problem child. *See* **question mark.**

problem recognition. The stage in the purchase decision process in which an individual or organization realizes that a difference exists between a desired state and the actual state; the difference can be created by an unmet need or a potential opportunity. [5]

problem-solving strategy. A means of getting information to use in making a purchase decision. [5]

producer agreement. *See* **agency contract**.

producer group. An organization of independent insurance producers that negotiates compensation, product, and service agreements with insurance companies. [8]

Producer Licensing Model Act. A model law that specifies the requirements an individual must meet to be licensed as an insurance producer. [8]

product. In the context of the marketing mix, the goods, services, and/or ideas that a seller offers to customers to satisfy their needs. [1]

product advertising. Any advertising designed to promote or focus on a specific product or service; includes direct response advertising and product awareness advertising. [10]

product awareness advertising. Advertising that seeks to stimulate demand for a product or service over time. [10]

product class. The entire group of products produced by a particular industry or industry sector. [6]

product concept. A verbal or pictorial version of a proposed product that includes its general form and a description of some of its features and benefits expressed in a manner consumers can understand. [6]

product design objective. In a comprehensive business analysis, a specification of a product's basic characteristics, features, benefits, issue limits, age limits, commission and premium structure, underwriting classes, and operational and administrative requirements. [6]

product development. The process of creating or modifying a product. [6]

product differentiation. The practice of distinguishing a product from competing products using its form, style, quality, or some other characteristic, such as price, distribution, or promotion, so that a customer understands and appreciates the difference. [1]

product form. A group of products within a product line that share certain basic characteristics. [6]

product imitation strategy. A product development strategy that attempts to simulate, as closely as possible, another company's successful product. Also known as a *me-too strategy*. [6]

product improvement strategy. A product development strategy that seeks to introduce new versions of existing products with significant differences to better satisfy customer needs. [6]

product innovation strategy. A product development strategy that involves developing products that provide completely new or different ways of satisfying customer needs. [6]

product item. A specific version of a specific product form within a product line. [6]

product life cycle (PLC). A concept traditionally used to describe the series of stages—introduction, growth, maturity, and decline—through which a product usually progresses, from its first appearance until its eventual withdrawal from the market. [6]

product line. A set of different products that are closely related because they (1) function similarly, (2) are marketed to the same target markets, (3) are priced about the same, or (4) are distributed through similar distribution systems. Also known as *strategic business unit*. [6]

product mix. The total assortment of products available from a company. Also known as *portfolio of products*. [6]

profitability analysis. The process of determining which company operations are losing or making money by comparing the sales an activity generates with the expenses incurred to generate those sales. [2]

profit center. *See* **strategic business unit.**

profit-oriented pricing objective. A pricing objective that focuses on the absolute or relative return that a company wants a product to generate. [7]

promotion. The activities that companies use to make customers aware of their offerings and to influence customers to purchase, and distributors to sell, a product. [1]

promotional pricing. A customer-driven pricing strategy in which a company sets lower-than-normal prices on certain products in an attempt to stimulate sales of all of the company's products. [7]

promotion campaign. Usually a short-term marketing program intended to achieve one primary goal, such as introducing a new product to a market. [9]

promotion mix. The specific blend or combination of promotion tools that a company uses to promote its products or services. [9]

proprietary brand. *See* **manufacturer brand.**

proprietary product. A product developed and managed by the company itself. [8]

prospecting. The process producers use to identify, contact, and qualify potential customers. [10]

prospect. A potential customer for a company's products or services. [10]

prospectus. A written document that describes specific aspects of a security, variable life insurance product, or variable annuity being offered for sale that, according to SEC rules must be provided to a potential purchaser of any such product. [11]

prudential regulation. A term used to describe solvency regulation in many countries other than the United States. [11]

psychographic segmentation. A method of dividing the total consumer market for a product or service based on multiple characteristics that describe consumers' attitudes, beliefs, opinions, values, lifestyles, activities, and interests. [3]

psychological need. A need that arises from a customer's social environment, such as the need for belonging, fulfillment, affiliation, and achievement. [5]

psychological pricing. A customer-driven pricing strategy based on the belief that customers find certain types of prices or price ranges more appealing than others. [7]

publicity. Any nonpaid-for communication of information that is intended to bring a person, place, thing, or cause to the notice or attention of the public. [9]

public source. An external source of purchase information that includes government agencies, associations, product-testing organizations, magazine and newspaper articles, and information available on the Internet. [5]

pull strategy. A promotion strategy designed to stimulate customer demand by giving customers an incentive to purchase a product, in effect "pulling" the product through the channel. [9]

pulsing pattern. A pattern for timing advertisements in which advertisements are distributed unevenly throughout a specified period of time. Also called a *bursting pattern.* [10]

purchase frequency. The number of times a product is typically purchased. [10]

purchasing power. A measure of a customer's ability to buy goods and services. Also known as *buying power.* [7]

push strategy. A promotion strategy designed to provide distributors with an incentive to sell a product, in effect moving (pushing) the product through the channel to customers. [9]

qualitative research. Marketing research that examines what people think and how they feel about the subject under study and the words they use to express their thoughts and feelings. Also known as *soft research.* [4]

quality business. *See* **well-written business.**

quantitative research. Research designed to generate concrete information about population characteristics and behavior that can be analyzed, summarized in the form of numbers, and projected to the population of interest with a known level of error. Also known as *hard research*. [4]

quantity discount. A rate structure that involves establishing premium rates graded by the size of the policy. [7]

question mark. A business unit or product line on the market share/market growth matrix that has a low market share in a high-growth market. Also known as a *problem child.* [2]

questionnaire. A data-collection instrument used to collect survey information by providing individual study participants with a specific set of questions that they are asked to answer. [4]

reach. In media advertising, the total number of people exposed to an advertisement in a given medium. [10]

reactive organization. An organization that tends to be more passive and cautious in responding to changes in the environment, rather than anticipating likely changes before they occur. [1]

readability requirement. A standard for insurance contracts imposed by states or other regulatory bodies that limits sentence length, word length, and the amount of technical jargon and legal language in the contract form. [6]

rebating. A sales practice, prohibited in most states, in which an insurer or insurance producer offers a prospect an inducement to purchase an insurance policy or annuity, and the inducement is not offered to all applicants in similar situations and is not stated in the policy itself. [11]

recall test. A post-testing method that measures how well customers remember advertisements. [10]

receiver. In the communications process, the person or group for whom a message is intended. [9]

recognition test. A post-testing method in which target market members are shown actual advertisements to which they were previously exposed and then asking them whether they remember the ads. [10]

reference group. Any group with which an individual identifies so closely that the individual adopts many of the beliefs, values, and norms held by the group as a whole. [5]

referral. *See* **referred lead.**

referred lead. A well-qualified prospect whose name a customer gives to a salesperson. Also known as a *referral.* [10]

registered person. *See* **registered principal** and **registered representative.**

registered principal. A registered representative who is an owner, partner, officer, manager, or director of a FINRA member and is actively engaged in managing the member's investment banking or securities business, including solicitation, conduct of business, or the supervision of registered representatives or other principals. Also known as a *registered person.* [8]

registered representative. A business associate of a FINRA member who is engaged in the investment banking or securities business, including soliciting the sale of securities or training securities salespeople, and has satisfied FINRA registration requirements. Also known as a *registered person*. [8]

registration statement. A document filed with the SEC to register a variable insurance product and other financial products subject to SEC regulation that contains detailed information about the variable product and the insurer, including specified financial statements. [11]

regulations. Rule or orders that explain or help implement the provisions of a state insurance code. [11]

reinstatement provision. A provision in a life insurance contract that gives the policyholder the right to reinstate the contract to fully paid-up status within a certain period of time after the policy has expired by paying all unpaid and outstanding premiums plus interest and satisfying any other requirements of the provision. [11]

relationship pricing. The practice of offering price reductions to customers who purchase multiple products from a company's product mix. [7]

reminder product advertising. A form of product awareness advertising used to reinforce customers' buying habits and a company's earlier promotion efforts by keeping the name of a mature product in customers' minds. [10]

renewal commission. A sales commission paid to an insurance producer on policies the producer sold that remain in force and the commission is equal to a stated percentage of each premium paid for a specified number of years after the first policy year. [8]

replacement. The act of surrendering or lessening the value of one life insurance policy or annuity contract to buy another life insurance policy or annuity. [5]

resident producer. An insurance producer who resides or maintains her principal place of business within a particular state and is issued a resident license by the state licensing authority. [8]

response hierarchy. A sequence of possible responses customers typically move through when exposed to promotions. [9]

response list. For direct mail campaign purposes, a list obtained from another company that includes names of people who have purchased products from the other company through direct response marketing. [8]

role. A socially expected behavior pattern that an individual in a particular position is supposed to follow. [5]

routine response strategy. A problem-solving strategy that typically involves decisions that are automatic or require little or no thought by customers making the purchase decisions. [5]

salaried sales agent. *See* **salaried sales representative.**

salaried sales representative. A company employee who is paid a salary for making sales and providing sales support. Also called a *salaried sales agent*. [8]

salary plan. A financing plan under which an insurer or agency pays a producer a pre-established monetary amount for work performed during a specified period of time in lieu of part or all of the commissions actually earned during that period. [8]

sales aid. Sales promotion material that can be used in conjunction with a sales presentation. [10]

sales analysis. The process of examining sales number to evaluate a company's current performance. [2]

sales-oriented advertising objective. An advertising objective that usually describes desired results in terms of an increase in sales or market share. [10]

sales-oriented pricing objective. A pricing objective that focuses on a specific level of unit sales or dollar sales that a company wants a product to generate. [7]

sales presentation. The promotional message a producer delivers to a prospect to explain the product or products recommended in a proposal, stimulate the prospect's interest in those products, and motivate the prospect to purchase the products. [10]

sales promotion. A form of promotion that uses incentive programs, that are usually monetary, designed to encourage distribution channel members to sell a product or customers to purchase a product. [9]

sample. For marketing research purposes, a subset of a population that a researcher studies to develop conclusions about the total population. [4]

SBU. *See* **strategic business unit**.

screening. In the product development process, a weeding-out process designed to evaluate new product ideas quickly and inexpensively in order to select those that warrant further investigation. [6]

search engine. A Web site that allows visitors to search for content on the Internet by inputting key words or topics and obtaining a numbered list of sites containing those words or pertaining to those topics. [8]

search engine marketing (SEM). The practice of advertising and marketing Web sites by means of search engines. [8]

search engine optimization (SEO). A method of search engine marketing by means of designing Web pages so that they meet search engine criteria for relevance for common key words and phrases resulting in as high a rank as possible in search results for targeted keywords. [8]

SEC. *See* **Securities and Exchange Commission.**

secondary group. A reference group that consists of members who share common interests or skills. [5]

secondary research. Market research already performed for another purpose, and often by another entity, that may apply to the present question or opportunity. [4]

Securities and Exchange Commission (SEC). A federal agency that has oversight authority over the securities industry, including the governance of the sales of securities. [8]

securities broker. A person or entity engaged in the business of buying or selling securities for the account of another. [8]

securities dealer. A person or entity engaged in the business of buying or selling securities for its own account. [8]

security. A document or certificate representing either an ownership interest in a business or an obligation of indebtedness owed by a business, government, or agency. [8]

selective distortion. The process by which people block out or modify information that conflicts with their preconceptions until it supports their perceptions. [5]

selective distribution. The level of distribution intensity that involves the use of only a few distribution channels relative to the number of prospects within a given market. [8]

selective perception. A person's decision to acknowledge certain pieces of information and ignore the rest. [5]

selective retention. The process by which customers remember and internalize information that supports their preconceptions. [5]

SEM. *See* **search engine marketing.**

sender. In the communications process, the creator or source of communication. [9]

SEO. *See* **search engine optimization.**

service. An activity that one party performs for another. [6]

service fee. An amount paid to a producer as compensation which is a usually small percentage, such as 1 or 2 percent, of the premiums payable after the renewal commissions have ceased. [8]

service mark. A word, phrase, symbol, design, or combination thereof, that identifies and distinguishes the services one party offers from those of others. [6]

service variance. One of the ways a company can offer tiered service to customers that involves varying the number and level of services a customer receives based on the customer's value to the company. [5]

shopping product. A product for which consumers are willing to exert the time and effort needed to gather information and compare products before purchase. [6]

single-employer group. A group made up of the employees of one company. [3]

single-variable segmentation. A method of segmenting a market using only one variable or characteristic, such as income level. [3]

situation analysis. An examination of the environmental forces that are likely to affect a company's marketing activities and actions consisting of three primary parts: (1) an environmental analysis, (2) an environmental forecast, and (3) an internal assessment. [2]

social class. A social division in which individuals or groups fit into a distinct societal hierarchy based on characteristics—such as wealth, education, and occupation. [5]

social environment. The demographic traits, values, beliefs, and shared and learned norms of behavior of various groups of customers who make up a population. [1]

soft research. *See* **qualitative research.**

span of control. A term that refers to the number of people a manager directly supervises. [2]

special-interest media. Media targeted to customers with an interest in a particular topic such as homes and home improvement, money or retirement issues, and sports and recreation. [9]

specialty advertising. A form of sales promotion that uses objects or articles imprinted with a company name or logo, address, phone number, and sometimes a slogan or sales message to promote a company, its producers, or its products. [10]

specialty product. A product that customers will make a special effort to obtain. [6]

sponsored link. A method of search engine marketing that involves a company paying a search engine a fee to be listed at the top of the search results page for certain keywords. [8]

Standard Nonforfeiture Law for Life Insurance. An NAIC model law which requires most individual life insurance policies to provide specified minimum nonforfeiture values. [11]

star. A business unit or product line on the market share/market growth matrix that has a high market share in a high-growth market. [2]

state insurance code. In the United States, state laws that regulate the business of insurance in a state. [11]

state insurance department. In the United States, a state administrative agency responsible for issuing certificates of authority and otherwise administering the state insurance code. [11]

statistical inference. A statistical process that allows researchers to draw conclusions and to make estimates and predictions about a population based on a sample taken from the population. [4]

status. The socially defined position an individual holds in relation to other members of a reference group. [5]

status-quo pricing. A behavior a company exhibits when it sets its prices for products at the general level its competitors establish. Also known as *meeting the competition.* [7]

steady timing pattern. A pattern for timing advertisements in which advertisements are distributed evenly throughout a specified period of time. [10]

STEP analysis method. *See* **PEST analysis**.

strategic business unit (SBU). An area of business that is distinct from other areas within a company that is operated as a separate profit center, has its own separate set or share of customers and competitors, has its own management, and is capable of having its own marketing strategy. Also known as a *profit center*, *division*, *product line*, or *line of business*. [2]

strategic marketing planning. The process a company uses to set its major long-term marketing goals and choose the overall strategies the company will follow to reach those goals. [2]

strategic window. The time period during which an optimum "fit" exists between a company's distinct strengths and the key requirements of a marketing opportunity. [2]

structured question. In a marketing research survey, a question that offers fixed alternatives. [4]

subculture. An ethnic, regional, religious, racial, age, or social group that exhibits characteristic patterns of behavior strong enough to set its members apart from others within the overall culture or society. [5]

Suitability in Annuity Transactions Model Regulation. An NAIC model regulation which requires producers to take specific measures to ensure the suitability of any purchase or exchange of an annuity contract which results in another insurance transaction, such as using the surrender value of an annuity to purchase another annuity or a paid-up life insurance policy. [11]

suitability requirement. A requirement that imposes a duty on producers to have reasonable grounds on which to believe that a specific product is suitable for a particular customer's needs. [11]

Suitability Rule (FINRA Conduct Rule 2310). A FINRA rule that requires members to have reasonable grounds for making an investment recommendation to a customer based on the facts disclosed by the customer as to his other security holdings, financial situation, and needs. [11]

Supervisory Rule (FINRA Conduct Rule 3010). A FINRA rule that requires broker-dealers to establish and maintain, in accordance with written procedures, a system to supervise the activities of their registered representatives and registered principals. [11]

surplus. The amount of assets that a company has over and above its policy reserves and other obligations. [7]

surrender charge. An expense charge imposed on some types of life insurance policies when the policyowner surrenders the policy. [5]

survey. A primary research data-collection method that typically uses structured forms, such as questionnaires, to gather data about a person's attitudes, knowledge, buying behavior, and preferences toward a particular topic, product, or service directly from the population being studied. [4]

SWOT analysis. A means of gathering and organizing information so planners can easily identify matches between a company's strengths and specific environmental conditions. The acronym SWOT stands for Strengths, Weaknesses, Opportunities, and Threats. [2]

syndicated research. Marketing research performed to obtain information about major topics that are of interest to many companies but would not be feasible for a single company to fund alone. [4]

tactical/action program. The element of a marketing plan that puts goals and strategies into action by describing: what activities are to be performed; how, when, and where these activities will be performed; who is responsible for performing each activity; how much each activity will cost and its expected results; the main elements of uncertainty involved; and how and how often the company will monitor and evaluate results. [2]

tactical marketing planning. The process by which a company translates its strategic marketing decisions into a set of specific, detailed, action-oriented activities the company will follow to reach its target market and satisfy customer needs. [2]

Taft-Hartley Group. *See* **negotiated trusteeship.**

target examination. A limited-scope examination, conducted by a state insurance department, of one or more lines of business or specific areas of an insurer's nonfinancial operations, such as its advertising materials. [11]

target market. A specific market segment in which a company focuses its efforts to market and sell products. [4]

target marketing. The process companies use to evaluate each identified market segment and then select one or more segments as the focus for their marketing efforts. [3]

target return objective. A profit-oriented pricing objective that typically sets a specific level of profit as an objective. [7]

technology. The application of knowledge, particularly scientific knowledge, to practical purposes. [1]

telemarketing. The use of the telephone to produce sales. [8]

third-party distribution system. A distribution system in which financial institutions or other organizations distribute to their own customers insurance products issued by other companies. [8]

tiered service. A customer relationship marketing strategy under which the service level an individual customer receives reflects the customer's value to the company. [5]

top-down approach to budgeting. A method for developing a marketing budget in which budgets are set at the corporate level, and marketing managers must divide available funds to cover all individual marketing activities. [2]

total customer benefit. The total of all the services, personal attention, recognition, and image the customer gains from the relationship that develops through repeated interactions with a company. [5]

total customer cost. The total of all the time, energy, and emotion a customer invests in a relationship with a company. [5]

trade advertising. Advertising directed toward distributors, often highly technical in nature, that describes the benefits to distributors of selling a company's products as well as the benefits to the customer of purchasing the company's products. [10]

trademark. A word, phrase, symbol, or design, or combination thereof, that identifies and distinguishes the goods or products of one party from those of others. [6]

trade sales promotion. Sales promotion efforts aimed at distribution channel members. [9]

trail commission schedule. *See* **asset-based commission schedule.**

twisting. A prohibited trade practice that occurs when an insurance producer misrepresents the features of a policy to induce a customer to replace an existing policy. [11]

tying arrangement. An organization conditioning the sale of one product or service on the sale of one or more of the organization's other products or services. [11]

unaided recall test. A type of recall test that establishes whether and how well an audience member exposed to a particular advertisement remembers the advertisement without prompting or clues. [10]

underwriting margin. The difference between the benefit costs—such as the cost of death benefits or health benefits—that the insurer assumes in its pricing and the product's actual benefit costs. [7]

undifferentiated marketing. A target marketing strategy that involves defining the total market for a product as the target market and designing a single marketing mix directed toward the entire market. Also known as *mass marketing*. [3]

unfair discrimination provision. A provision in a state insurance code designed to ensure that all individuals in the same underwriting classification are treated alike. [11]

Unfair Trade Practices Act. An NAIC model law which identifies a number of general insurer practices that are prohibited if committed (1) flagrantly, in conscious disregard of the law, or (2) so frequently as to indicate a general business practice. [11]

unique selling proposition (USP). A product attribute that is not offered or cannot be offered by competitors. [6]

unit supervisor. A sales manager responsible for recruiting, training, and supervising some or all of an agency's producers. [8]

unity of command. A management principle stating that employees should have only one manager to avoid confusion. [2]

unsought product. A product that most consumers are not actively seeking. [6]

unstructured question. In marketing research, a survey question that is usually open-ended and provides no answer choices. [4]

up-selling. A customer relationship marketing strategy that involves promoting a more powerful, more enhanced, or more profitable product than the one a customer originally considers purchasing. [5]

USP. *See* **unique selling proposition**.

utility. The ability of and the degree to which a product or service satisfies a customer's needs, often the true value of an exchange. [1]

value-based pricing strategy. *See* **customer-driven pricing strategy**.

variable cost. A cost that varies directly with changes in the amount or volume of a product sold. [7]

variable pricing. *See* **flexible pricing**.

variable subsidy plan. A financing plan in which a producer's commissions are multiplied by a predetermined percentage to determine the producer's compensation. [8]

vertical conflict. A form of channel conflict evidenced by the friction between an issuing company and members of its distribution channels. [8]

vested commission. A sales commission that is guaranteed payable to a producer whether or not the producer represents the company when the commission becomes due, even if the producer resigns or is terminated. [8]

voluntary trade association. A multiple-employer group that consists of individual employers that work in similar industries and have common business interests. [3]

want. In customer behavior, a desire to have more than is absolutely necessary to improve a condition that is unsatisfying. [5]

waste. In media advertising, the number of non-target market people exposed to an advertisement in a given medium. [10]

Web log. *See* **blog**.

Web site monitoring. The process of testing and tracking how customers use a company Web site. [2]

well-written business. A policy sale in which (1) the company (or producer) identifies the specific needs of the customer, and the customer recognizes that those needs are important, (2) the insurance product actually meets those needs, and (3) the customer is financially capable of paying the premiums. Also known as *quality business*. [5]

wholesaler. A sales intermediary appointed by an insurer to promote the insurer's products to third-party distributors and support market development. [8]

width of a product mix. A comparative measure of a company's product mix based on the number of different product lines or classes a company offers. [6]

withdrawal strategy. A type of marketing strategy under which a company sells or discontinues a business unit or product with the weakest growth and investment potential to better use its resources somewhere else. [2]

Index

N

O

P